Managing International Events

This book provides a comprehensive overview and examination of the international aspect of Events Management and the many challenges and complications that arise in the planning and delivery specifically of cross-border and cross-cultural events.

Authored by a current academic and ex-practitioner in the field, this book boasts an excellent balance of theory with practical advice and guidance. Chapters cover all the key concepts needed to manage and deliver an international event and fully reflect the current trends and issues facing the sector today. These include: sustainability, digital communication, social media, Big Data, corporate social responsibility, accessibility, security issues, and managing volunteers among many others. International case studies are included in each chapter accompanied by study questions and useful weblinks for further reading and research.

This will be of great interest not only to students and researchers of International Events Management, Tourism and Hospitality, but also to current practitioners in the Events sector.

W. Gerard Ryan teaches international event management at institutions around Europe and Scandinavia and continues to perform internationally as a musician. With three international event careers as a musician, a venue and festival manager, and an academic, he has developed a unique understanding of international events.

T0371841

'This timely and insightful publication is devoted to exploring international events from the outset. It has a clear vibe about it that offers understanding, explanation, analysis and examples from a myriad of international events. For educators and learners alike it's a highly focused, informed read; one that adds considerably to the canon of literature on events.'

Dr Graham Berridge, *Head of Department for Events, University of Surrey*

'An excellent textbook which provides substantial and detailed focus upon internationally focused events. This book will be a great resource to students and academics within event studies. The book contains some really good case studies and insights into international events from a theoretical and practical perspective.'

Dr Allan S. Jepson, *Senior Lecturer and Researcher in Event Studies, University of Hertfordshire*

'The author is to be congratulated for focusing on these significant, but in the literature so far, under-acknowledged dimensions of the events industry. This book will make a major mark on the knowledge 'landscape', and readers will benefit especially from its highly accessible integration of concepts and practice.'

Dr Paul Fallon, *Senior Lecturer in Tourism, Hospitality and Event Management, University of Central Lancashire*

Managing
International Events

W. Gerard Ryan

Routledge
Taylor & Francis Group

LONDON AND NEW YORK

First published 2021
by Routledge
2 Park Square, Milton Park, Abingdon, Oxon OX14 4RN

and by Routledge
52 Vanderbilt Avenue, New York, NY 10017

Routledge is an imprint of the Taylor & Francis Group, an informa business

British Library Cataloguing-in-Publication Data
A catalogue record for this book is available from the British Library

Library of Congress Cataloging-in-Publication Data
A catalog record has been requested for this book

ISBN: 978-1-138-57276-8 (hbk)
ISBN: 978-1-138-57277-5 (pbk)
ISBN: 978-0-203-70184-3 (ebk)

Typeset in Frutiger
by Newgen Publishing UK

Visit the eResources: www.routledge.com/9781138572775

This book is dedicated to the memory of Colin Lee –
a dedicated academic and all-round good man.

Contents

Contents

Contents

Figures

Figures

Tables

Case studies

Preface

This book has been written in response to the emergent global shift from a 20th century setting of study in higher education awards that focus on events management to a more realistic 21st century focus on international event management. It also responds to the major developments that have influenced the way in which international events themselves are delivered today.

My international events background and experience is long and multi-faceted and is best expressed in order of appearance: as a football supporter, a musician, a creative industries development manager, a venue and festival manager, and as an academic. To use a musical term, these influences may be reflected in the 'feel' of the book. I have been privileged to have been involved with and experienced international events that have brought the highest of highs and the lowest of lows on the terraces, in the audience, on stage, and in the wings. Fortunately, there has been a great deal of learning from all these experiences which contributes consciously and unconsciously throughout the text.

The book covers a broad selection of chapters that shed light on the genuine realities of being involved in international events on a number of levels. It is written from both an experience and research perspective, providing advice and tips complemented by academic research. As each of the eleven chapters unfolds, it becomes clear how much scope an international event covers and how topics that might at first appear to be insignificant prove to be central to the successful management and delivery of these highly complicated proceedings. In some cases, it has been necessary to focus in more detail on the contributing factors in order to provide a better understanding of how these influence the delivery of an international event.

The flow of the book is comparable to international event delivery and is set out in an orderly fashion. This does not mean it has to be read from beginning to end; each chapter is capable of being read on its own and the chapters can be read in any order. Whichever way is preferred, it will take the reader through the various processes an international event organiser will experience or need knowledge of in order to successfully deliver an international event. For further assistance, the book is separated into three parts as follows:

1. Planning and delivery (Chapters 1 to 3),
2. Internal forces (Chapters 4 to 6), and
3. External forces (Chapters 7 to 11).

Preface

There are some topics that could quite easily fit into more than one part. However, the parts assist in focusing the topics discussed and provide the reader with an additional approach to reading the book. They also provide academics with greater opportunity to plan semesters and design additional teaching materials around the various segments. The content of all three parts maintains a largely 'Western' approach to international events while providing the reader with a global perspective where possible on how international events activities differ across the world.

The book is written for international event students, academics, and researchers, but professional and amateur event organisers who want to understand the issues of international events in much greater detail will also benefit from the contents. With this in mind, it is appreciated that event 'manager' is too narrow a term for many of the activities discussed. Therefore, event 'organiser' is used to include the various levels of contribution to the delivery of an international event.

Since the turn of the century, international events have seen continued growth and during this time have evolved considerably. There have also been some very impressive achievements, particularly in the way in which audiences experience and engage with international events and how international events have responded to the various modern-day global developments. However, at the same time, there are aspects of international events that have not changed since the first known international event occurred. This is also a theme the book attempts to maintain throughout.

It is hoped that this book will prove to be a useful resource to a much wider audience and not merely be a companion to those specifically interested in the delivery of international events. However, if only the latter is achieved, the book will have served its purpose.

Acknowledgements

There are so many people that deserve to be acknowledged and thanked for their contributions, both knowing and unknowing, to the successful completion of this book. From tour managers, crew, band members, promoters, company directors, academics, and students, many have the right to be named. Even my old golfing friends who constantly chastised me around the course and those whose teaching style lies deep in the art of arguing toe-to-toe, all deserve to be acknowledged. However, there are a few people that stand out: in particular, my wife and family, Amanda, Charlotte, Hazel, and Annie, for their constant dedication and understanding, and without whom I would have completed the first draft much earlier; and my brother, Charlie, and sister, Bernadette, who have inspired me to keep going through the tough times. But there are many others from whom I have learned so much and to whom I owe a considerable amount of gratitude. These include the late Pete Fulwell, Susanne Burns, Dr Mike Jones, Dr Allan Jepson, Dave Jones, Eddy Grant, Dr Katy Vigurs and Professor Tehmina Basit. I must also mention close friends, Ian, Mike, Dave, and Alan, but especially my inspirational mate and workaholic John Murphy who probably instigated the path to constantly improving knowledge and developing a better understanding for everything from pop music to Plato. I would also like to tip my cap to Carlotta Fanton, Lydia Kessell, Judith Barrett and the following academic institutions: the Liverpool Institute for Performing Arts, the School of Popular Music at the University of Liverpool, and Staffordshire University.

Part 1

PLANNING AND DELIVERY

Chapter 1

What are international events?

Contents

1.1 Chapter overview

This chapter will provide an introduction to international event management and how technology is used to assist with delivery by clarifying some of the fundamental considerations surrounding international events that are often misunderstood. The chapter highlights the origins, value and importance of international events to strengthen the basic knowledge required when managing international events. This is intended to provide a foundation for the concept of international event management to eliminate the possibility of errors at a later stage.

1.2 Learning objectives

By the end of this chapter, the student will be expected to:

- Appreciate what is meant by international events
- Understand the origins of international events and how they have developed
- Explain the importance of international events and their effects
- Appreciate the scope of international events and their importance to individuals, communities and the wider population.

1.3 Introduction

Many of the world's most notable accomplishments are international events. The manner in which businesses, nations, and individuals meet, entertain, and trade continues to exemplify what can be achieved in a modern world. From religious gatherings of faith, to what for many are deeply fanatical gatherings of sport and politics, the draw of the international event is deep in passion, conviction, and to some, more important than life and death. Today, more people are attending, while more places than ever are planning and providing international events.

International festivals and events themselves offer a unique platform for cultural exchange, rejuvenation, or preservation (Jepson and Clarke, 2016). But while hindsight can demonstrate that many international events have existed for millennia, foresight is improving engagement through aspects of digital technology while advancing the key principles that have essentially remained unchanged. Now that the fourth industrial revolution is very much upon us – now commonly known as Industry 4.0 (I4.0) – all businesses have an opportunity to improve their entire value chain (Bordeleau et al., 2018). International events are absorbing aspects of I4.0 at every stage of the process, pushing the boundaries of event experiences far beyond the physical world. What can be produced in milliseconds today is a long way (not only in time), from the experience of the pioneers of the first notable international events.

1.4 Defining international events

In the 21st century, there are many examples of what could be considered an international event. Defining what an international event is should be relatively straight forward. Krugman and Wright (2006) suggest an international meeting involves the attendees crossing national borders, lasts at least two days plus travel time, has an attendance of 50 or more, and a business agenda utilising presenters. However, while this definition is focused on meetings, the more research that is conducted on the subject, the more variations in international events become apparent, making an appropriate definition much more complex. This is because many different examples of international events exist. For example, a government might consider an 'international event' to be one where at least 30% of the total delegates/visitors attending in person are international or non-domiciled visitors (Gov.uk, 2019). Then there are the all-pervading global major or mega events that are marketed, distributed, and promoted on a huge scale throughout the world, where the majority of the event's audience is at home watching on TV. These events are closing in on ticket sales of 10 million, but can estimate their broader audience in billions. Table 1.1 provides an indication of the size, reach, and cost of some recent major and mega international events.

On a more organic level, there are free-to-attend religious events that attract millions of pilgrims to one place from all over the world or the billions that follow the weekly religious schedule in local communities. There are community events that celebrate cultural activities, seasonal celebrations, business, political

Table 1.1 Size indicators of recent major international events

Event	Edition	Tickets sold	Broadcast rights	Total costs
		Millions	*US$ million*	*US$ billion*
Expo	Shanghai 2010	73	–	55
Olympic Summer Games	London 2012	8.2	2569	14
Football World Cup	South Africa 2010	3.1	2408	5.5
Asian Games	Guangzhou 2010	2	<752	18
Olympic Winter Games	Vancouver 2010	1.5	1280	7.5
European Football Championship	Ukraine/Poland 2012	1.4	1076	48
Commonwealth Games	Delhi 2010	1	52	6.1
Universiade	Kazan 2013	0.7	ca. 32	7.2
Pan American Games	Guadalajara 2011	0.6	<45	1.3
TOTAL		91.5	7462	162.6
MEAN		10.2	1066	18.1
MEDIAN		1.5	564	7.5

Source: Müller, 2015

and tourism activities that are globally coordinated, and private events that are just as international as any modern-day professional event.

So we begin to see that unlike international business where the focus is trading in or with other nations across borders, international events can be held in one place and still attract an international audience, either through actual visits or through the media. They can also be held in numerous places at the same time or tour from one nation to another. International events can originate from a single or a variety of cultures or they can begin as a local event and grow into an internationally recognised event.

There is of course, the basic definition of what an event is, which varies between academics (Bowdin et al., 2011; Chambers, 2003; Getz, 2005; Shone and Parry, 2013). However, it becomes difficult not to ascribe some aspect of an event with an international activity to even the most local of events. The key to the 'international-ness' of an event is not just having evidence of international engagement, as this is often already present throughout the local community because of human global mobility. To be properly considered an international event, the international-ness must be about management and/or the impact of the international aspect from a delivery perspective.

According to the Oxford English Dictionary (OED, 2016), to be 'international' requires inter-relations between two or more nations or organisations made up of nations, constituted by nations or national governments, and transcending national boundaries. A local event today can draw people from another culture or nation who can then attend without any great effort, engagement or knowledge of the organisers. Therefore, to accurately define an international event in the 21st century, or for an event to be accurately considered international, the event organisers must expressly manage the international characteristic.

There may be only a limited number of events that would need or even want to carry out research to highlight how international they are, so data is limited on the levels of international engagement. However, the structure of international society itself is changing and coupled with global tourism and the cultural demographic of communities around the world, it is difficult for any event to be held in the modern world without some influence of international participation because the volume of international movement and migration continues to rise. Population flows triggered by choice, demand or force across the world impact on even the smallest communities. The diversity of a community mix can be difficult to capture without considerable research, but a snapshot can be simply reproduced from the humblest of observations. Figure 1.1 shows the language options at a local community centre arrival screen. Without significant populations being present from each of these nations, there would be no need to provide such specific language facilities.

To take the example in Figure 1.1 a step further, Table 1.2 highlights the net migration figures in the most developed regions of the world with projections to 2100. To put these figures into perspective, between 1950 and 2015, the major areas of Europe, Northern America and Oceania have been net receivers of international migrants, while Africa, Asia and Latin and the Caribbean have been net senders, with the volume of net migration generally increasing over time. From 2000 to 2015, average annual net migration to Europe, Northern America and Oceania averaged 2.8 million persons per year (UN Department of Social and Economic Affairs, 2015).

Figure 1.1 Local community sign in screen

1.5 Origins of international events

It is possible to trace the roots of the earliest international events back to the Roman Empire and West Africa and to note the importance of the contribution international trading events have made in the development of the rest of the world. Gewald (2010) discussed the origins and growth of the earliest known international markets and trade fairs and it is evident how very similar in nature they are to contemporary international markets and trade fairs. The central place that was created was primarily to provide goods and services to its surrounding population. In the Jiangnan area of China, the market towns not only produced local products for the neighbouring population but also exported the products to other prefectures and even other countries (Chan *et al.*, 2015).

As far back as 4th century BC, Roman Empire tomb frescoes from the Campanian city of Paestum show paired fighters with helmets, spears, and shields in a propitiatory funeral blood-rite that anticipates early Roman gladiator games (Stone-Potter and Mattingly, 1999), a form of international audience entertainment. Figure 1.2 is an example of a later carving on display in northern England depicting Hadrian's victory celebrations as the Empire continued its march throughout Europe. These and earlier victories were often followed by gladiator games (Welch, 2007).

In the late 2nd century BC, North African trade routes were developed across the Sahara Desert with long waterless stretches between oases. These routes became known as the Gold Road where salt, textiles, beads, gold, ebony and ivory were traded between nations. Similarly, trade between Asia and Europe originates in the trading of silk, gems, horses, spices, paper and gunpowder via the Silk Road. People would meet in what became stop-off points along these trade routes, forming new communities and offering places of rest with open markets and trade fairs. The route spanned 5,000 miles from Chang'an the ancient capital of China (better known today as Xian) to the Roman Empire and beyond via Constantinople; now Istanbul. Figure 1.3 shows the distance travelled to market by some of the early merchants.

In other sectors of the industry, ritual or ceremonial activities such as missions and spiritual or Astrolatry gatherings such as the Nevruz provide indications of some of the earliest known international religious events. The ceremonial landscapes in the area around Salisbury Plain also contribute to early

Table 1.2 Migration rates in most-developed regions

Migrants in most-developed countries

Year	1950	1970	19190	2000	2005	2010	2015	2020	2030	2050	2075	2100
Net number of migrants (thousand)	738	3,563	7,163	13,247	15,774	16,431	11,683	11,756	11,365	11,551	8,663	776
Net migration rate per 1,000	0.2	0.7	1.3	2.3	2.6	2.7	1.9	1.9	1.8	1.8	1.4	0.9

Source: Data taken from UN Department of Social and Economic Affairs, Population Division, 2015

Figure 1.2 Victory carving from Hadrian's Wall

Figure 1.3 The Silk Road
Source: Sharma, 2015

evidence of international events and gatherings between 3000 BC and 2000 BC (Timewatch, 2017).

Each of these insights provides some indication of the importance of international events and their contribution to a developing world. Whether it is by ship, raft, on foot or on horseback, where international trade has led, culture and knowledge has followed. By considering these activities, the influence of international events on the fusion and expansion of the world and its people becomes more apparent.

Some of the largest international events have origins that can be attributed either to the continued efforts of individuals or quite simply, chance. Many renowned international events tend to have considerably modest origins when compared to what their scope eventually represents. For example, Hill (1996) explains that the first modern Olympic Games in 1896 would probably not have been held without the energy and determination of Baron Pierre de Coubertin. It was through his passion for sports education and his efforts to persuade the French to introduce physical education into schools that the idea to re-establish the modern Olympic Games came about.

The need to raise money for a community sports club or organisation through a number of fundraising activities is a typical example of the beginnings of a local event. These humble beginnings can lead to globally recognised events. In 1873 the All England Croquet and Lawn Tennis Club was gifted a pony roller. The roller was essentially donated as an incentive to look favourably on an application from a prospective member. In 1877 the pony roller broke and the club could not afford the £10 needed to pay for the repair. Consequently, the club decided to organise a tennis tournament for gentlemen in the summer of the same year (Mitchell, 2017). Tickets for the event were sold to 200 paying guests at a shilling each and 22 gentlemen paid a Guinea to participate. A silver challenge cup valued at 25 guineas was donated by a local magazine. The funds raised covered the cost of the tournament and the repair of the pony roller leaving the club with a total profit of £10 (Wikipedia, n.d.). The event is better known now as Wimbledon or The Championships and is the oldest and arguably the most prestigious tennis tournament in the world.

Probably the most unusual origin for an international event is that of the Tour de France. McGann (2006) explains that a group of advertisers set up their own sports newspaper in opposition to *Le Vélo* (The Bike), the leading French sports newspaper of the time, after disagreements with the main advertisers. This new newspaper was to be called *L'Auto-vélo* with the express intention of driving *Le Vélo* out of business. In stark contrast to *Le Vélo*'s green paper on which it was printed, *L'Auto-vélo* was printed on yellow paper.

In 1903 *Le Vélo* sued *L'Auto-vélo* claiming that its name was too close to theirs and as the subject matter was the same an infringement had been made. *Le Vélo* (the green one) won the case. After losing the lawsuit, *L'Auto-vélo* changed its name to *L'Auto* and quickly began to run out of funds. Just days after the lawsuit and in an attempt to reinvigorate sales, the newspaper announced 'the biggest cycling trail in the whole world' around France as a publicity stunt to raise money.

The Tour de France has grown to become the most famous bicycle race and one of the biggest international sporting events in the world. In 2016, the race covered 4,000km over 23 days, travelling through 660 cities in four countries reaching an altitude of 2,408m. Because of the nature of the event, it remains a free event for spectators to enjoy and attracts around 12 million spectators to the roadside and a global audience that reaches billions (BBC, 2014).

As international events began to capture the general public's attention, Chalkley and Essex (1999) observed that by the end of the 19th century, the

Olympic Games had emerged as the world's most prominent sporting event with a scale and significance that creates major challenges and opportunities for the organisation and infrastructure of host cities. This public attention consistently grew throughout the 20th century and along with growth, challenges and benefits have developed with time.

The benefits of the Olympic Games are numerous and can be put down to local investment in a city's infrastructure and facilities, increased tourism, and social cohesion. Challenges include the environmental impact the staging of the Olympics has on the planet. This and other environmental matters are discussed in more detail in Chapter 10. Moreover, because of the global audience and media exposure, the Games have often been used for political reasons. Berlin 1936, Munich 1972, Moscow 1980, and Atlanta 1996 are a few examples of Olympic Games that gained public attention for events off the field of play rather than sporting achievements on it.

1.6 The scope of international events

It should now be evident that international events are much more comprehensive than the modest explanation of something that crosses a border. The scope of international events in the 21st century pervades tourism, business, sport, religious, and political activities. Such events have a multitude of backgrounds and objectives and are often integrated into many other aspects of commerce. Although many are instigated by individuals who have no intention of creating an international interest, they contain so much more value that their importance far exceeds their original purpose. Some events (predominantly religious or spiritual events) are so old, the term 'international' did not even exist when they began.

We have established an understanding of what an international event requires for it to be considered international. From a delivery perspective, the event itself can be immobile, mobile or global. For example, the Musikmesse in Frankfurt is the international trade fair for musical instruments, sheet music, music production and marketing (Musikmesse, n.d.). This event is held every spring in Frankfurt am Main, Germany. This event attracts a global audience of traders and delegates to a single place. At the other extreme, events such as the Clipper Round the World Yacht Race is one of the biggest challenges of the natural world and an endurance test covering 40,000 nautical miles around the world (Clipper Round the World, n.d.).

Many international events fit into the category of international as they travel from country to country and include international participants. Generally, the best-known events tend to be sporting events due to media interest, global coverage, major sponsorship deals and advertising – the largest being the Olympics Games. Other examples include the quadrennial Fédération Internationale de Football Association (FIFA) World Cup, and the annual Fédération Internationale de l'Automobile (FIA) Formula 1 World Championship season. Table 1.3 provides examples of other major international events from around the world that have considerable significance throughout the world, but often originated as local events.

Planning and delivery

Table 1.3 A selection of international events from around the world

Event	Destination	Focus	When
Wakakusa Yamayaki	Nara, Japan	Social	January
Sundance Film Festival	Park City, Utah – USA	Film	
Carnivale Di Venezia	Venice – Italy	Culture	February
Mardi Gras	New Orleans, Louisiana – USA	Culture	
Sky Lantern Festival	Pingxi, Taiwan – Republic of China	Culture	
Rio Carnival	Rio De Janeiro – Brazil	Culture	
Holi	Mumbai, Delhi, etc. – India	Religious	March
St Patrick's Day	Global	Culture	
SXSW	Austin, Texas – USA	Music	
King's Day	Amsterdam – Netherlands	State	April
Snowbombing	Mayrhofen – Austria	Sport	
Songkran	Chaing Mai & Bangkok – Thailand	Calendar	
Stars of the White Nights	St Petersburg – Russia	Culture	May
Cannes Film Festival	Cannes – France	Film	
Glastonbury Festival	Pilton, Somerset – UK	Music	June
San Vino Wine Fight	Haro – Spain	Culture	
Download	Donington Park – UK	Music	
Tomorrowland	Boom – Belgium	Music	July
Tour de France	Paris – France	Sport	
Comic Con International	San Diego, California – USA	Literature	
Just For Laughs	Montreal – Canada	Comedy	
Edinburgh Festival	Edinburgh – Scotland	Culture	August
Edinburgh Fringe Festival	Edinburgh – Scotland	Comedy	
La Tomatina	Bunol, Valencia – Spain	Social	
Notting Hill Carnival	Notting Hill, London – UK	Culture	
Hajj	Mecca – Saudi Arabia	Religious	September
Oktoberfest	Munich – Germany	Culture	October
Austin City Limits	Austin, Texas – USA	Music	
Epcot Food & Wine Festival	Orlando, Florida – USA	Gastronomy	August – November
Diwali	Mumbai – India	Religious	
Dia De Los Muertos	Mexico City – Mexico	Culture	
Loy Krathong	Thailand	Religious	November
Mevlana Whirling Dervishes	Konya – Turkey	Remembrance	December
Krampusnacht	Tyrol – Austria	Culture	
Hogmanay	Scotland	Calendar	

While sporting events may attract the largest sums of money, media attention and global audience, there are events that have just as much of a claim to being the biggest international events in the world for different reasons. The Kumbh Mela Hindu festival in India is one of these events. This event occurs once every 12 years; although a Maha [Great] Kumbh Mela occurs every 144 years. The event has an estimated gathering of 80 to 120 million pilgrims throughout the six to eight week festival. The pilgrims gather at the sacred rivers in India in order to be cleansed of sins and seek salvation. Similarly, the annual Hajj religious pilgrimage to Mecca attracts an estimated 3.2 million. Of these, 1.4 million are said to be from Saudi Arabia with 1.75 million travelling from outside the country (Cheapflights.com, 2013).

One-off events also attract enormous attendances, particularly when people respond to special occasions such as state-based or similar national pride events. The 2011 Royal Wedding in London was one of the major broadcast events of the year, with over 24 million terrestrial viewers in the UK alone (Gorman, 2011). Police estimated a million people lined the wedding procession route from Westminster Abbey to Buckingham Palace (BBC, 2011). The royal couple kept the planning of the event in-house as it is attributed to Lady Elizabeth Anson who is the Queen's cousin. Lady Elizabeth also happens to be the founder of Party Planners, a London-based events company specialising in bespoke events for A-list celebrities.

Tragedies are just as likely to bring people together, whether that is responding to terror attacks, natural disasters, state funerals, or injustices when people gather to express their views on wars and human suffering. In these cases, events are often held simultaneously around the world. Examples of these include Live Aid which comprised official live events in seven countries and attracted an estimated global audience of 1.9 billion, across 150 nations (CNN, 2005); or the Arab Spring where young people drove a series of anti-government protests, uprisings and armed rebellions that spread across the Middle East in late 2010 (Ajami, 2011).

In recent years, anti-war protests have been simultaneously organised across the globe. In February 2003, some 60 countries hosted protests against the invasion of Iraq, creating massive gatherings of people worldwide for the same reason on the same weekend. Between 6 and 10 million people gathered together to protest in cities throughout Spain, Germany, Switzerland, Ireland, America, Canada, Australia, South Africa, India, Russia, South Korea and Japan. An estimated 3 million people gathered to march in Rome, which is the largest anti-war march ever recorded (Guinness World Records, 2003), while an estimated 1 million turned out in both London and Barcelona. These types of international events are covered in more detail in Chapter 7.

Other events are held in a single place but are considered international by virtue of either their content or interest. From business and education there is the unrelenting presence of the meetings, incentives, conferences and exhibitions or MICE industry, a specialised sector of international events. (See Chapter 9 for more details). International trade fairs, expos, conventions, and conferences attract businesses and delegates to specific destinations around the world. Every industry has their own string of events, but a typical example would be SXSW (South by Southwest) held in Austin, Texas, which is best known for its live events, seminars, main conference and extended festivals that celebrate and promote the convergence of the interactive, film, and music industries.

At the other end of the scale, the Music Cities Convention travels across the globe. It has been held seven times across Europe, Australia and North America. This event brings together 1500+ attendees from over 250 cities and 40 countries. Delegates from cities, governments and the cultural industries attend to explore the value of music in urban planning, quality of life, city policy and development strategies, exploring how music enhances economic development, creates jobs and drives tourism (Music Cities Events, n.d.)

Sporting events are largely spectator events where the spectacle is based around a single piece of action. The Grand National in Aintree, Liverpool, arguably the world's most famous horse race, began as a local attraction and has grown to a worldwide audience of 600 million (Kirkham, 2017).

National governance and politics is yet another sector in international events. Largely under the umbrella term of 'the public sector', there are numerous international events held annually around the world. Arguably the most significant global events include the G5, G8, G14, and G20 group of nations meetings. Surrounded by intense security, these events are possibly the epitome of complicated event organisation and secrecy.

More recently, the scope of an international event has tended to become much broader than the focus it originated for. As an event or the organisation grows, there comes with it a responsibility to give back to grassroots or local communities. For example, the Olympic Games now takes in a cultural and heritage agenda that includes art, history, and academic research (IOC, n.d.). FIFA provide a number of incentives around the world including a refugee and migrant assistance programme using football as a means of education and development for young people (FIFA, 2019). Even in the smallest of international events, their existence has become an opportunity to bring together individuals, groups, companies, governments and cultures. Particularly through music and sport, they often symbolise unity and can override political differences.

1.7 The value and importance of international events

The value and importance of international events is largely down to the organisers and the participants involved. Generally, it can be simply argued that an international event's value and importance depends on its reach. For those that are private affairs, the value and importance remain largely private to the local economy or community. However, for those that reach a global level the value and importance have a much bigger impact. International events can restore as well as divide communities and economies. They can provide security and jobs and even determine the direction of the local economy. International events have driven many changes in society such as inclusivity and broken down numerous boundaries for access. (This is discussed in more detail in Chapter 3). At the same time, international events can divide opinion, destroy communities and national economies and have massive environmental impacts that are often deliberately understated in the evaluation process (Getz, 2018).

To fully justify any value or (to some extent) the importance of an international event, it is necessary to consider the overall cost to the host. Due to the continuous expansion and development of the biggest international events, the cost of hosting tends to increase year-on-year and as Getz (2018) explains, a considerable amount of these costs may be omitted from the planning evaluation process, which brings into question the real reason for bidding to host the event in the first place.

Arguably, the most prominent reason given for bidding to host an international event is the financial return on investment. This is usually because it is the most beneficial way to gain public approval, particularly when the event is subsidised through taxes. However, the value or worth of an international event is not merely or solely about a financial return on investment. There are a number of other broader values that events can generate that provide much deeper significance. The non-monetary aspects are not always tangible and often these are the values with more meaning to participants and audiences alike. (See Case Study 1.1 for details on intangible cultural heritage).

Value from international events can be measured as a medium of exchange or considered as serving a specified purpose where satisfaction or return is assessed in terms of social impact or benefit, personal experience, audience involvement or participation, cultural impacts, usefulness or desirability. These concepts have been widely discussed as social return on investment (SROI). SROI is described as the application of a set of principles within a framework that is designed to recognise what is of value for different people in different situations and cultures (Nicholls *et al.*, 2012).

Because international events affect large numbers of people and the environment, it is important for the organisers to start any consideration for a new event by understanding the invisible effects. Profit may be the ultimate goal, but for an event to survive and retain the support of its audience, social values will need to form part of the delivery process.

Applying the principles of social value to an international event is a good place for international event organisers to start. According to Social Value UK (2016) the principles of social value provides the basic building blocks for anyone who wants to make decisions that take this wider definition of value into account, in order to increase equality, improve wellbeing and increase environmental sustainability. Figure 1.4 details the seven principles of social value that can be attributed to the reasons for holding an international event.

The value or importance of international events can also be considered in social terms where the occasion to meet and mingle with like-minded visitors is more important than the original activities within the event itself. Henley Regatta began in 1839 and has grown to around 600 competing rowing crews from universities, colleges, schools and independent rowing clubs from around the world. The event is promoted by many local businesses as the highlight of both the summer sporting calendar and the social season. Rather than resist the preference to socialise over following the rowing, the organisers have fully embraced these opposing values. Just like a social occasion, the most popular section at the event, the stewards' enclosure, has the strictest of dress codes. Moreover, drinking and spectating are not allowed to mix. The bar areas are laid out to maximise social engagement so they do not face the water (Canter and Fidler, 2017).

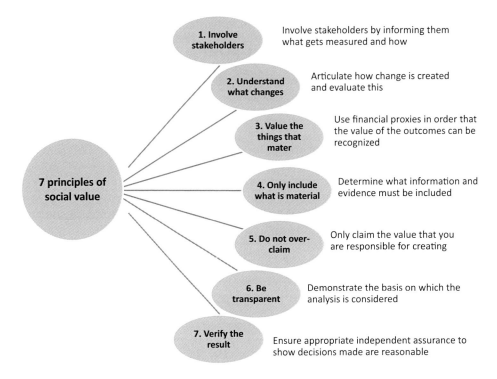

Figure 1.4 The seven principles of social value

Source: Adapted from Social Value UK, 2016

1.8 Summary

This first chapter has introduced us to the concepts of international events. A broad explanation has been provided of what international events are along with the various specialised niche groups that exist within the broader definition. The origins and scope of these various niches as best understood have also been explained. We have learned the value and importance of international events to communities and nations alike and how they can be used for objectives other than their original purpose. Finally, while international events can generate massive amounts of investment, there is also the need to consider their overall impact in order to deliver socially acceptable occasions.

Case study 1.1 The Prayagraj Ardh Kumbh Mela

There are few religious or spiritual events that attract crores of pilgrims from around the world. On the banks of the River Ganga, the Prayagraj Ardh Kumbh Mela which attracted 120 million Hindu devotees over 49 days was the Ardh Kumbh Mela in Prayagraj, Uttar Pradesh, India, from 15th January to 4th March 2019. Pilgrims at the Mela bathe in the waters. Hindus believe that doing so will cleanse them of their sins and help them attain 'moksha', setting them free from the cycle of birth and death. Kumbh Mela is a religious festival that is celebrated four times over the course of 12 years, the site of the observance rotating between four pilgrimage places on four sacred rivers in India. Each site's celebration is based on a distinct set of astrological positions of the Sun, the Moon, and Jupiter, the holiest time occurring at the exact moment when these positions are fully occupied (Encyclopedia Britannica, 2019).

The Kumbh Mela plays a pivotal role in the historical, cultural and spiritual heritage of India. Kumbh is a symbol of peace and harmony amongst all human beings. It also signifies the coming together of people from various cultures from all across the world and participating in the spectacle that is said to be the largest peaceful congregation of humanity. The importance of the Kumbh Mela was reflected when it was inscribed in the 'Representative List of the Intangible Cultural Heritage of Humanity' by UNESCO in 2017. This inscription reflects the significance of Kumbh worldwide. The Uttar Pradesh Government Allahabad Mela Authority has set up a permanent body to oversee the Kumbh Mela.

The event is said to blend the grand traditions of Kumbh with the deployment of modern techniques and solutions so that the kalpavasis, spiritual gurus, dignitaries, foreign visitors, and the pilgrims have a life-emancipating experience encapsulating the science of astronomy, astrology, spirituality, ritualistic traditions, social and cultural customs and practices, making it extremely rich in knowledge. Participating in the ritual of the holy bath at the Ghats is said to be an honour and a privilege. As per the Uttar Pradesh Government's vision, the ephemeral Kumbh city will be designed and build in consonance with the vision of Divya Kumbh, Bhavya Kumbh.

International events such as these require considerable organisation in order for them to pass without incident. Ample and knowledgeable security plans are required to ensure the protection of all attendees. Adequate infrastructures need to be in place to get everyone to and from the event.

Questions

1. How would you interpret 'intangible cultural heritage'?
2. How do you think the event organisers deal with the following?
   a. Adequate transport services
   b. Basic human needs, such as food, sanitation facilities, and health
   c. The clash between local communities and the onset of religious tourists
   d. Movement of people through the streets and the need for a bed
3. How might the organisers deal with lost and found, from people to mobile phones?
4. Would a more visible controlling contribution from the local government add to or detract from the event?

1.9 Useful websites

Lists of Intangible Cultural Heritage
https://ich.unesco.org/en/lists

International Covenant on Economic, Social and Cultural Rights
www.refworld.org/docid/3ae6b36c0.html

Silk Road revival initiative
http://nepalforeignaffairs.com/relevance-of-chinas-silk-road-revival-initiative-and-
    nepal/

World population prospects
https://esa.un.org/unpd/wpp/publications/files/key_findings_wpp_2015.pdf

Online community for the MICE (Meetings, Incentives, Conferences and Exhibitions)
    Industry
www.mice.com/

Event statistics
www.eventmanagerblog.com/event-statistics

References

Ajami, F. (2011). *From 9/11 to the Arab Spring*. Stanford, CA: Hoover Institution, Stanford University.
BBC (2011). Royal wedding watched by 24.5 million on terrestrial TV. Retrieved from www.bbc.co.uk/news/entertainment-arts-13248199 Accessed 15th June 2017.
BBC (2014). Are there four billion Tour de France viewers? Retrieved from www.bbc.co.uk/news/blogs-magazine-monitor-28264183 Accessed 30th June 2017.
Bordeleau, F. E., Mosconi, E., & Santa-Eulalia, L. A. (2018, January). 'Business Intelligence in Industry 4.0: State of the art and research opportunities'. Paper presented at the 51st Hawaii International Conference on System Sciences 2018, Waikoloa.
Bowdin, G., Allen, J., O'Toole, W., & McDonnell, I. (2011). *Events Management* (3rd ed.). London: Elsevier.
Canter, A., & Fidler, M. (2017). Blazers and bubbly – a Henley regatta photo essay, *The Guardian*. Retrieved from www.theguardian.com/sport/2017/jun/30/blazers-and-bubbly-a-henley-regatta-photo-essay
Chalkley, B., & Essex, S. (1999). Urban development through hosting international events: a history of the Olympic Games. *Planning Perspectives, 14*(4), 369–394. doi:10.1080/026654399364184
Chambers (2003). *The Chambers Dictionary* (2003 ed.). Edinburgh: Chambers.
Chan, T.-C., Pai, P.-L., Shaw, S.-L., & Fan, I. C. (2015). Spatiotemporal evolution of market towns in the Jiangnan area during the Ming-Qing dynasties of China. *Historical Methods: A Journal of Quantitative and Interdisciplinary History, 48*(2), 90–102. doi:10.1080/01615440.2014.995783
Cheapflights.com (2013). Top 10 crowd-drawing events from around the world. Retrieved from www.huffingtonpost.com/cheapflights/top-10-crowddrawing-event_b_3594312.html?slideshow=true#gallery/308336/6 Accessed 12th December 2016.

Clipper Round the World (n.d.). About the race. Retrieved from https://www. clipperroundtheworld.com/about/about-the-race Accessed 12th December 2016.

CNN (2005). Live Aid 1985: A day of magic. Retrieved from http://edition.cnn.com/2005/ SHOWBIZ/Music/07/01/liveaid.memories/index.html Accessed 12th December 2016.

Encyclopedia Britannica editors (2019). Kumbh-Mela. Retrieved from www.britannica. com/topic/Kumbh-Mela Accessed 10th November 2019.

FIFA (2019). Soccer Without Borders overcoming barriers in Uganda. Retrieved from www.fifa.com/about-fifa/who-we-are/news/soccer-without-borders-overcoming-barriers-in-uganda Accessed 10th November 2019.

Getz, D. (2005). *Event Management & Event Tourism* (2nd ed.). New York: Cognizant.

Getz, D. (2018). *Event Evaluation*. Oxford: Goodfellow Publishing.

Gewald, J. B. (2010). Gold: The true motor of West African history. An overview of the importance of gold in West Africa and its relations with the wider world. *Rozenberg Quarterly*, 1–14.

Gorman, B. (2011). 2 billion to watch the royal wedding worldwide? Really? Retrieved from https://tvbythenumbers.zap2it.com/1/2-billion-to-watch-the-royal-wedding-worldwide-really/90957/ Accessed 14th March 2018.

Gov.uk (2019). Broadband competition for event venues, Gov.uk. Retrieved from www. gov.uk/government/publications/broadband-competition-for-event-venues Accessed 21st January 2020.

Guinness World Records (2003). Largest anti-war rally. Retrieved from https://web. archive.org/web/20040904214302/http://www.guinnessworldrecords.com/content_ pages/record.asp?recordid=54365 Accessed 17th October 2018.

Hill, C. R. (1996). *Olympic Politics* (2nd ed.). Manchester: Manchester University Press.

IOC (International Olympics Committee) (n.d.). Culture and Olympic heritage commission. Retrieved from:www.olympic.org/culture-and-olympic-heritage-commission Accessed 10th November 2019.

Jepson, A., & Clarke, A. (2016). *An Introduction to Planning and Managing Communities, Festivals and Events*. London: Routledge.

Kirkham, J. (2017). The Grand National will be among the most watched TV events on the planet, *The Liverpool Echo*. Retrieved from www.liverpoolecho.co.uk/news/tv/grand-national-among-most-watched-12864656 Accessed 16th February 2018.

Krugman, C., & Wright, R. R. (2006). *Global Meetings and Exhibitions (The Wiley Event Management Series)*. New York: Wiley.

McGann, B., McGann, C. (2006). *The Story of the Tour de France Volume 1: 1903–1964*. Indianapolis: Dog Ear Publishing.

Mitchell, A. (Writer) (2017). Wimbledon. In T. Field (Producer), *BBC Radio 4,* Open Country. London: BBC.

Müller, M. (2015). What makes an event a mega-event? Definitions and sizes. *Leisure Studies*, 1–16. doi:10.1080/02614367.2014.993333

Musikmesse (n.d.). About Musikmesse. Retrieved from http://musik.messefrankfurt. com/frankfurt/en/aussteller/messeprofil.html Accessed 12th December 2016.

Music Cities Events (n.d). Bringing ideas together to create better music cities. Retrieved from www.musiccitiesevents.com/ Accessed 22nd May 2020.

Nicholls, J., Lawlor, E., Neitzert, E., & Goodspeed, T. (2012). *The Guide to Social Return on Investment*. London and Lincoln: Social Change UK.

OED (2016). *Oxford English Dictionary online*. Retrieved from https://www-oed-com. ezproxy.wlv.ac.uk/ Accessed 12th December 2018.

Sharma, T. (2015). Relevance of China's Silk Road revival initiative and Nepal. Retrieved from http://nepalforeignaffairs.com/relevance-of-chinas-silk-road-revival-initiative-and-nepal/ Accessed 27th March 2016.

Shone, A., & Parry, B. (2013). *Successful Event Management: A Practical Handbook* (4th ed.). London: Cengage Learning.

Planning and delivery

Social Value UK (2016). What are the principles of social value? Retrieved from www.socialvalueuk.org/what-is-social-value/the-principles-of-social-value/ Accessed 10th November 2019.

Stone-Potter, D., & Mattingly, D. J. (1999). *Life, Death, and Entertainment in the Roman Empire*. Ann Arbor, MI: University of Michigan Press.

Timewatch (Writer) & J. Gray (Director). (2017). *Stonehenge: A Timewatch Guide*. In J. Farren (Series Editor) *Timewatch*. London: BBC4.

UN Department of Economic and Social Affairs, Population Division (2015). *World Population Prospects The 2015 Revision (Vol. II: Demographic Profiles)*. New York: United Nations.

Welch, K. E. (2007). *The Roman Amphitheatre: From Its Origins to the Colosseum*. Cambridge: Cambridge University Press.

Wikipedia (n.d.). 1877 Wimbledon Championship. Retrieved from https://en.wikipedia.org/wiki/1877_Wimbledon_Championship Accessed 30th June 2017.

Chapter 2

The four pillars of international event delivery

Contents

2.1 Chapter overview

This chapter discusses the four pillars that international events are built upon: preparation, participation, communication, and legacy. Because international event management covers a multitude of business areas and disciplines, they can be extremely complicated to manage. International events will be dissimilar even when the main topic matter is the same. The four pillars cover the whole life cycle of an event and will assist in understanding the broader requirements of an international event to increase the likelihood of a successful outcome for all stakeholders.

2.2 Learning objectives

By the end of this chapter, the student will be expected to:

- Appreciate the full life cycle of an international event
- Understand the four pillars of international event management and their fundamental parts
- Recognise the various additional preparation considerations for international events
- Appreciate a number of decision-making processes appropriate to event delivery.

2.3 Introduction

The successful provision of all types of events is grounded in the quality of the planning and delivery processes. These two activities are habitually grouped together but are quite separate to each other and occur, for the most part, in a sequential fashion. Add to these the need for good communication and the legacy the event leaves behind, we then have the four pillars on which all great international events are built. Based on the topics discussed in Chapter 1, we can accept that creating a successful international event requires vision and an understanding of the specific area of business. The investment and preparation required to satisfy the call for an event to be international is by nature much greater. First and foremost, international events require a much longer lead-in period to allow for the more detailed preparation required.

2.4 The four pillars of international event delivery

For international events, there are more than a few unique tasks that need to be dealt with in the planning and delivery processes. The planning process largely precedes delivery, but with technological developments, opportunities exist

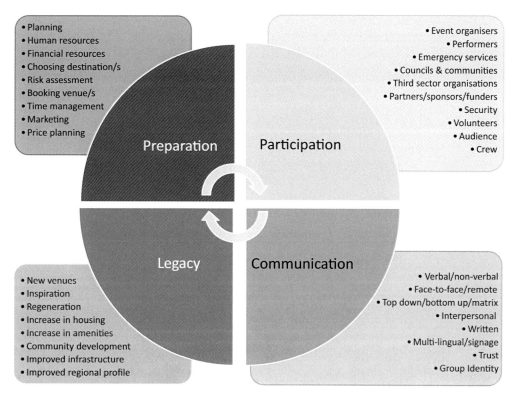

Preparation
- Planning
- Human resources
- Financial resources
- Choosing destination/s
- Risk assessment
- Booking venue/s
- Time management
- Marketing
- Price planning

Participation
- Event organisers
- Performers
- Emergency services
- Councils & communities
- Third sector organisations
- Partners/sponsors/funders
- Security
- Volunteers
- Audience
- Crew

Legacy
- New venues
- Inspiration
- Regeneration
- Increase in housing
- Increase in amenities
- Community development
- Improved infrastructure
- Improved regional profile

Communication
- Verbal/non-verbal
- Face-to-face/remote
- Top down/bottom up/matrix
- Interpersonal
- Written
- Multi-lingual/signage
- Trust
- Group Identity

Figure 2.1 The four pillars of international event delivery

for planning activities to exist during delivery phase. There are some planning-related activities (necessarily or otherwise), that may have to occur during the delivery stage, but these would have been highlighted during the planning stage. The two elements should by no means be treated as part of the same process. The event planning stage synchronises the necessary components in time to achieve a smooth delivery. However, some delivery activities may need to begin before the planning phase is completed due to the lengthy timescale of these activities. For example, the Olympic torch relay is considered part of the Games. Lasting for up to five months, the relay takes the torch to all six participating continents (Grant, 2014a). During this period, some of the most important planning activities are still being carried out. In fact, many stadia and other facilities are ordinarily still being built.

Figure 2.1 details many of the various aspects of the four pillars of inter-national event delivery, but the list is not meant to be exhaustive. These and other aspects will be discussed in more detail throughout this and other chapters.

For many event managers, managing international events is preferable to any other kind of event management. This may be for any number of reasons including:

- the diverse set of scenarios international events convey to a home location
- dealing and working with a mix of cultures

- the desire or need to travel
- a sense of combining work with pleasure
- the excitement and thrill of the challenge to bring an international event together
- experience, making certain individuals specialists in international event management.

Once you have decided this is your career choice, there are just a few more things to remember. An individual contribution is critical and the bigger the event, the bigger the stakes involved. The largest international events are highly-publicised and earnestly anticipated by the general public. Any failure is a potential disaster for the event itself, the organisers and the consequences can affect a nation for many years. Politicians, sponsors, the private sector, the public sector, the rich and the poor, the old and the young – and not forgetting the world's media – can all be relying on you. Get it right and it was just another day in the office. However, you might become a legend. Alternatively, if you get it wrong you might end up in prison. International events management is not the place for an easy ride, a nine-to-five work schedule, or free weekends. No pressure then, but they are just the reasons why those who deliver such events love them.

2.5 Preparation

There has never been a more appropriate saying when delivering events than fail to prepare, prepare to fail (Franklin, 2010). Identifying and effectively realising the jobs and challenges that need to be monitored or completed is what sets successful event organisers and event companies apart. The better prepared an event team is, the more likely there will be fewer complications down the line. It is not possible to remove all complications or challenges from an event and problems can and will occur in any event. However, better preparation and the completion of a risk assessment should mean minor rather than major adjustments closer to and during the event delivery phase and the ability to deal with whatever situation occurs.

As with any complicated event, there are a range of important activities that need constant monitoring to make the event successful. Beginning to create an itemised checklist from scratch is a good place to start, but would probably take as long as delivering the event itself. Once an itemised checklist begins to be compiled, it becomes difficult to avoid re-enacting the Monty Python Spanish Inquisition sketch (Dobrogoszcz, 2014). That is, every time the most important themes are listed, something else is added to the list. Therefore, it is a good rule of thumb to break the various processes down into a few basic headings to focus on the different aspects of the event. Bladen et al. (2017) discuss this as events operations, taking a project management perspective with event delivery broken down into manageable sections. Bowdin et al. (2011) discuss what they call the 'operations screen' and detail the skills and resources needed to deliver an event. This approach highlights the internal and external delivery processes involved in delivering an event and the risks in doing so. Berners (2017) recommends ensuring the event planning process follows a structural approach to managing events and that doing this will improve communications and pay dividends in the long term.

These examples highlight the various approaches available to event managers and even choosing which to follow can be considered part of the planning process. By starting with at least a trilogy of themes, the delivery challenge becomes more manageable. In the example in Figure 2.1, tasks or activities are placed within the suggested themes. By constantly monitoring the activities covered by preparation, participation and communication, the process of delivery becomes more effective. As the plan comes to life, what the event intends to leave behind (the legacy), also comes to fruition; even though legacy can also be included in a feasibility phase and decided much earlier. Legacy in such cases is then the starting point. This example is not based on one delivery task leading into the next; this would be covered in the preparation as part of the planning process. It is more about highlighting each activity within the theme to ensure each is incorporated into the workload and not overlooked. It is the breakdown of the what, who, why, where, how, and of course, when.

Each type of event will have its own particular requirements. Therefore, it is important to ensure the right balance is created between the needs of the event, to ensure the appropriate delivery, and not an over- or under-delivered plan. Certain events will require more technology than others, while another event might require extensive – and sometimes years of – preparation. For example, the Lucca Comic and Games Festival in Italy draws an audience in excess of 250,000. The city's natural population is estimated to be in the region of 90,000. This rise in population creates a host of issues for locals and organisers and while the money that flows in from increased spending, the local infrastructure is tested to the limit.

However big or small the event is, planning and preparation will usually follow the same general process. Creating a checklist is the perfect place to start planning as this will assist with what you want your event to achieve and should be used for guidance to highlight any potential requirements or points to be considered. Event lists are constantly added to and revised throughout the life of the event, but once you deliver your first event, you have a blueprint for the next.

To create an event checklist, it must include the following three key considerations:

• clear objectives
• sufficient time (to plan and deliver)
• clearly identified (and delegated) responsibilities.

Adding or removing actions in a checklist should always be considered to improve the efficiency, cost or overall delivery process. Based on Figure 2.1 above, Figure 2.2 provides some initial content for consideration that would come up in the initial implementation plan for an event.

Much of the work carried out during the preparation stages is experienced during the delivery stage. For example, planning for being paid in another currency will require the monitoring of the exchange rates. A shrewd decision may be to agree a fee based on an exchange rate for a period of time to avoid a loss at a later date. By doing so, any uncertainty in the fee is avoided. Alternatively,

---

Preparation

- Assembling the Team, Creating a Budget, Securing Dates and Timing, Assessing Travel Plans, Choosing Venue/s, Choosing a theme, Conducting Risk Assessments, Evaluating the Target Market, Deciding the Marketing Plan, Planning Arrangements, Construction Work, Groundwork/Preparations, Education & Training, Formation of Teams, Precautionary Measures, Legal Considerations, Rehearsals, Try Outs & Tasters, Dry Runs, Feasibility Studies, Lead In Times, Making Ready, Putting in Order, Necessary Qualifications

Participation

- Creating A Buzz, Sharing Information, Setting Appropriate Prices, Providing Unity, Obtaining Assistance, Attendance To the Event, Cooperation Between Individuals, Providing Support, Presence, Sharing Support, Protests, Concurrence, Encouragement, Joining In, Taking Part

Communication

- Verbal Communication, Written Communication, Correct Articulation, Interpersonal Skills, Multi-Lingual Skills, Implementing the Marketing Plan, Timing the Flow of Information, Making Connections, Making Contacts ,Team Meetings, General Intelligence, Support Links, Timely Transmissions, Providing Advice/Correspondence, Dissemination of Information, Expressions of Interest, Publication of Material, Providing/Reading Regulations, Creating Teams, Transfer of Information, Announcements/Correspondence, Marketing Material, Keeping In the Loop, Translation of Material, Social Networks

Legacy

- Type of Impact, Intangible Evidence, Tangible Evidence, New Venues, Improved Infrastructure, Increase in Housing, Increase in Amenities, Community Development, Regeneration, Improved Profile, Sustainable Development, Return on Investment, Skills Development, Increased Tourism, Civic Pride, Employment, Improved Mobility/Access

Figure 2.2 Itemised checklist for the development of an event implementation plan

the exchange rate will have to be monitored regularly and any fluctuation absorbed into the costs or enjoyed as a bonus.

It is common for many territories engaged in international events to trade in US dollars when another currency is less favourable. This is also often the case at sea where, in reality, no actual currency exists. International events are a core aspect of international cruises with musicians, performers, and event organisers being paid in US dollars. However, it is not unusual to find some companies being paid in something other than money when satisfactory monetary compensation cannot be agreed. Examples of this include payments in kilos of coffee in South American states or other luxury items. Import duty would still need to be paid as well as whatever transportation costs. These undertakings tend to be less popular today because of the complications involved, but the opportunity to negotiate any kind of payment is essentially down to the parties involved. Once the goods are exported their value can be much greater than the value of the local currency in another state.

2.5.1 Where and when to start

Event ideas can come from the humblest of beginnings and grow into global sensations. Many, of course, are created by governments and local authorities and become central to the communities they are intended for and much more.

Many international events come about from the success of local people or teams while others appear to have been part of the community for as long as everyone can remember. However they come about, there are people involved at every level of responsibility working throughout the year to ensure the next event is as good as, or better, than the last.

International events are quite often different from other international business activities because events come and go or exist for a specific length of time. A touring enterprise never guarantees it will return the following year; it builds all the risk into the success or failure of a seasonal or annual run. While most of the risks that exist when working in the global market are the same for all business activities, such as the need for constant political and financial stability, an international event manager will set their strategy with specific start and end dates in sight. The decision-making process for a business is more permanent.

For some touring organisations, these fluctuating conditions offer opportunities as circumstances can be favourable for long-enough periods to get in and out without the fear of long-term losses. Of course, the more successful an event becomes, the more contractually fixed the processes become; but even then, well written contracts can include clauses that allow the enterprise to get out before any major losses are incurred.

2.5.1.1 Choosing a date

Choosing a date to hold an international event can be both the simplest and most difficult of challenges. Some events are planned based on the seasons; others are fixed based on the availability of a date. Some organised events will be planned based on the availability of a venue, while others are offered out to venues to fit in with a particular touring programme. Whatever date is chosen, it is important to understand how much time is needed to successfully deliver the event.

The start date for planning an international event is often much earlier than first conceived. For example, London won the right to host the 2012 Olympics when Jacques Rogge made the final announcement in Singapore in 2005. The original feasibility study to put together the case to bid was conducted in 1996. However, Lee (2006) advises that in reality the preparations began even earlier, suggesting the decision for London to bid was made when Manchester's bid failed in 1993 – making a planning schedule of 19 years.

2.5.2 The golden thread

Once the decision has been made to go ahead with an international event, the key to delivering exceptional events that are well received is to produce, create, and follow a golden thread throughout the whole process. The golden thread can be compared to the x-factor, but is a managed concept. Exceptional event delivery is when the theme, design and content come together as one. Each aspect on its own can be considered to be well done, but once they are mixed, the event itself takes on a life and meaning of its own. The golden thread is essentially a theme or a message that continues throughout the event itself.

It can be transferred from one medium to another or can remain a constant throughout the event. It can be both obvious and sometimes quite subtle to the spectator, but when achieved, it holds the whole process together as it permeates the various elements of the event itself.

Essentially, this is what is meant when we talk about visionaries in the industry. These are the people who visualise the event in its completed form long in advance of any serious planning. It is then the job of the event organiser (who is often also the visionary), to implement these visions and make the imagined a reality.

2.5.3 Decision making

The art of decision making is an extremely broad topic and one of the important elements of international event management. How we arrive at our decision is an even more complicated process. It has been argued that almost any interesting cognitive function can be framed as a decision of some sort (Doya and Shadlen, 2012), while other studies suggest intuition plays an important role in every aspect of life and high intuitive skills positively contribute to the success of an organisation (Matzler et al., 2014). With these points in mind, it would be ill-advised to recommend how to make decisions. However, decisions will need to be made.

Throughout the life of an event, issues and problems will arise that require the event manager to make a decision. The challenge is to know if the correct decision is being made, particularly if the situation has never been experienced before. In extreme situations, panic can set in, the decision can appear more complicated and the pressure of responsibility can create a helpless sense of inability or impending disaster.

According to the Oxford Dictionary of Proverbs (Speake, 2015), there is an old exhortation or proverb that alludes to making decisions and has been used throughout the centuries to provide guidance on how to pay attention to small details . These may seem insignificant in themselves at the time, but if neglected can cause disaster at a later stage in the process.

The proverb reads as follows:

> For the want of a nail the shoe was lost,
> For the want of a shoe the horse was lost,
> For the want of a horse the rider was lost,
> For the want of a rider the battle was lost,
> For the want of a battle the kingdom was lost.

(Speake, 2015)

While this old proverb is a good rule of thumb to use and can develop management ability, it does not really address the stark reality of decision making. You could have metaphorically already have lost your horse and now need to make a decision on how best to save the rider.

There has been a deliberate attempt to avoid using the words 'right decision' in this process as it is often not a question of right or wrong. Some decisions can create both right and wrong consequences and the more serious or demanding it is, the more likely the decision will have multiple consequences for those involved. Correct decisions are based on a number of factors including: what are the actual circumstances of the time, what are the future implications, what might the consequences cost (monetarily and otherwise), how effective will the decision be and so on. Even doing nothing can be a calculated correct decision.

In order to make the correct decision, it needs to be an informed decision. So the first thing an event manager needs to consider is whether they have done anything like this before. Experience plays a great part in making the correct decision. If the answer is yes, then the options need to be weighed up based on this previous knowledge and an informed decision can start to be made on how to fix the issue or problem. If the answer is no, there may be no first-hand experience of a similar issue, then research needs to be conducted or advice sought on the issue or problem in order to make an informed decision. This can range from discussing the issue with someone else, asking for advice or referring to books or the internet. If there is no time to do any of these, a seat-of-your-pants decision may be required, which may sound irresponsible, but relies on the individual's true judgement and other life experiences.

2.5.4 RAG rating

To assist in the decision-making process, a popular means of managing large international event is to adopt a red, amber, green (RAG) rating to recognise how the effort from preparation to delivery is progressing. In international events, there is a need to consider multi-dimensional objectives where an activity is measured by a number of indicators. The RAG rating provides event managers with a succinct opportunity to plan the progress with specific accomplishments. The basic principle is to move, flag, prioritise, or group activities and tasks from positions of 'we will be' to 'we are'. The RAG rating assists in the recording of important milestones and highlights how a project, programme, or the event itself is performing. However, it becomes more significant as delivering the event becomes imminent.

Figure 2.3 highlights the three basic stages of the traffic light RAG rating: green, amber, and red. This can be extended to five ratings – green, green amber, amber, amber red, and red – depending on the level of activities involved. The five-rating option allows event managers to consider the readiness timeline and delivery in more detail and provides further preparation time to flag areas of concern or requiring progress.

2.5.5 Contingency planning

In every event there is the potential for many things to change and not go to plan. During the planning process, the organising team should be continually asking 'what if…?' This is the first stage in contingency planning and is normally covered as part of a risk assessment. Essentially, by asking 'what if…?' the organisers come to understand the key risks that may affect the event. There becomes a point when the problems established are covered by previous considerations. This is the point when the contingency planning has effectively exhausted itself. Therefore, contingency planning is the advanced preparation

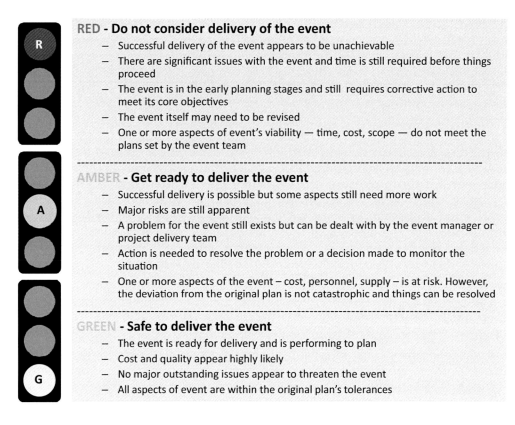

RED - Do not consider delivery of the event
- Successful delivery of the event appears to be unachievable
- There are significant issues with the event and time is still required before things proceed
- The event is in the early planning stages and still requires corrective action to meet its core objectives
- The event itself may need to be revised
- One or more aspects of event's viability — time, cost, scope — do not meet the plans set by the event team

AMBER - Get ready to deliver the event
- Successful delivery is possible but some aspects still need more work
- Major risks are still apparent
- A problem for the event still exists but can be dealt with by the event manager or project delivery team
- Action is needed to resolve the problem or a decision made to monitor the situation
- One or more aspects of the event – cost, personnel, supply – is at risk. However, the deviation from the original plan is not catastrophic and things can be resolved

GREEN - Safe to deliver the event
- The event is ready for delivery and is performing to plan
- Cost and quality appear highly likely
- No major outstanding issues appear to threaten the event
- All aspects of event are within the original plan's tolerances

Figure 2.3 A three-level RAG traffic light rating system

of action to meet unexpected events that could significantly impact the occasion should they occur. One way to view this is for every aspect of the event to have a contingency plan (Bridges, 2014).

Contingency planning does not mean investing in every given situation. Some situations are potentially more likely than others and these should be invested in. Other situations require an alternative plan to be put in place if a certain situation arises. There comes a point when it is simply impossible to go any further. For example, a sailing team in an around-the-world race cannot carry every spare part with them; some items will need to be left back at the home base or flown to the next destination. If something is needed during the stage that is not on board, the crew will have to be resourceful with what they have. The worst-case scenario will be that it will just take a little longer to fix. However, the team will have gone through the potential problems and planned for everything to the best of their ability. All the possibilities and various scenarios need to be considered so the team knows how to respond, even when any unlikely incidents occur.

Most contingency plans should be straightforward to think of and prepare for. However, while plans are simple to think of, staff may need constant reminders and regular training to ensure all are aware of the potential dangers if such difficulties were to occur. Fire drills are a good example, although most of this safety awareness will form part of inductions as employees join the company.

This is discussed in more detail in Chapter 5. Most, if not all, venues and event companies will appoint fire officers. Similarly, pre-event briefings should be standard practice before each and every event regardless of how often the events are held. Stewards, police, security, volunteers etc. should all experience the day/night briefing meeting prior to any shift. What everyone will learn as well as being prepared for are the things that have changed since the previous meeting or run-through.

To get contingency planning right, the organisers must consider the level of probability that something might occur against the level of impact on the event. These are the principles of risk management. For example, if a decision is made to hold an event outdoors, one of the first considerations will most likely be the weather. The role of the event manager is to deliver the event according to the event scope and organisational goals and objectives through the development of an event plan (Getz, 2012). The organisers will need to decide if inclement weather will affect these goals and objectives. However, some older festival attendees might argue that Woodstock '69 or Glastonbury '97 may have been considerably less memorable if the weather was benign. The organisers could have implemented a contingency plan that would have affected the continued delivery, but they would also have had to deal with the knock-on effects of implementing such a decision.

In some situations, contingency planning will mean making changes to planned activities or processes already in place. In other situations, it can mean delays with knock-on effects, leading to disruption and in the worst extreme, the consideration of cancelling the event itself. Although the cancelling of an event is the last thing any event manager wants to announce, it is surprisingly common. No event is safe from the possibility of cancellation, but good preparation will reduce the likelihood of this and the prospect of any number of other unwanted manifestations that are potentially much worse. If the likelihood of potentially serious consequences is established; be that by the organisers themselves or another responsible party (such as the health and safety inspectors or a natural phenomenon), then the delay, postponement or cancellation of an event is the prudent response.

In contrast to the rain effect discussed above (Woodstock '69 and Glastonbury '97), the wind can bring a whole different set of problems to event organisers and contingency planning can quickly turn into cancellation. In the summer of 2019 numerous festivals and events were cancelled across the UK at the last minute because of worsening weather. The Boardmasters festival in Cornwall, Houghton Festival in Norfolk, Blackpool Air Show, Bristol's International Balloon Fiesta, Wildside Festival Derbyshire, London Wildlife Festival at Walthamstow Wetlands, and the inaugural Women's Tour of Scotland cycling race were all cancelled around the same time due to 60mph ,gale force 10) wind forecasts. High winds are extremely dangerous at festivals because the tolerance levels of temporary structures are simply not adequate enough to withstand much speed (Gregory, 2019; Hawkins and Coles, 2019).

General wind forecasts can be observed, but accurate wind speed monitoring can only really take place on site and the organisers must respond with their weather management plan which will include contingency plans for high winds. Once the situation becomes so serious, regardless of the amount of investment, event organisers need to distinguish between making the correct decision,

Planning and delivery

Table 2.1 The Beaufort Scale

Beaufort Scale	Description	Average speed at 10m above ground		
0	Calm	Under 1 knot	Less than 1 mph	
	Light breeze	1 to 10 knots	0.7 to 12.2 mph	0.3 to 5.4 m/s
4	Moderate breeze	11 to 15 knots	12.3 to 17.8 mph	5.5 to 7.9 m/s
5	Fresh breeze	16 to 21 knots	17.9 to 24.0 mph	8.0 to 10.7 m/s
6	Strong wind	22 to 27 knots	24.1 to 31.0 mph	10.8 to 13.8 m/s
7	Near gale force	28 to 33 knots	31.1 to 38.3 mph	13.9 to 17.1 m/s
8	Gale force	34 to 40 knots	38.4 to 46.5 mph	17.2 to 20.7 m/s
9	Strong gale force	41 to 47 knots	46.6 to 54.7 mph	20.8 to 24.4 m/s
10	Storm force	48 to 55 knots	54.8 to 63.6 mph	24.5 to 28.4 m/s

Source: Adapted from Singleton, 2008

which may be to cancel the event, or risking the reputation of the company and the lives of others.

The strength of wind is the key for the event organisers to observe as this will indicate the point at which to consider making changes. Table 2.1 indicates the Beaufort Scale which is used to understand the different strengths of wind and their potential effects.

It is important for the organisers to remember that weather conditions can change quickly. Even in the event of bad weather, it may not be necessary to stop the whole event or cancel the show completely. Figure 2.4 shows how a wind action plan should be implemented. The event organisers should conduct regular weather forecast reviews in the run-up to the event and at any time a structure remains erect. If the speed of the wind goes beyond level five on the Beaufort scale, the organisers should prepare to halt operations until safe conditions have resumed. Once the situation has reached a level of concern, the organisers will need to conduct site safety meetings and review any risk assessment accordingly. If the situation remains critical and goes above level six, the organisers will need to consider preparations for full or temporary halt to the event. If the forecast or on-site conditions go beyond level six on the Beaufort Scale, the event may need to be cancelled or temporarily stopped and contingency plans and possible evacuation of the danger area to the designated refuge areas implemented.

Contingency planning should not be confused with implementing plan B. Contingency planning should first be considered as essentially keeping to plan A, but revising or reviewing the original plan slightly to keep plan A on track. Only in extreme circumstances does plan B come into effect. Contingency planning is something that constantly occurs throughout the life of an event. Musicians and actors have deps (deputies) who are able to jump in at short notice, travel plans can be revised due to delays, and suppliers often let you down. These are just a few typical examples of how good contingency planning keeps to the original plans with some alterations, and the show on the road.

Figure 2.4 Wind action plan

Source: Adapted from Grant, 2014b

2.5.6 Insurance

The ultimate contingency plan will be the insurance policy. Insurance is essentially transferring the risk to a third party, but the majority of events today cannot go ahead without the appropriate insurance being in place. Many specialist brokers exist who can advise on the correct insurance for the specific type of event. Everything from stallholders insurance to Christmas lights can be quite easily covered through an online application.

Venues and many event organisers today will not engage sub-contractors without proof of their public liability insurance. This is another important consideration for contingency planning as it remains the responsibility of the organisers to ensure that every sub-contractor is suitably insured and carries the correct paperwork to trade at the event. When concessions are provided at festivals, it is important for the organisers to do the rounds and check that every stallholder's paperwork is in order. It is poor practice to make assumptions when the consequences can be very serious.

2.5.7 Resilience

Being in charge of a task can bring great levels of responsibility that feed back into the overall delivery of the event. Such circumstances increase the pressure on individuals and teams to respond and deliver. Event organisers will soon discover their level of resilience as they encounter problems. Responsibility brings with it many levels of stress and the pressure can increase the closer the event gets to show time. However, while this may seem a little frightening to some, individuals are naturally able to build up their ability to respond to challenges and improve their performance after each and every experience. Resilience therefore is a skill that is developed with experience.

Resilience is required for a variety of situations that organisers will find themselves in. Every individual will react to situations in their own way, but there are conditions that put resilience to the test. Negotiating contracts, dealing with local communities, meeting celebrities, watching the weather, travelling or even commuting can all add pressure to the job. Resilience is also something that is acquired in a team and not always an individual requirement. The sense of a team in fact improves its individual members' levels of resilience. Clarke (2016) suggests there is a need for cross-disciplinary teamwork for complex but effective resilience-building solutions. At a more abstract level, the organisation may need to build a level of resilience in the face of a number of unpredictable conditions. Caralli (2011) lists a number of triggers that might require changes in resilience requirements that can all be considered relevant to an international event team under pressure. These include:

- changes in the organisation's mission, goals, objectives, or critical success factors
- changes in organisational lines of business or geographical operations
- changes in organisational structure, including staff changes
- changes that result in outsourcing services and assets or in changing current external entity relationships
- market and economic conditions
- social or political conditions, or geographically induced constraints
- identification of internal or external fraud or the realisation of risk and impact to the organisation
- redeployment or association of assets to new or different services
- identification of conditions that would result in exposure to new risks (via risk assessment processes).

Considering the many changes an event coordinator experiences during the life cycle of an event, it is no surprise that the role of an event coordinator was named as the fifth most stressful job in the USA (Elkins, 2017). However, that is not to suggest it is not rewarding. What international event organisers need to remember is that many situations can result in failure. Whether that is not receiving a contract or simply getting something wrong during the event process, stuff happens. Resilience is improved when failure occurs and individuals and organisations learn from the setbacks and adapt to any misfortune that is experienced. Following routines can be beneficial but not when it restricts the learning process or creates complacency.

2.5.8 Additional preparations for international events

Each sector of the event industry will have its own specific demands and each event will have its own unique set of circumstances. Much of the preparation is different from local planning and therefore not necessarily affected by international limitations. However, with international events, there are many more things to consider. Figure 2.5 provides an indication of the typical additional demands and considerations organisers will have to plan for when engaging

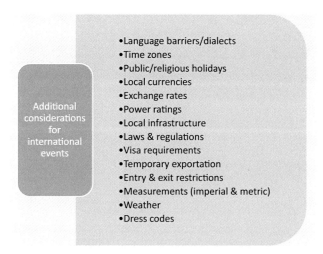

• Language barriers/dialects
• Time zones
• Public/religious holidays
• Local currencies
• Exchange rates
• Power ratings
• Local infrastructure
• Laws & regulations
• Visa requirements
• Temporary exportation
• Entry & exit restrictions
• Measurements (imperial & metric)
• Weather
• Dress codes

Additional considerations for international events

Figure 2.5 Additional demands on international event preparation

with international events. Several other demands will exist after the planning stages, but these will be specific to the event's location and type.

2.5.8.1 Language barriers and dialects

In international trade, one of the single most difficult barriers to trading overseas is language (Evans, 2012). However, language problems are not restricted to crossing international borders. Language can be a problem closer to home as people speak with different accents even in relatively close community groups. Language and understanding are really important because understanding a message depends on the language and tone used and how technical information is translated into recommended action (Purtle, Siddiqui, and Andrulis, 2011). Therefore, dialect differences can make communication difficult. Examples of dialect language barriers exist worldwide and travelling events will encounter these regularly along the way.

Chinese has a variety of dialects and languages with seven official languages and 59 other recognised languages that are commonly spoken; including Cantonese and Mandarin (Smith, 2018). Russia has 27 languages that are co-official and at least another 75 minority languages (Evans, 2012). In countries with many different cultures within them (the nations of the United Kingdom – England, Northern Ireland, Scotland and Wales – are a prime example) the language used may change to suit the local people or the culture (see Figure 2.6). It is also quite common to find mixtures of dialects in between the various destinations.

2.5.8.2 Time zones

Travelling through and dealing with different time zones can be extremely complicated and it is common for businesses that do so to keep track of the

Figure 2.6 Multi-language road signs from Scotland, Ireland, and Wales

different time zones. In order to distinguish which part of the workday their international colleagues are in, a number of clocks are positioned on the wall showing the time in each destination. For example, if there is a need for a wide-scale conference call, planning the call to meet everyone's schedule could become quite complicated. Being able to glance at a time zone clock can make planning such events much easier (Sapling, 2014).

Many international event organisations will stick to their local continent for business, but even doing this can involve the crossing of different time zones. Other businesses will stick to countries that speak the same language or come under the same jurisdiction, such as France or the UK who have many dependent territories. Some individual countries have numerous time zones such as USA, Canada, Russia and Australia. This can create problems with meetings when individuals use different time zones in their diaries or live events that use TV and the media. If one company in the USA uses EST (Eastern Standard Time) and another CST (Central Standard Time), the time of the meeting will appear to each individual as the same but will actually be slightly different.

Technology is making these issues much less of a problem. Data in calendars can now recognise some of these variances and offer options to sync the events, but caution is constantly necessary. Some places around the world do not follow the convention of hourly differences. Some are different by half an hour, 45 and even 15 minutes.

While nearly all countries have hourly time zones, some are half-hourly. Nepal is one of only two places in the world that has a quarter-hourly time zone; the other being the Chatham Islands. Nepal is 5 hours and 45 minutes ahead of GMT because it sets the meridian of Nepal Standard Time at Gaurishankar, a

Table 2.2 Time zone clocks, including the non-standard Kathmandu clock

London	New York	Los Angeles
17:20	12:20	09:20
Chatham Islands	Sydney	Singapore
07:05	04:20	01:20
Kathmandu	Berlin	Porto
23:05	18:20	17:20

mountain east of Kathmandu (Wong, 2015). Table 2.2 depicts different times as they appear at the same time in the various cities around the world.

2.5.8.3 Public, religious, cultural holidays/observations

Public holidays can work in the international event manager's favour as there is more opportunity for people to attend an event due to the additional free time. However, this will also lead to potentially higher delivery costs as many countries and businesses (especially the service industry) are either closed or charge more for working on public holidays. Religious holidays can be even more complicated as many faiths will observe very specific fasting and working restrictions that may have an impact on your own workforce. Some employees may need to attend religious events.

Each nation or territory will have its own cultural observations from Sunday closing, siestas, bank holidays, half-day trading, all having an effect on the preparations for international events. Businesses with national offices might have to close branches in one region. Again the UK is a prime example of these problems with the different nations observing public holidays on different days. For example, Scotland observes St Andrew's Day as a public holiday while St Patrick's Day is a public holiday in the Canadian province of Newfoundland and Labrador (for provincial government employees), and the British Overseas Territory of Montserrat. It is also widely celebrated by the Irish diaspora around the world, especially in the United Kingdom, Canada, United States, Brazil, Argentina, Australia and New Zealand (Cronin and Adair, 2002).

2.5.8.4 Local currencies

International business takes place through firms operating across national borders via different entry modes, such as wholly owned subsidiaries, joint ventures, strategic alliances etc. (Cook, 2018). Therefore, an agreed currency is needed to conduct any transaction. It is usual for business transactions to be conducted in the same currency as the event organiser's home state. If the organiser is based in the USA, the bills will appear in US dollars. If the company is based in mainland Europe, the bills will appear in euros and so on.

Transactions in international events still rely on cash. There are limits in what can be carried out of almost every country, so the need to know where you are travelling from and the restrictions is very important. This is discussed in more detail in Chapter 6. Border guards have the right to seize money. Moreover, some nations are not keen to receive currency from other places even when it is legal tender. Proffering Scottish money in England and vice versa can result in a refusal. Banks may also question depositors when the sums are over certain limits. Once again, it is important to check what customary activities there are in any given state.

2.5.8.5 Exchange rates

All foreign currency transactions are sensitive to fluctuations in what is commonly known as the exchange rate. This means that when agreeing fees and charges with a customer or supplier on one day the cost has the potential to rise or fall if the exchange rate changes the next. This may appear to be an insignificant issue as fluctuations on a daily basis tend to be minimal. However, when budgeting is done as part of the preparation process, the cost of a service or item may have changed significantly over the course of time.

For international event companies who regularly trade internationally the majority will keep to a single currency of choice for all financial transactions. This method allows for much better planning arrangements as the effect of the exchange rate is less of a concern to the company. In Europe, trading was made much simpler in 2002 with the introduction of the euro. However, out of the 50 nations across mainland Europe, 28 still use their own national currency. Table 2.3 provides a list of the nations and their particular currency.

Methods of electronic payment have made international transactions much more straightforward and include credit cards, debit cards and the ACH (Automated Clearing House) network which have been available since 1974. The exchange rate is then made in real time by the bank.

2.5.8.6 Power ratings and plugs

The majority of international events will be held in venues that are built for this very purpose. This means that using a venue that has an AC electricity grid connection is common practice for the majority of events. The different electric power supply ratings used around the world are important to know. The voltage and frequency of AC electricity power around the world are based on a number of voltage outputs. Therefore, there are variations from country to country. These range from 110v to 240v. Far fewer countries (about 20%) use a 110–120 V and a 60Hz rating but this does include the USA. The UK uses 230v and 50Hz.

To add to this complication, seasoned travellers will tell of the many different plugs and sockets in use around the world that are required to attach to the mains in each country. These are differentiated by a letter (A to N). Some territories use two or more and some bordering countries often use the same. Figure 2.7 displays a selection of the differences between different countries' plugs and sockets.

For many outdoor international events such as music festivals, there is the need to use generators to supply the necessary power. The event industry now recognises this as one of its biggest environmental challenges and some festival

Table 2.3 The currencies of the European nations

Country	Present currency	Sign	ISO 4217 code	Fractional unit
Albania	Albanian lek	L	ALL	Qindarkë
Andorra	Euro	€	EUR	Cent
Austria	Euro	€	EUR	Cent
Azerbaijan	Azerbaijani manat	₼	AZN	Qapik
Belarus	Belarusian ruble	Br	BYN	Kopeck
Belgium	Euro	€	EUR	Cent
Bosnia and Herzegovina	Convertible mark	KM	BAM	Fening
Bulgaria	Bulgarian lev	лв	BGN	Stotinka
Croatia	Croatian kuna	kn	HRK	Lipa
Cyprus	Euro	€	EUR	Cent
Czech Republic	Czech koruna	Kč	CZK	Halér
Denmark	Danish krone	kr.	DKK	Øre
Estonia	Euro	€	EUR	Cent
Finland	Euro	€	EUR	Cent
France	Euro	€	EUR	Cent
Georgia	Georgian lari	₾	GEL	Tetri
Germany	Euro	€	EUR	Cent
Greece	Euro	€	EUR	Cent
Hungary	Hungarian forint	Ft	HUF	Fillér
Iceland	Icelandic króna	kr	ISK	Aurar
Ireland	Euro	€	EUR	Cent
Italy	Euro	€	EUR	Cent
Latvia	Euro	€	EUR	Cent
Liechtenstein	Swiss franc	CHF	CHF	Centime,
Lithuania	Euro	€	EUR	Cent
Luxembourg	Euro	€	EUR	Cent
Republic of Macedonia	2nd Mcdn denar	ден	MKD	Deni
Malta	Euro	€	EUR	Cent
Moldova	Moldovan leu	L	MDL	Ban
Monaco	Euro	€	EUR	Cent
Montenegro	Euro	€	EUR	Cent
Netherlands	Euro	€	EUR	Cent
Norway	Norwegian krone	kr	NOK	Øre
Poland	Polish złoty	zł	PLN	Grosz
Portugal	Euro	€	EUR	Cent
Romania	4th Romanian leu	lei	RON	ban
Russia	Russian ruble	₽	RUB	Kopeyka

(*continued*)

Table 2.3 Cont.

Country	Present currency	Sign	ISO 4217 code	Fractional unit
San Marino	Euro	€	EUR	Cent
Serbia	Serbian dinar	РСД	RSD	Para
Slovakia	Euro	€	EUR	Cent
Slovenia	Euro	€	EUR	Cent
Spain	Euro	€	EUR	Cent
Sweden	Swedish krona	kr	SEK	Öre
Switzerland	Swiss franc	CHF	CHF	Centime
Turkey	Turkish lira	₺	TRY	Kuruş
Ukraine	Ukrainian hryvnia	₴	UAH	Kopiyka
United Kingdom	Pound sterling	£	GBP	Penny
Vatican City	Euro	€	EUR	Cent

Source: Miaschi, 2017

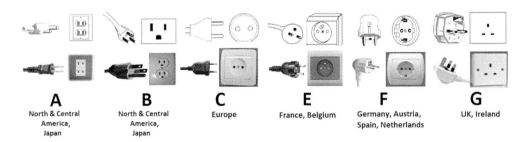

Figure 2.7 A selection of plugs and their corresponding sockets

organisers have been fortunate enough to make changes to either offset or reduce the carbon waste. This is discussed in more detail in Chapter 10. Melt in Germany and Glastonbury in the UK have both fitted permanent renewable solar power systems on their sites (Johnson, 2012). The current impact is limited but it shows the event organisers' green intentions and a possible future outlook for recurring outdoor events.

2.5.8.7 Local infrastructure

As an event travels from region to region, the organisers will experience a number of means of access to venues and event sites. Most modern event spaces have taken into consideration the transportation of equipment making the whole process of gaining access a matter of timely planning. Venues in more remote areas can create considerably more difficult to access. Interstate travel is usually a straightforward process as all big cities are connected through major road links. The general infrastructure problems that are caused tend to be much closer to the venue.

Many towns and cities have narrow streets and pedestrian walkways making them difficult to navigate. Others have time restrictions on access for any vehicle but public transport. Market towns across Europe can be particularly problematic due to the narrow streets and hills. Modern cities have created additional problems for event organisers by pedestrianising the roads. For example, the world-famous Cavern Club's main entrance is situated in the centre of Liverpool and is accessed via a pedestrian street with limited access to vehicles (see Figure 2.8).

Many ski resorts have motorised vehicle policies and a total ban on anything but electric vehicles. Swiss car-free ski resorts include Bettmeralp, Braunwald, Mürren, Riederalp, Rigi, Sass Fee (since 1951), Stoos, and Wengen. In Italy, a car free policy exist in Chamois with cable car access only. Courmayeur also has a car-free centre. Avoriaz is the one French ski resort that claims that it is totally car-free. Les Arcs, La Plagne, Valmorel, Valmeinier, Plagne Soleil, Belleplagne, and La Norma and Ax-Bonascre in the Pyrenees are also listed as car-free (Harneis, 2016). These places often become international venues holding numerous international events during the year. Gaining access needs to be planned well in advance to ensure the necessary equipment can be transported and set up in good time.

Figure 2.8 The world-famous Cavern Club entrance, Liverpool, UK

Similar to holding international events in mountainous regions, event organisers will seek out unique event spaces and deal with the complications they bring after the space has been chosen. These include open spaces in woods, parks, and farms, or even on the top of many famous landmarks. Many buildings such as museums and galleries that were never intended for international events are maximising their space and availability by hosting events for the corporate market. This can mean that access requires a great deal of investigation prior to the event if the space has not been used in an event capacity before.

2.5.8.8 Local laws and regulations

As events travel from nation to nation, it is important that the organisers are aware of any changes in the law or regulations that may affect the delivery of the event. These can include speeding restrictions, age of minors, alcohol limits, opening hours and parking. These basic considerations could all have massive consequences on the delivery of an event and could place the organisers in serious trouble with the authorities and even lead to a spell in prison.

Some laws that would today be considered unusual still exist. For example, dancing in some states is banned on a Sunday. 'Tanzverbot' is the German term for a dancing ban. The state or canton governments in countries such as Germany and Switzerland continue to have laws that ban the act of dancing (Wikipedia, n.d.). Even in the UK the 1780 Sunday Observance Act, which threatened any paid-for 'publick entertainment on the Lord's Day' with a £100 fine was only repealed in 2000 (Bloom, 2016).

Similarly, many American states continue to impose a number of dance-related bans. As in the UK, many of the bans are from old legislation, but it is prudent to check if your event is likely to infringe any aspect of the law.

2.5.8.9 Visa requirements

A large number of countries require visitors to apply for a visa in order to gain entry. Some countries are seeking to remove restrictions while others are seeking to impose them. Whatever the situation, it is always important to check before any travel arrangements are made as to what the existing state of affairs is for the whole team who are to travel. It is an easy oversight to assume the national status of a colleague simply because you have worked with them for a period of time. Visa requirements are discussed in more detail in Chapter 6.

What is most significant for touring events is that it is most likely a working visa that is required and not the basic tourist visa. Attempting to gain entry to a state with the wrong visa can result in being refused entry. Added to this is the cost and time it takes to obtain a work visa. The touring company will need to ensure that the cost is worth the effort. To put this into context, it has been suggested that Elvis Presley never toured outside of the USA because his manager Colonel Tom Parker (real name Andreas van Kuijik), was an illegal immigrant and would not have been able to get back into the USA (Barrow, 2003).

If the time and effort it takes to secure a visa for a given territory does not deter, there are many other regulatory deterrents to travel besides a travel visa requirement. Lawson and Roychoudhury (2016) discovered that people can be harassed, detained, and summarily denied entry by border control agents on even the slightest suspicion of criminal activity (Nikiforuk, 2013).

2.5.8.10 Temporary exportation

Travelling internationally with equipment can include a requirement for special documentation to leave the country of origin, enter the destination country, and return with the goods without having to pay duty each time a border is crossed. The international documentation for this temporary exportation is an ATA (Admission Temporaire/Temporary Admission) Carnet or simply a Carnet. A Carnet allows event organisers to take items in and out of many countries without having to pay customs duties or taxes. For international events, a Carnet is the equipment's passport. They apply to most non-perishable goods, providing ease of entry, exit, and re-entry. The agreement between countries saves the event organisers time and money. Twelve months' coverage is standard with most UK ATA Carnets across participating countries worldwide (ata-carnet.uk, n.d.). See Chapter 6 for more information on crossing borders with equipment and the necessary travel documentation.

2.5.8.11 Entry and exit restrictions

There are a variety of restrictions an international event organiser will have to deal with when entering or leaving a nation. These will depend on the particular nations involved but can create last minute issues. The main issues for international events include:

- individuals being stopped at the border and refused entry
- equipment being held at customs due to inadequate paperwork
- animals being quarantined
- transport vehicles failing local regulation or compliance orders.

International events personnel being stopped and refused entry at borders is a common occurrence. The reasons can be politically or religiously motivated, while health and criminal convictions have also proved to be reasons to deny access. Muslim singer Cat Stevens, who changed his name to Yusuf Islam, was refused entry to the United States in 2004 on 'national security grounds'. However, this received a great deal of press resulting in it being deemed a mistake. Colin Powell, the Secretary of State at the time later apologised (Smith, 2014).

For many musicians travelling with their instruments, the long-running issues over ecologically threatened woods such as Brazilian rosewood have also caused difficulties at the border. CITES (the Convention on International Trade in Endangered Species of Wild Fauna and Flora) introduced laws and put restrictions on how certain woods were traded across international borders. The latest laws mean it remains possible to travel with instruments freely as long as the total weight is not over 10kg (22lbs) of rosewood and other regulated woods (Glynn, 2017).

Drivers of transportation vehicles should be aware of the various requirements as they travel from country to country. There are numerous differences in the requirements for travelling in different places. Tyres may have to be changed seasonally, and the drink-driving law on how much alcohol is permitted in the blood can be a very serious issue. Some nations have zero, or close to zero, limits. Scotland, for example, has lower limits than England and Wales. The most problematic, however, are the south-east European states as they vary from zero tolerance (in Romania, Georgia, Czech Republic, Moldova, and Hungary) to 0.05% (in Turkey, Bulgaria, Greece, Syria and Serbia) (DrinkDriving.org, n.d.). A careless approach to these regulations can be disastrous to the event even the day after as significant amounts of alcohol will remain in the blood. Many nations, such as the Scandinavian states, have regular morning checkpoints with police breathalysing drivers.

2.5.8.12 *Measurements (imperial and metric)*

Most countries around the world use the metric system of measurement. Only Myanmar (Burma), Liberia, and the United States have yet to adopt the International System of Units as their official system of measurement for weights and measures (ChartsBin, 2010).

Whatever system is used, clear communication will remain paramount to ensure that the correct details are supplied. De Seife (2007) may have satirised the consequences of providing the wrong measurements for a Stonehenge model in the film *This is Spinal Tap*, but even a few centimetres' miscalculation can turn into costly repairs and ruin a stage plan.

2.5.8.13 *Local weather*

The weather has been discussed earlier in the chapter, but when travelling inter-nationally, it becomes an even more unpredictable factor and should never be taken for granted, particularly if the event is touring. Disruption to travel plans is a common enough experience even without the contribution of the weather, but when the elements are added to the mix in today's cautionary advice procedures, everything in the event's plans can be affected. Usually, regular reviews of the weather conditions should be enough to make alterna-tive arrangements and keep things on track, but this can lead to very last-minute changes to travel plans.

Considering that many international events travel from place to place, any set-up and close-down plans for outdoor events are constantly affected by the weather. The setting up of most outdoor events and their temporary demount-able structures (TDS) will be affected by every aspect of the weather. Wind, rain, sun, snow, and thunder and lightning all need to be considered. The con-dition of the ground can change depending on the weather during the event and make any kind of movement unadvisable. If the event is on high ground, there is a chance that low cloud cover could be an issue due to poor visibility. Figure 2.9 takes a venue from the north-west of England to highlight how the weather can be different on high ground from one day to the next. Visibility in

Figure 2.9 A change in the weather, Houghwood Golf Club, Billinge, UK

the top image is clearly for many miles, while visibility in the bottom image is no more than 20 metres.

As with local infrastructure issues discussed above, the local weather conditions may affect access. Other measures may need to be undertaken to ensure access remains possible even in the event of bad weather. Temporary surfacing for vehicles and those on foot may need to be prepared.

There may also be a need to weatherproof equipment for certain outdoor events as the equipment may need to be in position for a number of days. Protection from the elements at all times needs to be considered in the set-up arrangements. The need for contingency planning throughout the event will be paramount as equipment failures due to the weather are not uncommon.

2.5.8.14 Dress codes

A good rule of thumb for dress codes is, when in Rome, do as the Romans do. Fashion cannot be the most important consideration when travelling to some parts of the world due to the need to observe certain regulations. Understanding dress codes when visiting other countries is an essential part of travelling for mutual respect and tolerance. In some countries, dress codes are a very sensitive area. In 2016, *The Telegraph* newspaper offered the advice summarised in Table 2.4.

It is essential to respect traditional dress codes when in countries such as Pakistan or Iran. Following local dress codes, particularly for Western women, is essential to avoid aggressive behaviour from locals or unwanted attention from men. Saudi Arabia and other Middle Eastern countries are among the strictest in the world and some countries like Iran and Iraq use special police to enforce the required dress codes (Dwankowski and Huseby, 2017).

Most Middle Eastern countries require women to cover up and wear a head scarf. But while merely clothing your collarbone is enough in Jordan, just an inch of shoulder skin could get you arrested in Iran. Men are usually fine in

Table 2.4 A selection of dress code rules from around the world

Camouflage ban

In some Caribbean countries, including Jamaica, Barbados, Trinidad and Tobago, St Lucia, as well as in Saudi Arabia, it is illegal to wear camouflage clothing.

Driving with sandals

Probably not advised in any case in any country, but this is a criminal offence in Spain.

Bikinis in the street

In some parts of Spain it's against the law to wear only a bikini or swimming shorts in the street. Some local council authorities, including Majorca, impose fines if people are caught wearing swimwear away from the beach on the seafront promenade or adjacent streets.

Fancy dress

In Greece, some fancy dress costumes may be regarded as offensive and therefore against public decency laws.

High heels

Greece's historic sites, such as the Acropolis, have banned the wearing of high heels for fear of causing damage to ancient monuments.

Make-up on men

Back in 2010, seven men who walked into a fashion show in Sudan were arrested for being 'indecently dressed' by wearing make-up for the show, an act deemed 'offensive' by a court judge.

Facial hair

The 21st century saw the return of facial hair across Western cultures. Attitudes vary greatly from East to West. Some religions consider a full beard to be absolutely essential while others consider them unhygienic. Japan's wartime rule over South Korea created a continuing source of resentment for the moustache.

Source: Based on Kim, 2016

long trousers, and women carry shawls for a quick conservative fix (CNTraveler, 2009). However, when visiting new places for the first time, it is important to consider reviewing all the information on specific territories before entering their jurisdiction.

2.6 Participation

Participation in and at international events can be described as being across the event and through the event. It also occurs on a number of levels that include management, non-physical contributions, working on the day and actually taking part. Participation is essentially all the elements which make up a particular event. Each and every event is an interconnecting network of activities. Depending on the size of the event, creating a number of different layers can contribute to ensuring each aspect of the event is delivered to a satisfactory level of competence and care. Roles also range from being involved at the centre of the event – be that on a stage for music and theatre or on a field of play for sporting events. It takes in the perimeter of the event space that may be the venue building or the temporary structure's fencing, and sometimes spreads beyond the event's immediate footprint, moving out to the surrounding area. There is also non-participation and deliberate exclusion which is discussed in more detail in Chapter 8.

2.6.1 Being involved

Being involved in an international event can be a perplexingly entangled and complicated process. This is why it makes sense to have a separate management team or committee of organisers to handle the various necessities of the planning process, leaving those who are engaged directly with the event to focus on their role. However, it is accepted that this is not always possible to achieve.

The planning process overlaps considerably with the delivery of the event when other stakeholders physically contribute to the event itself and assist in making it happen. While the two have different aims, schedules, and purposes, a lot of synergy is required between the two as the sum of the parts increases. Figure 2.10 highlights the various contributions from a range of participants that make an event happen. In this diagram, the emphasis is on a sense of equal contributions, something that larger events use as motivation for some of the less glamorous or mundane tasks. Many of these contributing elements connect much more with some than they do with others and this is reflected in the way they are arranged/grouped within the figure. While it is not meant to be a representation for all international events, it is indicative of many.

While an equal contribution and inclusive viewpoint is commendable and keeps engagement and morale high, it is important to understand that international events are heavily hierarchical. Although a sense of equal contribution is often the objective, without a strong hierarchy of management, it would be impossible to complete the necessary planning and delivery requirements on

Figure 2.10 Contribution of participants to make international events happen

budget and on time. Figure 2.11 provides an example of the management structure for a typical international event.

With so many activities being organised at the same time, the work is usually broken down into sections. In this way, for example, the plans for the streets to be cleaned after the event can be arranged by one line of responsibility at the same time that another team is planning promotional activities. Therefore, the aim of the management team should be to first specify and allocate tasks and operating methods to ensure the smooth running of the event to a satisfactory level for the participants, whilst at the same time ensuring the safety of all those involved. The management team must also consider the event's sustained creation of value for the owners, employees and other stakeholders.

Once the event is over, its legacy becomes the priority – but this still forms part of the preparation process. For continuing events, the event's long-term future and to some degree the region are also critical considerations in the

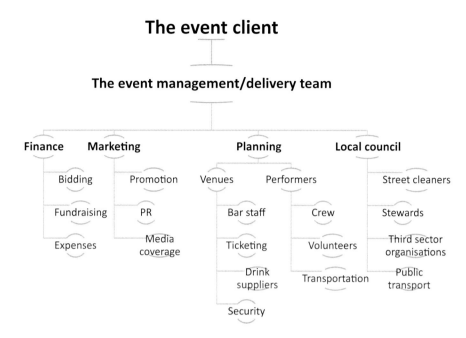

The event client

The event management/delivery team

Finance	Marketing		Planning		Local council
Bidding	Promotion	Venues	Performers		Street cleaners
Fundraising	PR	Bar staff	Crew		Stewards
Expenses	Media coverage	Ticketing	Volunteers		Third sector organisations
		Drink suppliers	Transportation		Public transport
		Security			

Figure 2.11 A hierarchy management structure of an event delivery team

planning stages. However, none of these tasks are what might be considered part of the live event.

2.6.2 The run-up to the start

In the run-up to the start of an event, particularly those which include a per-formance of some kind, a sense of expectation is evident. The organisers are ensuring all the planning is in place and a sense of handover begins to develop. Even this part of the event includes a great deal of planning, with many large events having events-within-events for very specific build-up activities. Boxing, for example, has an undercard made up of less significant bouts on the same bill as a main boxing match. Many sporting finals now include performances from other celebrities to raise the atmosphere within the venue before the start and during intervals. For many spectators and participants, superstitious routines are played out. Favourite clothes are worn, lucky charms are kissed. A milestone has been reached, a bridge is about to be crossed and all the preparations and arrangements come to an end. A metamorphosis occurs. Those involved from this point on are getting into a different mindset. The activities of those who have contributed to make the event happen begin to lessen. The stage is set, and the participants take over responsibility to deliver.

Once an event is underway, a whole new set of circumstances prevails. The experience is so unique, it is normal for the organisers to experience a sense of personal ownership in the event itself. How the experience feels can be described in detail by those who attend and take part in the lived experience of the event. Often the experience is so of the moment, one's normal sense of time and place disappears.

Many international events of all kinds are said to take spectators on a roller-coaster of emotions. Event organisers work on these emotions and have developed ways of providing experiences beyond that of any normal place, service or product; they have moved into offering dreams and emotions where it seems the only thing that limits us is our imagination (Berridge, 2012). However, as we each have different responses to situations, satisfaction cannot always be guaranteed for everyone.

2.6.3 The communication link

The final consideration of participation in this section is how preparation, participation and communication are continuously linked throughout the process. While we have discussed the release in the experience above and how change-over is achieved as the event begins, much of the actual process of preparation continues on through the participation process and through the communication process. For example, travel plans remain relevant throughout the event and tour itineraries are also ongoing. Financial planning turns from expenditure to income while contingency planning is on always ready to step in. It is the preparation that was completed that is keeping the event together through the communication process. Without this, much of the event would simply fall apart. Figure 2.12 highlights how the features of preparation and participation continue to cross over in an iterative manner. It remains important for the organisers to understand how these overlap. The iterative process between preparation, communication, and participation means each is constantly informing the other until a specific result is achieved.

Sometimes, the iterative monitoring process can go awry and even the best planning can result in failure when these processes are poorly carried out. The Champions League Final in Cardiff 2017 between Real Madrid and Juventus was celebrated as a success. However the local pubs and shops in Cardiff city centre said they lost huge sums of money. Local people had been advised by the local council to avoid the city centre as 170,000 fans were expected in the city for the match. One food shop owner said it was one of the worst weekends on record (Meechan, 2017). Everything had been planned to the last detail. However, a miscalculation on when the fans would arrive and leave the city and the advice communicated to locals to stay away rendered the place a ghost town for most of the day. The error destroyed any opportunity for local traders to make a profit, highlighting the importance of up-to-date and informed communication throughout the preparation and participation processes.

2.7 Communication

Bernard Haitink, the renowned Dutch conductor, once explained that his teacher described conducting as *luft sortieren*, or 'arranging the air' (BBC, 2019). International event management can also appear to be a similar experience as

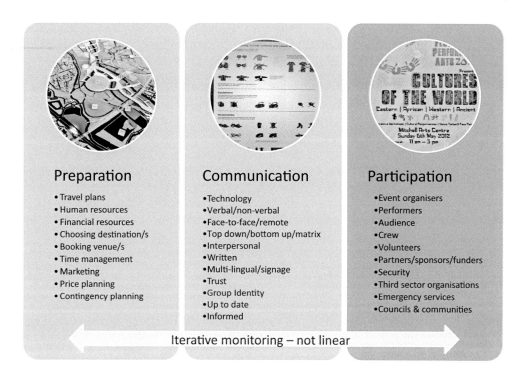

Preparation

- Travel plans
- Human resources
- Financial resources
- Choosing destination/s
- Booking venue/s
- Time management
- Marketing
- Price planning
- Contingency planning

Communication

- Technology
- Verbal/non-verbal
- Face-to-face/remote
- Top down/bottom up/matrix
- Interpersonal
- Written
- Multi-lingual/signage
- Trust
- Group Identity
- Up to date
- Informed

Participation

- Event organisers
- Performers
- Audience
- Crew
- Volunteers
- Partners/sponsors/funders
- Security
- Third sector organisations
- Emergency services
- Councils & communities

Iterative monitoring – not linear

Figure 2.12 Sub-sectors of the continuous communication process

it is not that dissimilar from the role of a conductor. The various communication levels of an international event are brought together in much the same way a conductor communicates with an orchestra. Dealing with the various people, personalities, instruments, and sections places many demands that require great skill, knowledge, and leadership to keep everything together in pursuit of the common goal.

As can be seen from Figure 2.12, there are many different layers and methods of communication that are required to deliver an international event. Fortunately for international events, communication goes way beyond just the use of verbal communication and good communicators tend to do very well in the event industry. Good communication will find itself being the centre of success, while at the same time poor communication finds itself at the centre of failure. For communication to be efficient and objectives to be achieved, strong relationships must be formed between clients and vendors (Halsey, 2010).

Methods of communication include verbal, non-verbal, virtual and physical methods. Any one of these methods will be best suited for the different types of message that need to be sent during the delivery of an international event. So there is no surprise that an emphasis exists on ensuring communication is accomplished to meet the requirements of the intended outcome.

To put the depth of communication that exists when delivering international events into some kind of perspective, we should consider how the majority of international events are delivered. Most of the work is dependent on what other people are doing and what each individual does is largely for someone else. Furthermore, each event demands the dedicated services of seasoned professionals who are tasked with ensuring the event is delivered safely to the best of their ability. However, many of these professionals are self-employed and will go from one event to another, usually within the same discipline and with only a verbal agreement to bind them. For example, a stage manager on a world tour with a famous rock band will complete the tour and go and work with a different artist on another tour with a different group of professionals. Each individual's ability to communicate goes far beyond their verbal ability.

A good manager can see or hear a job being well done in events; there is often little need to 'over talk' a situation. The combined communication that is created throughout the event is largely implicit and focused directly on the task in hand. This leads to trust in an individual that is built up within a team and created by the combined level of communication throughout all of the work that is completed. An individual's contribution is essentially communicated back to the team not by a manager, but by their own personal management and completion of their own responsibilities.

We can consider good communication from a people management perspective and how event managers are able to connect with people to bring the best out of a team through leadership. This is largely done through social communication where the message comes from one individual to another or a group of people. This can be put down to the correct choice of words, the time of day, how much pressure is on each individual, the workload, and the time available to complete the task with consideration for the context of the exchange. In an international events context, the sender of the message must be aware of any cultural differences that exist and how the language will be interpreted when translated to another.

Another key aspect of communication is how each of the different businesses involved in an event come together using a number of communication channels. This is of particular importance when distance, language barriers, and different cultural values exist. A relatively new feature in today's workforces are the closer bonds being achieved through social media building relationships across the different companies involved. Almost as soon as people begin to communicate, they share their social media details and create even stronger connections.

There is communication through the use of technology and its implementation throughout and beyond the term of an event. Much of this is used as a marketing tool and usually dealt with through a dedicated department. But again, the information involved is crucial to the correct message being transmitted. Often one of the main difficulties is communicating to multiple audiences through the same channels.

Whatever the style or type of international event, organisers need to understand that each event is both a means and an opportunity to communicate with an audience. In international events, the content itself is the main communication tool that gets the potential audience interested in attending. However, the event itself can override the content when the communication process between the event and local stakeholders goes awry. This is discussed in more detail in Chapter 8.

2.7.1 Flags and national anthems

Arguably two of the most significant processes of communication and identity at many international events are the flying of national flags and the playing of national anthems. The flying and position of flags have many protocols while national anthems pay respect to hosts, winners, teams, and dignitaries. Both the flying of flags and the playing of national anthems are taken very seriously, and in order to avoid a diplomatic incident, it is imperative to observe the correct etiquette and procedure to ensure the right message is communicated.

2.7.1.1 Flags

The standard protocol for national flags is first for them to be of equal size and displayed on staffs of equal height, each in a position that is not inferior to any of the other flags or ensigns. Every event venue should respectfully fly all of the flags of any nation involved in the event. It is imperative to position the flag correctly from the flagpole side. For example, the French tricolour has blue closest to the flagpole, while the Union Flag has a correct way up. In the top half of the flag nearest the flagpole, the wider diagonal white stripe must be above the red diagonal stripe, so that Scotland's St Andrew's Cross takes precedence over Ireland's St. Patrick's Cross (Bartram, 2002).

Flags should always be raised and lowered in a dignified manner. The flying of a flag is used to signal the beginning of an event, or the arrival of a VIP. To make it all the more complicated, this is done on the flagpole. For this to happen, it is important to ensure a flag unfurls correctly and this is done by folding the flag in a particular way. In fact, the folding of a national flag in public is a ceremonial event in itself which involves up to eight people. Some nations use a square folding technique while others use a triangular or a gatefold technique. The Union Flag is folded and then rolled.

2.7.1.2 Folding flags

The square fold begins with two downward central horizontal folds from the bottom to the top to make a long rectangular strip. These are followed by two upward folds from right to left, one downward fold from right to left and one upward fold from right to left. Other folds such as the gatefold and the triangular fold start the same. It is the long horizontal folds that are different. It is necessary to always pull the flag taut. Figure 2.13 illustrates the four different folding techniques discussed, with the Canadian flag illustrating how eight people contribute to a ceremonial flag-folding event. Alongside this is the United States' triangular folding of the stars and stripes, with the folding and rolling of the Union Flag and the gatefold of the national Australian flag also shown.

Due to the importance of etiquette and correct positioning at international events, flags should not be used for general decoration unless they follow the strict criteria described here. Coloured bunting or other forms of decoration

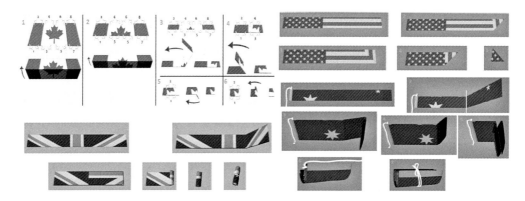

Figure 2.13 Different methods for the ceremonial folding of a national flag

Source: Author, based on Wikihelp, n.d.

that reflect the colours of the nations involved would add to the effect without being discourteous to any other contributing nations. Pendants can be placed on tables with other forms of national identity, adding to the overall design.

When displaying the national flag with flags of several other countries on a stage or for the media behind a lectern, the guest flags should be arranged in alphabetical order to the right of the host national flag, from the audience or observer's view. The national flag will always be on the left, furthest from the speaker.

2.7.1.3 Flags at half-mast

The flying of a flag at half-mast is an indication of communal or shared mourning. The flag at half-mast is meant to signify the flying of an invisible flag of death at the top. The usual flag is then positioned two-thirds of the way up the flagpole. Some flags are never meant to fly at half-mast as they represent a constant in a nation.

In the UK, the Royal Standard (or Banner), for example, represents the constant of the monarch and is flown over whichever abode the sitting monarch is in residence at. It is never reduced to half-mast. However, after a public outcry and misunderstanding of this protocol, the Royal Family flew the Union Flag at half-mast over Buckingham Palace in 1997 after the death of Princess Diana. The Queen was resident at Balmoral in Scotland at the time.

When a flag represents more than just the country, these are not reduced to half-mast either. The flag of Saudi Arabia includes representation for the Shahada or the Islamic creed. Iranian and Iraqi flags represent the Takbir, or 'God is Greatest', while Afghanistan's includes both the Shahada and the Takbir, indicating the oneness of God (Kandur, 2017).

There is a great deal more protocol involved with the use and position of flags on vehicles, yardarms, buildings, uniforms, and in processions. The flaginstitute. org provides detailed information on the correct protocol for each of these as well as a number of other important uses of flags during ceremonies at international events.

2.7.1.4 National anthems

It is a custom to perform the national anthem as part of any ceremonial proceedings. The audience is obliged to stand during the playing of all national anthems while some male attendees can be expected to remove headwear. If the headwear is casual or considered unisex like a baseball cap, women can also be expected to remove them.

Making sure the correct anthem is played is a carefully managed part of international events that can go wrong at the highest level. During an international football match between France and Albania in 2019, a mix-up saw the national anthem of Andorra played by mistake. The faux pas resulted in a seven-minute delay as Albania refused to start the match without the error being rectified (Beswick, 2019).

The task of playing the correct national anthem is made all the more complicated when countries go through a massive political upheaval and change their national anthem. Russian gold medal winners at the biathlon world championship in Austria in 2017 had to sing their national anthem themselves after an old, Yeltsin-era anthem was played by mistake (BBC, 2017).

While the national anthem plays an integral part in many national events, there are those who believe that the playing of the national anthem should be reserved for international events. In the USA, Bennett (2016) and (Smalera, 2017) question whether a crowd still needs to hear the national anthem played before all 82 NBA games, 162 baseball games, 18 CFL games and 16 NFL games when they are only between state and not national teams.

2.7.1.5 Using national anthems for protest

In August 2016, the national anthem in the USA was used to highlight other issues in the country. Colin Kaepernick and Eric Reid, the American football stars, used the playing of the national anthem to 'take a knee' in protest about issues of race, activism, and free expression after the police shootings of black men (Mindock, 2019). Kaepernick stated, 'I am not going to stand up to show pride in a flag for a country that oppresses black people and people of color' (Whyke, 2016).

These actions led to Kaepernick becoming the face of Nike's 'Just Do It' campaign for 2018 (The Telegraph, 2018), although the protests ended with the NFL. reaching a grievance settlement. Terms of the settlements were not disclosed, and the players and the league reached a confidentiality agreement (Mather, 2019).

This was not the first time American athletes have used their national anthem as a means of protest. Over fifty years ago, two American athletes gave Black Power salutes on the podium as they collected their Olympic medals in Mexico City in 1968. Tommie Smith and John Carlos said their clenched fists showed the solidarity of black America. The pair wore no footwear to represent those living in poverty and had human rights logos on their jackets (Chulani, 2018). Also, during the 1972 Summer Olympics in Munich, West Germany, Vincent Matthews and Wayne Collett turned away from the American flag and with hands on hips, chatted casually until 'The Star Spangled Banner' had finished (Carlson, 2010).

2.8 Legacy

The fourth pillar of international events is legacy. Legacy can be measured in a number of ways including financial, physical, intellectual, and emotional. Event organisers and academics have learnt over the years that the assumption that the objectives of legacy are to be constructive and bring added value to the event can be outrageously incorrect. When legacy is poorly managed, planned or implemented, the results can be devastating.

International events are held for a variety of reasons. The bigger and greater the reach of the event, the more emphasis there tends to be on legacy. In most circumstances, this means a method of quantifying what the event will leave behind. According to Hiller (2006), the legacy of large-scale events is the post-event consequences. The International Olympics Committee (IOC) (n.d.) claim that Olympic legacy includes the long-term benefits of the Games to the host city, its people, and the Olympic Movement before, during and long after the Olympic Games.

In a large-scale publicly funded event, legacy usually includes the added demand of publicly measuring the event's sustainability in terms of the triple bottom line (TBL). Much of this is discussed in more detail in Chapter 3. TBL includes:

- the efficiency of the investment being made
- the impact the event has on the environment
- the social equity or consideration for all.

Smaller international events tend to have fewer negative economic issues, but even the smallest of international events should be able to quantify some kind of ongoing value or return from the event as a form of legacy. For all events, legacy can be described as developing some kind of ongoing benefit for the community. The bigger international events may seek evidence of increased tourism, infrastructure investment, business growth, and enhanced recognition as a global city or nation. For more local international events, legacy can be expressed in increased community engagement, improved understanding, the removal of barriers and even the provision of activities for hard-to-reach or excluded groups.

Appreciating the broader economic and social bearing of legacy from events is highly challenging because of the manner in which legacy is presented. A new venue built specifically for an event is a typical example of legacy. However, whether this is deemed a positive or a negative impact will depend on a number of factors. One group may suggest a positive impact because of the added value to the community for social activities. Another group might suggest a negative impact due to a loss of trade, while another group may protest against the new venue's impact on their day-to-day lives. Communities seek transparency when it comes to investment and while legacy is included as one of the four pillars of international events, it is the responsibility of the organisers to provide this transparency.

2.8.1 Economic impact analysis

Common methods of determining legacy impacts from international events are through an economic impact analysis or a cost-benefit analysis. These tend to be the method of measurement preferred by economists involved in advising governments prior to undertaking a major financial commitment in order to justify the investment. The economic impact analysis examines the effect of an event on the economy. The content is usually quite detailed and will include a number of different impact levels, taking into consideration how a local community is affected as well as the wider impact on the whole country. An economic impact analysis usually measures changes in business revenue, business profits, personal wages, and jobs (Weisbrod, 1997). A cost-benefit analysis, on the other hand, considers the strengths and weaknesses of alternatives by seeking to find the best approach to achieving benefits while minimising the spend. Again, the data generated by an event can be for a region or a country. The benefits are calculated as a value increase in consumption from the local population, while the costs will be related to the factors of production needed to organise the event (Taks *et al.,* 2011; Jiménez-Naranjo *et al.,* 2016).

While it may appear to be more beneficial to adopt a cost benefit analysis when public money is involved, events that receive the biggest investment from the public purse tend to favour adopting an economic impact analysis. Taks *et al.* (2011) observed that a lot of the data is generic and often grossly over-estimated. Many of the benefits from the event are not event-related but considered returns on investment. Such examples include potential social benefits from new buildings or the probability of improved living conditions, and increased tourism. However, these returns are not guaranteed and not fully experienced until long into the future. As it takes so long for the return to be quantified or the benefit to be measured it is difficult to challenge the supposed aspirational assumptions or reprehend any flaws observed in the data.

In order to provide a more publicly transparent approach to legacy, Preuss (2015) proposed four questions that require clear inclusion in the process. These were:

- What should be considered as legacy?
- Who, as in which stakeholders, are affected by the changes?
- How will legacy eventually affect the quality of life?
- When does the legacy start to create value?

A cost-benefit analysis is preferred by the general public and other analysts as it affords a much more immediate and logical representation of the costs in contrast to benefits. (Barget and Gouguet, 2010) suggest it is not enough to calculate only the economic effects of a project without assessing their social utility for the population. Urban strategies of any kind should pay attention to the establishment of economic functions, social integration and the sustainable re-use of post-physical legacy (Chen, 2012).

2.9 Summary

This chapter has discussed in detail the four pillars of international event management. It has been shown that the content of each of the pillars is wholly dependent on the numerous different aspects of the international event itself.

The four pillars are central to the successful delivery and satisfaction of everyone involved in international events. Each individual pillar provides support for the others while the level of engagement with each is again dependent on the event itself. At one end of the process, the amount of planning and preparation required to deliver international events cannot be over-emphasised, while at the other, the importance of what the event leaves behind and the quality of communication carry just as much importance. The methods of participation may differ considerably, but each plays an important role in the success of the event.

Case study 2.1 Communicating on site with PMRs (personal mobile radios). Correct procedure

It is often taken for granted at many large-scale events that PMRs, or walkie-talkies as they are commonly known, will be used to communicate on site during the event. Police, lifeguards, security and many other event personnel are seen with a device as part of their uniform. PMRs are the preferred choice of contact for outdoor events where many staff are spread over a large area or the absence of a mobile signal can interfere with the communication and so separate responsible crew from the rest of the team. PMRs also have no additional charges for their use. Fortunately, they are an ideal and a largely artless means of communication, and everyone knows how to use them, right?

The principles of use may be very simple, but if required in an emergency, the receiving of precise information through a sent message becomes all the more critical. Where is the incident? What is the problem? How many people are involved? What is the help that is required? How serious is the problem? The emphasis on understanding the communication being transmitted becomes much more acute. The safe delivery of a message can be interrupted by any number of interferences such as background noise, nerves, tone of voice, the speed of speech, the incident itself, volume control, range limitations or equipment failure.

Questions

- List a number of situations in which it is appropriate to use walkie-talkies over other forms of communication.
- What are the limitations of walkie-talkies over other forms of communication?
- If you were the communications manager, how would you decide the people to carry PMRs when they are in limited supply?

2.10 Useful websites

Plug voltages by country
www.worldstandards.eu/electricity/plug-voltage-by-country/.

World plugs map
www.iec.ch/worldplugs/map.htm

Legacy strategy approach
www.olympic.org/~/media/Document%20Library/OlympicOrg/Documents/
    Olympic-Legacy/IOC_Legacy_Strategy_Full_version.pdf?la=en

Getting things done
https://gettingthingsdone.com/

Event management software
www.getapp.com/customer-management-software/event-management/

Advice for women travelling abroad
www.gov.uk/guidance/advice-for-women-travelling-abroad

References

ata-carnet.uk (n.d.). ATA Carnet Information Centre. Retrieved from www.ata-carnet.uk Accessed 13th September 2019.

Barget, E. & Gouguet, J.-J. (2010). Hosting mega-sporting events: Which decision-making rule? *International Journal of Sport Finance 5*(2), 141–162.

Barrow, A. (2003). The colonel: the extraordinary story of Colonel Tom Parker and Elvis Presley. *The Spectator 293*, 56–57. London: The Spectator (1828) Limited.

Bartram, G. (2002). 'A Guide to Flag Protocol in the United Kingdom.' London: AGM of the National Association of Civic Officers.

BBC (2017). Wrong national anthem played for gold medallists. Retrieved from www.bbc.co.uk/news/video_and_audio/headlines/39020854/wrong-national-anthem-played-for-gold-medallists Accessed 3rd November 2019.

BBC (2019). Prom 60: Vienna Philharmonic and Bernard Haitink. Retrieved from https://learningonscreen.ac.uk/ondemand/index.php/prog/1453FC60?bcast=130041942 Accessed 12th September 2019.

Bennett, D. (2016). Why national anthems should be reserved for international events. Retrieved from www.sportsnet.ca/football/nfl/national-anthems-reserved-international-events Accessed 3rd November 2019.

Berners, P. (2017). *The Practical Guide to Organising Events*. London: Routledge.

Berridge, G. (2012). Event experience: A case study of differences between the way in which organizers plan an event experience and the way in which guests receive the experience. *Journal of Parks and Recreation Administration 30*(3).

Beswick, E. (2019). Macron apologizes to Albania after wrong national anthem played at football match. Retrieved from www.euronews.com/2019/09/09/macron-apologizes-to-albania-after-wrong-national-anthem-played-at-football-match Accessed 3rd November 2019.

Bladen, C., Kennell, J., Abson, A. & Wilde, N. (2017). *Events Management: An Introduction*. Oxon and New York: Routledge.

Bloom, D. (2016). Theresa May tried to keep a 220-year-old law that banned dancing on Sundays. Retrieved from www.mirror.co.uk/news/uk-news/theresa-tried-keep-220-year-8741994 Accessed 13th August 2019.

Bowdin, G., Allen, J., O'Toole, W. & McDonnell, I. (2011). *Events Management*. London: Elsevier.

Bridges, T. (2014). 'Exploring contingency planning for adverse weather conditions: How well do event managers plan for inclement weather?' Masters of Business (MBus), Unitec Institute of Technology, New Zealand.

Caralli, R. A. (2011). *The CERT Resilience Management Model: A Maturity Model for Managing Operational Resilience*. Boston, MA: Pearson Education.

Carlson, M. (2010). Wayne Collett: Athlete who staged a Black Power protest at the 1972 Olympic Games. *The Independent*. Retrieved from www.independent.co.uk/news/obituaries/wayne-collett-athlete-who-staged-a-black-power-protest-at-the-1972-olympic-games-1956018.html Accessed 5th November 2019.

ChartsBin (2010). International measuring system of units by country. Retrieved from http://chartsbin.com/view/d12 Accessed 19th June 2019.

Chen, Y. (2012). Urban strategies and post-event legacy: The case of summer Olympic cities. Conference paper, AESOP (Association of European Schools of Planning) 26th Annual Congress, Ankara, Turkey, 11th–15th July 2012.

Chulani, N. (2018). Black Power salute: 50 years on how much has changed? *The Guardian*. www.theguardian.com/sport/video/2018/oct/17/black-power-salute-50-years-on-how-much-has-changed-video-explainer .

Clarke, D. J. (2016). *Dull Disasters? How Planning Ahead Will Make a Difference*. Oxford: Oxford University Press.

CNTraveler (2009). Etiquette 101: Dress Codes. Retrieved from www.cntraveler.com/stories/2009-09-08/etiquette-101-dress-codes Accessed 8th March 2018.

Cook, G. (2018). *The Routledge Companion to the Geography of International Business*. London: Routledge, Taylor & Francis Group.

Cronin, M. & Adair, D. (2002). *The Wearing of the Green: A History of St. Patrick's Day*. Oxford: Routledge.

de Seife, E. (2007). *This is Spinal Tap*. London: Wallflower.

Dobrogoszcz, T. (2014). *Nobody expects the Spanish Inquisition: cultural contexts in Monty Python*. Lanham, MD: Rowman & Littlefield.

Doya, K. & Shadlen, M. N. (2012). Decision making. *Current Opinion in Neurobiology, 22*(6), 911.

DrinkDriving.org (n.d.). Worldwide blood alcohol concentration (BAC) limits. Retrieved from www.drinkdriving.org/worldwide_drink_driving_limits.php#bac_limits Accessed 19th June 2019.

Dwankowski, C. & Huseby, E. M. (2017). Dress codes around the world. https://ndla.no/en/node/81154?fag=56850 Accessed 8th March 2018.

Elkins, K. (2017). The 10 most stressful jobs in America. Retrieved from www.cnbc.com/2017/01/11/most-stressful-jobs-in-america.html Accessed 20th August 2019.

Evans, N. (2012). Language barriers and international trade. Retrieved from http://smallbusiness.co.uk/language-barriers-and-international-trade-2110138 Accessed 8th March 2018.

Franklin, B. (2010). Quotation from Franklin, Benjamin on Planning. Retrieved from http://link.galegroup.com/apps/doc/A234834198/ITOF?u=salcal2&sid=ITOF&xid=02fa9285 Accessed 8th March 2018.

Getz, D. (2012). *Event Studies: Theory, Research and Policy for Planned Events*. Oxford: Routledge.

Glynn, L. (2017). A guide to the CITES law on rosewood guitars. Retrieved from www.pmtonline.co.uk/blog/2017/05/19/a-guide-to-the-cites-law-on-rosewood-guitars Accessed 19th June 2019.

Grant, A. (2014a). Mega-events and nationalism: The 2008 Olympic torch relay. *The Geographical Review, 104*(2), 192–208.

Grant, E. (2014b). Guidance for the management & use of stages and related temporary event structures. Retrieved from https://www.stages.co.uk/userfiles/files/EventStructuresCodeofPractice.pdf Accessed 14th September 2019.

Gregory, A. (2019). UK weather: More festivals cancelled as thunderstorms and 60mph winds to batter UK. *The Independent.* Retrieved from www.independent.co.uk/news/uk/home-news/uk-weather-forecast-latest-temperature-festival-cancelled-storms-wind-flooding-roads-boomtown-a9051031.html Accessed 14th August 2019.

Halsey, T. (2010). *Freelancer's Guide to Corporate Event Design from Technology Fundamentals to Scenic and Environmental Design*. Burlington, MA: Focal Press, Elsevier.

Harneis, R. (2016). Car-free ski resorts: Greener, safer, quieter. Retrieved from www.onthesnow.co.uk/news/a/582108/car-free-ski-resorts-greener-safer-quieter Accessed 14th August 2019.

Hawkins, J. & Coles, J. (2019). Boardmasters 2019 organisers explain exactly why event was cancelled. Retrieved from www.somersetlive.co.uk/news/uk-world-news/boardmasters-2019-organisers-explain-exactly-3198750 Accessed 14th August 2019.

Hiller, H. H. (2006). Post-event outcomes and the post-modern turn: The Olympics and urban transformations. *European Sport Management Quarterly, 6*(4), 317–332.

IOC (International Olympics Committee) (n.d.). Legacy. Retrieved from www.olympic.org/olympic-legacy Accessed 18th October 2019.

Jiménez-Naranjo, H. V., Coca-Pérez, J. L., Gutiérrez-Fernández, M. & Sánchez-Escobedo, M. C. (2016). Cost–benefit analysis of sport events: The case of World Paddle Tour. *European Research on Management and Business Economics, 22*(3), 131–138.

Johnson, C. (2012). *The Power Behind Festivals. A Guide to Sustainable Power at Outdoor Events*. Green Festival Alliance.

Kandur, J. L. (2017). Flags flying at half-mast. Retrieved from www.dailysabah.com/feature/2017/01/07/flags-flying-at-half-mast Accessed 5th November 2019.

Kim, S. (2017). Air France headscarf row: what not to wear when visiting Muslim countries. *The Telegraph.* www.telegraph.co.uk/travel/advice/dress-code-guide-for-muslim-countries/

Lawson, R. and Roychoudhury, S. (2016). Do travel visa requirements impede tourist travel? *Journal of Economics and Finance, 40*(4), 817–828.

Lee, M. (2006). *The Race for the 2012 Olympics*. London: Virgin books.

Mather, V. (2019). A timeline of Colin Kaepernick vs. the N.F.L. *The New York Times.* www.nytimes.com/2019/02/15/sports/nfl-colin-kaepernick-protests-timeline.html

Matzler, K., Uzelac, B. & Bauer, F. (2014). Intuition: the missing ingredient for good managerial decision-making. *Journal of Business Strategy, 35*(6), 31–40.

Meechan, B. (2017). Champions League: Cardiff businesses count the cost. Retrieved from www.bbc.co.uk/news/uk-wales-south-east-wales-40161554 Accessed 12th November 2018.

Miaschi, J. (2017). The currencies of the European nations. *WorldAtlas*.com

Mindock, C. (2019). Taking a knee: Why are NFL players protesting and when did they start to kneel? Retrieved from www.independent.co.uk/news/world/americas/us-politics/taking-a-knee-national-anthem-nfl-trump-why-meaning-origins-racism-us-colin-kaepernick-a8521741.html Accessed 3rd November 2019.

Nikiforuk, C. (2013). Sexism at the border: a personal account. Retrieved from http://rabble.ca/news/2013/04/sexism-borderpersonal-account Accessed 17th July 2019.

Preuss, H. (2015). A framework for identifying the legacies of a mega sport event. *Leisure Studies, 5*(8), 643–664.

Sapling (2014). The ultimate guide to the time zone clock – part 3. Retrieved from www.sapling-inc.com/blog/synchronized-clock-systems-blog/the-ultimate-guide-to-the-time-zone-clock-part-3 Accessed 8th March 2018.

Planning and delivery

Singleton, F. (2008). The Beaufort scale of winds – its relevance, and its use by sailors. *Weather, 63*(2), 37–41.

Smalera, P. (2017). Let's stop playing the national anthem before sporting events. Retrieved from https://qz.com/1087013/lets-stop-playing-the-national-anthem-before-sporting-events Accessed 3rd November 2019.

Smith, C. (2018). The seven barriers of communication. Retrieved from https://guides.co/g/the-seven-barriers-of-communication/37300 Accessed 8th March 2018.

Smith, O. (2014). Nigella Lawson: Odd cases of refused entry to the US. Retrieved from www.telegraph.co.uk/travel/destinations/north-america/united-states/articles/Nigella-Lawson-odd-cases-of-refused-entry-to-the-US Accessed 19th June 2019.

Speake, J. (ed.) (2015). *Oxford Dictionary of Proverbs*. 6th ed. Oxford: Oxford University Press.

Purtle, J., Siddiqui, N. J. & Andrulis, D. P. (2011). Language issues and barriers. In Statler, M. & Penuel, K. B. (eds) *Encyclopedia of Disaster Relief*. Newbury Park, CA: Sage Publication.

Taks, M., Kesenne, S., Chalip, L., Green, B. & Martyn, S. (2011). Economic impact analysis versus cost-benefit analysis: The case of a medium-sized sport event. *International Journal of Sport Finance, 6*(3), 187–203.

Telegraph, The (2018). NFL protest player Colin Kaepernick chosen by Nike as face of new campaign. Retrieved from www.telegraph.co.uk/american-football/2018/09/03/nike-choose-colin-kaepernick-first-nfl-player-kneel-us-anthem Accessed 4th November 2018.

Weisbrod, G. (1997). Measuring economic impacts of projects and programs. Retrieved from https://docplayer.net/8208616-Measuring-economic-impacts-of-projects-and-programs.html Accessed 15th August 2019.

Whyke, S. (2016). Colin Kaepernick explains why he sat during national anthem. www.nfl.com.

Wikihelp (n.d). How to fold a flag. Retrieved from www.wikihow.com/Fold-a-Flag Accessed 5th November 2019.

Wikipedia (n.d). Dancing ban. Retrieved from https://en.wikipedia.org/wiki/Dancing_ban Accessed 13th August 2019.

Wong, T. (2015). How time zones confused the world. Retrieved from www.bbc.co.uk/news/world-asia-33815153 Accessed 8th March 2018.

Chapter 3

Evaluating international events

Contents

3.1 Chapter overview

This chapter discusses the various methods and processes involved in international event evaluations, what an evaluation should consist of, provide, and the reasons for undertaking one. It considers the sources of information evaluations utilise in order to identify the factors most likely to impact an event and its immediate community from before it begins to beyond the delivery process.

It also considers the darker side of international event evaluations and how they are used to support specific event objectives and abuse the very principles of independence and objectivity that the process of evaluation is meant to uphold.

3.2 Learning objectives

By the end of this chapter, the student will be expected to:

- Understand the various ways in which evaluations can be used
- Understand the timing of evaluations and their objectives
- Be able to choose a suitable evaluation method for any aspect of international event management
- Appreciate the different components of evaluations and how they are used to support an event.

3.3 Introduction

Event evaluation is a central aspect of international event delivery. Evaluations are not afterthoughts nor are they something just tacked on to the end of an event. The evaluation of an international event is, in simple terms, an opportunity for review, and can be focused on any or every aspect of an international event. An evaluation should critically scrutinise set features or every aspect of an event. Torkildsen (2005) considers evaluation to be one of a six-stage approach to programming and as an opportunity to provide the clear establishment of an event's goals.

The process of evaluation involves collecting and analysing information, reviewing activities, characteristics, and outcomes. The overall purpose of conducting evaluations is to make judgements. to improve effectiveness, and/or to inform the decision-making process (Patton, 1987). When used appropriately, an evaluation can be defined as the holistic assessment of an event through the utilisation of a broad range of measures and approaches to determine value and impacts in an agreed or prescribed context (Brown *et al.*, 2015).

Evaluations, therefore, are, in part, an essential management function of information gathering and feedback through which processes can be improved, goals more effectively attained, and by which organisations can learn and adapt (Brown *et al.*, 2015).

3.4 Types of evaluation

For many international events, the evaluation process is restricted to the economic impact analyses (O'Sullivan *et al.*, 2009; Richie, 1984; Sherwood, 2007) that were discussed in Chapter 2. The most likely reason for this is because such analyses are a stakeholder requirement, particularly for government and tourism agencies (de Grosbois, 2009). This approach, however, fails to account for a number of important factors including the impact of the event on the host community as well as the impact on the natural environment, such as water and energy use and waste generation (Sherwood, 2007).

In reality, there are a number of evaluation types that can be used to study events. Each evaluation type can be used for a diverse range of objectives. The reason for so many types of evaluation is that they are central to the development of business and can be suited to different times within the event life cycle. Table 3.1 provides details on what the various evaluations are used for, how they are most suited and when to use them.

Each evaluation an international event adopts should be guided by its own particular objectives. Table 3.1 provides a solid backbone from which to start, but much more detail is required in order to complete a well-focused evaluation. Most city councils produce guidance on planning events which include consideration of the evaluation process. However, these all tend to be reflective and fixed on what to do once the event has been delivered. It is important for international events to consider the wider strategic objectives and planning of the organisation, and should underpin their activities with rigorous evaluations associated with quantifiable measurements (Crowther, 2010).

Using Table 3.1 as a starting point, each evaluation process should be formed around one of three phases:

- the pre-event phase
- the transitive phase
- the post-event phase.

Each phase of the evaluation process is seeking specific information and will devise a number of indicators to direct attention to certain data. These can take the form of feasibility or design indicators in the pre-event phase, or success indicators, gap indicators and achievement indicators in the transitive or post-event phases. These measurement indicators serve to provide more detailed and attentive evaluations.

3.4.1 Measurement indicators

Whichever evaluation is being undertaken, the format of the evaluation needs to be designed. An evaluation should include a number of indicators that will effectively highlight the presence (or not) of something. These may be targets the event is seeking to achieve or benchmarks it must meet. Each indicator used is meant to prescribe the type of data required. While this is a method to ensure the data collected is specific, it can also produce criticism if certain indicators

Table 3.1 Types of event evaluation method

Type of evaluation	What it is	When to use	What it shows	Why it is useful
Formative evaluation	A means of judging the value of an event while the programme activities are beginning to form or in progress.	During the development of a new event	Whether the proposed elements of the event are likely to be needed, understood, and accepted by those involved	It allows for modifications to be made to the plan before the full implementation begins Maximises the likelihood the event will succeed
Evaluability assessment	A review of a proposed event to assess if the objectives are adequately defined and achievable	When an existing event is being modified to adopt to the target audience or being used in a new setting	The extent to which an evaluation is possible, based on the goals and objectives	
Needs assessment	A review process to determine needs, or 'gaps' from previous events and the next delivery			
Process evaluation	This determines whether the event's activities have been implemented as planned	As soon as the event begins During the operation of an existing event	How well the event is working The extent to which the event is being implemented as designed	Provides an early warning for any problems that might occur Allows event organisers to monitor how well their event plans and activities are working
Event monitoring	A continuous review of activities		Whether the event is accessible and acceptable to the target audience	
Outcome evaluation	Assesses the progress or outcome objectives that the event is meant to achieve	After the event has reached its target audience	The degree to which the event is having an effect on the target audience	Tells whether the event is being effective in meeting its planned objectives
Objectives-based evaluation	Focuses on generating information for accountability and decision making			

	Description	When	What it measures	Benefits
Economic evaluations	A systematic review of the resources being applied to the event	At the beginning of an event	What resources are being used for the event and their costs (direct and indirect) compared to outcomes	Provides event organisers and funders a way to assess cost relative to effects
Cost-effectiveness evaluation	Compares the relative costs to the outcomes (effects) of at least two options or courses of action	During the operation of an existing event		Can be used to gain credibility and/or support for organisers
Cost-benefit analysis	Assesses the available options to determine the most economically beneficial approach			
Cost-utility analysis	A form of financial analysis to guide procurement decisions			
Impact evaluation	An assessment of how the intervention being evaluated affects outcomes, whether intended or unintended	During the operation of an existing event at appropriate intervals	The degree to which the event meets its ultimate goal on an overall rate of engagement	Provides evidence for use in policy and funding decisions
Summative evaluation	Attempts to identify possible problems that have occurred and adjust the process accordingly	At the end of an event		

Source: Based on CDC, n.d.

have been excluded. For example, there are many approaches to measuring the sustainability of an event, with most models designed to assess subsets rather than sustainability as a whole (Dolf and Teehan, 2015).

An evaluation of a major international event may collect vast amounts of data that highlight how environmental targets are being met only to avoid critical information in the overall balance of the evaluation. As there is currently no standard protocol or method to assess the eco-sustainability of events, it is common for data to be deliberately neglected by the organiser (Boggia *et al.*, 2018; Scrucca *et al.*, 2016).

The carbon footprint created by travelling attendees to international events or the destination of waste once it has left the venue are two examples of data that are conspicuous by their absence in environmental studies. Environmental issues are discussed in more detail in Chapter 10.

3.4.2 Types of measurement indicator

Before embarking on the evaluation process, it is important to set out which performance or measurement indicators are to be used. There are potentially thousands of measurement indicators to quantify and monitor every inch of a working international event project. From finance and process metrics to people and customer metrics, it can be easy to lose track of the event by focusing too much on the evaluation and not on the task in hand. There is also a good possibility that by adopting the wrong approach the purpose of the evaluation will be lost in the process. Parmenter (2010) suggests many companies work with the wrong type of measure simply through ignorance as there are really only four types of performance measures:

1. Key result indicators (KRIs) that tell you what you have done based on previously set objectives
2. Result indicators (RIs) that just tell you what you have done
3. Performance indicators (PIs) that tell you what to do
4. Key performance indicators (KPIs) that tell you what to do to increase performance dramatically.

Performance indicators can become very useful in event delivery when there is a partnership between public and private sector organisations. Responsibilities for monitoring spend and performance in meeting the event's objectives can be lost in grey areas of responsibility if these are not specifically allocated. Governments around the world now tend to create local organisation companies to deliver large-scale events to create an arm's length approach to the delivery process. This is in effect a government's way of avoiding any conflict of interest issues and direct responsibility for the event, but it also maintains the workings of open market forces.

The use of public funds to deliver events can be extremely controversial and create a backlash from communities and groups. Some communities can see spending on events as a waste of money and would prefer to see taxpayers' money spent on more tangible projects such as improving school budgets or fixing roads. However, when used appropriately, Whitford (2014) suggests that performance indicators can be advantageous to the wider community by demonstrating a real commitment to public interest, transparency, accountability, and a responsiveness to local issues beyond political rhetoric.

3.5 The phases of event evaluations

The process of event evaluations most commonly occur in one of two primary stages: pre-event evaluations to provide an appraisal of the events feasibility and post-event evaluations for review or improvement purposes. However, as can be seen from Table 3.1, it is common for many event evaluations to occur during the event itself. These tend to take the form of monitoring activities, but may also be used to generate information for accountability and decision making. For repeating events, any evaluation will usually include an assessment of the successes and failures of previous events.

Due to limited resources (both financial and human), many companies involved in international events may not have a formal approach to evaluation and instead adopt a continuous method of review. This approach for many sole traders and SMEs is essentially the precarious but necessary approach of busy professionals not having the time or resources available to dedicate to such activities. The level of evaluation in such circumstances comes down to what is remembered and learned from experience.

3.5.1 Pre-event evaluations

Pre-event evaluations will highlight the value of an event while the program activities are beginning to form or in progress. A pre-evaluation is essentially a learning curve that on paper should lead to the most efficient, effective, competent and well-organised processes in event delivery. A pre-event evaluation allows for modifications to be made to the plan before the full implementation begins. When you consider the depths of organisation that international events require, the majority succeed in achieving their objectives. However, even with the most detailed methods of evaluation, things can still go seriously wrong. Pre-event evaluations maximise the likelihood the event will succeed.

Therefore, the purpose of pre-evaluation is not about ensuring things will not go wrong, but instead a method of agreeing and working to a number of set standards that when adhered to ensure things will not go wrong or, if they do, a plan is in place to deal with them. Pre-event evaluation will assist in informing whether the proposed elements of the event are likely to be needed, understood, and accepted by those involved.

3.5.2 Consultation processes

Many international events will begin with a consultation process. These will exist at a number of levels during the pre-evaluation phase, often beginning in boardrooms and eventually being taken directly to the people in their communities. Every city council will promote their desire to engage effectively with local communities and consultations are a good way of getting to a whole community to gauge opinions and gather information in a short space of time. In the event of a public consultation, it provides councils with the opportunity to communicate directly with local people about the development and design of any proposed large-scale event.

3.5.3 Types of consultation method

Consultations can take the form of a number of communication processes and, often, does not require a physical presence in the community. Many consultations will utilise a variety of methods in order to reach as many of a target population as possible. Whichever form of consultation method chosen, specific expertise will be required to conduct the process effectively.

3.5.4 Websites

The method of consultation often considered the most cost-effective is through a company website. However, this requires both access to and the ability to use a computer. Therefore, there is the potential for exclusion as many elderly or low-income members of a community may not have the relevant access to equipment required.

3.5.5 Surveys

Surveys enable the event organiser to collect large amounts of data and can be used to cover areas considered too sensitive for other forms of consultation. Surveys can be conducted over the phone or in person. A much greater emphasis will be placed on skilled operatives in collecting information through surveys as they can be very difficult to analyse. Surveys are usually best used as a support method to other means or mixes of consultation.

3.5.6 Focus groups

If an event has any complex issues that require more depth of analysis, focus groups provide the event organisers with the opportunity to delve deep into the problem. Focus groups may require more than one representative group and considerable time, effort, and a lot of people to effectively produce the necessary returns. The beauty of focus groups is that they can provide surprising results due to their usually spontaneous nature.

3.5.7 Public consultations

Public consultations tend to be a formal opportunity for community members to meet face-to-face with more senior members of the international event planning team. The event organisers' plans and strategies can be discussed in the community itself, with an opportuniy for details to be explained. Any concerns can be raised and dealt with providing the event organisers with the opportunity to build relationships with the local community. Of course, problems can arise if the public consultation process is dominated by any negative issues. Figure 3.4 highlights the nine stages that would ensure a quality consultation process for an international event.

Evaluations are also conducted because of the amount of people involved in the delivery process. Everything to do with international events can arguably be improved through an evaluation. So much so, that Brown *et al.* (2015) suggest that evaluation is an essential management function of information gathering and feedback through which processes can be improved, goals more effectively attained, and from which organisations can learn and adapt. Because of the economic and social impact that international events have on locations and their respective communities, a pre-event evaluation is not only a means of understanding the overall impact of the event, it has become a necessary function of the delivery process.

3.5.7.1 Transitive evaluations

Transitive evaluations include some kind of activity or decision during the event itself. The activity might result in no action being taken. What is important is the act of monitoring or surveillance. With some processes within an international event, it is necessary to respond to a situation as it is happening in real time. Most of the decisions in such situations should be common sense. Security, stewards, and volunteers are continually being tasked with transitive evaluations. Any kind of inspection during the event is a typical example of a transitive evaluation being carried out. Transitive evaluations allow event organisers to monitor how well their event plans and activities are working and keep the plans in order. Chapter 5 provides more information on the role of staff at events.

The main reason for using transitive evaluations is to improve the quality of the event. Moreover, many potential problems that might occur later in the delivery process can be avoided. Crowd management or responses to the weather are typical examples. However, what event organisers do not want to do is make a situation worse through bad judgement. On-the-spot decisions are a form of transitive evaluation and experience plays a vital role in getting these right. There is very seldom a second chance to reverse a decision in real time once it has been made. For example, setting aside culpability, the decision by police to open the Leppings Lane gate at Hillsborough in 1989 just minutes before a fatal crush (Scraton, 2016), or the pilot's decision to make a third attempt to get the Manchester United team home after a European match in 1958 (Cavendish, 2008; Evans, 2001) are both testimony to this.

Another form of transitive evaluation is the conducting of surveys. Volunteer motivation and satisfaction (Barron and Rihova, 2011; Farrell *et al.*, 1998; Kwok *et al.*, 2013; Lee *et al.*, 2014; Vetitnev, 2018), customer engagement (Gopalakrishna *et al.*, 2017; Johnson, 2018), and team performance (Ericksen and Dyer, 2004; Mancini, 2018; Woods, 2013) are just a few examples of how transitive evaluations can assist in the performance of a team and the delivery of an event while it is still live. The data gathered will assist in understanding these critical aspects of international event delivery and contribute to the post-event evaluations data for further review.

3.5.7.2 Post-event evaluations

Once an event is over, event organisers have the opportunity to review how everything went and begin to make plans for the next one. Essentially, a post-event evaluation is considering the degree to which the event met its objectives. It will consider how the event performed based on the agreed set or level of standards and assess what went wrong, why, and if any 'unknowns' occurred. At the same time, the evaluation will include what went well. With this information, the organisers can decide if anything needs to be reviewed, changed or improved for subsequent events. With the increase in digital communication, a great deal of data is captured that will assist in this process. With this in mind, it is important to note that Chi et al. (2018) observed that the event's benefits might appear less appealing than they were in the pre-event evaluation, making it difficult to gain similar levels of support in the post-event stage.

The event organisers will be seeking answers to a lot of questions and the size of the team involved will affect the level of investigation. There are a number of areas the event organisers should be seeking information from. The formula for conducting a successful post-event evaluation is asking the right questions. Initial reports may be focused on marketing, communications, finances, overall team performance and timing. Once these have been discussed or reported upon, the team may move on to what went well, what did not go so well, who shone, who struggled, what would be done again, what needs to change, should the event grow, should it move, and so on and so forth.

Within the finance discussion or report, the reviewers may consider expenditure against return on investment. There may be discussions about suppliers or whether the timing of the event could be improved by booking or purchasing things earlier. The marketing report might discuss what platforms were used and whether the response met the expected results. Website traffic and social media may fall under marketing and due to the various analytic tools available with social media, apps, and website design, a very good report can be produced to inform the team. This will assist in preparing targets for the next event.

All the data collected by means of the evaluations processes used will contribute to providing evidence for future use, in policy decision making, and provide vital data for any funding applications the organisers may choose to make to improve the event next time round.

3.6 Evaluation through experience

As explained above, many international event organisers are not in a position to conduct formal evaluations, but still continue to include the basic principles of evaluation within their organisation. The most proficient event organisers have masses of evaluation ability and rely on their professional experience to ensure their standards are maintained. When necessary, an event organisation with a small team will learn very quickly how to adapt and develop as they go. This approach works well in a small team as guidance and advice circulates between the team members.

Many of the activities in international events are service-based, making the evaluation in the support organisations largely based on the quality of service provided. When the company consists of a handful of staff, the evaluation process is communicated verbally in a real and sentient manner. There is no list of questions or desired outputs; the focus is on hard work and maintaining a quality of service.

The simple reality for many international event support organisations and small businesses is that they can be deeply reliant on their performance. If they are a new entrant without a strong engagement history or network, they could be judged to be only as good as their last performance. An evaluation process, no matter how small, can be the difference between success and failure. It can be as little as a conversation based around doing the same things as well as the last time, or making some marginal changes to improve productivity.

3.7 Large-scale event evaluations

In spite of the high costs involved just to put forward a bid to host a large-scale international event, the interest shown by cities around the world (with the backing of the host country) is still quite robust. With this in mind, there is substantial attention paid to and investment in evaluation of large-scale events at every stage of the process. Right from the outset, bid preparations can be counted in years, while the total course of preparation and delivery is actually over a number of decades.

Large-scale international events often include major construction projects that literally change the local landscape. Because of the size and impact of these projects, international design competitions are generally commissioned. These contribute to the planning, evaluation, and marketing of the event. Once the winning design has been chosen, models are built at a scale of 1:1000 to illustrate the proposed design and its impact on the main development area. These are then used to highlight the key sites in the project and are displayed for public viewing close to the development site. Figure 3.1 is the scale model from the London 2012 Games displayed to the public prior to the Games in a local library close to the main venues in Stratford, east London.

The design decisions may be reviewed and evaluated over a period of time and scale models allow the organisers to consider impacts such as wind patterns, design aesthetics, emergency access, traffic and transport efficiency, and satisfaction levels from local residents and visitors. The availability of models for public evaluation and broader consultation activities plays a major role in developing community relations. A sense of inclusion is created and can ultimately contribute to the organiser's commitment to building a partnership with the local community with concern for the long-term improvement of quality of life in the region. Figure 3.2 shows the scaled model of a large section of Expo 2000 in Hannover, Germany, and the subsequent developed site.

Figure 3.1 London 2012 site model displayed to the public in the local Stratford library

Figure 3.2 The 1:1000 scale model and the real Hannover Expo 2000

International events will bring a variety of effects to the local community and these cannot always be explained in financial terms. Disruption to normal working activities is often a highly sensitive area for the local community as the impact felt during the event is real and immediate. The impact of the event's financial cost is often much more difficult to sense, even though it is partly borne by the individual members of the communities involved, paid for out of their taxes. The decision for organisers to make is what to include in any evaluation and how the information gathered will be processed and made available to those affected by the event.

3.7.1 Olympic evaluations

The ultimate in evaluation processes and demands is contained within the Olympic Games procedures. When such events are championed as breathing new life into deprived and run-down areas, the evaluations themselves become a key aspect of the Olympic delivery process. Right from the beginning as each city applies to host the Olympic Games, the IOC has a set of processes for the evaluation each application has to follow. These are provided to examine the candidature applications from cities applying to host the Olympic Games. They enable a thorough assessment of the candidate cities' applications and serves as a guide for the IOC Members as to what to vote on when choosing a host city. It is the first indication of the IOC's impression of the bids made available to the public. Each host city is also afforded the opportunity to respond to the report.

The IOC provides an evaluation commission to review each application as part of the application process. As defined by the Olympic Charter, the evaluation commission's mandate is to:

- Analyse the candidature files and guarantees submitted by the cities
- Carry out a site visit to each city
- Produce a report highlighting the opportunities and challenges of each bid city with a strong focus on sustainability, legacy, and athletes' experience, using the analyses, as well as a number of external independent studies.

(IOC, n.d.)

Even though these are the preliminary application phases of the bidding process, the evaluation procedure is highly detailed. Each candidate city needs to provide the evaluation commission with detailed information of their plans for the event. Each bidding city is assessed on the same four areas. These are:

1. The Games Concept
2. The Games Experience
3. The Paralympic Games
4. The Games Delivery.

Once the visits by IOC representatives to the candidate cities have been completed, the Evaluation Commission will complete and release their report on their findings. Each section of the report produced by the evaluation commission will contain comments on the opportunities and the challenges that exist in the application. For example, the IOC Evaluation Commission report for the 2026 winter Games was released in May 2019 after the visits were completed in March and April the same year. Stockholm-Åre and Mila-Cortina were the two bidding cities. Stockholm-Åre's bid contained a total of 71 opportunities and 49 challenges, while Milan Cortina's bid contained a total of 79 opportunities and 24 challenges (IOC, 2019). A selection of opportunities and challenges that the Evaluation Commission observed along with the city's vision for the event from each bid are highlighted in Table 3.2.

Once the live phase of the event has ended, the proposed legacy is meant to commence. Legacy is discussed in more detail in Chapters 2 and 4. The value of a legacy is arguably the most difficult aspect of the bid to evaluate. This is because a great deal of the legacy impact takes time to take effect. Legacy also has to meet the needs of multiple components at the same time (Preuss, 2019), which complicates the task of gathering information. Therefore, any evaluations of legacy outcomes have to complete a test of time and can only be assessed long after the event.

The IOC (2017) advises that legacy outcomes should be evaluated based on the event's specific vision, objectives, and from a local context. These would have been set out in the bid along with a set of key performance indicators (KPIs). The IOC believes this approach will allow success in delivering the legacy vision to be evaluated. Figure 3.3 provides an overview of how this is should be achieved.

3.7.2 Negative legacy

For bidding cities, it is important to remember that positive legacy is not always achieved. Not only can the perspective of some stakeholders be negative, the actual impact could turn sour. Once a large-scale event has been approved, the eventual impacts created, positive or negative, will cut right through every aspect of life making them hard to ignore. While a whole nation can be affected through the many cultural, economic, environmental, political, physical, and social changes the Olympics bring about, it is the local community who will most likely endure or benefit from the major structural impacts.

Table 3.2 A Games vision with a selection of opportunities and challenges for the 2016 candidature cities

City	Vision	Selected opportunities	Selected challenges
Stockholm-Åre	Stockholm-Åre 2026's vision is to create transformative Winter Games for the future that: Encourage more physical activity and sports participation to promote a healthy lifestyle among Swedish youth	Build on Sweden's strong sustainability platform to become a true world leader in sustainability	Additional work and further engagement are needed on how specific Games programmes would support the long-term vision of the regions and national government
	Create a more united, integrated, and inclusive society for all Swedes	Promote sport, health, and physical activity in Sweden at a time when historically strong sports participation is declining, especially among young people	Limited information on capacity of public transport from Stockholm to other venue cities, particularly travel to Åre and Sigulda; advanced planning and assistance from the organisers will be key
	Highlight Sweden's diversity and culture and promote the country as a great place to visit and do business	The Games could act as a catalyst for national goals of social development and inclusion/ integration	Hotel capacities are limited in Falun and Åre, where almost all star-rated rooms would be needed for Games stakeholders and spectators would need to rely on alternative accommodation
	Reaffirm Sweden's recognised leadership in sustainability	Central Stockholm provides a dynamic inner-city atmosphere	
	Present an authentic and magical Swedish Olympic Winter Games experience for all stakeholders	Stockholm can leverage its technology proficiency to enhance the spectator experience	

continued

Table 3.2 Cont.

City	Vision	Selected opportunities	Selected challenges
	Create a new and responsible hosting model, setting new standards for innovation, sustainability, creativity and fiscal responsibility for future Olympic Winter Games	Spectators will benefit from a very efficient public transport system to access competition venues within Stockholm. Ticketed spectators will travel for free with public transport on the day of the event within the Stockholm region	
Milan-Cortina	The vision of Milan-Cortina 2026 is to deliver memorable Olympic Winter Games that embrace sustainability, using Italy's experience, passion and heritage in winter sports to inspire athletes and deliver many long-term benefits for sports and society. The vision is underpinned by five key goals that will deliver a range of benefits:	Promotion of sport, health, and physical activity in the whole of Northern Italy (focus on children born after 2010)	Competition schedule should be reviewed once the final capacities and temporary lighting have been further assessed
	1. Games for all providing a positive experience for the entire population	Northern Italy can further boost its position as a major winter sport and tourism destination (well defined goals)	The timetable suggested for certain events was modelled on the PyeongChang 2018 and Beijing 2022 competition schedules and needs to be reconsidered for a European time zone
	2. Sustainable development and cooperation in the macro-alpine region	Games can enhance the attractiveness of the mountain region as a place to live and work, to reverse the trend of de-population (including improved physical and digital infrastructure)	

Table 3.2 Cont.

City	Vision	Selected opportunities	Selected challenges
	3. Promotion of the Olympic spirit and values	Olympic Village development aligns well with Milan's need to meet growing demand for affordable university accommodation	Suggestion of hosting World Championships for the sliding sports test events will generate unnecessary costs for the OCOG; only existing or limited-scale test events should be considered
	4. Development of Italy's Alpine and Dolomites region into a major sports and tourism hub		
	5. Strengthening of the Olympic brand and the benefits of Olympic Agenda 2020		

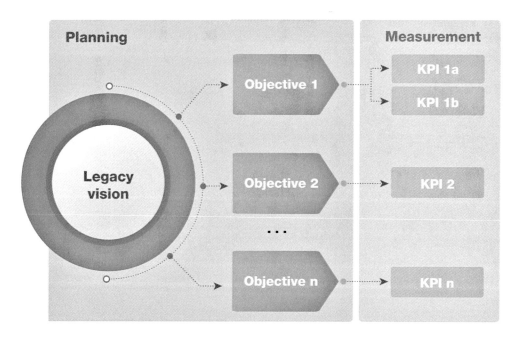

Figure 3.3 Calculating the Legacy Measurement from an Olympic Games evaluation
Source: IOC, 2017

Negative Olympic legacy is nothing new. Most of the sports facilities for the 1968 Winter Games in Grenoble, France, were demolished after the Games rather than assume any maintenance costs. It took the taxpayers of Quebec over30 years to pay off the huge deficit from the 1976 Montreal Games, while several stadia built on the former Athens airport for the 2004 Games were simply abandoned (Chappelet, 2013).

The objectives of structural changes from events are all intended to be positive in the long term. However, even from the outset, this will not always be the perspective of many members of the local community. It is often they who comprehend the impact more than the event organisers. This is where consultation becomes central to the understanding of how an international event fits in with the culture and needs of the immediate and larger community. International events will set out the criteria for how evaluations will meet the needs of the host. However, slight changes in the wording can often be overlooked.

As part of recent revisions to the vision of the Olympic movement, the term 'social responsibility' was removed from its working principles and replaced with 'sustainability' (Bayle, 2016). On the one hand, this can be perceived as a move forward in the world of single-use plastics and unnecessary waste. On the other, social responsibility incorporates sustainability as it is a duty every individual has to perform to maintain a balance between the economy and the ecosystems (Nieuwenhuis, 2018; Scheinbaum and Lacey, 2015). The evaluation measure in this example could be perceived to have been revised to allow applicants more room in the evaluation process.

Negative impacts make the visibility of evaluations central to the event's success. Figure 3.4 highlights how impact evaluations can explain legacy from

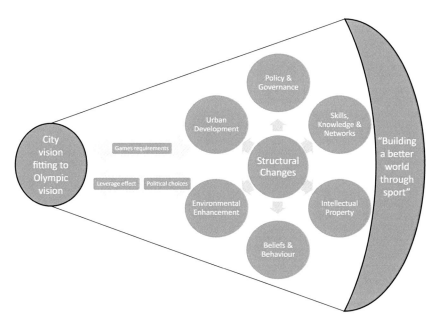

Figure 3.4 Analytical tool for the evaluation of Olympic Games legacy

Source: Based on Preuss, 2019

the point of view of causality and change, explaining how legacy is created and what is the specific role played by the hosting of the Olympic Games (IOC, 2017).

The statement 'building a better world through sport' is part of the Olympic ideal and strategic vision. The concept is that by using sport as a tool for social change, the IOC and its partners implement various activities across the globe. These include humanitarian assistance, peace-building, education, gender equality, and the environment (IOC, 2013). However, it is important to appreciate that while international sport is brought to the people by some of the largest corporations in the world, it is based on something that belongs to everyone anyway, and the suggested changes are basic values that should not have to be paid for or appropriated by a single organisation.

3.8 International event funding applications

There are many pots of funding that assist charities, local business, and third sector organisations in delivering their contribution to international events. In some cases, the event organising body is the funding applicant. Each call for funding applications is extremely specific in who and what the funding pot is targeted towards. Each award will provide detailed criteria on how each application is evaluated. Usually, an award is granted on three specific criteria:

- Relevance
- Quality of the activities
- Management of the project.

The relevance of the project focuses on the contribution of its expected results to the objectives of the call as well as the innovative nature of the project. The quality of the activities determines how the project will be implemented in practice, and how likely it is to reach its objectives. Other possible criteria might include the cost effectiveness of the proposed action, the sustainability of the project after funding has ceased, and the expected impact at local, regional, national and international levels. The management of the project evaluates the extent to which the structure and management of the project will ensure effective implementation of the project including sufficient allocation of human resources with clear and adequate distribution of tasks between the project team members (EUSurvey, 2019).

For much larger applications, the award criteria may seek detailed information on a return on investment (ROI) and specify the particular areas of return that are considered most important. The wider issue with this kind of evaluation is the lack of certainty it provides. Estimating returns can be controversial when the outputs are based on various data from future projections. Projected outcomes from an international event cover a number of areas including:

- Employment opportunities
- Economic growth
- Tourism generation
- Enhanced business innovation
- Improved business investment

- Increased business opportunities
- Increased property prices
- Improved local/national facilities
- Impact on local infrastructure.

More recently, areas such as the promotion of tourism and regional development have both become pivotal in the bidding process for companies to be able to deliver their event with the assistance of local government support (Ryan, 2014). Because of these impacts, the event's value needs to be transferred beyond its intangible perspective. Therefore, it has become important for organisations to ensure an evaluation process is undertaken.

3.9 Weighting criteria

When using evaluations to distinguish funding or grant applications, weighting certain criteria within a bidding process (a process which most funding organisations apply) can purposefully exclude or include activities the funder wishes to ensure are a prominent factor in the awarding of the grant. For example, a new event company may struggle to provide evidence of generating tourism through its events when compared to an established event company with previous funding success. Updating funding criteria is a regular occurrence in itself and can catch some companies outside the new evaluation process.

Weighting can be carried out through a points system with points being awarded for the quality, relevance, and management of the application. If 100 points are available for the whole application, the relevance section may be worth up to 50 points with a minimum threshold of 30 while the remaining sections worth 20 and 30 points each. Applications that fall below any indicated minimum threshold would be immediately rejected.

Other weighting can be applied by scoring sections on top of a given score. For example, an application might favour match funding where other 'clean' money is also secured to support the event. Clean money means that it must not come from another funding body, but is sourced from the private sector. Certain calls for funding insist on a minimum contribution of match funding, then score the section appropriately. Scoring multiples may force the bid to secure more clean money through the weighting process. If weighting is a multiple of 1 to 5, the weighting is multiplied by the scoring for the assessment as follows:

- 1–10% match funding: multiply score by 1
- 11–19% match funding: multiply score by 2
- 20–34% match funding: multiply score by 3
- 35–49% match funding: multiply score by 4
- 50% and over match funding: multiply score by 5.

The scores from each section of a bid are all added together to give the final value. In this example, there is good reason to reach 50% match funding, but also no additional benefit in going any higher.

3.10 Triple bottom line

Towards the end of the 20th century, a greater emphasis was placed on the social and environmental impact of events. Large-scale international events are frequently funded through the public purse making events and evaluations politically charged. This has resulted in concerns over transparency, economic estimations, misleading results, and expected future gains that might occur.

Evaluations end up overriding reality as agencies and consultants primarily present positive and promising results (Giulianotti and Klauser, 2011; Hosenball and Whitesides, 2013; IFSEC Global, 2014; Kirchner, 2014). The phrase 'the triple bottom line' (TBL) and its effects are discussed in more detail in Chapter 11, but it is relevant to introduce it here to expand on the importance of evaluations.

TBL is a simple and increasingly popular way to organise thoughts and action on sustainability (Mitchell *et al.*, 2008). It is attributed to the English businessman John Elkington. He proposed the idea that companies should prepare for three separate, but absolutely necessary basic levels of evaluation and that they should be conducted and considered in equal measure, stressing the phrase 'what you can't measure you are likely to find hard to manage' (Elkington, 1998, p. 72). The three basic levels of evaluation are the three 'p's: people, profit and planet. The first is a measure of how socially responsible an organisation has been throughout its operations. The second focuses on the business's financial activities while the third is a measure of how environmentally responsible the company is in conducting its affairs (Hindle, 2008). It is only when an event follows a TBL approach to measure the financial, social and environmental parts that a greater expectation towards equity and public transparency involved in hosting events is demonstrated (Emery, 2010). Figure 3.5 provides an overview of the TBL measures of performance.

Transparency is of great importance within an events context because of the role of power and decision-making. It is often a small team of people within

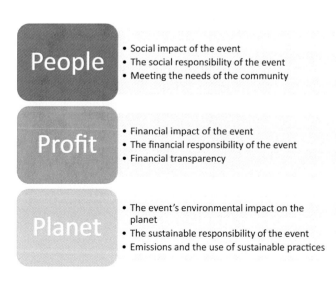

Figure 3.5 TBL measures of performance

the public sector making decisions on behalf of local people (Jepson and Clarke, 2014). Although it should be noted that Fredline *et al.* (2005, p. 4) stressed that the triple bottom line approach does not provide a completely holistic evaluation of all of the impacts events create. There are a number of conditions too difficult to be realistically captured through TBL, such as the potential to generate long-term impacts on destination image and investment in the region through media exposure, and the difficulty to reliably and consistently measure the different performance impacts.

3.11 Consequences of evaluation abuse

The process of international events can be a bit of a mystery. Donald Rumsfeld's famous quote provides a fair explanation of the bidding and delivery process, and can help decipher how the eventual decisions are made to choose a host city or nation:

> There are known knowns. There are things we know that we know. We also know there are known unknowns. That is to say, we know there are things that we don't know. But there are also unknown unknowns. The ones we do not know we don't know.
>
> (Donald Rumsfeld, 2002)

Rumsfeld's approach is based on an analysis technique referred to as 'the Johari window' that helps people better understand their relationship with themselves and others through interpersonal awareness. A major international sporting event necessitates the spending of billions of dollars and the potential for corruption is very real. The IOC for example, has been labelled 'about as corrupt an organisation as there is on this planet' (Fogel, 2019). The history of international event bids, awards, and the eventual awarding of contracts is full of examples of both proven and alleged acts of corruption (Matheson *et al.*, 2017). This is discussed in more detail in Chapter 8, but concerns about cost overruns or corruption may prompt officials to limit the release of accurate data (Baade and Matheson, 2016)

Arguably, one of the disagreeable if not the most publicly offensive activities in the management of international events is the misleading of the public for capital gain through event evaluations. There is a great deal of trust placed in the actions and contributions of professional evaluators, but with the possibility of personal gain provided through interested parties, the opportunities can be very tempting. Crompton *et al.* (2001) suggest that two major consequences exist when professionals fail to recognise and expose abuses in economic impact analyses as follows:

- mischievous studies create precedents that subsequent sponsors feel compelled to follow and,
- the rightful discrediting of evaluations as valuable tools.

With public money funding international events, political corruption in the form of bribes, cronyism, nepotism, parochialism, and embezzlement have all been witnessed in the delivery of international events. Alongside these abuses, the question whether modern large-scale and mega events produce only positive impacts on a given economy was considered as long ago as the early 1980s (Giulianotti and Klauser, 2011). Since then, much more attention has been paid to economic evaluations and their use in international events, largely due to excessive levels of corruption.

The impact of international events can be considerable on a number of levels and not all of these impacts is positive. To get around this issue, the method or means of evaluation can be politically charged and follow a set of planned outcomes or predetermined policies. Foley *et al.* (2012) discussed this by drawing on the Habermas (1976) notion of *legitimation crisis,* noting that events are increasingly influenced by wider political aims. Considering that the success or failure of an event can depend upon the particular criteria by which it is evaluated, it is necessary to consider an event's success or failure in the context of the evaluation method used, and where possible, have independent research conducted.

Another form of evaluation abuse is bias. Chan *et al.* (2015) noted that economic impact studies are often biased in their tendency to exaggerate economic benefits in order to gain credibility and support for the event's organisers. While Giulianotti and Klauser have stated:

> The main problem of economic impact studies resides in the fact that analyses are only as good as the experts conducting them. The process of assessing the economic impact of events is unfortunately very controversial and has negative connotations due to the biases that frequently occur when the process is driven by subjective and naïve approaches or political pressure.
>
> (2011, p. 250)

Evaluations will remain an area of disagreement within the international events community, as those who wish to see an international event pass any tests put before it may place unethical opportunities ahead of the greater good.

3.12 Summary

This chapter has discussed the importance of evaluations and their effect on international events. We have learned that there are several ways to evaluate an event depending on its size and impact and that evaluations can cover some distinctive aspects of an event during delivery as well as covering the effects of the event long after it has finished. We have also learned that evaluations can have different objectives and, depending on the chosen method of evaluation, various results can be obtained. Moreover, when evaluations are politically motivated, there are often more questions than answers by the time the process has been concluded.

Case study 3.1 IAAF World Athletic Championships norovirus outbreak

During the 2017 IAAF World Athletic Championships in London an outbreak of the norovirus hit many of the competing teams resulting in numerous athletes not being able to arrive at the start to compete in their events. At least 30 athletes and team members at the world athletics championships were reported to have been infected. The teams included athletes from Botswana, Germany, Canada, Ireland and Puerto Rico. Germany was hardest hit with nine athletes pulling out of their respective competitions and competitors who arrived later in the competition being allocated other hotels outside of the original plans as a precautionary measure. At least seven Canadian athletes were affected.

One athlete, Isaac Makwala, Botswana's leading 400 metres contender, was prevented from competing, while the Botswana team was refused entry to compete in the 200 metres final. The IAAF said Makwala had shown symptoms of the virus. The team doctor, however, refuted these claims explaining a number of errors. Makwala stated, 'They say they are waiting for the medical results but I don't know because they didn't test me. I don't know what, which medical results they are waiting for.' However, the German triple jumper Neele Eckhardt who was allowed to compete then collapsed due to gastroenteritis during the event and finished last in the final held on the following Monday. The governing athletics body, IAAF, said: 'We have followed strict hygiene protocol, ensuring that those affected are not in contact with other guests and all public areas have been thoroughly sanitised.'

Questions

1. What additional safeguards could the event organisers have put in place to assist with the outbreak and competing athletes?
2. Could the organisers have dealt with the issue differently to allow the suspected infected athletes, who were later found to be unaffected, to compete and restricting those who were unwell, being allowed to compete? If so, what actions could have been implemented?
3. What does the way the organisers dealt with the outbreak suggest?

3.13 Useful websites

Olympic evaluation commission website
www.olympic.org/evaluation-commission

IOC Report Evaluation Commission Olympic Winter Games 2026
https://stillmed.olympic.org/media/Document%20Library/OlympicOrg/Games/
    Winter-Games/Games-2026-Winter-Olympic-Games/Report-of-the-IOC-
    Evaluation-Commission-2026-LO-RES.pdf#_ga=2.17823673.107244893
    0.1567228951-1681617141.1567228951

18 Key Performance Indicator (KPI) Examples Defined
www.clearpointstrategy.com/18-key-performance-indicators/

Family Arts Festival event evaluation toolkit
www.familyarts.co.uk/wp-content/uploads/2015/05/Family-Arts-Festival-
    Evaluation-Toolkit.pdf

References

Baade, R., & Matheson, V. (2016). Going for the gold: The economics of the Olympics. *The Journal of Economic Perspectives, 30*(2), 201. doi:10.1257/jep.30.2.201

Barron, P., & Rihova, I. (2011). Motivation to volunteer: a case study of the Edinburgh International Magic Festival. *International Journal of Event and Festival Management, 2*(3), 202–217. doi:10.1108/17582951111170281

Bayle, E. (2016). Olympic social responsibility: a challenge for the future. *Sport in Society, 19*(6), 752–766.

Boggia, A., Massei, G., Paolotti, L., Rocchi, L., & Schiavi, F. (2018). A model for measuring the environmental sustainability of events. *Journal of Environmental Management, 206*, 836–845.

Brown, S., Getz, D., Pettersson, R., & Wallstam, M. (2015). Event evaluation: Definitions, concepts and a state of the art review. *International Journal of Event and Festival Management, 6*(2), 135–157. doi:10.1108/IJEFM-03-2015-0014

Cavendish, R. (2008). The Munich air crash: February 6th, 1958. *History Today, 59*(2), 15.

Center for Disease Control (CDC) (n.d.). Types of Evaluation. Retrieved from www.cdc.gov/std/Program/pupestd/Types%20of%20Evaluation.pdf Accessed 28th August 2019.

Chan, T.-C., Pai, P.-L., Shaw, S.-L., & Fan, I. C. (2015). Spatiotemporal evolution of market towns in the Jiangnan area during the Ming-Qing dynasties of China. *Historical Methods: A Journal of Quantitative and Interdisciplinary History, 48*(2), 90–102. doi:10.1080/01615440.2014.995783

Chappelet, J.-L. (2013). Mega sporting event legacies: A multifaceted concept. *Papeles de Europa 25*, 76–86.

Chi, C., Ouyang, Z., & Xu, X. (2018). Changing perceptions and reasoning process: Comparison of residents' pre- and post-event attitudes. *Annals of Tourism Research, 70*, 39–53. doi:10.1016/j.annals.2018.02.010

Crompton, J. L., Lee, S., & Shuster, T. J. (2001). A guide for undertaking economic impact studies: The Springfest example. *Journal of Travel Research, 40*(1), 79–87. doi:10.1177/004728750104000110

Crowther, P. (2010). Strategic application of events. *International Journal of Hospitality Management, 29*(2), 227–235.

de Grosbois, D. (2009). Assessing the socio-cultural impact of special events: frameworks, methods, and challenges. [Report]. *Journal of Tourism Challenges and Trends, 2*(2), 39+.

Dolf, M., & Teehan, P. (2015). Reducing the carbon footprint of spectator and team travel at the University of British Columbia's varsity sports events. *Sport Management Review, 18*(2), 244–255.

Elkington, J. (1999). *Cannibals with Forks: The Triple Bottom Line of 21st Century Business*. Oxford: Capstone.

Emery, P. (2010). Past, present, future major sport event management practice: The practitioner perspective. *Sport Management Review, 13*(2), 158–170. doi:10.1016/j.smr.2009.06.003

Ericksen, J., & Dyer, L. (2004). Right from the start: Exploring the effects of early team events on subsequent project team development and performance. *Administrative Science Quarterly, 49*(3), 438–471. doi:10.2307/4131442

EUSurvey (2019). Call for proposals EAC/S17/2019. Retrieved from:https://ec.europa.eu/eusurvey/runner/SmallMusicVenues Accessed 29th August 2019.

Evans, R. (2001). Munich air crash inquiry clouded by diplomacy: Dispute over suppressed evidence after the Busby Babes disaster in 1958 strained relations between Germany and Britain. *The Guardian*. Retrieved from www.theguardian.com/uk/2001/aug/25/football.robevans

Farrell, J. M., Johnston, M. E., & Twynam, G. D. (1998). Volunteer motivation, satisfaction, and management at an elite sporting competition. *Journal of Sport Management, 12*(4), 288–300. doi:10.1123/jsm.12.4.288

Fogel, B. (Writer) & S. Mullervy (Director). (2019). A review of WADA bans and the IOC response. *PM*. Live 9th December 2016. London: BBC Radio 4. Retrieved from https://learningonscreen.ac.uk/ondemand/index.php/prog/14EFDB3E?bcast=130788436 Accessed 10th December 2019.

Foley, M., McGillivray, D., & McPherson, G. (2012). *Event Policy*. Oxford: Routledge.

Fredline, L., Raybould, M., Jago, L., & Deery, M. (2005, July). 'Triple bottom line event evaluation: A proposed framework for holistic event evaluation'. Paper presented at the Third International Event Conference, The Impacts of Events: Triple Bottom Line Evaluation and Event Legacies, UTS, Sydney.

Giulianotti, R., & Klauser, F. (2011). Introduction: Security and surveillance at sport mega events. *Urban Studies, 48*(15), 3157–3168. doi:10.1177/0042098011422400

Gopalakrishna, S., Malthouse, E. C., & Lawrence, J. M. (2017). Managing customer engagement at trade shows. *Industrial Marketing Management*. doi:10.1016/j.indmarman.2017.11.015

Habermas, J. (1976). *Legitimation Crisis*. Trans. and ed. by T. McCarthy. London: Heinemann Educational.

Hindle, T. (2008). *Guide to Management Ideas and Gurus*. London: Profile.

Hosenball, M., & Whitesides, J. (2013). Reports on surveillance of Americans fuel debate over privacy, security. Retrieved from www.reuters.com/article/us-usa-wiretaps-verizon/reports-on-surveillance-of-americans-fuel-debate-over-privacy-security-idUSBRE95502920130607 Accessed 12th August 2019.

IFSEC Global (2014). Role of CCTV cameras: Public, privacy and protection. Retrieved from www.ifsecglobal.com/video-surveillance/role-cctv-cameras-public-privacy-protection/ Accessed 20th March 2018.

IOC (International Olympics Committee) (n.d.). Evaluation commission. Retrieved from www.olympic.org/evaluation-commission Accessed 13th June 2017.

IOC (2013). Building a better world through sport. Retrieved from www.olympic.org/videos/building-a-better-world-through-sport Accessed 5th September 2019.

IOC (2017). Legacy strategic approach: moving forward. Retrieved from https://www.olympic.org/~/media/Document%20Library/OlympicOrg/Documents/Olympic-Legacy/IOC_Legacy_Strategy_Full_version.pdf?la=en Accessed 3rd September 2019.

IOC (2019). Report: IOC evaluation commission Olympic Winter Games 2026. Retrieved from www.olympic.org/news/ioc-releases-evaluation-commission-2026-report Accessed 2nd September 2019.

Jepson, A., & Clarke, A. (2014). The future power of decision making in community festivals. In I. Yeoman, Robertson, M., McMahon-Beattie, U., Backer, A., & Smith, K. A. (eds), *The Future of Events and Festivals*, 67–83. London: Routledge.

Johnson, C. (2018). Automating customer engagement with big data analytics. *Health Management Technology, 39*(3), 21.

Kirchner, R. (2014). *Surveillance and Threat Detection: Prevention Versus Mitigation*. Waltham, MA: Butterworth-Heinemann.

Kwok, Y., Chui, W., & Wong, L. (2013). Need satisfaction mechanism linking volunteer motivation and life satisfaction: A mediation study of volunteers' subjective well-being. *Social Indicators Research, 114*(3), 1315–1329. doi:10.1007/s11205-012-0204-8

Lee, C.-K., Reisinger, Y., Kim, M. J., & Yoon, S.-M. (2014). The influence of volunteer motivation on satisfaction, attitudes, and support for a mega-event. *International Journal of Hospitality Management, 40*, 37.

Mancini, S. (2018). Assignment of swimmers to events in a multi-team meeting for team global performance optimization. *Annals of Operations Research, 264*(1–2), 325–337. doi:10.1007/s10479-017-2735-5

Matheson, V.A., Schwab, D., Koval, P. (2018) Corruption in the bidding, construction and organisation of mega-events: An analysis of the Olympics and World Cup. In: Breuer, M., Forrest, D. (eds) *The Palgrave Handbook on the Economics of Manipulation in Sport*. Cham: Palgrave Macmillan.

Mitchell, M., Curtis, A., & Davidson, P. (2008). Evaluating the process of triple bottom line reporting: Increasing the potential for change. *Local Environment, 13*(2), 67–80.

Nieuwenhuis, R. (2018). Social responsibility. *Science, 360*(6396), 1411–1411.

O'Sullivan, D., Pickernell, D., & Senyard, J. (2009). Public sector evaluation of festivals and special events. *Journal of Policy Research in Tourism, Leisure and Events, 1*(1), 19–36. doi:10.1080/19407960802703482

Parmenter, D. (2010). *Key Performance Indicators (KPI): Developing, Implementing, and Using Winning KPIs*. Hoboken: John Wiley & Sons.

Patton, M. Q. (1987). *Qualitative Research Evaluation Methods*. Thousand Oaks, CA: Sage Publishers.

Preuss, H. (2019). Event legacy framework and measurement. *International Journal of Sport Policy and Politics, 11*(1), 103–118.

Ritchie, J. R. (1984). Assessing the impact of hallmark events: Conceptual and research issues. *Journal of Travel Research, 23*(1), 2–11.

Rumsfeld, D. H. (2002). *Department of Defense News Briefing – Secretary of Defense Rumsfeld. February 12, 2002 11:30 AM EDT*. http://archive.defense.gov/Transcripts/Transcript.aspx?TranscriptID=2636.

Ryan, W. G. (2014). The end of the rainbow? A case study of community events in Liverpool (UK) Community Festivals and Events. In A. Jepson & A. Clarke (eds), *Exploring Community Events and Festivals,* 224–237. London: Routledge.

Scheinbaum, A., & Lacey, R. (2015). Event social responsibility: A note to improve outcomes for sponsors and events. *Journal of Business Research, 68*(9), 1982–1986.

Scraton, P. (2016). *Hillsborough: The truth (updated edition)*. Edinburgh: Mainstream Publishing.

Scrucca, F., Severi, C., Galvan, N., & Brunori, A. (2016). A new method to assess the sustainability performance of events: Application to the 2014 World Orienteering Championship. *Environmental Impact Assessment Review, 56*, 1–11.

Planning and delivery

Sherwood, P. (2007). *A Triple Bottom Line Evaluation of the Impact of Special Events: The Development of Indicators* (Doctoral thesis). Victoria University, Melbourne, Australia.

Torkildsen, G. (2005). *Leisure and Recreation Management* (5th ed.). London: Routledge.

Vetitnev, A. (2018). The influence of host volunteer motivation on satisfaction and attitudes toward Sochi 2014 Olympic Games. *Event Management, 22*(3), 333–352. doi:10.3727/152599518x15239930463145

Whitford, M. (2014). Principles to practice: Indicators for measuring event governance performance. *Event Management, 18*(3), 387–403. doi:10.3727/152599514x14038805493437

Woods, M. (2013). *Beyond The Call: Why Some of Your Team Go The Extra Mile and Others Don't Show* (2nd ed.). Chichester: Wiley.

Part 2

INTERNAL FORCES

Chapter 4

Strategic use of international events by authorities

Contents

4.1 Chapter overview

This chapter provides an introduction to the key issues involved in the strategic use of events by authorities. It looks at how state authorities intervene in the delivery of international events at various levels of governance. It considers how urban regions have grown and how they compete with other local, national and international regions. It also considers the different methods of securing the staging of the biggest international events and how regions have used these occasions as a catalyst for urban regeneration.

4.2 Learning objectives

By the end of this chapter, the student will be expected to:

- Understand the various levels of intervention authorities can provide international events
- Understand the broader role of authorities in delivering international events
- Appreciate the broader issues that the bidding process can bring to a nation.

4.3 Introduction

Governing authorities are meant to effectively govern, direct and regulate at various levels (locally, regionally and nationally), depending on their remit, on behalf of the people they represent. Within this remit, an authority's role is to represent and connect with the people. Events of all kinds are a central feature of a governing authority's social and business development activities. This is so much so today that many larger cities and towns now have a dedicated events department and destination management organisations that focus solely on attracting business and tourism through international events. In recent years, the exposure that is generated through the various media channels and global communications by international events has played an important role, driving many governing authorities to become increasingly engaged with international events.

4.4 State intervention

Government or state intervention in the economy is generally restricted to measures that support or enhance industrial infrastructure (Jones, 2010). State subsidy for events through financial assistance, delivery support and/or direct involvement with international events therefore eventually becomes a key factor in the growth of modern-day nations, cities and towns. International event delivery and two different methods of engagement – for profit and not-for-profit – regularly come together and work side-by-side to ensure large-scale events are delivered safely and with minimum disruption to the day-to-day lives of local residents.

As we will discover, state intervention is unavoidable on many levels of international event delivery and this contribution is essential to the survival of many community-facing events. However, it is also important to begin this chapter with a note of caution. Many questions remain unanswered over the vast amounts of time and public money states devote to securing international events. Moreover, research suggests many of the anticipated benefits that persuade nations to support bidding activities never materialise. Rojek (2014), for example, suggests that global events are placebos. They distract Western populations from facing the difficult debates and decisions on taxes and resource redistribution (from the North to the South), which are the true solutions to the ills of the world.

Authorities use international events for a range of economic, political and social objectives. Dodds and Joppe (2001) suggest that such events are one of the three main components of development plans, along with infrastructure and marketing image. Therefore, international events have become an important channel of cultural symbolism at a global level, with sporting events, cultural events, and business forums helping to generate and circulate symbolic value (Colombo and Richards, 2017). Many city authorities have realised the value of investing in international events. For example, Singapore's economy and socio-cultural scene have been revitalised, largely by the nation's recent public and private sector investments in arts and cultural infrastructure (Pei-Chin and Coca-Stefaniak, 2010), including major international events such as the Formula One Grand Prix (since 2008) and the Youth Olympic Games (2012).

The breadth of influence that international events can have in a region will ultimately depend on the organising authority's ability to effectively promote whatever the attraction may be. Effective local information services increase visitor awareness of places to visit and things to do. This leads to attracting non-residents to the region, increasing the length of stay and raising the level of spending (Carbone and Yunis, 2005).

Foley et al. (2012) suggest that state intervention is provided through subsidy, direct provision and/or regulation to alleviate urban deprivation, enhance physical health, contribute to moral welfare, secure social integration and foster self-improvement. All of these objectives can be addressed and potentially achieved through hosting a recognised international event. However, there is a dichotomy with the bigger international events. That is, according to Barrios et al. (2016), the costs will change during the life of the event and the public will be burdened with higher taxes to pay for it.

In light of the increased level of negative responses to the hosting of many large-scale international sporting events (Abend, 2014; Bauer, 2017; Bayle, 2016), the need for governments to make realistic fiscal and economic announcements has never been greater. The initial public predictions of a £1.8 billion total cost during the bidding process for the London Olympics were subsequently revised to become a £9.3 billion 'final' cost, after the Games had been awarded (House of Commons Public Accounts Committee, 2008). Not a small discrepancy in any fiscal prediction, but made all the more questionable when other additional items of expenditure remained outside the official budget for the event (Jennings, 2013). Foreseeable requirements for public sector funding were excluded from the estimates at the time of the bid to host the Games, so giving an unrealistic picture of the expected costs (House of Commons Public Accounts Committee, 2008).

Public events, spaces and venues are funded by central and municipal governments throughout the world and play an important role in the cultural lives of their citizens (Urban Task Force, 1999). However, state intervention also has a duty of care and, depending on the ruling administration's perspective, the event's impact can be considered negligible. As well as permitting social gatherings, a ruling administration also has the ability to cancel or even remove events from the social and cultural calendar.

4.5 The banning of events

It would be considered harsh in Western-style democracies for any nation to have a ruling administration that considered the cancelling of festivals, public gatherings and events without good reason, but this is what happened in the UK in the 19th century. The 1871 Fairs Act, which sought to amend the existing law relating to fairs in England and Wales, saw the abolition of hundreds of fairs and events in England and Wales (see Figure 4.1). The Act stated:

> [25th May' 1871.] WHEREAS certain of the fairs held in England and Wales are unnecessary, are the cause of grievous immorality, and are very injurious to the inhabitants of the towns in which such fairs are held, and it is therefore expedient to make provision to facilitate the abolition of such fairs.
>
> (Hansard, 1871)

How the crown came to the conclusion that these events were unnecessary may never be fully understood. One suggestion was that the decline of the fairs marked a great shift in British society, as it came decisively under the influence of industrial capitalism, the modern state, and the embourgeoisement of the working classes (Barnett, 2013). It could also have been due to the loss of traditional sites in town centres, or an attempt to curtail the growth of travelling fairs. However, fairs could only be abolished if there was no public opposition to this. If the notice of abolition was greeted with public outrage and pressure, the Secretary of State had the power to rescind the request from the local authorities (University of Sheffield, 2015).

In the United States, too, fairs were banned. From around 1745 fairs were held in Trenton Township, New Jersey in April and October for the buying and selling of livestock and other products. Initially promoted by King George II, after five years the legislature declared them illegal (Sanders, 2019). More recently, careful control of events such as protests, rather than banning them outright, is common practice throughout the world. The banning or censoring of international journalists from reporting on events or their preparation is also widespread throughout the world, particularly where human rights are a concern. However, the banning of activities can also create internationally newsworthy events as protestors use the international media to highlight their cause.

[34 VICT.]   *Fairs.*   [CH. 12.]

CHAP. 12.

An Act to further amend the Law relating to Fairs in England
and Wales.   [25th May 1871.]

A.D. 1871.

WHEREAS certain of the fairs held in England and Wales are
unnecessary, are the cause of grievous immorality, and are
very injurious to the inhabitants of the towns in which such fairs are
held, and it is therefore expedient to make provision to facilitate the
abolition of such fairs:

Be it enacted by the Queen's most Excellent Majesty, by and
with the advice and consent of the Lords Spiritual and Temporal,
and Commons, in this present Parliament assembled, and by the
authority of the same, as follows:

1. This Act may be cited as "The Fairs Act, 1871."   Title.

2. In this Act the term " owner " means any person or persons,   Definition of " owner."
or body of commissioners, or body corporate, entitled to hold any
fair, whether in respect of the ownership of any lands or tenements,
or under any charter, letters patent, or Act of Parliament, or otherwise howsoever.

3. In case it shall appear to the Secretary of State for the Home   Secretary of State may, on representation of magistrates, with consent of owner, order fair to be abolished.
Department, upon representation duly made to him by the magis-
trates of any petty sessional district within which any fair is held,
or by the owner of any fair in England or Wales, that it would be
for the convenience and advantage of the public that any such fair
shall be abolished, it shall be lawful for the said Secretary of State
for the Home Department, with the previous consent in writing of
the owner for the time being of such fair, or of the tolls or dues
payable in respect thereof, to order that such fair shall be abolished
accordingly: Provided always, that notice of such representation,   Notice of representation to be published in newspapers.
and of the time when it shall please the Secretary of State for the
Home Department to take the same into consideration, shall be
published once in the London Gazette, and in three successive weeks

[*Public.—12.*]   1

[CH. 12.]   *Fairs.*   [34 VICT.]

A.D. 1871.   in some one and the same newspaper published in the county, city,
or borough in which such fair is held, or if there be no newspaper
published therein, then in the newspaper of some county adjoining
or near thereto, before such representation is so considered.

Order of Secretary of State to be published in newspaper.   4. When and so soon as any such order as aforesaid shall have
been made by the Secretary of State for the Home Department,
notice of the making of the same shall be published in the London
Gazette, and in some one newspaper of the county, city, or borough
in which such fair is usually held, or if there be no newspaper
published therein, then in the newspaper of some county adjoining
or near thereto, and thereupon such fair shall be abolished.

LONDON : Printed by GEORGE EDWARD EYRE and WILLIAM SPOTTISWOODE,
Printers to the Queen's most Excellent Majesty. 1871.

Figure 4.1 The Original Fairs Act, 1871

Source: legislation.gov.uk, n.d.

Borders and migration (USA), human rights (Hong Kong), LGBT (Russia) and economic justice (France) are just a handful of examples.

4.6 The shifting metropolitan landscape

To understand how international events today have been created or developed, it is necessary to undertake a quick review of recent decades, and changes in the urban landscape in particular. In this context, the period after the 1960s provides evidence of change throughout the established world in both economic and urban development.

Urban development is a system of residential expansion that creates spaces for people to live. Within this development is a process which includes intentional interventions from governing bodies to benefit the local population. These include recreational activities and ultimately, the establishment, provision or delivery of international events. Thriving towns and cities are an essential element of a prosperous national economy. The gathering of economic and human resources in one place stimulates innovation and development in business and industry (Open University, 2019).

As populations grow, incredible amounts of investment, both public and private, is poured into the future of a region to maximise the opportunities that either already exist or are considered necessary to improve the quality of living. Over time, the activities that exist in cities and towns are often considered a reflection of the place itself and form the basis of the area's growth. However, developments in the mid-20th century that were generated by the globalisation of economic processes created a wave of change that spread throughout the world. Many major cities and towns throughout the world suffered from a long-term decline while others benefited.

How deep the effects of this changing landscape were on each place often depended on the industries that had built the city in the first place. Pike *et al.* (2016) created a typology of place by analysing key differences between UK cities, having identified the key factors in relation to a city's decline. They proposed a variable level of resistance to decline by categorising three different types of city: 'Core', 'Over-shadowed' and 'Freestanding' cities. The amount of decline a city experienced was dependent on a number of factors. For example, the risk of recent relative decline was lower for cities with:

- More highly qualified people among its working age group
- No nearby larger city attracting away service trade
- Faster rail access to London
- Little history of dependence for work on mining/manufacturing.

Pike *et al.* (2016) also suggested that the manner in which regions have declined varies from place to place, proposing two types of decline – absolute and relative. Absolute decline refers to the outright reduction in population or employment. Relative decline is a comparison of performance to similar places with under-performance in relation to comparators.

These definitions fit many comparable examples around the world, in particular, cities that are suffering from a change in how and where goods are produced. Improved global transport links, low-priced imports and cheaper labour in developing economies began to turn long-standing boomtowns around the world into ghost towns, with their major employers closing the large factories that were the heart of the region's economy. This brought poverty to the region and created a brain drain of those fortunate enough to be in a position to relocate. Urban decline has been described as a fairly normal process affecting more than one in four cities in the world between 1990 and 2000 (Bernt, 2009). Cities across the world that were built on industry and manufacturing all suffered from this shift in global trade and industry – for example, in Sweden, Italy, the UK, Spain, and the USA.

For some time towards the end of the 20th century, many regions throughout the world had no answer to the decline being experienced. But as vast spaces became vacant, events of all sizes became one of the solutions to the problem. This constituted a complete reversal from the Victorian approach of removing festivals and events from public spaces. In response to the global restructuring of industry in the 1970s and 1980s, the elected governments of economically depressed cities increasingly adopted growth-orientated local economic development policies (Loftman and Nevin, 1996), many of which included international events.

The demand by authorities to attract international events has introduced new opportunities for the organisers. Many international events today that are synonymous with their place of origin have become so popular, they are able to move to other countries and still receive enormous support. American Football held four matches in London during the 2019/20 season with reports suggesting they were the most in-demand tickets across the entire league (Finnis, 2018). For cycling, it has become more regular for the Tour de France to start in one of

Figure 4.2 Le Tour caravan that precedes the race – Yorkshire, England, 2014

the surrounding countries and in 2018, the Giro D'Italia went much further with the first three stages being held in Israel. Figure 4.2 shows the Tour de France caravan that precedes the race on the first day of the 2012 event in the heart of Yorkshire, England.

4.7 The authority's function in delivering events

As a nationally or locally elected authority's role includes representing its people, it will undertake a number of roles when facilitating, supporting or delivering international events. Besides providing operational support, authorities can be the source of income for events delivered by third parties or bid directly to host international events. Once an event reaches a certain size, there is no avoiding an authority's involvement. The first point of communication with an authority from an event organiser is usually the application for a licence to hold the event. For small events, this usually requires very little engagement between the parties, but as the event grows, the process becomes much more detailed, with the relationship becoming more engaged the bigger the attendance numbers at the event.

In the UK, providing the event attendance is for licensable activities, below a certain number for each day (usually 500), and temporary in nature – i.e. a one off event for up to a week – temporary applications can be made to the local council. If attendance at the event grows, or the circumstances do not meet the requirements of a temporary licence, the involvement of the authority will increase. Roads may need to be closed, streets may need to be cleaned immediately after the event; and the overall safety of the public, always paramount, becomes more manageable with the support of the local council.

If the event's attendance goes into thousands, the organisers will revise their communication plans and be in regular communication with the local authority and the emergency service representatives in the region. To ensure that good planning and communication is possible between these bodies, it is essential for the event organisers to have in place an emergency command system to manage communication, resources, and responsibilities in order to implement essential strategies in a crisis or an emergency. These communication processes are discussed in more detail in Chapter 5.

Meetings during the planning stages at this level take on a much more significant role and will have in attendance representatives from all the necessary authorities including local councils, the emergency services, third sector organisations and any other body or stakeholder that either needs to inform or be informed in a responsible capacity in the event of an emergency situation.

Local authorities unsurprisingly have access to all the requirements to effectively deliver large scale events. The six attributes or strategic requirements for an international event, people, skills, knowledge, infrastructure, power and resources are readily available to a local authority. These are also discussed in more detail in Chapter 5. With all of these requirements at their disposal, how an authority responds to the demands of providing quality international experiences with the use of public funds can ultimately be the making or breaking of an event.

4.8 Destination management

Another key responsibility of national and local authorities is destination management. Destination management is a relatively recent phenomenon that has numerous definitions. Effectively, destination management involves the coordinated and integrated management of a destination in terms of a number of regular activities. These include: attractions and events, facilities, transportation, infrastructure and hospitality resources (Mill and Morrison, 2012). These are important to international events as they are core concepts of international event delivery. Destination management is considered a professional approach to guiding all of the efforts in a place that has decided to pursue tourism as an economic activity (Morrison, 2013).

Many governing authorities also believe that through the various interventions of destination management, the wellbeing of society can be improved (Braithwaite and Drahos, 2000). Many events can be delivered with minimal concern for a local community and will meet all the objectives of the planners. However, large-scale international events come with considerably greater demands. They are both welcome and unwelcome in the view of the public. The pressure to satisfy supporters, placate dissenters and keep the media onside makes the task of delivery much more problematic. The benefits of success and the potential for substantial exposure is largely what the proprietors of the biggest international events want the authorities to focus on. However, international events are often used as an opportunity to highlight other issues local and national authorities would prefer not to be attached to the event. The international media events attract can encourage the act of coat-tailing events to gain media exposure.

Social movements can use the media at major events to draw attention to issues they deem important by organising public demonstrations near the event site. If the demonstrations create a big enough impact, the demonstration can become the newsworthy story. Such activities include human rights and environmental protests (see Chapter 10).

Local and national authorities can find themselves in an unusual position when it comes to dealing at the highest level of the event industry. The aspiration to secure the larger mega or hallmark events can bring into question disparities in state spending. Residents tend to have good memories when it comes to cuts in services and the potential commitment to financial expenditure a major event brings with it. The public-private relationship can be further obstructed due to the conflicting agendas each will have. There are many similarities each side will have, including the need for economic value and the importance of social capital (Aldridge *et al.*, 2002). Furthermore, international events are perceived by authorities as a means of providing for residents. However, such events often cause a great deal of disruption to the day-to-day lives of the host community, from disrupting commuting and the school run to compulsory purchase orders of residential property and the adverse effects on an individual's health.

But while a commercial event company will usually trade in a specific area of the event industry, events are not the ultimate priority for an authority. An authority's focus is on delivering public services way beyond those of the events sector, including collecting taxes, housing, street cleaning, social care and education. Even when event industry specialists are involved in negotiations on behalf of the authority, there will always be these underlying differences between commercial activities and civic responsibilities. Having said that, treating councils as partners puts in the spotlight the role local authorities play in moving the event industry forward (Gonzalez, 2017).

The draw of large-scale international events can also put the authority in turmoil. Horne (2007) detected that, even during times of austerity, developers in the event industry have been able to extract public subsidies and tax holidays from governments desperate for their business, while the same governments have been cutting back, sometimes severely, on social welfare spending. Budgets that had previously been unavailable in one spending round have miraculously been revived when the opportunity to host a major extravaganza presents itself.

On an international level, it is without doubt that the principal large-scale and mega events will attract and eventually deliver the media exposure tourist destinations desire, which is why the events are so sought after by administrations around the world. They can raise the international profile of a place and provide opportunities for regeneration.

4.9 Build, redevelop, and redesign

As governments seek more cost-effective methods of event delivery, the last 20 years has seen the redevelopment of many sports venues, with space designated for hospitality a key feature. It is rare in today's understanding of the use of space for new venues to be built without dedicated hospitality areas or for events to be held without infrastructure that is fit for purpose.

The future planning of major events often includes the redesign of venues and stadia, and the local authority or national government taking control of them. In most cases, the venues are handed back to the local residents as sports facilities. History suggests that this does not always work out as the plan or bid suggested. Many previous Olympic host cities have a multitude of vacant and derelict venues that stand as legacy to the event. Converting a stadium originally designed for a single event is a massive undertaking and requires excellence in future planning. One particular success was the conversion of the stadium for the XVII Commonwealth Games in 2002. The venue was converted from an athletics stadium into a football stadium, and is now home to Manchester City Football Club.

There are a number of complications that converting the athletics stadium into a football stadium brought, however – most notably, the running track around the pitch and the fact that the original stadium was not enclosed. Over a nine-month period, the venue was converted from a 41,000-seat athletics stadium to a 50,000-seat football stadium. The stadium was enclosed with seating, and the track was removed. In order to make the venue more compatible with football, the ground was lowered by 6 metres, with 90,000 square metres of earth removed, and a lower seating section installed to provide 24 additional rows of seating (Dite, 2019). Figure 4.3 shows the difference between the two stands, with the original on the left of the picture.

Figure 4.3 Before and after the City of Manchester stadium conversion

Source: Based on images from Tony Smith and Wikipedia, n.d.

4.10 Access to funds

One of the more attractive – if costly and uncertain – approaches used by governing authorities (both local and national) to transform derelict spaces, kick-start redevelopment, attract new investment or even just to be seen to be contending is to officially bid to host an international event. More recently, the links between globalisation and attracting activities such as international events to a particular location has become part of what is known as the 'new urban politics' (Ancien, 2011; Cochrane *et al.*, 1996; Foley *et al.*, 2012; Hodson and Marvin, 2009). See Chapter 9 for more details.

The approach some authorities now take towards events has resulted in some destinations being dubbed 'eventful cities'. The concept developed out of the basic observation that cities are using events to achieve a growing range of policy objectives, including economic growth, image change, social cohesion, and physical redevelopment (Richards and Colombo, 2017). Considering that political opinion was previously highly sceptical of financial intervention in the arts and cultural activities which form the backbone of the event industry, this has been a fundamental reorientation of municipal strategy. Previously, spending taxpayers' money on such intangible social activities was considered outside the realm of civic responsibility. There was a lack of appreciation for or an understanding of the value these activities bring.

The duty of care to ensure the survival of local cultural activities is a recent phenomenon (Minihan, 1977). Even a relatively recent perspective on international events that are subsidised by local or national governments might conjure up conceptions of cultural activities that are provided in the interest of particular sections of the community. Information about subsidy for events-related activities struggles to reach many grassroots organisations; the information might be readily available, but its sharing and promotion is at best random. Organisations such as local orchestras, theatre and dance companies, venues, galleries or minority groups are eligible to receive funding based on their ability to prove their engagement with the community. However, in the early stages of arts funding the fact that access to these limited funds was largely communicated by word of mouth, meant that the recipients were often closely linked to those involved in distributing the funds.

The recipients of arts and cultural funding, central to many international events, shift and change very slowly as the practice of setting up organisations eligible to receive the support is infrequent compared to commercial business. However, authorities have developed the funding process over the years in an attempt to be inclusive rather than exclusive, while also claiming that the process is more transparent. Previously, applications were decided on the whim of a committee. Today, criteria that are aligned to a points system or value-weighting have become the standard procedure for applications. These are not all without dissatisfied applicants, but the decision-making process can, in most cases, be quantified for all to see.

The lion's share of available funding for such activities today requires a great deal of evidence to prove a return on investment. Previously, the hosting of an event was about creating a moment in time or something for a community or group of communities. The event was something that happened usually as a one-off occasion and was experienced by those who attended. The hosting of large-scale urban events is no longer just about the occasion. Viehoff and Poynter commented:

> The role of the large-scale urban event has gone from constituting a highly significant moment for the transformation and history of the city to presenting a much more instrumental function, as a support element for the necessary updating of the brand image of the city, regardless of the type of physical transformation that may be produced as a consequence of its celebration.
> (Viehoff and Poynter, 2015)

It becomes apparent, however, that gaining access to funds for events is often based on the ability to lobby. Lobbying is when the legislators, or in this case the funding bodies, are influenced by discreet communications from organisations (or their representatives), on their funding allocations. In Scotland, for example, Behr and Brennan (2014) discovered that direct government funding remains skewed towards the national performing companies such as Royal Scottish National Orchestra, Scottish Opera and Scottish Chamber Orchestra. Data from funding body Arts Council England suggests that the subsidy provided to organisations based in London is more than double that of organisations based in every other region (i.e. north, south-east, south-west and the Midlands), in terms of both the amount of funds awarded and the number of organisations funded (Arts Council England, 2019).

Outside of London: many major metropolises in the UK have now managed to transform themselves from the dominance of industry and production to services and consumption (Viehoff and Poynter, 2015). This is often achieved in conjunction with the hosting of international events. The annual Birmingham

Christmas Market, for example, brings in more than 5 million visitors a year and has become the centrepiece of Birmingham's festive calendar (Bentley, 2019). This renaissance of space and reuse of buildings for arts and cultural purposes is evident throughout the world. The Basilica Building in Hudson, New York, Hotel de Goudfazant in Amsterdam, The Spinnerei, Leipzig, Mikser House in Belgrade, and the Russell Industrial Centre, Detroit, are all examples of the redevelopment of space where industry once thrived. Today, the hosting of international events and exhibitions is the catalyst for regeneration.

4.11 Bidding for events

One of the leading pressures placed on local and national governments is to provide or attract international events to the region. Hosting major international events is considered a high-ranking economic activity and while pressure may come from residents to both hold and avoid the hosting of international events, each and every authority will face competition from neighbouring cities, regions and nations. Event bidding can be considered to occur within a specialised marketplace in which owners (or sellers) control the rights to host an event and bidders (or buyers) compete for those rights (Getz, 2004). However, the value in becoming a host venue, host city or host nation has never been more debated.

The greater the international reach the event delivers, the greater the investment committed. Shoval (2002) observed that events are being used as the means to finance large-scale construction projects in an era of growing inter-urban competition as places compete to strengthen their global status. This pursuit of status forces large cities and nations to seriously consider making formal bids to host international events, with the largest of them demanding the provision of spectaculars that include major construction projects and entertainment at a cost of billions of dollars to the host nation.

To host an event such as the Olympic Games requires many years of careful and precise planning. It requires the bringing together of all the relevant organisations, authorities and stakeholders, working together as one united team, to ensure that the event leaves behind a positive, long-term and sustainable legacy (IOC, n.d.). However, using mega events such as the Olympic Games as a means for economic growth has been widely debated. Many economists believe that the increasing cost of hosting the Olympics greatly outweighs any economic or social benefit gained from hosting the event (Bremer, 2016). However, the social benefit lies in the feel-good factor created in the aftermath of large events, and sporting triumphs can provide political momentum to incumbent governments (Jennings, 2013).

Over the last 30 years, there has been an exponential growth in the number of cities and nations bidding to host all kinds of international events. Considering the prospective benefits international events are believed to bring to a destination, including increased tourism, new infrastructure and development, financial investment, enriched destination image, and regional promotion, international sporting events in particular have proved to be a major attraction for the modern urban destination. This has made bidding for large-scale events a foundation of municipal strategy, even though history suggests that achieving a financial return on investment from such events is unlikely. To get around this problem, civil authorities and bid representatives tend to focus on the positive aspects of a number of other causative factors that are presented to host city populations on the basis of legacy commitments in such a way that the financial return on the investment becomes a secondary matter.

Each bidding process for international events is unique to the type of international event involved. Some events are targeted at cities while others are targeted at nations. The main types of event that include bidding processes are for meetings, exhibitions and conventions, political events, and sporting events. Some cities and even nations will group together to create regional bids, while other events are reserved for member organisations. Whereas bidding to host the Olympic Games is available to all cities, FIFA only takes bids from Member Associations (MAs). Similarly, bidding for some events will be at the discretion of the national government while others are open to all commercial bidders.

The majority of bidding activities to host international events pass with little interest from people or the media. Venues and destination management organisations will be processing bids for business events on a regular basis with limited media attention. However, as the event size and reach is increased, so is the interest in the cost and potential knock-on effects. This is because not all international event returns are positive and the negative returns can have much deeper and longer-lasting effects on a region, with particular attention being placed on its less fortunate groups. The uncertainty involved in hosting international sporting events and the robust application process have proved to be the most contentious of all bidding and hosting undertakings.

Undelivered assurances from major bids that incorporate aid and inspiration for the young, the poor and those in need of employment are typical recurring themes that are frequently unsuccessful. Successful bidding nations have been criticised for economic hardship which has left the majority of newly built venues abandoned (Gibson, 2015; Kennelly, 2016; Staufenberg, 2016). Table 4.1 lists the various areas of return that can be created from the hosting of international events. These will attract much greater interest from the media when public money has been used to create the area of return.

Once a region decides to enter the bidding process, the investment to compete in the bidding process is committed to the cause and only one bid (sometimes multi-national) will secure the right to hold the event. Therefore, as there is only one winner, there are numerous applications where a city or nation will have invested vast sums of public money with no means of return. In recent years, the City of Paris alone suffered three failed bids to host the summer Olympic Games of 1992, 2008 and 2012. Between 1990 and 2016 there were 13 Olympic host cities; 67 cities submitted 99 bids with even more producing preliminary bids that did not progress beyond the preliminary stage (Oliver and Lauermann, 2017).

The reasons for cities or nations to formally engage in such intricate investments and bid to host international events are a complex web of local, national and international demands, needs and aspirations (Strohmayer, 2013).

Of course, some international bidding processes are more commercial than others. The Olympics and FIFA World Cup require substantial assistance from central government. For Union des Associations Européennes de Football (UEFA) competitions, the bid is largely a commercial process for the national football

Table 4.1 Areas of return through the delivery of international events

Area of return	Sub-category: Positive	Sub-category: Negative
Residents	Social cohesion Residents' wellbeing Sense of achievement Creation of good memories Social activities	Displacement Lack of interest Social exclusion Non-delivery of promises Disruption to daily life
Place	Improved image destination Enhanced reputation Positive media coverage Projected attendance figures	Poor destination image Poor/over attendance Reduced reputation
Political	Retention of power Civic pride Educational opportunities Cultural awareness Business development Personal legacy International politics	Civic dissatisfaction Human rights protests Loss of power Sustainability matters
Financial	Tourism spend Property value growth Job creation Trade development Inward investment	Inadequate use of resources Debt from construction Increased rental costs Ongoing cost of delivery
Urban regeneration – infrastructure	New facilities and venues New roads and transport links Company relocation	Unsuitable infrastructure Vacant premises

associations, but there will be costs incurred by the state which usually relate to policing, waste management and general safety outside of the stadium.

4.12 Hosting international recurring events and finals

Each of the major sporting individual and team disciplines engages in international competition. Even at grassroots level, events will take place at a national, regional and local level, but still regularly require an international management process. Depending on the level and reach of these events, international competing finals will be hosted annually, biannually, or quadrennially. Triennial events also exist, but not usually in the world of sport. However, there are numerous sporting events that follow quadrennial and biannual cycles. Most famously, the Olympics and the FIFA World Cup are held quadrennially, while volleyball, diving, taekwondo and table tennis all have major biennial gatherings.

The hosting of many sporting tournament finals and business events has proved to be very popular with authorities and can act as a first phase in bidding for international events. Many organising bodies now put out tenders for nations to bid for the privilege to host a broad spectrum of events. International trade fairs, trade shows, and conferences can bring massive financial benefit to a region and many of those international companies that have an annual meeting with a global presence move from continent to continent to satisfy the demands of their members. The regional arenas and expo halls then work together with local authorities to secure the event. It is common practice for most internationally recognised business associations with an international membership, both large and small, to put out bid tenders for partnerships to work together with local organising committees to bear the financial and organisational responsibilities of the association's annual meeting.

In sport, the practice of putting hosting opportunities to a bid is widespread. Ten countries entered formal bids to host the Fédération Equestre Internationale (FEI) World Championship events in 2022. This followed a move by the FEI to offer to break up the traditional World Equestrian Games (WEG) format and invite interest in hosting single or combined disciplines (Radford, 2019). There are bidding opportunities for event management partners in World Sailing events. These are naturally exclusive to cities with facilities by the sea. Many national golf tournaments similarly allow bidding for clubs to host the event. The Irish Open has regularly been held in both Ireland and Northern Ireland. Athletics, rugby league and union, judo, and many more all rotate the host nation for annual international finals between member states.

4.12.1 Hosting UEFA finals

In December 2016 UEFA, the organising body for association football (soccer) in Europe launched an open bidding procedure for national football associations (on behalf of the venues/football clubs) to express their interest in hosting one of the four club competition finals: the UEFA Champions League, the UEFA Europa League, the UEFA Women's Champions League and the UEFA Super Cup. Each bidding association is allowed a maximum of one bid per final. This means that if two or more clubs from one nation express an interest, the national association must select one to go forward. Clubs had until 27th January 2017 to express interest and to submit a full bid dossier to UEFA by 6th June 2017. A full bid dossier is over 150 pages long. The selection of hosts was made three months after the deadline (UEFA, 2016).

For the 2019 finals, UEFA received 14 bid dossiers from ten member associations to host UEFA club competition finals in 2019 (UEFA, 2019). Table 4.2 highlights the competitions, bidding clubs with average attendance figures for each tournament.

The bidding process to host a European final is highly complex and follows strict regulations set out by UEFA on the basis of Article 50(1) of the UEFA Statutes (UEFA, 2016). The regulations are aimed at setting a clear and open bidding procedure over a three-stage procedure and include:

- An Initiating Phase, during which each of the UEFA member associations can declare their interest to bid
- A Bid Dossier Development Phase, during which each Bidder develops its Bid Dossier based on the Bid Requirements; and
- An Evaluation Phase, during which the Bid Dossiers submitted by Bidders are evaluated by UEFA.

Table 4.2 UEFA completion finals and bidding venues, 2019

UEFA Champions League	UEFA Europa League	UEFA Women's Champions League	UEFA Super Cup
Azerbaijan: Baku, Olympic Stadium **Spain: Madrid, Estadio Metropolitano***	**Azerbaijan: Baku, Olympic Stadium** Spain: Seville, Estadio Ramón Sánchez-Pizjuán Turkey: Istanbul, Beşiktaş Stadium	**Hungary: Budapest, Ferencváros Stadium** Kazakhstan: Astana, Astana Arena	Albania: Tirana, National Stadium France: Toulouse, Stadium de Toulouse Israel: Haifa, Sammy Ofer Stadium Kazakhstan: Astana, Astana Arena Northern Ireland: Belfast, Windsor Park Poland: Gdansk, Arena Gdańsk **Turkey: Istanbul, Beşiktaş Stadium**
Average attendance: 49,304 per match Final attendance: 63,272	Average attendance: 35,677 per match Final attendance: 51,370	Average attendance: 1,586 per match Final attendance: 19,487	Average attendance: N/A Final attendance: 38,434

*Winning hosts are shown in **bold**

Source: Based on UEFA data, 2019

The total timescale between announcing invitations to tender and announcing the venue to host a European football final is about ten months. Considering the amount of paperwork required for a single event, the preparation time is very tight. The venue then has 20 months to prepare to host two teams who will not be known until a month before the event itself. This is discussed in more detail in Chapter 10. These final few weeks see a scramble by fans for flights, hotels and tickets with the corresponding providers adjusting their pricing, particularly once the point of departure becomes known.

4.13 Bidding to host the Olympic Games

The bidding process for either of the Olympic Games (summer or winter) is long, expensive, full of protocol and lobbying, but remains the biggest sporting extravaganza in the world. Organising committees are brought together to produce proposals for the IOC which demands not only the support of the committee, but also the serving government and its people.

The eventual hosting of the summer or winter Olympic Games is arguably the biggest event any country might undertake. The cost to host is astronomical and ever rising. The six Games (both summer and winter), held between 2004 and 2014 cost on average US$8.9 billion. This figure does not include any road, rail, airport or hotel infrastructure, which often cost more than the Games themselves. Furthermore, whatever the proposed budget, cost overrun is found in all Games, without exception (Flyvbjerg *et al.*, 2016). Therefore, creating a return on investment requires enormous effort from the organisers who have to pursue an ever growing break-even point in order to keep up with the IOC's contractual requirements.

The International Olympic Committee (IOC) franchises the event to cities to host and in return receives a fee from the host. This means that there is no actual cost to deliver the event borne by the IOC. The reality is that, while openness is at the heart of the IOC's processes, economic data about the event tends to avoid addressing very important factors. Aside from infrastructural issues, according to Bull (2018), in 2014 Oslo dropped out of the bidding process for the 2022 Winter Olympics after a Norwegian tabloid newspaper published a leaked copy of the IOC's Olympic rider. See Chapter 5 for more detailed information on riders.

The reason for dropping out is said to have been related to mounting public opposition to the bid, and the disclosure of the rider was not the main factor in the city's decision. However, the document stipulated many demands including:

- IOC members get a cocktail reception with the Norwegian royal family
- Exclusive use of special road lanes
- Priority treatment at airports and hotels.

Since more information about the real cost to host the Games has come to the public's attention, the bidding process has come under pressure in recent years with public votes and referendums contributing to a number of cancelled bids. A key distinction in public discourse is that people were not opposed to the idea of the Olympic Games. Instead people showed concern for the concessions they must make to host the month-long event (Bauer, 2017). Hosting an event of this size from a national perspective can seem gratuitously expensive and, from a global perspective, tremendously harmful to the environment (see Chapter 10). However, the Games continue to succeed in obtaining widespread support around the world.

A record number of 204 nations were represented at the 2008 Summer Olympics in Beijing (BOCOG, 2010) and a well-planned event has the potential to convey a diverse set of benefits and opportunities to the host region and country. With this in mind, it is common sense for feasibility studies to begin some time before any formal bid is considered by the host nation. In 1993, after the then President of the IOC had described Manchester's chances of hosting the 2000 Olympics as 'very, very high' (BBC, 1993), they received very little support during the vote. The Games were eventually awarded to Sydney. In light of this failure, London conducted its first feasibility study for the 2012 Games in 1997 (Lee, 2006).

The current bidding process is based around two main phases which are governed by the Olympic Charter Rule 33 and its bye-laws, 'Election of the host city' (IOC, 2015b). These are:

1. The election of any host city is the prerogative of the Session
2. The IOC Executive Board determines the procedure to be followed until the election by the Session takes place. Save in exceptional circumstances,

such an election takes place seven years before the celebration of the Olympic Games

3. The national government of the country of any applicant city must submit to the IOC a legally binding instrument by which the said government undertakes and guarantees that the country and its public authorities will comply with and respect the Olympic Charter
4. The election of the host city takes place in a country having no candidate city for the organisation of the Olympic Games concerned.

For any nation, rule 3 is an extremely powerful demand and provides an indication of the size of the commitment being made. However, once the decision to proceed has been made, the actual bidding process may begin. This commences with the Invitation Phase which is not a formal commitment to bid, but rather an expression of interest and an opportunity for the host applicant to gauge the public's response. Once a city progresses to the candidature process, three more stages need to be completed as part of a formal commitment to bid (IOC, 2015a):

A. The Invitation Phase (not a formal commitment to bid)
B. The Candidature Process (a formal commitment to bid)
   I.   Stage 1: Vision, Games concept and Strategy
   II. Stage 2: Governance, Legal and Venue Funding
   III. Stage 3: Games Delivery, Experience and Venue Legacy.

During the candidature process, the IOC will make formal inspection visits to each candidate city at various times during the planning stages. This is included in the candidate city's budget for the event. These visits normally take four days at a time and a candidate city can expect multiple visits during the course of a bid and numerous subsequent visits if granted permission to host. Tokyo, for example, experienced eight visits during its early preparations for the 2020 Games with London accommodating ten visits during the whole preparation stages (Morgan, 2018; Pavitt, 2019).

In 2017, after three withdrawals from the bidding process (Budapest, Hamburg, and Rome), only two cities remained: Paris and Los Angeles (Butler, 2017). In response to this, the IOC Executive Board met in Lausanne, Switzerland, to discuss the possibility of naming two winners. On June 9th, 2017 the IOC formally proposed electing the 2024 (Paris) and 2028 (Loss Angeles) Olympic host cities at the same time thereby allowing both remaining cities to prepare to host the event. The 2028 Summer Olympics is scheduled to take place from 21st July to 6th August 2028 in Los Angeles, California. While most host cities have seven years to prepare for the Olympic Games, due to the review in the bidding process and the announcement procedure, Los Angeles will see an additional four years of preparation time.

This unprecedented move provides Los Angeles with a total of eleven years for preparations, but also highlights the IOC's concerns about the withdrawals by introducing two major changes in the bid procedure. The IOC will advance funds to a Los Angeles Organising Committee in view of the longer planning period and to increase participation and access to youth sports programmes in the city of Los Angeles in the years leading up to the Games (IOC, 2017).

It is notable that during a previous round of bidding for the 2022 Winter Olympics, a similar situation occurred when Krakow, Lviv, Oslo and Stockholm withdrew their applications (Abend, 2014). This resulted in a two-way battle between Beijing, China, and Almaty, Kazakhstan, to host the Games. Beijing was ultimately declared the winner. Unlike Los Angeles, Kazakhstan were not given the opportunity to host the following Olympics. Prime Minister of Kazakhstan Karim Massimov made a speech with a key message that Almaty was not a risk choice for 2022, but a golden opportunity to prove that smaller advancing nations can successfully host the winter Games (Wilson, 2015). Unfortunately, his words did not instigate a review of the rules like that of Los Angeles.

4.14 Competitive dialogue

In order for an event to acquire funding or be approved for delivery when a bidding process is required, the local authority or organising body will usually seek to qualify and quantify (in the application process) the suitability of the host through competitive dialogue. Competitive dialogue is a process that is used in large and or complex procurements. The basis of competitive dialogue is that the initial applications are judged and removed on the basis of 'most economically advantageous tender' (MEAT). In other words, all delivery partner applications and all potential solutions can be considered for tender, although not if a bidder has been eliminated at an earlier stage. Once all the bids have been duly considered, a final competitive tender is made from the shortlist of bidders, followed by a contract being awarded to a winning bid. Each awarding body will have its own set of criteria with minimum requirements on top of the MEAT. The further along the bidding process the bid proceeds, the more important these other criteria become until the final vote is cast or ballot is counted by the members of the organising council or committee.

The Olympic Games are delivered by an organising committee (OC), which utilises its own version of competitive dialogue for all the contract drafting and negotiations needed to host the Games. When the Games delivery process began in 2006, it was Britain's first major competitive dialogue tender to take place under new EU procurement rules. The infrastructure budget, set at £2.4 billion at the time of the bid to stage the Games in 2005, increased to over £9 billion in 2007 (Freshfields Bruckhaus Deringer, 2015). However, even with such control placed on spending for the thousands of contracts, agreements and licences, not all recent Games have turned a profit and overspending, waste, and controversy have meant fewer applications and more retracted interest. Reality has proven that it is not just hosting that costs so much, it is the maintenance of the space once the Games have left town.

4.15 Adhering to the proposal

The widening awareness of the opportunities international events can bring to their host will mean each will have a different purpose for its decision to bid. Once a destination has secured the rights to deliver an international event, the organising committee designates how and where the investment is to be made.

The finer detail of many winning bids has come under much scrutiny as much of the investment and potential benefits and losses are long-term and designed to occur after the event as part of the events legacy. Horne (2007) suggests that in their enthusiasm to host and support sports mega events, politicians and other senior bureaucrats often encourage the fiction that they do not know as much as the public about things that actually form the background to the bid.

Much of the initial investment may go into the building of new facilities as well as improving transport links. This part of the investment is frequently self-evident and requires little clarification. Other aspects of the investment programme are ambiguously presented and wrapped around the writing skills of the authors. For example, Russia claimed that 90% of the initial investment for the 2018 FIFA World Cup was intended for developing transport, tourism and technical infrastructure for the long-term needs of cities and communities (Müller, 2017). The long-term needs were unspecific and how the tourism data was measured separately from other tourism investment has never been adequately shown.

How these claims are quantifiably evidenced remains indefinable. Such important returns on investment narratives appear to be common practice in bidding applications for the major international events. Tomlinson (2014) argues there are widespread gaps between legacy claims and the realities of recurring Olympic bids. The truth of legacy claims, particularly about returns on investment, will always prove elusive without systematic post-event research over realistic extended periods.

4.15.1 Global economic effects

The last 20 years have seen a significant shift in public support for events and other cultural activities. After the global depression of the 1970s, events and festivals became a region's method of celebrating the improved economy. Bianchini and Parkinson (1993) put this down to a trend in the 1980s towards the de-centralisation of social issues from central government to local governments. European and arts-based funding began to broaden its reach to the less high-brow events and local festivals blossomed while the larger hallmark events came within reach of more local authorities.

(García, 2004) advised that the high levels of investment required to produce hallmark cultural events and infrastructures were not framed in an assessment of long-term cultural legacies or coherent strategies that sought to secure a balanced spatial and social distribution of benefits. Since the global economic downturn of 2008, areas such as an event's social benefits have moved further down the pecking order in a broader shift away from thinking of the arts as cultural activity in need of subsidy and towards treating them as part of the creative economy (Behr and Brennan, 2014).

International sporting events advocate much potential but the ensuing 'return on investment' is not applicable to all stakeholders. Two of the biggest international sporting events, the FIFA World Cup and the Olympic Games, whilst signifying development and progress in the modern world, magnify the many social divisions and inequalities that exist in and around the host destination, regardless of whether it is a city for the Olympic Games or a nation (or set of nations) for the FIFA World Cup. The events' arrival and subsequent departure have proved to be the cause of community displacement, serious public disorder and in some cases ongoing debt.

The majority of international events are ultimately a means of adding to the host destination's tapestry of social activity. The return on investment is grounded in creating better places to live and work with the long-term goal of improving a sense of identity for local residents with increased levels of civic pride. But not all international events are hosted by authorities or even targeted at the tourist or people from outside the region. On a local scale, such funding is the lifeblood of the arts and culture of many destinations and can reach much deeper than economic returns or visitor attractions. Local funding can assist in a region's re-development by maintaining activities that reflect their identity and bring isolated communities together.

4.16 Summary

This chapter has considered the strategic use of international events by authorities as well as some of the protocols that are central to the proper and respectful delivery of international events. It has considered the values authorities place on the processes of international events, particularly on how the various procedures, processes and dialogue impact on the event itself. We have learned that international events require the intervention of the authorities at different levels depending on their size, the roles that authorities undertake in supporting international events, as well as how they approach creating international events for cities, regions and nations.

Case study 4.1 Liverpool International Garden Festival 1984

Land use planning and development control are, arguably, the instruments that have provided the primary means of intervention by governments in shaping the nature of development on behalf of society (Carbone and Yunis, 2005). International events have proved to be a model means of instigating change, both physically on the landscape and socially within society.

The Expo 1984 Liverpool, more commonly known locally as the International Garden Festival is one such event. The aim of the event was to revitalise tourism and the city of Liverpool which had suffered cutbacks and had recently endured riots in the streets. The original idea came from the then Conservative Environment Minister Michael Heseltine. The Garden Festival was one of the first major projects undertaken by the Merseyside Development Corporation, a body set up to regenerate Liverpool in the early 1980s in the wake of the Toxteth riots (Coslett, 2014). The festival itself was hugely popular, attracting over 3 million visitors.

Figure 4.4 Map of the Liverpool International Garden Festival 1984

The event was recognised by the Bureau International Des Expositions on the 24 June 1982. Much of the site, which was situated in the old South Docks area, was derelict in the years before the Expo and underwent an extensive renovation project in preparation for the event (Bureau International des Expositions, n.d.).

Questions

1. What should be considered before awarding an internationally recognised event to a city?
2. What prior concerns might exist when allocating derelict land to an international event?
3. Why is what happens after the event has finished important?

4.17 Useful websites

UEFA tenders & bids
www.uefa.com/insideuefa/documentlibrary/tenders/index.html

Bidding for events
www.leoisaac.com/evt/top074.htm

Event protocol
https://event-protocol.co.uk/

Internal forces

Festivals Australia
www.arts.gov.au/funding-and-support/festivals-australia

Olympic Games candidature process
www.olympic.org/all-about-the-candidature-process

Flag code faqs
www.ushistory.org/betsy/faq.htm

References

Abend, L. (2014). Why nobody wants to host the 2022 Winter Olympics. Retrieved from http://time.com/3462070/olympics-winter-2022/ Accessed 19th November 2015.

Aldridge, S., Halpern D., & Fitzpatrick, S. (2002). Social capital. A discussion paper London: Performance & Innovation Unit, Cabinet Office, UK.

Ancien, D. (2011). Global city theory and the new urban politics twenty years on: The case for a geohistorical materialist approach to the (new) urban politics of global cities. *Urban Studies, 48*(12), 2473–2493. doi:10.1177/0042098011411945

Arts Council England (ACE) (2019). Project Grants: all awards offered 01 April 2019 – 31 May 2019. Retrieved from www.artscouncil.org.uk/arts-council-national-lottery-project-grants/project-grants-data Accessed 11th June 2019.

Barnett, R. (2013). This parliament of monsters: London's spectacular fairs. Retrieved from https://sickcityproject.wordpress.com/2013/09/09/this-parliament-of-monsters-londons-spectacular-fairs/ Accessed 5th June 2019.

Barrios, D., Stuart, R., & Andrews, M. (2016). Bringing home the gold? A Review of the economic impact of hosting mega-events. *CID Faculty Working Paper No. 320, July 2016.* Cambridge, MA: Center for International Development at Harvard University.

Bauer, A. (2017). Referendums Becoming New Olympic Reality. Retrieved from http://aroundtherings.com/site/A__59144/Title__Referendums-Becoming-New-Olympic-Reality/292/Articles Accessed 7th June 2019.

Bayle, E. (2016). Olympic social responsibility: a challenge for the future, *Sport in Society. 19*(6), 752–766.

BBC (1993). 1993: Green light for Manchester Olympics. Retrieved from http://news.bbc.co.uk/onthisday/hi/dates/stories/july/13/newsid_2502000/2502947.stm Accessed 24th May 2017.

Behr, A., & Brennan, M. (2014). The place of popular music in Scotland's cultural policy. *Cultural Trends*, 1–9. doi:10.1080/09548963.2014.925282

Bentley, D. (2019). This is why Birmingham's German Christmas Market is coming earlier in 2019. *Birmingham Mail.* Retrieved from www.birminghammail.co.uk/whats-on/whats-on-news/birmingham-german-market-earlier-2019-17096417 Accessed 13th November 2019.

Bernt, M. (2009). Partnerships for demolition: the governance of urban renewal in East Germany's shrinking cities. *International Journal of Urban and Regional Research, 33*(3), 754–769.

Bianchini, F., & Parkinson, M. (1993). *Cultural Policy and Urban Regeneration: The West European Experience*. Manchester: Manchester University Press.

BOCOG (Beijing Organizing Committee for the Games of the XXIX Olympiad) (2010). *Official Report of the Beijing 2008 Olympic Games, Volume II. LA84 Foundation.* Available online at LA84 Foundation Digital Library Collection. https://digital.la84.org/digital/collection/p17103coll8/id/44358/rec/89 Accessed 20th June 2018.

Braithwaite, J., & Drahos, P. (2000). *Global Business Regulation*. Cambridge: Cambridge University Press.

Bremer, A. (2016). *A Cost-Benefit Analysis: The Economic and Social Effects of the Rio 2016 Olympics.* Economics and Business, Kalamazoo College, Senior Individualized Projects Collection.

Bull, A. (2018). Nobody can afford to host the Olympics but at the IOC the largesse never stops. *The Guardian*. Retrieved from www.theguardian.com/sport/2018/oct/23/olympic-games-host-ioc-money Accessed 12th January 2019.

Bureau International des Expositions. (n.d). EXPO 1984 LIVERPOOL. Retrieved from www.bie-paris.org/site/en/1984-liverpool Accessed 5th June 2019.

Butler, N. (2017). Exclusive: IOC vow to 'further adjust' candidature process after Budapest 2024 withdrawal. Retrieved from www.insidethegames.biz/articles/1047403/exclusive-ioc-vow-to-further-adjust-candidature-process-after-budapest-2024-withdrawal Accessed 27th May 2018.

Carbone, G., & Yunis, E. (2005). Making tourism more sustainable: A guide for policy makers. Nairobi: UNEP Division of Technology, Industry and Economics.

Cochrane, A., Peck, J., & Tickell, A. (1996). Manchester plays games: Exploring the local politics of globalisation. *Urban Studies, 33*(8), 1319–1336. doi:10.1080/0042098966673

Colombo, A., & Richards, G. (2017). Eventful cities as global innovation catalysts: The sónar festival network. *Event Management, 21*(5), 621–634. doi:10.3727/152599517X15053272359077

Coslett, P. (2014). The Places. Retrieved from www.bbc.co.uk/liverpool/content/articles/2009/04/28/local_history_garden_festival_feature.shtml Accessed 14th July 2015.

Dite, C. (2019). Etihad Stadium, Manchester: A successful two-stage design approach converted an athletics venue into a football stadium. Retrieved from www.arup.com/projects/etihad-stadium Accessed 27th June 2019.

Dodds, R., & Joppe, M. (2001). Promoting urban green tourism: The development of the other map of Toronto. *Journal of Vacation Marketing, 7*(3), 261–267.

Finnis, A. (2018). It's now harder to get a ticket for a London NFL game than a Beyoncé concert – so where next for American football in the UK? *The Telegraph*. Retrieved from www.telegraph.co.uk/american-football/2018/10/11/now-harder-get-ticket-london-nfl-game-beyonce-concert-next/ Accessed 11th June 2019.

Flyvbjerg, B., Stewart, A., & Budzier, A. (2016). The Oxford Olympics study 2016: Cost and cost overrun at the Games. *Said Business School WP 2016–20.* doi.org/10.2139/ssrn.2804554

Foley, M., McGillivray, D., & McPherson, G. (2012). *Event Policy*. Oxford: Routledge.

Freshfields Bruckhaus Deringer (2015). Appointing the Olympic Delivery Authority's delivery partner. Retrieved from www.freshfields.com/globalassets/services-page/construction-and-engineering/publication-pdfs/major-projects-initiative-.pdf Accessed 10th June 2019.

García, B. (2004). Cultural policy and urban regeneration in Western European cities: Lessons from experience, prospects for the future. *Local Economy: The Journal of the Local Economy Policy Unit, 19*(4), 312–326. doi:10.1080/0269094042000286828

Getz, D. (2004). Bidding on events: Identifying event selection criteria and critical success factors. *Journal of Convention & Exhibition Management, 5*(2), 1–24. doi:10.1300/J143v05n02_01

Gibson, O. (2015). Olympic legacy failure: inspiring London 2012 message has become a millstone. *The Guardian*. Retrieved from www.theguardian.com/sport/blog/2015/jul/05/olympic-legacy-failure-london-2012-message-millstone Accessed 25th July 2016.

Gonzalez, M. (2017). The city is the venue, Access All Areas. Retrieved from: https://accessaa.co.uk/great-run-the-city-is-the-venue/ Accessed 7th December 2017.

Hansard (1871). *Fairs Act 1871 c. 12 (Regnal. 34_and_35_Vict)*. London.

Hodson, M., & Marvin, S. (2009). 'The new urban politics of ecological security – the 'systemic' reconfiguration of London's socio-technical networks?' Paper given at: Unmaking England? Is London Delinking from its Peripheries – International Workshop, 15th–16th January 2009, Manchester.

Horne, J. (2007). The four 'knowns' of sports mega-events. *Leisure Studies, 26*(1), 81–96. doi:10.1080/02614360500504628

House of Commons Committee of Public Accounts (2008). *The Budget for the London 2012 Olympic and Paralympic Games*. London: House of Commons, The Stationery Office.

IOC (International Olympics Committee) (2015a). *Candidature Process Olympic Games 2024*. Geneva: International Olympic Committee.

IOC (2015b). *Olympic Charter*. Retrieved from https://stillmed.olympic.org/Documents/olympic_charter_en.pdf Accessed 10th June 2019.

IOC (2017). Los Angeles declares candidature for Olympic Games 2028 – IOC to contribute US$1.8 billion to the local Organizing Committee. Retrieved from www.olympic.org/news/los-angeles-declares-candidature-for-olympic-games-2028-ioc-to-contribute-usd-1-8-billion-to-the-local-organising-committee Accessed 23rd March 2018.

IOC (n.d.). Olympic Games candidature process. Retrieved from www.olympic.org/all-about-the-candidature-process Accessed 6th June 2019.

Jennings, W. (2013). Governing the Games: High politics, risk and mega-events. *Political Studies Review, 11*(1), 2–14. doi:10.1111/1478–9302.12002

Jones, M. (2010). The UK music economy. In P. L. Guern & H. Dauncey (Eds.), *Stereo: Comparative Perspectives on the Sociological Study of Popular Music in France and Britain*, 75–89. Florence: Routledge.

Kennelly, J. (2016). *Olympic Exclusions: Youth, Poverty, and Social Legacies*. New York: Routledge.

Lee, M. (2006). *The Race for the 2012 Olympics*. London: Virgin books.

legislation.gov.uk (n.d.). Fairs Act 1871, Chapter 12. Retrieved from www.legislation.gov.uk/ukpga/1871/12/pdfs/ukpga_18710012_en.pdf Accessed 23rd March 2019.

Loftman, P., & Nevin, B. (1996). Going for growth: Prestige projects in three British cities. *Urban Studies, 33*(6), 991–1019. doi:10.1080/00420989650011708

Mill, R. C., & Morrison, A. M. (2012). *The Tourism System* (7th ed.). Dubuque, IA: Kendall/Hunt Publishing.

Minihan, J. (1977). *The Nationalization of Culture: The Development of State Subsidies to the Arts in Great Britain*. London: Hamish Hamilton.

Morgan, L. (2018). IOC Coordination Commission set to conduct sixth inspection of Tokyo 2020 preparations. Retrieved from www.insidethegames.biz/articles/1067243/ioc-coordination-commission-set-to-conduct-sixth-inspection-of-tokyo-2020-preparations Accessed 10th June 2019.

Morrison, A. M. (2013). Destination management and destination marketing: The platform for excellence in tourism destinations. Retrieved from www.lyxk.com.cn/fileup/PDF/2013-1-6.pdf Accessed 13th June 2019.

Müller, M. (2017). How mega-events capture their hosts: Event seizure and the World Cup 2018 in Russia. *Urban Geography, 38*(8), 1113–1132. doi:10.1080/02723638.2015.1109951

Oliver, R., & Lauermann, J. (2017). *Failed Olympic Bids and the Transformation of Urban Space: Lasting Legacies?* New York: Palgrave McMillan.

Open University (2019). *Study Session 5 Urbanisation: Trends, Causes and Effects*. Retrieved from www.open.edu/openlearncreate/mod/oucontent/view.php?id=79940&printable=1 Accessed 5th May 2019.

Pavitt, M. (2019). Tokyo 2020 primed for latest IOC inspection as preparations ramp up for Olympic and Paralympic Games. Retrieved from www.insidethegames.biz/articles/1079459/tokyo-2020-primed-for-latest-ioc-inspection-as-preparations-ramp-up-for-olympic-and-paralympic-games Accessed 10th June 2019.

Pei-Chin, T., & Coca-Stefaniak, J. A. (2010). Cultural urban regeneration practice and policy in the UK and Singapore. *Asia Pacific Journal of Arts & Cultural Management, 10*(7).

Pike, A., MacKinnon, D., Coombes, M., Champion, A., Bradley, D., Cumbers, A., et al. (2016). Uneven growth: Tackling city decline. York: Joseph Rowntree Foundation.

Radford, S. (2019). 10 venues vie to host 2022 world championships: two bids for full Games, *Horse & Hound*. Retrieved from www.horseandhound.co.uk/news/world-equestrian-games-2022-bids-690050 Accessed 13th November 2019.

Richards, G., & Colombo, A. (2017). Rethinking the eventful city: Introduction. *Event Management, 21*(5), 527–531. doi:10.3727/152599517X15053272358997

Rojek, C. (2014). Global event management: A critique. *Leisure Studies, 33*(1), 32–47.

Sanders, P. (2019). County and state fairs. Dictionary of American History. Retrieved from www.encyclopedia.com/history/dictionaries-thesauruses-pictures-and-press-releases/county-and-state-fairs Accessed 29th May 2019.

Shoval, N. (2002). A new phase in the competition for the Olympic gold: The London and New York bids for the 2012 Games. *Journal of Urban Affairs, 24*(5), 583–599. doi:10.1111/1467–9906.00146

Staufenberg, J. (2016). Olympic legacy: Haunting pictures show past Games buildings left to crumble. *The Independent*. Retrieved from www.independent.co.uk/sport/olympic-games-buildings-rio-de-janeiro-crumble-pictures-world-berlin-beijing-sarajevo-a7176171.html Accessed 30th April 2017.

Strohmayer, U. (2013). Non-events and their legacies: Parisian heritage and the Olympics that never were. *International Journal of Heritage Studies, 19*(2), 186–202. doi:10.1080/13527258.2012.669391

Tomlinson, A. (2014). Olympic legacies: recurrent rhetoric and harsh realities. *Contemporary Social Science, 9*(2), 137–158. doi:10.1080/21582041.2014.912792

UEFA (2016). UEFA club competition finals 2019: bid regulations. UEFA.com. Retrieved from www.uefa.com/MultimediaFiles/Download/uefaorg/General/02/42/99/42/2429942_DOWNLOAD.pdf Accessed 21st December 2018.

UEFA (2019). Evaluation report: UEFA club competition finals 2019. UEFA.com. Retrieved from www.uefa.com/MultimediaFiles/Download/OfficialDocument/uefaorg/Regulations/02/50/17/48/2501748_DOWNLOAD.pdf Accessed 8th Novemvber 2019.

University of Sheffield (2015). National Fairground and Circus Archive. Retrieved from www.sheffield.ac.uk/nfca/researchandarticles/historyfairs Accessed 5th June 2019.

Urban Task Force (1999). *Towards an Urban Renaissance*. London: HMSO.

Viehoff, V., & Poynter, G. (2015). *Mega-event Cities: Urban Legacies of Global Sports Events*. Oxon: Routledge.

Wikipedia (n.d.). City of Manchester stadium. Retrieved from https://en.wikipedia.org/wiki/City_of_Manchester_Stadium

Wilson, S. (2015). Beijing to host second Olympics in a mere 14 years. Retrieved from https://webcache.googleusercontent.com/search?q=cache:8i8A9x7gjCcJ:www.staugustine.com/article/20150801/NEWS/308019963%3Ftemplate%3Dampart+&cd=1&hl=en&ct=clnk&gl=uk&client=firefox-b-d Accessed 3rd May 2017.

Chapter 5

Staffing international events

Contents

5.1 Chapter overview

This chapter looks closely at the contribution people make in delivering international events. It considers the training and recruitment methods, and the multitude of roles that are required to ensure international events are planned and delivered safely, as well as the various means of employment. The chapter considers how international event organisations deal with the changing need for staff by considering the pulsating nature of events, zero-hour contracts, codes of conduct, and the various contracts, riders and agreements used in the industry. This chapter also considers how ethics play an important role in maintaining the various principles of creating a good place of work. The chapter also considers how large groups of support staff such as volunteers, stewards, security guards and marshals are engaged and trained and how the many support organisations needed to deliver large-scale events come together and share the countless challenges that must be overcome to ensure the successful delivery of an international event.

5.2 Learning objectives

By the end of this chapter, the student will be expected to:

* Understand the working environment of international events
* Recognise the different responsibilities of people working in an event
* Appreciate the importance of training staff for the various roles required to deliver international events
* Understand how appropriate staffing and planning contributes to the safety of the event.

5.3 Introduction

Every international event is unique. What remains a constant throughout is the need for co-production between a range of staff and organisations who are directly involved in the delivery. These efforts are made by a variety of stakeholders. The amount of people (human resources) required to deliver an international event can range from a small community of volunteers working – often without seeing it as such – as part of the non-profit sector for the benefit of the local community or a set of like-minded societies, to a mass of teams and departments managing billion-dollar budgets and multiple sectors, organised by heads of state, eminent celebrity figures, steering groups, supervisory boards, contractors and committees that can make the calculating and management of all those involved an enormous task of ingenuity. In Chapter 2 we looked at the planning and preparation of international events. The most important aspect of planning and preparation is the people involved in carrying out these tasks. Therefore, this chapter will focus on how international events are brought together and delivered, and the roles involved.

5.4 The working environment

Anyone who gets to work on an international event will come to an understanding that the work is hard, the hours are long, but the rewards can be worth all the effort. You get to work with inspirational people, create amazing experiences for people and no day is ever the same. No international event organiser is the same, and everyone takes a different path to get into the industry (Walker, 2017). International events represent a fascinating and challenging area of work in terms of the structure and dynamics of the employment environment (Baum *et al.*, 2009). This employment environment is so broad there are essentially very few trades that do not engage with the event industry on one level or another.

   The event sector itself is said to be one of the fastest growing areas of most Western nations' economies. Cities and nations are developing their infrastructure to accommodate and take advantage of the numerous opportunities that exist to host international events. This has taken the form of upgrading existing stadia, building new commercial venues and, as discussed in Chapter 4, developing neglected spaces to incorporate event opportunities for local communities. Each of these activities requires the specialist skills and knowledge of people working or training to work in the event industry.

5.5 Building the team

Tomlin (2013) suggests that the keys to success in building any event workforce are:

- Attention to detail
- Brilliant recruitment and selection
- Brilliant induction and training
- Brilliant communications and engagement
- Allow people to bring their true personalities to the role
- Allow leaders to role-model and lead – leaders need to be the change they need to see happen.

   The sheer size of some organisations, as well as the difficulties in managing unusual organisations in the event industry, make human resource management a complex issue to deal with in practice (Hoye *et al.*, 2018). International events will have paid members of staff, including management, unpaid volunteers, and executives who work both with and without compensation. Once the main organising team of players have been identified and assembled, other stakeholder engagement from emergency services, city councils, international liaison, third sector organisations, advisors, local business and community groups may all contribute to the final delivery of the event. The whole event process will be influenced by the age, regularity, irregularity, size, location, and timing of the event itself (Holmes and Smith, 2009).

Internal forces

One particular area of caution in the delivery of an international event is the creation of departmental silos. Larger international events will have so many activities going on that they will have to be broken down into tactical actions for different parts of the organisation to focus upon. In doing so, it is necessary to create teams of employees. Teams will gel and even see competition within the organisation. This can lead to restricting knowledge sharing, with one team who might seek to be better informed than another. Priority from managers can inadvertently be given to one team or section of an organisation who go on to insulate themselves from other parts of the organization, so creating internal silos (Saberton, 2018).

Silos can devastate an organisation. It is important to develop unified leadership to encourage trust, empower, and break managers out of the 'my department' mentality and into the 'our organisation' mentality (Gleeson and Rozo, 2013). Otherwise, different department objectives, budgeting, and responsibilities can lead to diluting the common vision and narrowing the focus of team leaders and managers, leading to a lack of awareness of the main aims within the organisation (Saberton, 2018).

5.6 SKIPPA, the six attributes of an international event

There are six attributes an international event will require to provide the best possible experience for its stakeholders. These are easily remembered by using the mnemonic SKIPPA, which lists the attributes as:

- Skills
- Knowledge
- Infrastructure
- People
- Power, and
- Assets.

Figure 5.1 provides further details and the characteristics related to staffing international events. The responsibility of staffing or finding the right people for international events is principally the task of a human resource (HR) department. Ultimately, it is the people who are employed who prove to be the productivity and efficiency of the organisation. Therefore, building the team to deliver the event becomes a critical factor very early on in an event's life cycle. However, many event organisations do not have a HR department. Sharing responsibilities is a quite normal way for lots of international event organisations to achieve their goals.

In the world of international events, the range of organisations involved is quite extensive. From non-profit organisations that exist to develop communities, meet the needs of identifiable and discrete groups in those communities and work for the public good, to private companies who ultimately exist to create wealth for individuals (Hoye et al., 2018). Applying SKIPPA to the production and delivery of an international event will assist in ensuring the whole array of tasks is well prepared for.

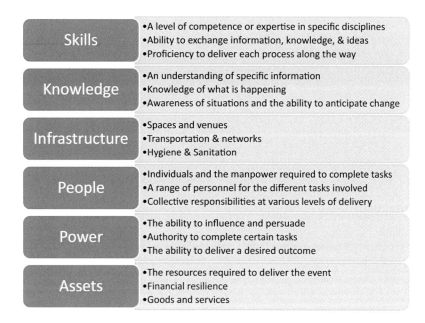

Figure 5.1 SKIPPA, the six characteristics for international event delivery

Resources and infrastructure are central to all business, but when building a team, people, skills and knowledge are very much intertwined. The amount of research into international event skills and leadership qualities is a reflection of the rapid growth and worldwide demand for events professionals (Fletcher *et al.*, 2009; Padron and Stone, 2019; Stone *et al.*, 2017) For many international events, simply understanding the responsibilities required demands specialist knowledge, and some of the more specialised roles need additional professional advice, e.g. financial and or legal advice. Skilled workers are usually sourced through dedicated organisations specialising in the various required trades. In international events, many skilled workers are sourced through word-of-mouth. Their appointment to work on or as part of the event is usually through contractual agreements. However, many of these are verbal or agreed on the shake of a hand.

As well as resulting from a formal bid to host, international events can also grow from an individual's passion. This provides a wealth of inherent challenges created by the individual's own success. Organisers can often find themselves out of their depth when suddenly they no longer know all the people involved by name. An event's growth can be rapid and quite unexpected. An individual's knowledge and skills are tested and the need to find people with other specialist knowledge and skills increases. For any business that grows, it is normal for responsibilities to become fragmented into departments. In such cases, event organisations will be required to share management responsibilities across various departments to deliver the event.

International events, and in particular mega events, can require the management of an army of paid staff and volunteers. They are complex logistical operations that are reliant upon advance planning and wide-ranging programmes of investment in the construction of infrastructure, venues and facilities (Jennings, 2012a). For this reason, mega events will appoint a figure who has a long-established relationship with that type of event. These individuals may also tend to have other interests outside of the event that align with the role. For example, the LA2028 organising committee is made up of US basketball, football and other sports club owners as well as athletes who previously competed in the Games (Downey, 2019; Wharton, 2019). London 2012 appointed Lord (Sebastian) Coe, formerly known as Seb Coe, a double gold- and double silver-winning Olympic athlete. With his mix of athletics success and previous political appointments, he became the standout figure to fulfil the role of heading up the eventually successful London bid to host the 2012 Summer Olympics. Coe's ongoing success has led to him subsequently being appointed president of the International Association of Athletics Federations (IAAF) in 2015.

Similar to this approach, sports teams are often lead by individuals who have come through the ranks of the club as players. The experience gained from a long-standing dedication to the profession is often essential to success. Once in position, the new manager or coach will appoint ex-teammates or people they had worked with previously to fill the assistants' or backroom staff positions. Similarly, these roles are usually vacated when the previous incumbent leaves the post.

The use of power in the delivery of international events is multi-faceted. People-power is the biggest contribution for all events, but without the power to motivate, very little would be achieved. Power as influence can be used to open doors, gain access to funds, and encourage decision makers. Once an event is in production, the ultimate role of power is about strength of mind and the ability to keep the planning and delivery on track by avoiding unnecessary complications and delays. For a society where sport is a vital component of national identity, sporting events, and the places where they are held, become spaces for political agendas and ideologies, and also for the control of social relations (Moufakkir and Pernecky, 2015).

There is also the power of the people as communities and unity of mind which can overcome great challenges and initiate change in the most difficult of circumstances. For example, the act of the 14-year-old schoolgirl Greta Thunberg to take time off school to demonstrate outside the Swedish parliament in 2018, holding up a sign calling for stronger climate action, led to an international demonstration in September 2019. Hundreds of thousands of young people took part in worldwide protests in response to Greta Thunberg's demands for action on climate change (Russell *et al.*, 2019; Siddique *et al.*, 2019).

In the world of international events it is also important to recognise that the existence of power sometimes has nothing to do with individuals: it is created by the event itself. Events can reach deep into a community, with both positive and negative consequences. Religious and political events can tear communities apart or bring them together. Sporting rivalries in single cities or across national borders generate intense hatred through the adoption of one colour over another. Music festivals and carnivals trace their roots to emancipation or the raising of awareness for global problems.

5.7 Employ or contract?

One of the predominant reasons for hosting an international event is employment. For many of the positions the event will need to fill, there will be a decision on whether to offer a contract of employment or to contract the work to a third party. As the majority of the companies engaged in the event industry are either sole traders or SMEs (small and medium-sized enterprises), the full range of employment options discussed above will be put into use.

Many of the jobs that need to be filled before, during and after the event will follow the regular pattern of employment the event industry has adopted the world over for many years. This is what makes the event industry such a unique working environment. One organisation might have the overall responsibility for delivering the event. They will then in turn engage with a large number of contracted organisations to supply the multitude of resources required to make it happen. Each of these organisations will specialise in an aspect of the event's needs. Figure 5.2 shows a representative example of a selection of the organisations that could be involved in such an arrangement. In this example, a large-scale outdoor festival has been used as the sample. However, it is possible to amend the suppliers to fit any kind of international event.

Because of this unusual employment process, how the international event industry operates on an annual basis needs to be considered. It was Toffler (1990) who came up with the phrase 'pulsating organisations' for businesses with regularly expanding and contracting workforces over their commercial life cycle. The event industry fits perfectly into this model. Event organisations will have a core, usually small team of workers who will be fully employed throughout the

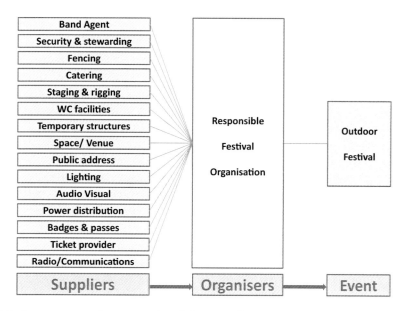

Figure 5.2 A representative example of the suppliers contracted in to assist in the delivery of a large-scale outdoor festival

Source: Adapted from Ryan and Kelly, 2017

Internal forces

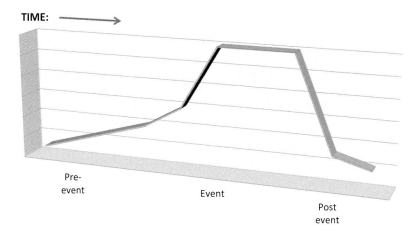

Figure 5.3 The rise and decline of staff requirements, or a pulsating event workforce
Source: Adapted from Toffler, 1990

year on a normal employment contract. They are often just the owners of the business. As the event draws near and during the period when the event is in full flow, the need for staff increases and an influx of personnel is required to cover the numerous posts needed to deliver the event. Figure 5.3 emphasises the changing requirements for personnel during the life cycle of an event.

Filling the multitude of positions required for the event as a whole is shared between the contributing suppliers. The pressure will remain high throughout the process and, once again, good lead-in times and planning will be required to ensure all the necessary positions are covered as the event moves through its various levels of employment need.

5.8 Contracts and agreements

As with a number of international event management matters, proper legal advice should always be sought. Dealing with contracts and agreements is certainly one of those matters. In the grand scheme of things, there is not that much difference between the two, but contracts can become less flexible in light of a disagreement. International events tend to lean more towards contracts as a trail of responsibility is necessary at all levels. Agreements, however, can form the basis of many arrangements within an event organisation.

5.8.1 Zero-hour contracts/gig economy

Pulsating organisations that operate in the event industry make use of zero-hour contracts to fill the various positions that become available for short periods of time in the event life cycle. The case of Carmichael v. National Power plc decided that a casual/zero-hours worker was self-employed and thus excluded from most of the basic employment statutory rights (Leighton and Painter, 2001). There remains a great deal of debate over the use of zero-hour contracts across all industries as a whole and there are very good reasons to dislike these types of employment arrangements. However, they are well suited to the people who work in the event industry.

Many of the forces that are coupled with zero-hour contracts are highly stressful for families and individuals on low incomes. The effects are growing economic insecurity, low productivity, diminished autonomy and worrying levels of personal debt (Fleming, 2017). The effects of this were portrayed in Ken Loach's 2019 film *Sorry We Missed You*, described as a 'piercing drama' about a zero-hours-contract driver (Abraham, 2019). The event industry, like many others, is very much dependent on these types of arrangements, but usually with personal satisfaction from those engaged in them.

Many of the people in international events on zero-hour contracts have never been unemployed. Due to the seasonal and/or pulsating working practices, events have a need for zero-hour contracts. Stewards, bartenders and waiting staff are just a few examples of the roles that zero-hour contracts are used for, but even some of the top positions in international events are filled in the same way. Many skilled personnel are registered with local and national agencies and take on work in events as and when it is offered. Other individuals are so well respected within their specialist area they are contacted directly to check that their availability matches with that of other events. These individuals will move from one event to another or jump from tour to tour on an ad hoc and perfectly satisfactory zero-hour contract basis.

The type of staff who live a permanent life on zero-hour contracts include: steel monkeys (scaffolders), roadies (crew), stage managers, lampies (lighting engineers), soundmen (sound engineers), truckies (truck drivers), chuck wagons (caterers), musicians, drummers, and humpers (stage hands). Each skilled specialist transfers across events taking breaks and holidays as and when it fits with the next offer of employment. McCabe and Savery (2007) observed a similar approach in other sectors with workers moving both job role and sector undertaking different tasks, gathering knowledge, experience, and competencies as they go.

Zero-hours contracts are also known as casual contracts. They are for what is known as 'piece work' or 'on call' work which in essence means you work for the company as and when the need arises. Therefore, zero-hour work is work with no guaranteed hours. Employers who employ staff on zero-hour contracts are able to avoid many of the usual rights assigned to an employee of a company. However, the employer does remain responsible for health and safety of staff on zero-hours contracts.

In the UK, the rights of both employers and employees is further explained on the government website (Gov.uk, n.d.) as follows:

* Employees remain on call to work as and when an event might need them
* The employer does not have to give them work every day
* The employee does not have to do work when asked
* Employees are entitled to statutory annual leave and the National Minimum Wage in the same way as regular workers.
* Employers cannot do anything to stop a zero-hours worker from getting work elsewhere.
* Employees can ignore a clause in their contract if it bans them from looking for work or accepting work from another employer.

All-in-all, the argument over zero-hour contracts may never be overcome. The demand for zero-hour contracts in the event industry will remain a complication, but while many in the industry engage with them without a second thought – and on first-rate pay that reflects their specialist skills, experience, ability, and knowledge – their removal will be problematical for the industry.

5.8.2 Riders

An essential aspect of many international events is an attached rider. Described by the OED as follows:

> A supplementary clause in a performer's contract specifying particular requirements for accommodation, food, drink, etc. Also (chiefly British): the items so specified or provided; (hence) an additional fee paid in kind to a performer, usually in the form of food and drink.
>
> (OED, 1989)

A rider is not usually in the part of a contract before the signatures. It metaphorically rides on the back of the contract and includes a variety of 'comfort' requirements. Many famous stories exist about the strange and unusual demands placed in riders, but as was discussed in Chapter 4, they are not reserved solely for performers. The cost of a business rider can run into huge sums of money and actually be the deciding factor in ruining the deal.

5.9 Codes of conduct

A code of conduct is intended to make clear in a statement the rules, values, ethical principles and vision of a business or organisation. Having a code of conduct provides those involved with clear standards and expectations of how to perform when representing the business as an employee. A code of conduct can be an important part in establishing an inclusive culture, but it is not a comprehensive solution on its own. An ethical culture is created by the organisation's leaders who manifest their ethics in their attitudes and behaviour (McMillan, 2012).

It is good practice for international event organisations to set out their code of conduct for casual staff such as volunteers and stewards or even officials to be guided by a set of key principles. This might include setting out the importance of their role and the type of involvement these recruits have during the event. Codes of conduct offer a guide for all of the interactions and tasks that may be included.

Compiling a code of conduct can be a complicated process. Knowing what to include and exclude becomes a critical factor prior to its release. Points to consider include whether the company's principles and vision are expressed appropriately. Is the content inclusive for all employees? Has the right tone been adopted in the document?

When reading through codes of conduct for international events, in particular business events such as conferences, a common phrase that appears in the text is: 'The following Code of Conduct is based on the example policy published by

Geek Feminism, created by the Ada Initiative and other volunteers. The website offers organisers example policies suitable for most open source computing, or technology-related conferences (Geek Feminism, n.d.). The example policy provides information on a number of headings including:

- An introduction
- Anti-harassment policy text
- Short, medium and long public versions
- Enforcement
- Reporting
- Anonymous and personal reports
- Internal version for conference staff
- Conferences in which difficult topics are included
- License and attribution.

Once a code of conduct has been written, all future materials will need to reflect the text within it. This then allows the organisation to demand that all members of the workforce, regardless of their level of engagement, comply in accordance with the condition of their engagement or employment.

There may of course be times when it is not possible to comply with an organisation's code of conduct. Lunday (2010) suggests there are times when the code may be unrealistic or may not address the range of a business's activities or even set the wrong tone. Codes may suffer from numerous weaknesses that undermine their effectiveness and place a company's reputation of integrity at risk. This is possible when the organisation is present in several territories with different standards on moral or ethical principles. Moreover, complacency within the organisation may cause issues not to be properly observed or updated.

Without a positive culture of support, codes of conduct can be useless. Therefore, codes of conduct require the full commitment of the organisation and the workforce to be functional. The code may also have to change or evolve in tandem with the organisation. Over longer periods of time, organisational cultures change and organisations will need to adopt new approaches to working practices and staff morale.

5.10 Training and recruitment

All of an event's workforce, regardless of their pay or position, should be expected to know their responsibilities and in return expect to be managed competently. Therefore, having a proper and fit for purpose training programme in place is central to both the experience and the retention of those with reason to show a full commitment to the event and the organisation. In order to better recruit and retain paid staff and volunteers, there is a need to identify the means by which to enhance their overall workplace satisfaction or the volunteer experience (Costa *et al.*, 2006). The reputation of an event or company can quickly wear away if the management of paid staff and volunteers turns out to be an unsatisfactory experience. Deploy too many volunteers and there is often nothing to do, deploy too few staff and the event is in danger of

Figure 5.4 London 2012 Games Maker uniform processing

succumbing to a host of health and safety issues. Add to this the basic needs of any individual and it becomes clear why a sound programme of recruitment and training needs to be in place.

During the training and recruitment process, many large-scale international events will provide uniforms and dress their volunteers in the corporate colours of the event. This in itself can be an enormous undertaking. The 70,000 Games Makers for the 2012 London Olympic and Paralympic Games were chosen from an initial 250,000 applications. The successful applicants then had to attend training sessions and arrive for uniform fitting; a process that began in September 2010. Six months prior to the start of the event, training and uniform distribution began. Figure 5.4 shows one of the London Organising Committee of the Olympic Games (LOCOG) venues for issuing Games Makers with uniforms.

5.11 Volunteers

Non-technical event volunteers are generally employed in behind-the-scenes roles to assist with the smooth running of the event. There is no doubt as to the importance of their contribution. Recruiting, retaining, and managing volunteers are some of the most challenging tasks for any event organisation. As with most aspects of events, early planning is essential to the success of the operation. Many events will attract large numbers of people who are prepared to volunteer. Determining the applicant's suitability for a role is a big challenge as time is usually limited and applicant numbers are high.

Due to the rise in demand for volunteers, there are numerous online volunteer management applications now available. Also, there is now a range of companies who offer the software to build a dedicated volunteer database.

Volgistics	Software for volunteer recruiting, tracking and coordination
Timecounts	Recruit, schedule and track volunteer time
eCoordinator	Volunteer management solution
Zoho Creator	Low-code platform to build custom business apps
Volunteer Impact	Better Software and Better Support
VolunteerLocal	Organize, manage, schedule and communicate with volunteers
MobileServe	Volunteer Management Software
DonorSnap	Contact database and donor management tools for fundraisers
GovPilot	e-Government management solution
EveryAction	A unified CRM for nonprofits
Get Connected	Mobile-friendly volunteer management software
Mobilize	Community and member management software
Greater Giving Event Software	Fundraising solution for non-profits
KeepnTrack	Visitor, student, & volunteer management software
SignUpGenius	Volunteer management & event planning made simple
InitLive	Staff/Volunteer management tool built for events!
Giveffect	All-in-one, web-based nonprofit management software
VolunteerKinetic	Volunteer workforce management
CiviCRM	Open source CRM for nonprofits, civic sector & advocacy orgs
Track It Forward	Time tracking for volunteers
VolunteerMark	Cloud-based volunteer management software for nonprofits
Volunteer Tracker	Volunteer management software for schools
NewOrg	Online data management solutions for nonprofit organizations
Offero	Volunteer and event management solution for local government
Optimy	Customer-oriented sponsorship & grant management software

Figure 5.5 A list of volunteer management software apps and their focus

Figure 5.5 lists a selection of volunteer management software readily available online to international event organisers.

Organising volunteers into teams and communicating with them will be some of the first things to consider once they arrive on site. An appropriate app can make this experience easier to manage. Then the organisation will have to consider logging volunteer hours and consistently identifying volunteer opportunities, scheduling breaks etc. to avoid having clusters standing around with nothing to do. Inactivity and a lack of responsibility deflates morale and will impact on volunteer retention. However, the first problem the event organisers will face will be deciding the correct number of volunteers required.

Knowing the number of roles to fill to create a balance between work and people will make a massive impact on the overall job, and the experience, engagement, and satisfaction levels of those who sign up to volunteer for the event. It is critical to remember that while volunteers are not on the payroll of the event, they are also not free labour. It is essential not to underestimate volunteer expenses when setting the event budget. A number of reimbursable expenses should be accounted for in the plan.

A central aspect of third sector engagement with international events is the placement of volunteers. Many large-scale events will recruit their own army of volunteers. In fact, the need for volunteers at major events has led to the release of volunteer registration alongside or even before ticketing information is released. International events are now relying on the likelihood that oversubscription for tickets or not being able to afford to pay for the price of a ticket will encourage people to sign up to volunteer instead. In 2019, for example, UEFA released online a list of the various venues across Europe where the Euro 2020 games would be played. Prominent on the same webpage was the information to register to volunteer (UEFA.com, 2019).

The deployment of volunteers at international events has become more and more prevalent in the 21st century. From the Olympic Games to local community festivals, a diverse range of events are heavily dependent on volunteers for their operations (Smith *et al.*, 2014). It would be fair to suggest that because of the global accessibility of events, organisers see volunteers as a pivotal factor in the survival and development of many events around the world.

One of the more understandable explanations for their deployment is cost. Strigas and Jackson (2003) suggested that volunteers make sense economically as they cut the operational costs of hosting. The immediate advantage to the audience is that lower costs equate to cheaper tickets. Whatever the bottom line, the most important themes for responsive volunteers include motivation, commitment, and satisfaction. Each of these matters will have an effect on the retention and overall performance of those offering up their free time for little or no financial gain.

Understanding why people volunteer for events is a much studied subject that has yielded many reasons from altruism, experience, travel, self-interest and personal beliefs (Costa *et al.*, 2006; Holmes and Smith, 2009; *The Independent*, 2012; Nichols and Ojala, 2009; Paraskevaidisa and Andriotis, 2017; Rattan, 2010; Smith *et al.*, 2014; Strigas and Jackson, 2003). Whatever the reasoning and as we will discover in this chapter, volunteers no longer have to be exclusively sourced from local residents. There is no doubt that the increased desire for people to volunteer has benefited the event industry as a whole.

From the organisation's perspective, the characteristics sought in a volunteer's personality tend to be common across all international events. The role of a volunteer will always involve direct contact with other people and, quite often, volunteers are the first point of contact for the audience, performers and guests. Therefore, the type of person sought should be welcoming, friendly, and polite. There will always be a requirement for volunteers to show a willingness to help out with a variety of tasks, to be reliable, and to show initiative. It is often the case that volunteers will also be required to have some leadership ability, as teams of volunteers are created for the larger events.

In return, volunteers are often provided with a great deal. If the event is large, then the minimum that should be expected is the opportunity to receive quality training. Then there is the individual's own personal development from being involved. Moreover, much of the training received is transferable and can be used in CVs and future job applications. Many businesses today are just as receptive to voluntary experience as they are to paid work experience, even placing the unpaid work ahead of paid work as the individual contribution is all the more valuable when made without monetary gain.

The reimbursement of expenses and daily sustenance should be expected in any voluntary role, but this cannot be taken for granted at some smaller events. However, every volunteer with the right attitude will leave the event with improved knowledge of some sort. Whether the overall experience was good or bad is another matter, but the general consensus of most volunteers is that they learn a lot and meet people who become lifelong friends.

5.12 Calculating volunteer numbers

There is no simple answer to predicting the number of volunteers required; the eventual number will be based on the specifics of the event itself. Questions the organisers will need to answer include:

- What is the predicted attendance for the event?
- How many venues does the event cover and how widespread is it?
- How long will the event be on for?
- How big an issue are the security concerns
- What is the overall profile of the event? Spectators, participants etc.

From the event organiser's perspective, they may want to register as many volunteers as possible and have more than one person doing the same role. There is always going to be a number of drop-outs that is impossible to avoid. From a volunteer's perspective, there is an important balance between being stressed from over-responsibility and being fed up because there is nothing to do.

For large-scale international events, some employees and those who volunteer to assist during the event will require specialist training in the build-up to the event. Some of the biggest sporting events rely on an army of volunteers to get fans safely in and out of the event. The success of the 2012 Olympics was principally ascribed to the efforts of 70,000 volunteers (Crumpton, 2012; Mackintosh et al., 2016).

According to Sport England, there are 2 million adults who give up at least one hour a week to help out at their local club or at events. It is no exaggeration to say that without them, grassroots sport would wither and die (Slater, 2017). The important role the volunteers played at London 2012 was expressed in the 'Games Maker' name bestowed upon them. It was estimated that the Games Makers contributed 8 million hours of voluntary work behind the scenes during the event (The Independent, 2012).

Being a volunteer is not just about signing up and turning up on the day or for the duration of the event itself. Larger events require further commitment long before the event begins. Attending training days is central to the quality of service provided. Having the right answer to questions from spectators is essential in 21st century events. This breeds confidence in spectators and improves the overall quality and experience of the event.

For London 2012, the Games Maker volunteers and other paid employees were expected to attend a series of 'orientation' training events specific to their role and dedicated location, highlighting the crucial part they would play while building confidence in what they could deliver together. The pre-event training days had to communicate some complex themes and learning goals established by a vast number of stakeholders, yet still deliver an event that motivated, inspired and reinforced their retention up to and during Games time (Engage for Success, 2012). The training events provided an introduction to the heritage and importance of the Games, as well as an insight into what working at

London 2012 would be like. The sessions covered the different Olympic sports, the venues where the events would take place and the different roles each Games Maker would undertake (Degun, 2012). The task of training so many volunteers is itself a serious task and the Games chief executive, Paul Deighton, admitted that training the Games Makers was the biggest challenge that his organisation has faced in the lead-up to the Games

5.13 Training themes

The key themes to the training are customarily based around security, and health and safety. Training requires an uncomplicated means of understanding with a widespread level of knowledge. This is largely achieved by training people in important protocols through a variety of potential situations. Real examples should be discussed where possible. A common method to explain complicated scenarios is to use memorable acronyms or mnemonics.

Volunteers may not be receiving any financial reward for their efforts, but the importance of their role and the level of responsibility do not diminish. For example, security at events will always be a major consideration. Most large-scale events will provide guidance on security with specific models in training sessions and handbooks. LOCOG provided Games Makers at London 2012 with pocket guides that highlighted some of the foremost procedures.

LOCOG also devised memorable slogans and mnemonics for the Games Makers of the 2012 Olympics. The aim was for everyone to feel engaged so they had an unbreakable connection to the Games to inspire passion and support (Tomlin, 2013). Part of that process was to remember the acronym 'I DO ACT': be Inspirational, Distinctive, Open, Alert, Consistent, and act as part of a Team (see Figure 5.6).

Another typical example of mnemonics for highlighting training is the HOT procedure. When faced with unattended items, workers are asked to consider 'HOT' as a means of dealing with the situation. Is it Hidden, Obviously suspicious

Think... I DO ACT

- **Inspirational**
  - Behave in a way that inspires others
- **Distinctive**
  - You provide the personal touch – let yourself shine through
- **Open**
  - Be approachable and honest to people
- **Alert**
  - You are the host , so be aware of people's needs
- **Consistent**
  - Welcome every person as an individual
- **Team**
  - You are central to a united team – mark your mark

Figure 5.6 The 'I DO ACT' mnemonic used for all Games Makers

Source: Based on Games Maker training presentation, 2011

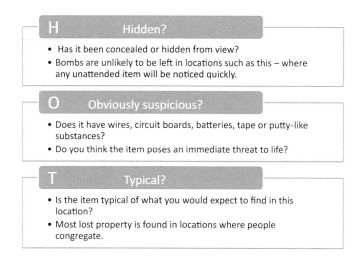

Figure 5.7 The HOT protocol for unattended items

Source: Based on LOCOG training, 2011

or Typical for the location within which it is in? Figure 5.7 provides further explanation of the protocol for unattended items in the HOT mnemonic.

There are a number of training themes international events should provide for volunteers. These are similar to those that many large organisations offer to all staff through an induction process. These would normally include:

- Hazards and risks in the workplace
- Special equipment for the role
- Safety at work practices
- Work health and safety legislation
- Emergency procedures
- First aid and other emergency contacts.

The training of volunteers and stewards at international events should cover a broad area to ensure communication and understanding for everyone involved is to the highest possible standard. Many roles will require additional training and this would be provided after the first levels of training have been completed. However, it is important to remember that training does not stop after induction. Many international events will have full-time stewards, volunteers, marshals and other regular staff who will be provided with training throughout their engagement with the event provider. Table 5.1 highlights many of the key themes that will be covered during a training programme for marshals, volunteers and stewards at events

By adopting these key principles to volunteer training, volunteers become empowered and are provided with a good understanding of the organisation and its values. From here, the event organisation can go on to provide inspiring volunteering opportunities that stimulate the activities of the volunteers involved. This encourages a good working experience and brings them back

Internal forces

Table 5.1 Key themes for marshals, volunteers, and stewards at events

Security, health and safety	Selling or canvassing whilst at work	Hazards, incidents, and injuries	Contact with the media, confidential information
Always the most important aspect of any event. All workers should receive the appropriate training for their level of responsibility.	Volunteering at events has been used to get close to customers. Engaging in personal business is not allowed and can lead to removal from the event.	An incident of any kind needs to be reported in the correct fashion. International events will have documentation to be completed depending on the level or seriousness of the incident in question	Media contact should always be advised against unless specifically requested. Accuracy of information will maintain the good relationship between all stakeholders.
Use of mobile phones during work	*Working with young people, children, and vulnerable adults*	*Searches and other security requests*	*National anthems and cultural awareness*
Visual impressions speak volumes and while some roles require the use of mobile phones, these are usually issued and should only be used in emergencies or as part of the role.	All people at an event should be treated with care. How any action may be perceived should be considered. Safeguarding is essential for all. Disabilities are not always visible.	Both spectators and staff will undergo searches when arriving and sometimes when leaving an event. Failure to consent to reasonable requests could lead to further consequences.	Respect should be the first thing on everyone's mind at all times. International events engage with many cultures and consistency is expected and protocols should be visibly observed.
Dress code, uniforms, personal belongings, and accreditation	*Workforce conduct, photographs, and VIP's*	*Protecting the brand and unwanted commercial access*	*Work patterns throughout the event*
Personal property can be very difficult to protect and advice should be to avoid loss. Presentation is part of the visual aspect of the event while proper accreditation is vital to the overall security of the event,	Volunteers will be asked to maintain a code of conduct during the event. It is not appropriate for any staff to be seen taking photographs during an event and, while being in the presence of VIPs can be exciting, respect should be paid at all times.	Most international events come with sponsorship and merchandising. Therefore volunteers are often the first point of support. Other companies may attempt to ambush the event or undertake unauthorised commercial activities.	For some longer international events, patterns of work and rosters will be created. Volunteers need to ensure arrival in good time and good communication about availability throughout the event.

year after year, even encouraging their friends to join up and remain involved on an ongoing basis.

5.14 Stewarding and security

The need to engage security and stewarding staff is often overlooked at some smaller international events, particularly at the embryonic stage. This is because, for many international events, arrangements to appoint a professional security firm or to even have any kind of visible safety staff is not a legal necessity. There is, of course, the ignorant belief that 'it'll never happen to us' which seems evident at many international events. On the other hand, larger international events may need to convey a frontline presence of security and stewards with a constant visibility that is paramount to the overall experience and satisfaction of those attending. Some political and sporting events could not be held without the visible presence of mass security and police on the ground and in the air.

Depending on the draw of the event and the nature and/or personality of those involved, the event may even necessitate plain-clothed as well as uniformed teams. With these things in mind, it becomes very clear that the cost of ensuring safety at an international event can be tremendously high. However, once they are deployed, the responsibility for many of the event organiser's biggest concerns is delegated to the team of security providers.

It is not usual for security and stewards to have access to the stage or field of play: this is the area being protected. Access to the field of play is exclusively reserved to a limited group involved in the event. With the exception of certain circumstances, such as the protection of perimeters, individuals, or when there has been an invasion of the pitch or stage area, security personnel and stewards remain in the backstage public spaces.

From a lay perspective, the difference between security and stewarding (or even stewarding and volunteers for that matter), is not always plainly defined. They appear to be doing very similar roles. In the UK, the main difference between the two is that stewards can be contracted by the organiser to complete their role while security staff must be trained, pass an exam, and hold a licence. Stewards are often responsible for activities such as crowd management, advice, and general spectator support while security personnel will guard premises, property, and people (SIA, 2018). The 'Security at Events Guidance' document defines the threefold role of security and Figure 5.8 highlights the main areas of responsibility.

In public events when security is required to cover any of these activities, they can only legally be undertaken by licensed personnel. In the UK, security staff will receive their licence after training from the Security Industry Authority (SIA) under the Terms and Conditions of the Private Security Industry Act 2001.

If the decision to have security staff and stewards at an event is made, the organisers will have to plan well in advance the ratio of security staff to stewards required based on a number of factors. As discussed in Chapter 2, this is normally calculated as part of a risk assessment prior to the event plan being completed. The risk assessment data will inform the final number of stewards and security personnel the event will require to satisfactorily meet any health and safety requirements. Every event and space will be different

Figure 5.8 The threefold role of security

and even when it is the same venue with a repeat event, some adjustments will need to be considered. The main factors to consider each time the event is held will include:

- The number of visitors on each day
- The timing of the event – day, night and for how long
- The age of the audience and if children/juveniles are present
- The nature of the event
- If alcohol is available
- Standing, seated or both
- The quality of access to the venue
- The size and shape of the venue
- The type of venue
- The amount of emergency exits
- If the event is indoors or outdoors or both
- Any other concerns with the position or access of the event.

Once the data has been gathered from the risk assessment, the organisers can work on the amount of support required. There is no definite rule to guide event organisers on these numbers, but as a basic rule of thumb an indoor event should ensure:

- At least one steward for every 20 people standing
- At least one steward for every 50 people seated.

The ratios will be higher for outdoor events and consideration should be given to all the points above. The number of security personnel required will again be dependent on the type of event. However, in any country like the UK where security is a licensed role, they will be provided by a dedicated security contractor who will guide any event organiser on the necessary numbers required based on the event itself.

It is also important to ensure that security and stewards are clearly identifiable. The wearing of uniforms for visible security is common. Stewards should be provided with high-visibility tabards or bibs stating their role. This will contribute to the attendees' experience by reducing any delay in the case of an emergency and providing peace of mind to spectators and attendees.

It is also important to consider, depending on the size of the event, the point at which security for the event begins. This will vary in both in time and in distance. Furthermore, not all security is human. Much of the specialist equipment used to assist security staff to ensure the safety of events is the first line of defence. Examples of this include: surveillance cameras, x-ray machines, scanners, transport vehicles, visible weapons, specialist clothing, and perimeter fencing. Then there is the communication between national and other law enforcement agencies around the world. This is discussed more generally in Chapter 7.

Instead of the 'it'll never happen to us' approach, every event organiser should believe that nothing will go wrong with their event while at the same time having a plan and preparing for the worst-case scenario. Since the events of 11th September 2001 (more commonly knowns as 9/11), there is considerably more focus on international events as a point of attack from terrorist groups. This is put into perspective when it is considered that logistically complex hostage-taking events have fallen as a proportion of all terror events, while logistically simple, but deadly, bombings have increased as a proportion of deadly incidents (Enders and Sandler, 2005).

There are many reasons for employing a dedicated security contractor, not least that it is usually stated in a contractual agreement. However, outside of contractual arrangements, deploying security at events brings a number of benefits. These include:

- The physical presence for peace of mind during the event
- To deter the possibility of an attack occurring in the first place
- 24-hour monitoring of space and equipment – buildings, parking, rented goods etc.
- Continuous protection of spectators and those taking part during the event
- Close and distance personal protection – athletes, celebrities, politicians, venues etc.
- Prevention of theft from employees, volunteers, and other personnel
- Crowd management and some control if necessary
- General behaviour when alcohol is available.

5.15 Marshals

Many international sporting events will require a skilled team of marshals to undertake a number of key roles to ensure the safety of participants and spectators. Unlike security staff and stewards, marshals will often have access to some parts of the field of play. Events that are conducted on streets such as bike races, marathons and motor races all rely on the skills of marshals. Much of

Internal forces

their role is route management and requires a detailed examination of the route prior to the event or stage of the event. Even after many planning inspections have been completed, marshals will conduct further inspections on the day of the event to see if anything has changed and needs further consideration or revision.

International cycling events are a good example of the deployment of marshals as they have historically been made up of a convoy of vehicles and activities as they pass through each stage of the event. The caravan, as it is known, is a chain of many elements including inspection vehicles, police, a promotional/marketing convoy, race commissionaires, the media, special guests, support services, team cars, race doctors, the competing teams, ambulance services and a cleaning team. It can take over three hours for the whole convoy to travel through a small town with normal conditions, and much longer over hills and mountains. Figure 5.9 is a diagram of a typical Tour de France convoy.

Before the convoy sets out, the route will be sealed off from the public and teams of marshals will be positioned throughout the route. It is normal for cyclists to be travelling at speeds of up to 60 kilometres per hour in groups of over 100 so both visual and aural warnings emphasise the potential danger as they approach. In these dangerous circumstances, street furniture such as bollards, traffic islands, barriers, and road signs are permanent structures that could cause a fatal collision. Obstructions in road cycling are managed by marshals with whistles and flags to assist the cyclist visually and aurally. The whistles are blown in short blasts at repeated intervals while the flags are waved above the marshal's head from side to side as the cyclists approach the obstruction.

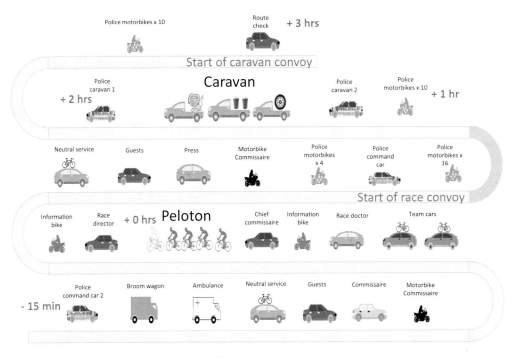

Figure 5.9 The Tour de France convoy

Source: Author, based on Gough and Taylor, 2014

Road junctions are also managed and teams of marshals on motorbikes control each junction ahead of the race itself as it nears and passes through. A popular method is to use a caterpillar chain where a team of six to ten motorcyclists ride the route at a set distance apart. The first one will stop at the junction and wait for the next rider to stop behind them. Once the second rider is stationary, the first rider moves off to the next junction and so on. This is much safer, as avoiding the overtaking manoeuvres removes the possibility of collisions.

Track motor racing is also synonymous with the positioning of marshals and the Le Mans 24-hour race marshals have a broad range of responsibility during the event. The most visible task is the variety of flags they must wave to denote different conditions during the 24-hour race. Marshals at motor racing events can be in charge of a number of responsibilities, including:

- Ensuring competitors' safety by displaying the right flags
- Intervening quickly when incidents occur, such as a car leaving the track or an accident, and take care of towing or lifting vehicles stuck on the gravel
- Cleaning up the track, by clearing debris, sweeping, or absorbing spills
- Protecting people like medics who attend incidents on the track.

In an event where the possibility of a serious accident could occur day or night, the Le Mans 24 marshals are effectively the event management team's boots on the ground. They keep the race manager in the loop in real time and if necessary provide written reports, shouldering substantial responsibility as these assist in the general health and safety of the event and can even be used to decide sanctions on drivers during the race (Lemans.org, 2019).

5.16 Third sector engagement

The third sector is a term used to describe a range of organisations that are neither public sector nor private sector. These community and voluntary organisations play a vital role in the delivery of many international event services. Their contribution is arguably the most valuable resource in international event management. It originates from a broad range of support agencies and organisations that contribute to the overall safe and acceptable delivery of events. From providing volunteers to liaising with local residents, their contribution is often very much underestimated. They are the secret army of operations, the glue that binds events, the people with a local understanding or effectively the nails in the ancient 'want of a horseshoe nail' proverb in Chapter 2.

Many third sector organisations (TSOs) have been around for over a hundred years providing support to local people and businesses. The third sector is largely made up of not-for-profit community groups and voluntary organisations. They work in partnership with other organisations, agencies, and individuals to improve services and collaboration between stakeholders and promote a number of community impacts. Table 5.2 provides an indication of the types of organisations and the various trading statuses. They have become one of the cornerstones of international event success. It is difficult to reach a conclusion on the value of the third sector, but without their input, international events

Table 5.2 Types of organisation and trading status

Types of organisation	Types of trading status
Community group	Charitable trusts
Co-operative	Companies limited by guarantee
Faith groups	Community interest companies
Grant-making trust	Industrial societies
Housing association	Mutual societies
Private club	Not for profit trade associations
Residents' group	Provident societies
Social enterprise	Registered charities
Sports organisation	Self-help groups
Tenants' group	Unincorporated groups
Voluntary organisation	

would be a completely different experience and cost the paying spectator considerably more to attend.

As international events became more reliant on human resources, largely due to health and safety requirements, the third sector contribution has ensured the survival of countless events. Commercial sporting events in particular could not exist on the same financial scale without third sector intervention.

The National Audit Office (NAO, 2010) explains that TSOs are generally:

- Independent of government
- Value-driven
- Reinvest any surpluses generated in the pursuit of their goals.

For TSOs to be independent of government is an important part of the history and culture of the sector. It can allow them to get much closer to the community as a sense of trust is built over a period of time. This is evidenced through their value-driven goals as they are motivated by the desire to achieve social goals (for example, improving public welfare, the environment or economic wellbeing), rather than the desire to generate a profit. Because they re-invest any surpluses, TSOs are sometimes called 'not-for-profit organisations'. A better term might be 'not-for-personal-profit' because in many cases, TSOs need to make surpluses (or 'profits') to be financially sustainable.

5.17 Volunteer tourism (voluntourism)

As already discussed, finding and engaging staff and support workers to assist with the delivery of international events is an enormous undertaking. More recently, concepts such as volunteer tourism or voluntourism have emerged that have proved to be useful sources of personnel for international events. With the greater mobility of people, the concept is currently one of the fastest-growing travel trends. It consists of individuals using their annual leave or free time to work for international development programmes such as UNICEF, Save the Children, CARE International, and World Vision. In this context, it has come under a great deal of criticism, largely due to the lack of long-term commitment, short-term altruistic gain and a lack of relevant skills being brought to volunteer sites (Freidus, 2017). However, international events can be a much better fit. Due to the requirements of both international events and volunteer tourism, there are numerous benefits that are well suited to both the event and the tourist.

While the concept is available for all, youth travellers are travelling more frequently to a wider range of destinations, looking for different cultural and social experiences, interested in outdoor and sports activities, music-related events, and the social and environmental impacts of travel (Pompurová et al., 2018). The available opportunities and their suitability for 'voluntourists' of all ages and tastes are extensive as the broad scope of international events covers culture, art, religion, and politics. The idea of being part of an international event rather than just a spectator has propelled the voluntourism movement into a powerful alternative to the archetypal holiday by the beach.

The motivation for voluntourists is multifaceted, but life experience and life-long learning would be two key drivers. These might include the opportunity to meet new people and create new friendships, possibly even develop new skills and form new life perspectives (Smith et al., 2014). There is also the added knowledge that once the trip is over, a personal sense of value is experienced through the individual's contribution to humanity. In a time when conservation and the earth's continued existence are high on the global agenda, transforming tourism from a capitalist expression of wealth to a global community of environmentally aware participants is a new approach to the post-holiday conversation. Not forgetting, of course, voluntourists receive free access to the event, promotional materials, clothing, and the chance to rub shoulders with celebrities who might be participating in the event.

5.18 Sharing the challenge

Managers of international events will face numerous challenges in the planning of an event. The bigger its scale, the more complications and responsibilities there are to deal with. The world's biggest sporting events have become complex and transformative undertakings over the past 30 years, with costs often exceeding US$10 billion (Müller, 2015). Therefore, it is to be expected that major challenges of one sort or another will also occur during the planning process. Many of these challenges can be quite unremarkable in many respects, but can also develop into more serious problems if not managed correctly. So the term 'managing international events' refers to a whole team of managers, organisers or coordinators who deal with the challenges encountered in each segment.

Major events will have detailed management structures with specific responsibilities distributed between units. The FIFA World Cup is a prime example because of the broad range of departments and various levels of management (see Figure 5.10).

When applying to host the FIFA World Cup, a local organising committee (LOC) is set up. If their bid is successful, the detailed structure is put into place. The supervisory board will make the strategic decisions on preparations for the tournament and these will be implemented by particular departments through the managing board that oversees the operations and financial teams

Figure 5.10 Organising structure for FIFA World Cup 2018, Russia

Source: Based on FIFA, 2018

in preparation for the event. The supervisory board convenes as the need arises, while the managing board would meet once a quarter (FIFA, 2018).

As these types of mega events are funded largely through taxpayers' money, it is usual for the organising boards to be made up of government officials and other senior officers. The head of the supervisory board for Russia in 2018 was Vladimir Putin with the deputy prime minister operating at the next level.

For many smaller organisations and events, the structure is naturally much less complicated. They will still require a number of departments and a team of managers to effectively deliver an international event with the key responsibilities further down the chain being managed by different individuals. This way, the constant organisation of each department is maintained. The diagram in Figure 5.11 depicts a typical mid-sized international event management team and the departments required to deliver an international event.

In most mid-sized organisations, the administration, finance and marketing teams are customarily based in the organisation's home country and contribute to the day-to-day running of the company from there. The production team is more hands-on with the event itself. In smaller companies, it is usual for individuals to double up and assume at least two of the roles listed. Therefore, the production manager may also be the financial manager. The smaller the organisation, the more roles the individuals involved will undertake.

5.19 Public–private partnerships

Trends in the provision of infrastructure development over recent years indicate that the private sector is playing an increasingly important role in the procurement process (Marcus *et al.*, 2002). With many international events, the amount of money involved sees governments looking for alternatives to simply spending

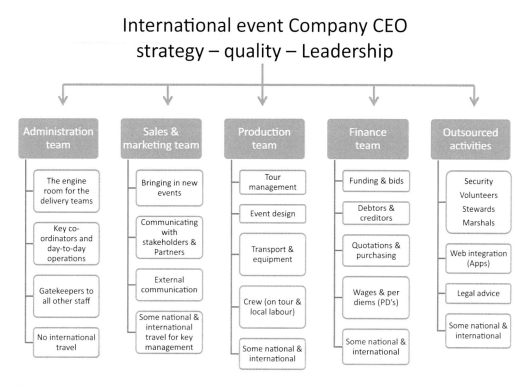

Figure 5.11 Typical mid-sized international event management company structure

public money. The work involved requires another level of human resource management, particularly when the event is very large-scale, expensive, and becomes part of the host's landscape long after the event itself has past. For many potential host nations eager to be involved, this has become a major challenge where it is evident that the demands of hosting are way above the nation's ability to provide. With the introduction of procurement routes through public-private partnerships, more nations are now in a position to transfer many of the initial costs to the private sector and simultaneously use international events as a means of developing major construction projects. Managing these complex projects – for example, building new infrastructure such as transport links and venues – is a major undertaking and can bring considerable disruption to the host community. The management of such projects demands specialist knowledge and a considerable amount of risk.

Build-operate-transfer (BOT) is a model where a company is appointed to assume responsibility for much of the infrastructure for the event by bringing together construction, operation, and maintenance. The big construction companies will contribute private investment into the project in return for the operation of the construction over a period of time (such as 20 years), shifting the financial risk from the public to the private sector (Jennings, 2012b). By doing so, the construction company can generate a return on its investment. However, the use of BOT projects has been strongly criticised for irrational construction schedules, the involvement of those who lack of experience in operating large-scale venues, and huge cost overruns (Chan, 2010; Chinyere, 2013; Hu *et al.*, 2008)

5.20 Emergency command structures

We will discuss in Chapter 9 how the developing world has changed the delivery of international events and the overall implications of this, but one particular implication for international events is the likelihood of an attack on the event itself and the possibility of this developing into a major incident. Event organisers are not expected to take control of major incidents as they will not have access to the specialist resources necessary to do so. However, they are expected to have prepared for such circumstances during the planning stages and to have appointed the appropriate team in consultation with the emergency services. Ultimately, the reason for an emergency command structure is to hand responsibility for a major incident over to the most experienced, professional, and knowledgeable people in order to ensure the highest level of safety is provided to everyone present at the event.

Such management processes recognise that in very serious situations there may be a need to coordinate the handling of an incident at three specific levels of control or command: strategic, tactical, and operational. In many international events, this management structure is referred to as gold, silver, and bronze command. Many international event organisers have accepted this model of control and implement it from a very early stage in the planning process. However, in preparation for a major incident during liaison with the emergency services, it is advised that clarification is sought to determine which the preferred approach is in the local area (The Purple Guide, 2012).

It is important to understand that, as the name suggests, the gold (strategic), silver (tactical), bronze (operational) command structure is role-based rather than grade-based. Each role or responsibility is allocated according to skill, expertise, location, and competency (Home Office, 2018). However, while there can be a number of bronze and silver commanders, there is only ever one gold commander who holds ultimate responsibility for the handling and outcome of the incident. If a serious incident were to occur at the event, the event organisers would assume supporting roles for the command structure, providing information and assistance as necessary.

Understanding what is considered a critical incident is also important as an event organiser should not be implementing a process when it is unnecessary. However, if the evidence is clear, appropriate advice would be to suggest it is better to declare an incident, take the appropriate action and then retract the call, rather than do nothing and increase the potential for escalation. Therefore the organisers should consider a critical incident as an incident outside of their usual business activity that can result in serious consequences.

5.20.1 The command structure

According to the UK Home Office's guidance (2018), the gold commander is ultimately responsible for the handling and outcome of the incident and sets the strategy for dealing with it. They determine the strategy for managing an incident including any tactical parameters that the silver or bronze commanders should follow. The gold commander must retain strategic oversight of the incident. While gold commanders should not make tactical decisions, they will be responsible for ensuring that any tactics deployed are proportionate to the risks identified, meet the objectives of the strategy, and are legally compliant.

The silver commander is responsible for producing the tactical plan following the strategy set out by the gold commander. There can be more than one silver commander, but each must have a clearly defined and logged remit. The bronze commander takes the operational decisions necessary to accomplish the silver commander's tactical plan. As with the silver commander, there can be more than one bronze commander as long as each has a clearly defined and logged remit. For example, an incident may require a bronze operational commander,

Table 5.3 Gold, silver, and bronze command responsibilities

Gold command – strategic

Open decision log and record all decisions taken – Define the overall intention – Determine what resources are needed – Determine specialist skills required – Agree and advise silver commander of the strategy – Identify and liaise with other partners (such as the emergency services, her majesty's revenue and customs, border force, other government departments) – Appoint gold support staff, and any tactical advisors – Approve silver commander's tactical plan before implementation – Throughout the incident, review and update the strategy depending on information received and the events which occur and relay further strategic decisions to silver commander – Maintain objectivity throughout the incident – Ensure the command structure is in place and monitor its effectiveness – Monitor the effectiveness of silver commander's tactical plan – Keep informed of any developments – Keep any strategic reference group or duty board members appraised of the incident and developments – Formally close CI (record in decision log) and advise silver commander – Lead the formal de-brief

Silver command – tactical

Open decision log and record all decisions taken – Appoint deputy / support staff / tactical advisors – Establish the instigation of critical incident management procedures – Brief gold commander and take their strategic instructions – Appoint officers to undertake business as usual while you are a silver commander – Obtain and agree gold commander's strategy – Coordinate the tactical plan – Coordinate the change-over of staff and commanders including your own – Liaise closely with bronze commander and obtain regular updates – Brief staff and keep them updated – Ensure the bronze commander operations meet with the strategic and tactical plan – Provide regular updates to gold commander and take their further instruction on the strategic handling of the incident – Continually review tactical plan – Attend formal de-brief – Collate all records of the incident including decision logs – Ensure staff health and welfare is considered – Partake in formal de-brief

Bronze command – operational

Open decision log and record all decisions taken – Appoint deputy / support staff / tactical advisors – Conduct initial and ongoing risk assessments as the incident progresses – Ensure resources are deployed as directed by the silver commander – If the incident continues over a long period, ensure handover period is sufficient – Assist or liaise with other agencies and services as required at scene or at bronze commander level – Ensure relevant records are completed and collated including any records that have a bearing on the incident – Refer the media to press office or media bronze commander – Provide regular updates to silver commander and take their further instruction – Ensure staff are briefed and updated – When the incident is ended stand down as the bronze commander – Partake in formal debrief

Source: Based on UK Home Office advice, 2018

a bronze communications commander and a bronze logistics commander. Table 5.3 provides a more detailed explanation of the responsibilities of each commander within the levels of command.

It may be necessary to set up an emergency operations centre that can be either a physical location or a virtual location connected by telephone and video links. An operations centre supports the emergency response and the major incident communications activities. By allowing the decision makers to communicate directly and by keeping them abreast of the unfolding situation with the most current information, the most appropriate decisions can be made without delay.

Once the incident is over, a formal debrief should be held with the findings written up into a formal report. The lead debrief officer should pay particular attention to making recommendations for the best way to inform future commanders on how the situation was managed, how a similar situation could be averted, and ultimately how the incident was concluded.

5.21 Summary

This chapter has taken a close look at the way human resources are deployed across a wide variety of roles at international events. The chapter has provided an in-depth review of how people contribute to the safe construction and delivery of international events of all sizes. We have learned how clearly specified roles and responsibilities improve the level of communication at international events, and the important contribution made by those who are often considered to be less important in the grand scheme of event delivery. We have also learned the importance of training and that it is how members of staff engage with the event that often makes the difference between a negative and a positive experience for both staff members and those attending the event.

Case study 5.1 L'Eroica volunteers

One of the biggest challenges any international event organiser will face is the recruitment of a team of volunteers. Some of the biggest issues include getting the right number of volunteers, balancing the boring and attractive tasks, and ensuring each volunteer has enough responsibility to remain engaged with their task. There are thousands of mid-sized events that require the assistance of hundreds of responsible volunteers. Most importantly, the event organisers want to see their volunteers turn up and when they do, complete the task they have been charged with undertaking.

In 1997 in Gaiole in Chianti, Italy, 92 hunters of feelings and emotions gave life to the first edition of L'Eroica as they set out in a rainbow of vintage bikes and wool jerseys to cycle the dusty white roads of Tuscany. Each year ever since, on the first Sunday of October, the magic of an event lost in time is repeated across challenging routes traversing magnificent landscapes with unforgettable stops for refreshments involving thousands

Figure 5.12 L'Eroica hashtag illumination

of passionate Eroici. Today, there are 13 events taking place all over the world between March and October every year. The events include:

- Eroica Japan
- Eroica Britannia
- Eroica South Africa
- Eroica California
- Eroica Montalcino
- Eroica Hispania
- Eroica Limburg
- L'Eroica Italy
- Eroica Germania
- Eroica Dolomiti.

Considering the advances in cycling technology today, this international event has become one of the most authentic and dedicated challenges with good-spirited participation. L'Eroica itself was inspired by classic cycling and aimed to rediscover the roots of an extraordinary sport. Over the years, the Eroica vision and values have been shared with the world, creating new events for both classic and modern bikes.

The role of the volunteer is not only helping the riders on-site but also out and about throughout the ride route. Volunteers need to keep the riders safe along the routes as well as guide them along the way. The organisers suggest that being part of the team will gift each individual with a unique experience. The volunteers are much loved by the riders for helping support their endeavour as they undertake one of the various routes of the challenge. For the volunteer, the reward will be more than just a pass to the festival and well-stocked goodie bag.

Many L'Eroica volunteers return year after year to offer their support. Many attend the festival with family and friends to volunteer together. There are many volunteering positions available before, during and after the event to suit many availability options but all with the key aim of making L'Eroica the focal point of many conversations (https://eroica.cc).

Questions

1. What can the organisers do to make sure they have enough volunteers on the day to meet their own safety standards for the event considering last minute no-shows?
2. How should the organisers decide who takes on the more responsible jobs?
3. How can the organisers make sure the volunteers communicate between each other and the team leader to ensure each of the stations is adequately staffed?
4. How should the organisers deal with breaks and rotating the volunteering roles?
5. Why do you think the volunteers for this event continue to return and even volunteer for other events around the world?

Case study 5.2 Applying SKIPPA to international event delivery

Create an international event for 1,000 spectators or delegates and apply SKIPPA's six attributes to provide the best possible experience for the events stakeholders. Consider the following:

- How many people (staff) will be required to host the event
- Where will the event be hosted?
- What broader infrastructure plans will be required?
- Are there any specialist skills required by the staff?
- What are the areas of specific knowledge required?
- Who will be the key influencers involved
- What is the estimated budget?
- What equipment will be required for the event?

5.22 Useful websites

Zero-hour contracts: the good, the bad, the context
https://uniofglos.blog/eventsglos/2018/11/05/zero-hour-contracts-the-good-the-bad-the-context/

Volunteer advice and support
www.majorevents.govt.nz/resource-bank/workforce-and-volunteers-for-events/

Geek Feminism conference anti-harassment policy
https://geekfeminism.wikia.org/wiki/Conference_anti-harassment/Policy

Planning for incidents and emergencies
www.hse.gov.uk/event-safety/incidents-and-emergencies.htm

Security at events guidance
www.sia.homeoffice.gov.uk/documents/licensing/sia_security_at_events.pdf

Job advice –Worksmart
https://worksmart.org.uk/

References

Abraham, R. (2019). Cannes: Ken Loach's Sorry We Missed You — a piercing drama about a zero-hours-contract driver. *The Financial Times*. Retrieved from www.ft.com/content/1ba039f0-7893-11e9-be7d-6d846537acab Accessed 19th September 2019.

Baum, T., Deery, M., Hanlon, C., Lockstone, L., & Smith, K. (2009). *People and Work in Events and Conventions: A Research Perspective*. Wallingford: CABI.

Chan, P. C., Patrick, T. I., & Daniel, W. M. (2010). Critical success factors for PPPs in infrastructure developments: Chinese perspective. *Journal of Construction Engineering and Management, 136*(5), 484–494.

Chinyere, I. I. (2013). Comprehensive objectives for PPP projects: Case of Beijing Olympic Stadium. *International Journal of Business and Management, 8*(9).

Costa, C. A., Chalip, L., Green, C., & Simes, C.. (2006). Reconsidering the role of training in event volunteers' satisfaction. *Sport Management Review, 9*(2), 165–182.

Crumpton, N. (2012). Olympics showed real meaning of integration. *Campaign*, 14–15.

Degun, T. (2012). Training 70,000 Games Makers is the biggest challenge so far, admits London 2012 chief Deighton. Retrieved from www.insidethegames.biz/articles/15755/training-70000-games-makers-is-the-biggest-challenge-so-far-admits-london-2012-chief-deighton Accessed 23rd March 2017.

Downey, R. (2019). Who's Who on the LA 2028 Board of Directors. Retrieved from https://goldencitygamescom.wordpress.com/2019/03/15/whos-who-on-the-la-2028-board-of-directors/ Accessed 9th May 2019.

Enders, W., & Sandler, T. (2005). After 9/11: Is it all different now? *Journal of Conflict Resolution, 49*(2), 259–277. doi:10.1177/0022002704272864

Engage For Success (2012). London 2012 Games Maker orientation events. Retrieved from https://engageforsuccess.org/london-2012-games-maker-orientation-events Accessed 8th May 2017.

Internal forces

FIFA (2018). LOC organizational chart & functions. Retrieved from http://img.fifa.com/mm/photo/tournament/loc/02/90/10/56/2901056_big-lnd.jpg Accessed 23rd February 2018.

Fleming, P. (2017). The human capital hoax: Work, debt and insecurity in the era of uberization. *Organization Studies, 38*(5), 691–709. doi:10.1177/0170840616686129

Fletcher, D., Dunn, J., & Prince, R. (2009). Entry level skills for the event management profession: Implications for curriculum development. *ICHPER-SD Journal of Research, 4*(1), 52.

Freidus, A. (2017). Volunteer tourism: What's wrong with it and how it can be changed. Retrieved from http://theconversation.com/volunteer-tourism-whats-wrong-with-it-and-how-it-can-be-changed-86701 Accessed 23rd March 2018.

Geek Feminism (n.d.). Conference anti-harassment policy. Retrieved from https://geekfeminism.wikia.org/wiki/Conference_anti-harassment/Policy Accessed 10th May 2019.

Gleeson, B., & Rozo, M. (2013). The silo mentality: How to break down the barriers, *Forbes*. Retrieved from www.forbes.com/sites/brentgleeson/2013/10/02/the-silo-mentality-how-to-break-down-the-barriers/#75da88e68c7e Accessed 20th January 2020.

Gough, J., & Taylor, C. (2014). Tour de France 2014. Retrieved from https://letour.yorkshire.com/ Accessed 3rd March 2016.

Gov.uk (n.d.). Contract types and employer responsibilities. Retrieved from www.gov.uk/contract-types-and-employer-responsibilities/zero-hour-contracts Accessed 9th May 2019.

Holmes, K., & Smith, K. (2009). *Managing Volunteers in Tourism*. Oxford: Elsevier.

Home Office (2018). *Critical Incident Management. Version 12.0*. Retrieved from https://assets.publishing.service.gov.uk/government/uploads/system/uploads/attachment_data/file/736743/critical-incident-management-v12.0ext.pdf Accessed 30th October 2018.

Hoye, R., Smith, A., Nicholson, M., & Stewart, B. (2018). *Sport Management* (5th ed.). Oxon: Routledge.

Hu, W. F., Chen, J. G., & Zhao, M. R. (2008). 'Dispute administration and resolution in international construction projects'. Paper presented at the International Conference on Multi-national Construction Projects, Shanghai, China.

Independent, The (2012). London 2012: Olympics success down to 70,000 volunteers. Retrieved from www.independent.co.uk/sport/olympics/news/london-2012-olympics-success-down-to-70000-volunteers-8030867.html Accessed 27th March 2018.

Jennings, W. (2012a). *Mega-Events and Risk Colonisation: Risk Management and the Olympics Centre for Analysis of Risk and Regulation*. London: London School of Economics and Political Science.

Jennings, W. (2012b). *Olympic Risks*. Basingstoke: Palgrave McMillan.

Leighton, P., & Painter, R. W. (2001). Casual workers: still marginal after all these years? *Employee Relations, 23*(1), 75–93. doi:10.1108/01425450110366282

Lemans.org. (2019). 24 Heures du Mans – Safety: the role of marshals and their flags. Retrieved from www.lemans.org/en/news/24-heures-du-mans-safety-the-role-of-marshals-and-their-flags/52086 Accessed 17th June 2019.

Lunday, J. (2010). Typical weaknesses of codes of conduct. Retrieved from www.corporatecomplianceinsights.com/typical-weaknesses-of-codes-of-conduct/ Accessed 10th May 2019.

Mackintosh, C., Darko, N., & May-Wilkins, H. (2016). Unintended outcomes of the London 2012 Olympic Games: Local voices of resistance and the challenge for sport participation leverage in England. *Leisure Studies, 35*(4), 454–469. doi:10.1080/02614367.2015.1031269

Marcus, J., Gameson, R., & Rowlinson, S. (2002). Critical success factors of the BOOT procurement system: Reflections from the Stadium Australia case study. *Engineering Construction and Architectural Management, 9*(2), 352–361.

McCabe, V. S., & Savery, L. K. (2007). 'Butterflying' – a new career pattern for Australia? Empirical evidence. *Journal of Management Development, 26*(2), 103–116.

McMillan, M. (2012). Codes of ethics: If you adopt one, will they behave? Retrieved from https://blogs.cfainstitute.org/investor/2012/02/20/codes-of-ethics-if-you-adopt-one-will-they-behave/ Accessed 24th June 2018.

Moufakkir, O., & Pernecky, T. (2015). *Ideological, Social and Cultural Aspects of Events.* Oxon: CABI.

Müller, M. (2015). The mega-event syndrome: Why so much goes wrong in mega-event planning and what to do about it. *Journal of the American Planning Association, 81*(1), 6–17. doi:10.1080/01944363.2015.1038292

National Audit Office (NAO) (2010). What are third sector organisations and their benefits for commissioners? Retrieved from www.nao.org.uk/successful-commissioning/introduction/what-are-civil-society-organisations-and-their-benefits-for-commissioners/ Accessed 13th June 2019.

Nichols, G., & Ojala, E. (2009). Understanding the management of sports events volunteers through psychological contract theory. *Voluntas, 20*(4), 369–387. doi:10.1007/s11266-009-9097-9

OED (1989). *The Oxford English Dictionary.* Oxford: Clarendon Press.

Padron, T. C., & Stone, M. J. (2019). Leadership skills in event management courses. *Event Management, 23*(2). doi:10.3727/152599518x15403853721321

Paraskevaidisa, P., & Andriotis, K. (2017). Altruism in tourism: Social exchange theory vs altruistic surplus phenomenon in host volunteering. *Annals of Tourism Research, 62*, 26–37.

Pompurová, K., Marčeková, R., Šebová, L., Sokolová, J., & Žofaj, M. (2018). Volunteer tourism as a sustainable form of tourism—The case of organized events. *Sustainability 2018, 10*(1468).

Purple Guide, The (2012). The Purple Guide to health, safety and welfare at music and other events. Retrieved from www.thepurpleguide.co.uk/ Accessed 23rd March 2017.

Rattan, J. (2010). Managing volunteers in tourism: Attractions, destinations and events. *Tourism Analysis, 15*(3), 395–396.

Russell, B., Sage, A., & Webster, B. (2019). Thousands of pupils and workers walk out in global protests demanding action on climate change. *The Times.* Retrieved from www.thetimes.co.uk/article/thousands-walk-out-in-global-protests-demanding-action-on-climate-change-qchtx06rz .Accessed 20th September 2019.

Ryan, W. G., & Kelly, S. (2017). The effects of supply chain management (SCM) activities and their impact on festival management and the customer experience. . In A. Jepson, Clarke, A. (Eds.), *Power, Construction, and Meaning, in Communities Festivals and Events,* 109–128. Oxon: Routledge.

Saberton, M. (2018). Avoiding operational silos. Huddle.com. Retrieved from www.huddle.com/blog/breaking-operational-silos/ Accessed 20th January 2020.

Security Industry Authority (SIA) (2018). *Security at Events Guidance.* Retrieved from www.sia.homeoffice.gov.uk/Documents/licensing/sia_security_at_events.pdf Accessed 14th June 2019.

Siddique, H., Marsh, S., & Naaman, Z. (2019). Global climate strike: Greta Thunberg and school students lead climate crisis protest. *The Guardian.* Retrieved from www.theguardian.com/environment/live/2019/sep/20/climate-strike-global-change-protest-sydney-melbourne-london-new-york-nyc-school-student-protest-greta-thunberg-rally-live-news-latest-updates Accessed 21st September 2019.

Slater, M. (2017). How unpaid volunteers make the sports world go round. Retrieved from www.bbc.co.uk/sport/20567861 accessed 21/10/2017.

Smith, K. A., Lockstone-Binney, L., Holmes, K., & Baum, T. (2014). *Event Volunteering. International Perspectives on the Event Volunteering Experience.* New York: Routledge.

Internal forces

Stone, M. J., Padron, T. C., Wray, M. L., La Lopa, J. m., & Olson, E. D. (2017). Career desires and expectations of event management students. *Journal of Hospitality and Tourism Management, 32*, 45–53. doi:10.1016/j.jhtm.2017.04.005

Strigas, A., & Jackson, N. (2003). Motivating volunteers to serve and succeed: design and results of a pilot study that explores demographics and motivational factors in sport volunteerism. *International Sports Journal, 7*, 111–121.

Toffler, A. (1990). *Power Shift*. New York: Bantam Books.

Tomlin, J. (2013). Using power of the games to inspire lasting change – Sharing lessons from the Games Makers Programme and managing over 70,0000 volunteers for the Olympics and Paralympics. Retrieved from www.attend.org.uk/sites/default/files/Jean%20Tomlin%20-%20lessons%20from%20the%20Olympics%20Volunteering%20Programmeapproved.doc Accessed 11th May 2019.

UEFA (2019). Euro 2020 ticket and venue update. Retrieved from www.uefa.com/uefaeuro-2020/ Accessed 12th June 2019.

Walker, M. (2017). 7 signs you were born to work in events. Retrieved from www.eventbrite.co.uk/blog/7-signs-you-were-born-to-work-in-events-ds00/ Accessed 11th May 2019.

Wharton, D. (2019). LA 2028 Olympic organizing committee staff gets some fresh faces. Retrieved from www.latimes.com/sports/olympics/la-sp-la2028-expands-staff-20190425-story.html Accessed 9th May 2019.

Chapter 6

Crossing cultures and crossing borders

Contents

6.1 Chapter overview

This chapter covers many of the conditions that are associated with crossing borders and cultures when involved with international events. Language and cultural differences present considerable challenges for international events and their organisers. A summary of the world's cultures is therefore discussed. However, as discussed in Chapter 1, the integration of different cultures in the same place is part of the changing world. It is no longer necessary to cross a physical border to encounter these different cultures. This chapter discusses this in more detail. It is also fully appreciated that in some places, different cultures exist in the same street, providing both complications and opportunities to international event organisers.

6.2 Learning objectives

By the end of this chapter, the student will be expected to:

- Appreciate the importance of cultural values and the impacts on individuals of travel
- Understand the complications of crossing borders for different nationalities
- Recognise how cultural differences can pose as barriers and opportunities to international events
- Understand the main concerns about crossing borders and the impact of international events, and how other influences follow.

6.3 Introduction

We live in a world that is characterised by events and other trading activities conducted and developed across national boundaries. The global marketplace is essential to the success of many international events and it is necessary to have an understanding of the various cultures, customs, and values of these highly individual societies the event engages with. The influence of these trading activities and cultural norms penetrates much deeper than just crossing borders as travelling will include direct interactions with people from different cultural backgrounds. This movement across borders will bring with it stimuli that will have an impact on those who travel and those who are encountered along the way (see Figure 6.1 for the variety of languages used on a café's welcome sign at an international event). Globalisation, as is discussed in Chapter 9, has increased the number of international events resulting also in an increase in cultural engagement. These cultural stimuli will be different in many respects and the engagement is able to affect the people in the recipient area as well as those visiting.

Events can exert a strong influence on the community in which they are held, and when an event is transposed from its place of origin into a new community,

Figure 6.1 A welcome greeting expressed in many languages outside a café at an international venue

its ideas are transposed with it, both positive and negative, with potentially significant consequences for that new host community's values, rituals, thoughts, and ways of life. Culture is the distinctive ideas, customs, social behaviour, or products of a particular nation, society, or people (OED, 2016). These different ways of life create a sense of belonging, and international events are capable of cultivating as well as corrupting them.

6.4 Hurry up and wait

It makes sense to begin this chapter with an explanation of the experience of being involved in delivering international events. There is the constant pressure of deadlines followed by phases of inactivity and calm. This is essentially the supply chain of the event coming together at different stages in the event life cycle. Phases of inactivity are usual and have to be accepted as part of the planning process.

When travel is necessary, the complications involved in crossing borders intensify the 'hurry up and wait' condition. There is the demand from timetables to arrive at a place by a certain time, only to have to wait for the next phase in the journey. Allowing for delays is part of good planning, but these also contribute to the hurry up and wait experience. When travelling by air, it is recommended to arrive at the airport two hours prior to check in. Modern flight times factor in delays in the schedule to meet arrival targets, and anyone with travel experience who travels by road or rail without factoring in delays does so at their peril.

Delays mean more waiting time, but if these potential issues are not factored into the journey, the possibility of bigger problems further down the line becomes more likely. Missed transfers, traffic jams, and cancellations can lead to a number of undesirable situations including increased costs, changes of plan, postponements and/or cancellations.

The wait part of the cycle is not normally something to look forward to, but it does present the event organiser with the opportunity to catch up on outstanding tasks. This requires organising work around the busy periods. As time pressures are experienced at one part of the journey, the slack in the other makes up for the inability to work. Travelling presents numerous opportunities to get on with outstanding work, providing the motivation to do so is not removed by the distraction of the immediate surroundings. Motivation is just as easily lost when travel fatigue kicks in, the personal focus is low or when the stress of travel is overbearing. However, even when the motivation is there, it is not always possible to complete the tasks most pressing as communication can be limited when there is no available network or Wi-Fi, or when the person you need to speak to is in an incompatible time zone.

6.5 Crossing cultures

International events can largely be considered as transcultural. In line with the true meaning of the word, they transcend the limitations of borders as they contain elements common to many different cultures. This does not mean that attention to different cultures should be overlooked; on the contrary, many international events are deeply sectarian. However, it does suggest that international events are largely acceptable to all cultures as they fit well with the broader interests of human society.

6.5.1 Understanding the basics of culture

Academics at Yale University have created a database listing the outline of world cultures. According to Human Relations Area Files (HRAF, 2017), the cultures of the world can be broken down into eight distinct areas, namely, Africa, Asia, Europe, Middle America and Caribbean, the Middle East, North America, Oceania, and South America. However, the database suggests that within each of these areas, there are up to 50 different categorised cultures.

As we travel across borders with events, it is important to appreciate and acknowledge what culture is. Culture is a multifaceted concept that contributes to the many characteristics of an individual, state, or form of identity. It is often deep rooted and permeates a society whilst remaining concealed to outsiders apart from the more obvious visible or tangible examples. The language, skin, and hair of two individuals may be alike, but this should never be taken as meaning their values or customs will be too. Understanding culture, being sensitive to the differences and nuances in people from country to country, is fundamental to success in the international marketplace (Solomon, 2009).

Culture and customs are sometimes only truly understood from experience; although considerable documentation about differing cultures is available to prepare for the experience itself. Odello (2012) recommends that in order to understand the meaning and significance of a people's culture or a cultural identity, it is pertinent to refer to other disciplines such as anthropology, ethnology, and the social sciences. Triandis (1989) suggests that a country's culture is a key environmental force that shapes its people's perceptions, dispositions, and behaviours. The foremost Western explanation of culture is provided by Tylor (1871), who described culture as a complex whole comprising of knowledge, belief, art, morals, law, customs, and many other capabilities and habits.

These cultural beliefs and ways of life have developed slowly over time and are often averse to change. More recently, communities themselves have changed, with migration introducing new and distinct cultures. With this in mind, Flannery (1972) observed that cultural evolution provides a socio-environmental situation where increasing linearisation and meddling are high, and the end result is further centralisation. The resulting disappearance of some people's cultural values and the significance now attached to identity can create both an opportunity and a challenging agenda for many international events.

6.5.2 The good the bad and the ugly

Visitors, travellers, and migrants have a range of reactions to 'crossing cultures' when moving from one cultural environment to another (Davies and Fitchett, 2004). When crossing into a different culture, not only can the visitor bring new experiences, it is important that touring events take into consideration the culture of the societies where they are being hosted. Emotional stresses experienced when encountering new cultures can disorientate, undermining the ability to perform, and result in culture shock. People are used to their normal living environment and a sudden change can be bewildering if no proper preparation has been made. Ward (2001) described culture shock as the effect of psychological and social processes that are experienced through intercultural contact.

An individual's ability to deal with these cultural differences along with the absence of family and friends outside of their natural surroundings can have both positive and negative effects on their ability to do business. Doran (2002) considered the effects of cultural differences between East and West and suggested that visitors coming from an 'eastern culture' might experience high levels of culture shock when moving to a 'Western culture', and vice versa. Globalisation (Chapter 9), is of course reducing many of the cultural differences that exist, but even the growth of international influence does not fully erase the deeper cultural values. One's normal way of life can be affected by the massive, visible differences in income levels, education and spending.

Certainly, one of the good aspects of cultural development is when groups of cultures come together in their local communities to share their way of life and values. Such events go a long way to remove ignorance and promote understanding. Figure 6.2 is typical of a local event that highlights how

Figure 6.2 An event poster from a local event focusing on cultural inclusion

communities use their different cultures to bridge the gaps between them by coming together in planned events to learn from each other.

6.5.2.1 Trojan horses?

One of the most infamous stories in crossing borders and cultures is the tale of the Trojan horse when a giant horse of polished oak had been left outside the gates of Troy. Assuming it was a gift, the Trojans towed the giant horse inside (Philips and Whannel, 2013). Hidden inside were the troops of the Greek army, intent on opening up the city to invasion. The story aligns with international events as it signifies how the crossing of cultures brings more than what is initially evident or observable on the surface.

The touring of international events can add a great deal of risk to the project, particularly when the event is breaking boundaries. In these circumstances, not knowing what the reception will be at the other end can create a lot of apprehension. However, the effect of anticipated events can have much more extensive influences on the destination community. In some cases, new audiences have long awaited the arrival of visiting events based on these cultural influences that are enveloped into the event itself or when the hidden characteristics bring about deep levels of change. Touring bands from Western cultures have influenced less developed or restricted cultures through music, fashion and attitude.

The 1980s was a time when crossing a border to perform in certain countries was considered a political act. China, South Africa, the former USSR, and some

South American countries were all on a banned list to performers from the political West (McAlpine, 2018). Some academics believe that Western music opened the gates to many communities and led the way to cultural changes around the world. This wave of touring bands encouraged and nurtured the new sense of optimism, freedom, and individuality that was intensifying at the time. It also served as a means of protest against the failing Soviet regime (Lengyel, 2014). Previously, much music and many touring bands from the West had been banned from the nation. Alexei Yurchak the Russian emigré and author suggested that the policy backfired stating that 'the measures it proposed to curb the spread of Western music helped to create the conditions that enabled its further expansion' (Happy, 2016).

As well as breaking boundaries, music is well documented for causing revolutions and riots. A performance of Daniel Auber's opera 'La Muette de Portici' in 1830 in Brussels instigated a revolution that resulted in the secession of the southern portion of the Kingdom of the United Netherlands and the establishment of Belgium as an independent state (Loomis, 2012). The premier of Stravinsky's 'Rite of Spring' in Paris in 1913 allegedly caused a riot (Willshire, 2013) and Christian groups, primarily in the southern United States took to the streets to burn records of The Beatles in response to John Lennon's remark that the Beatles were 'more popular than Jesus' (Murrmann, 2014).

6.5.2.2 Cultural shift

The diversity and way of life of a particular nation, its different societies, and its people will impact on the types of events that are available in any given region. Respect for cultural diversity whether implicit or explicit is something that all international event organisers should be mindful of during the planning phase of an event. On a global level, this has become known as 'glocalisation', which is discussed in more detail in Chapter 9. However, glocalisation is about adjusting a product to accommodate the user or consumer in a local market, rather than respecting the much deeper-held values and customs international events encounter.

When events of any kind tour or visit foreign places, they are generally well accepted and pass without incident in and out of each territory they visit. An appraisal of cultural practices as borders are crossed is often unnecessary as mutual values exist in the territories being visited throughout the world. However, in some instances something considered conventional or acceptable in one nation may be considered illegal or insulting in another. In such cases significant effort is required to ensure that nationalistic interests are not provoked and local, cultural or national values are observed.

Different cultures can be disorientating when first experienced and the less democratic the political system, the more likely it is that problems will be experienced by the touring event at some point during the visit. Even in what have long been considered stable democracies, some people remain deeply concerned about a cultural threat from foreign visitors and actually have a sense of fear or hostility towards other cultures (McLaren, 2002).

In recent years, this cultural threat problem has been reignited with reactions to Donald Trump's presidential campaign under the slogan of 'America First' and the UK's decision to leave the European Union. These political developments appear to have incited deeper discrimination towards minority groups and have resulted in increased hate crimes, racist and homophobic attacks (Perraudin, 2019), the cancellation of events (Arthur, 2018), and the use of international events such as football matches for a return to violent and destructive behaviour, as well as expressions of far right extremism (Arnold and Veth, 2018; Georgiev, 2017; Horobin, 2016).

Even in local communities within Britain individuals have experienced a cultural shift due to the effects of political uncertainty and change. The effects of Brexit, the term used to describe Britain's exit from the EU is impacting on the multi-cultural expansion in some cities. One local individual commented:

> Racists have always been there, but Brexit seems to have brought out the really ugly side and made people feel more emboldened to actually come out with these really ugly views.
>
> (White, 2014)

Such developments in a nation's attitude to those considered foreigners or outsiders will impact on the plans of touring events. When the safety of anyone involved with the event is jeopardised, the organisers are forced to review the tour plans. Travelling or venue security arrangements will come under review if the organisers have good reason to believe the event can be attacked. For example, assaults on worshippers have increased in recent years with religious settings being easy targets for rogue attacks.

6.5.2.3 Symbolic borders, division, and symbolic actions

The crossing of a border, for most of the world, is a straightforward concept that requires time and some documentation to pass through. In many parts of Europe and Scandinavia, the process is often unnoticeable as physical borders between most European countries have been removed and only exist as lines on maps. An area known as the Schengen Area, named after the Schengen Agreement of 1985, signifies a zone where 26 different European nations acknowledge the abolishment of their internal borders for free and unrestricted movement in a drive towards continental integration (Schengen Visa Information, n.d.).

Cultural borders and differences can, however, exist in much smaller spaces when borders are more symbolic and serve to highlight tensions that exist or previously existed within the local community. Gated communities, peace lines, check points, and defensive walls have existed for millennia and often remain part of a city's impression. Many are ancient relics while others remain a visible or sometimes invisible boundary between political, sporting, and religious perspectives. Such divisions remain significant for international events as being associated with one side can exclude acceptance in another. Bridging this divide requires clear evidence of impartiality and the careful management of words and actions during the visit.

Similarly, crossing a border to take an international event to a disputed territory can have an adverse impact and create a hostile response that brings about global calls to boycott the event. For example, a group called the Boycott, Divestment, Sanctions or BDS movement works to end international support for Israel because of its policy towards Palestine. Any event planned to visit Israel will be scrutinised by the group and its supporters. Singers Lana Del Rey and Lorde both cancelled planned tours in 2018 after heeding calls from BDS campaigners not to perform in the country. Fashion designer Vivienne Westwood and Pink Floyd singer Roger Waters were among dozens of figures who urged the BBC to oppose Israel's hosting of the contest in Tel Aviv in 2019 (Osman, 2019). In France there were street demonstrations while anti-Israel protesters disrupted a live performance on French TV by the Israeli singer who had won the competition in 2018 (Pavia and Bremner, 2019).

6.5.3 Managing the cultural compromise

Distinctive cultures are evident throughout the world. However, they have never been restricted to their place of origin and cultural diversity is now a visible factor in every major city. As events are usually constructed around the ideas, beliefs, customs and social behaviour of the people who initiated them, cultural values can be vividly as well as unintentionally infused into an event. Individuals, groups, majorities and minorities can all instigate cultural events in the places they live.

It is not usually the intention of events to divide people or places, but overlooking cultural values is the first step to instigating a negative reaction. Some societies' abiding fight against the disappearance of traditions are well documented, none more so than for those of indigenous populations becoming minorities in the home states. The long-standing actions of the native Indians of America or the Aborigines of Australia are two prime examples. A number of indigenous groups have reacted to this evaporation of native culture by instigating their own events, reintroducing their culture to their now multi-cultural homelands. Many of these events have gone on to attract an outside, international audience.

A day of national celebration is something most countries hold to mark an occasion of importance for the people of the nation. These events are often a celebration of independence from or victory over another nation. Switzerland's National Day remembers the alliance formed in 1291 between the cantons Uri, Schwyz and Unterwalden as it began to gain independence from the Holy Roman Empire (Zimmer, 2000). Independence Day in the United States recognises the declaration of independence from the Kingdom of Great Britain in 1776 (Armitage, 2007). While these events are largely domestic occasions, the ongoing proceedings tend to attract an international audience, most notably through tourism and the visiting diaspora.

At the same time, some countries' national celebrations reveal how complicated the management of these events can be. Tacit knowledge in local communities can expose the varying levels of engagement in the way people celebrate the occasion. Symbolic interaction, as a sociological concept, presupposes that members of a group have their own detached individual perspective on how they should act in a given situation (Lal, 1995). Partisan and even xenophobic perspectives can be bottled up for a long time as the underlying reality remains contained in the privacy of the minority group's social interactions.

As the Western world becomes more appreciative of human rights and the right to individual expression, the views of these previously muted groups have begun to express the long-standing matters of identity more vocally. Highlighting these matters has reached many international events and the event organisers are thus faced with additional difficulties to overcome. Activists who reflect a growing disquiet from a minority group can create major challenges when the organisers overlook their concerns.

For example, after tensions had been rising for some time over a planned event, the port of Mangonui in the North Island of New Zealand banned a replica of Captain Cook's ship from docking. The occasion was part of the Tuia 250, which was a US$10 million series of events. The ship was meant to dock to mark 250 years since the explorer's arrival (Russell, 2019). Similarly, citizens of Australia have also reacted critically to the annual Australia Day celebrations on 26th January. Mackaness (1960) explains the date is the anniversary of the arrival of Captain Cook in Sydney, Australia, in 1788 with a fleet of eleven convict ships from Great Britain and the first governor of New South Wales. The raising of the Union Flag there symbolised British occupation of the eastern half of the continent. Kwan (2007) suggests the first ever recognition of the event by all the Australian territories was not until the sesquicentenary anniversary in 1938. The celebrations have always been seen to disregard the much broader communities that exist in the country and, of course, the indigenous population.

Aborigines and others with sympathetic values have always considered the day offensive and instead hold their own events to highlight an alternative perspective. Tippet (2009) explained that the 26th January 1938 was declared an Aboriginal Day of Mourning. Fifty years later it became known as Invasion Day or Survival Day. The controversy has gained momentum with protests against the date being held throughout the country. Chan (2017) suggests that the nation is in support of a day of celebration for the nation and that it should be called Australia Day. However, an alternative date that allows all Australians to celebrate without prejudice is going to be required for the day to be representative of the entire nation and its people.

6.5.4 Preconceived perspectives and perceptions

Perspectives on the different cultures, people and places around the world, both positive and negative, can be conceived or imagined. Different opinions of many cultures are based on historical facts of nations, political stability, hearsay, and even fake news. However, it is only when a place has been visited and the culture experienced first-hand that a real understanding of a place, its culture, and its people can develop. Carder and Machida (2017) go as far as to suggest that travelling not only increases social awareness, it enhances people's recognition of foreign affairs as an important issue. Figure 6.3 provides an indication of cultural expectations typical of a wedding ceremony in two vastly different cultures. Each of these events celebrates a lifetime achievement in very much the same way but relevant to their individual culture.

Figure 6.3 Cultural wedding DJs from India and Europe

6.6 Crossing borders

Crossing international borders can be challenging. Not only does the act stimulate emotions of anticipation, fear, anger, sadness, and joy, to do so with ease will require a lot of preparatory work. Even when everything is in order, delays are usually inevitable, particularly when the journey is for work purposes. Strict rules and laws mean that procedures have to be observed and paperwork has to be checked. For individual delegates going to conferences or trade shows, the experience should be very similar to a vacation. However, as soon as paid work, goods, and/or money become involved, the activity becomes much more complex and can be extremely complicated.

6.6.1 Getting there

Aside from the environmental issues which are discussed in Chapter 10, travelling abroad comes with a range of consequences and tensions that can be both positive and negative for those having to do the travelling. Alongside the already discussed experience of new cultures, the routine of life at home can be something that is craved to be absent from or anticipated to be assumed again. For many individuals who tour the world with events, both of these emotions are experienced simultaneously. There is the great desire to travel, while at the same time there is the emotion of being torn from family and friends and the safe social environment people call home. Of course, these emotions of desire will depend on a number of contributing factors which are discussed here.

To many individuals involved in touring with international events, the actual act of travelling itself can be one of the most stressful aspects of the occupation. Ivancevich *et al.* (2003) suggest that the individual and organisational reasons for travel influence the type and amount of stress with which business travellers contend. Even though travel is a central aspect of the job, delays, other people, and the lack of control mean that even the most travelled of international event organisers can still experience high levels of stress when crossing borders.

The more proficient event organiser with experience will have ways of reducing the amount of stress through their understanding of airports, routes, travel times, and the necessary preparations required before leaving home. Of course, the more successful an individual or business becomes, the more the company can spend on making the travelling experience less stressful. This might begin with purchasing the additional fast-track and excess baggage options, and taking advantage of online check-in prior to boarding aircraft to remove the hassle at check-in and the gate. For longer distances, there are business or first class flights, or the more privileged may hire limousines or charter private jets. However, with the growing sustainability debate which is discussed in more detail in Chapter 10, these investments are coming under intense scrutiny.

As well as the skills required to get smoothly from one place to another, the tour/event organiser/team is expected to possess the knowledge of how to transport everything that is required for the event. As with any occupation, the person undertaking the role of tour manager will be a specialist in the type of event involved. Knowing the pitfalls whilst getting to the location as well as the most appropriate means of travel for whatever is being transported is half the journey. What is being transported will depend on the type of international event. Generally, this can be broken down into three specific areas of care; the transport of people, equipment, and wildlife. The increased security procedures at airports have created much higher demands on travelling across borders and the more complicated the event content, i.e. people, equipment, wildlife and destination/s, the more intricate the travel plans and paperwork required.

Each country of origin will provide foreign travel advice for their citizens who need to visit another country with updates being regularly made on the destination. There are a number of risks that can change very quickly that would influence the advice. The most common include:

- Politics
- Weather
- Disasters/Force majeure
- Civil unrest, and
- Disease.

6.6.1.1 Politics

Political events in a given territory are usually predictable, but can still change very quickly. In these circumstances, the individuals' own government would normally provide advice or warnings on whether travel is advisable. Similarly, if an individual happens to already be there, advice on how safe it is to stay is normally quick to arrive.

6.6.1.2 Weather

As was discussed in Chapter 2, the weather can be devastating to events and, if anything is bound to change, it is probably the weather. However, weather forecasts have to be observed even though they usually include changeable conditions. For the weather to affect travel or the event itself, it would normally have to be extreme. With the technology available today, extreme weather such as storms, heatwaves, and downpours are generally predicted and then tracked for many weeks before they hit an area. Places that suffer from regular weather disruption, such as monsoons and droughts, can also be planned for in advance.

6.6.1.3 Disasters/force majeure

Disasters or force majeure are wholly unpredictable and cannot usually be factored into the travel plans. However, they should always be included in any legal documentation and contracts to avoid liability for any investment made by participants.

6.6.1.4 Civil unrest

Civil unrest does not usually affect international events unless of course the civil unrest is the international event being organised. Civil unrest in most cases is short-lived and often localised but can turn into an ongoing national situation. For example, during Hong Kong's Anti-Extradition Law Amendment Bill protests, international sporting events, pop concerts, fashion shows, and international conferences were all cancelled, postponed, or moved out of the semi-autonomous Chinese territory after months of demonstrations (Ng, 2019). Similarly, the Spanish venue IFEMA Feria de Madrid hosted the UN climate summit COP25 in 2019 after it was cancelled due to protests in Santiago, Chile. The organisers had just 18 days to stage the event which usually takes at least 18 months (Wood, 2019).

6.6.1.5 Disease

It remains the traveller's responsibility to have up-to-date information about the risks involved when travelling abroad. Anyone travelling, particularly to areas where there is a possibility of contracting an infection, should make all the necessary preparations to protect their health. This can include understanding seasonal threats, receiving preventative inoculations prior to travel for known hazards, and purchasing specialist repellents to protect from insect bites. Incidents of health in the events location such as a rapid spread of an infectious disease within a short period of time will force organisers to reconsider their travel plans. The World Health Organisation (WHO) provides regular updates on global health issues in order to prevent and control the effects of any infection spreading. The WHO advises all individuals planning travel to seek advice on the potential hazards in their chosen destinations and understand how best to protect their health and minimise the risk of acquiring disease. Forward planning, appropriate preventive measures and careful precautions can protect their health and minimise the risks of accident and of acquiring disease (WHO, 2019).

6.6.2 Transporting people

The event industry is heavily reliant on gatherings and face-to-face meetings. Therefore the need to travel is without question. Getting people to wherever the event is should not bring too much difficulty for the organisers; it is largely a case of ensuring the travel arrangements are all in place in good time. This can include purchasing tickets, arranging transfers, applying for visas, and making sure any travel restrictions are overcome.

Anyone travelling should ensure they have appropriate travel insurance before they travel. There are some restrictions on securing travel insurance that could affect the trip including: the age of the passenger, medical history, and the destination. For anyone travelling by air having to declare a manageable ailment, such as diabetes or asthma, a Fit to Fly certificate may be required. Pregnant women will also need a certificate to travel with most airlines after the 28th week of pregnancy. Most insurance companies provide detailed information on the different levels of cover and what certification may be needed before cover is issued.

As for the person who is travelling, organisers should be aware of restrictions that could be placed at the border. These include:

- An individual's religious or ideological belief
- The individual's health
- The individual's nationality
- The type of business
- Type of goods being transported as baggage, and
- A criminal record.

6.6.2.1 Religious and ideological belief

The level of travel restrictions placed on individuals due to their religious beliefs varies greatly. However, not all restrictions are enforced by the destination as they can also be imposed by the state of origin. In places where these restrictions exist, many can be overcome with special validations under very limited circumstances. The best-documented example in recent years of restrictions to travel based on a person's religious belief was the Presidential Proclamation 9645 for Protecting the Nation from Foreign Terrorist Entry into the United States. This proclamation restricted entry into the United States to seven Muslim-majority countries (Trump, 2017).

Travel restrictions have also been placed on individuals wishing to speak at events when the views or ideologies being expressed are considered controversial in the eyes of the governing power. These events can be considered as inciting violence which is a criminal offence. One of the prohibited actions under a global definition of terrorism is creating a serious risk to the health and safety of the public or any section of the public (Player *et al.*, 2002). Even for academic debate where freedom of speech is fundamental to the functioning of institutions, speakers can be stopped at the border when the fear of controversial and offensive ideas being advanced overrides the importance of the event.

6.6.2.2 The individual's health

For most international event organisers, travelling and an individual's health are not a major cause for concern as only the obvious health issues will restrict the ability to travel. Some ailments may only restrict the traveller from flying, such as deep vein thrombosis, chronic obstructive pulmonary disease, risk of stroke or recent surgery. In such cases, if travel is necessary for individuals in these circumstances, alternative forms of travel would have to be arranged. Otherwise, the only other restriction would be if the individual contracted an infectious disease prior to travel. In situations where a global threat to people's health is possible, intensive monitoring of the circumstances is required. Considering coughing and sneezing in crowded public places, can exacerbate the risk of spreading any virus, international events can become no go zones from a public health perspective and cancellation becomes a serious consideration for the organisers. International events can be the cause of turning an epidemic into a pandemic.

In the worst cases, viruses that are deemed zoonotic, meaning they are transmitted between animals and people, have the potential to bring the international event industry to a standstill. In late 2019, the coronavirus or COVID-19 pandemic that began in Wuhan in the Chinese province of Hubei forced the cancellation of many major international events in 2020. In these circumstances, it is very difficult to know who may be infected and the event organisers have very little time to respond to the threat. Delegates with the virus may be unaware at the point of travel that they are infected.

In one such case, the cancellation of the event came about because of the organisers' attempts to allay concerns about the spread of the virus at their event. By announcing stringent health and safety measures that included a ban on handshakes, and taking attendees' temperatures upon arrival, the Mobile World Congress in Barcelona fell victim to its own precautions. The event was expecting more than 100,000 delegates from 200 countries across the four days of the conference. However, on news of the planned health and safety measures, the biggest names in mobile communications who had been monitoring the situation pulled out forcing the whole event to be cancelled (Sweeney, 2020).

6.6.2.3 The individual's nationality

There is no doubt that while the business world of international events is global, we still live in a world of restricted movement. Every individual will hold a passport or identity card and these are checked on leaving and entering a country to make sure a person is legally entitled to cross the border. If the journey is permissible, all travel documents must be valid for the whole duration of the trip and penalties are imposed on those who do not comply with any of the many potential constraints. There are restrictions to entry in every country around the world. Therefore, an individual's nationality is the only way to know if the person is restricted from entering another country.

What might appear to be a straightforward trip for a member of the event team can change if the individual is not in possession of a particular passport and/or visa. This is also discussed in Chapter 3. The colour of a passport can mean the difference between a relatively straightforward passage through customs and borders, or additional delays, or even being refused entry without additional documentation. With this in mind, those eligible will hold and travel with more than one passport for ease of movement across different borders. For many regular international travellers with dual nationality and expatriates, obtaining an additional driver's licence can be beneficial. However, even in the 21st century, if the individual is not white, there will be stories to be told from the travel experience. For example, on a recent trip, the Olympic legend Mo Farah was the victim of racial discrimination. Flying back from the Rio games he was sent to the back of the queue by an airline official who, according to his wife, refused to believe he had a business class ticket (Onuzo, 2016).

For anyone wanting to avoid the need for a visa, data indicates that an individual currently needs to hold passports for 14 countries to have access to the whole world (Henley & Partners Passport Index, 2019a). These are: Afghanistan, Angola, Azerbaijan, Republic of Congo, Mali, Maldives, North Korea, Singapore, Syria, Turkmenistan, Turkey, Uganda, United States, and Vanuatu.

The passport the individual holds can be very significant at the border as different countries have different arrangements with each other. The number of countries that can be visited without a visa by an individual depends on the passport-issuing country's arrangements throughout the world with other countries. Table 6.1 indicates the countries ranked by the Henley Passport Index as the top ten at the beginning of 2020. This is the original ranking of all the world's passports, with each scored according to the number of destinations their holders can access without the need of a prior visa.

6.6.2.4 The type of business

In the event industry, there are a number of circumstances that will affect an individual's ability to travel unrestricted across a country's border particularly in the event of trade barriers on certain products. International trade barriers place restrictions on the import and export of certain products which affect trade and the exhibitions and events that go with them.

While political events are regularly accompanied by protestors, and sporting bodies place restrictions on the movement of supporters, the trading of certain products at events can also add complications for the organisers. For example, 116 people were arrested for offences including aggravated trespass and obstruction of the highway at Europe's biggest arms fair, Defence & Security Equipment International (DSEI) in London in 2019. The event connects governments, national

Table 6.1 Henley Passport Index scores

Rank	Country	Score	Rank	Country	Score
1	Japan	189	6	Belgium	183
	Singapore			Canada	
2	Finland	187		Greece	
	Germany			Ireland	
	South Korea			Norway	
3	Denmark	186		United Kingdom	
	Italy			United States	
	Luxembourg		7	Malta	182
4	France	185	8	Czech Republic	181
	Spain		9	Australia	180
	Sweden			Iceland	
5	Austria	184		Lithuania	
	Netherlands			New Zealand	
	Portugal		10	Latvia	179
	Switzerland			Slovakia	
				Slovenia	

Source: Based on Henley & Partners Passport Index, 2019b

armed forces, and the global defence and security supply chain and attracts some 35,000 delegates and exhibitors to the Excel Centre in London for the biennial trade show which has long been a focus for protestors (Sabbagh, 2019).

6.6.2.5 Type of goods being transported as baggage

As long as the goods being transported are not restricted at the point of exit or entry, it is possible to transport almost anything as baggage. What can be transported depends on where the journey begins and where it ends. What can be transported for free depends on what it is and the total weight of baggage. There are long haul and short haul variations, but if in doubt it is advisable to declare the items to customs.

All countries provide a duty-free allowance on a number of items that is largely designed for personal consumption. Banned or restricted goods such as meat, dairy or plant-based products will need to be declared and require extra documentation for entry, all of which needs to be presented at the time of travel. It is normal for the goods being transported for events to return with the travellers, but if any items are carried for sale, a duty will have to be paid.

It is possible to carry cash across a border, but all countries will also impose a restriction on the amount of cash that can be carried without needing to be declared. The EU restriction is €10,000 while the United States has a $10,000 restriction. Any larger amounts will require extra documentation to be presented.

6.6.2.6 A criminal record

One of the clarification points at job interviews is if applicants have a criminal record. For international events there are a number of circumstances where this could be problematic, particularly when international travel is involved. People with criminal records are not usually barred from entering a country. However, it is important to know if a criminal record would determine the right of entry and if the criminal record demands the need for an entry visa.

Any country that does require an entry visa in the events destination list will ask in the documentation whether the applicant has a criminal record. The applicant will have to state the nature of the offence and the consequences in the visa application.

Every country provides detailed information on what is required from an individual to gain entry through their border security whether a visa is required or not. The USA, for example, currently advises the following for people who have been arrested by any law enforcement agency:

> We do not recommend that travelers who have been arrested, even if the arrest did not result in a criminal conviction, have a criminal record, certain serious communicable illness, have been refused admission into, or have been deported from, the United States, or have previously overstayed under the terms of the Visa Waiver Program, attempt to travel visa free under the Visa Waiver Program. The Rehabilitation of Offenders Act does not apply to US visa law and spent convictions, regardless of when they occurred, will have a bearing on a traveler's eligibility for admission into the United States.
>
> (US Embassy & Consulates in the UK, n.d.)

6.6.3 Transporting equipment

In this case, equipment is the collective term for all the tangible items an international event requires. Whether an event company is exhibiting at a trade show or touring as part of a live show, getting the necessary equipment through the various customs and border checks is something all international event organisers will have to prepare for well in advance.

A rule of thumb is that, for most international events, large items are provided by the event organiser as part of the event in the host country. This includes stands and furniture for exhibitions, PA and lighting systems, and backline for music events which consists of amplifiers and drum kits. The exhibitor or touring band would then bring their own personal items or products to complete the set-up for the show. However, this is not always the case and in many cases, the whole show needs to be transported around the world.

Many items will travel as cargo and, if the event company is not transporting the equipment themselves, many international carriers specialise in the transportation of different types of equipment the event or the participant would use. The driver of the vehicle is legally responsible for the safety of the vehicle and any load being carried. The insurance policy for the vehicle should include cover for the carriage of dangerous goods.

Motor sports employ teams of technicians whose job is not only to maintain the equipment, but also to transport it and set it up at the venue. Some of the items being transported will be on the list of restricted goods. Prohibited goods cannot pass through the border, while restricted items require special licences or permits before being allowed through. While the list of prohibited items is too long to cover, a good example is the many thousands of gas cylinders transported for international events. Individuals providing concessions travel to international events every day without incident. International sporting competitors use caravans and motorhomes to travel to competitions. They will also have experienced the need to declare the type of gas being carried at seaports and the regulations during the event. In the UK, everyone carrying gas cylinders in a vehicle in the course of their work has to follow basic legal safety requirements (BCGA, 2017). Figure 6.4 shows the various types of labelling a vehicle must display.

Certain international events can take advantage of sharing baggage through the use of marine fares which allow 40kg instead of 20kg. Event organisers have been known to use one container for personal use and another for transporting equipment. Marine fares extend beyond the ship's crew and include staff employed to work on a vessel such as entertainers. For touring events, the added baggage can assist with support for the maintenance team.

Exhibitions often include bulky items which in many cases have to be transported ahead of the individuals travelling. The biggest touring bands not only have a number of articulated lorries loaded with musical equipment; they will have the lighting, sound, and stage designed and in the more extreme cases have all of this built specifically for the tour. Exhibitors may also carry samples of their goods in their baggage through customs to get them to the show. Each country will have its own rules on what goods can be taken over a border

| Category 1 | Category 2 | Category 3 | Category 3 |

Transport category	Hazardous property	UN Division	Examples of industrial gases in category
1	Toxic	2.3	N/A
2	Flammable	2.1	Acetylene, hydrogen, propane, propylene.
3	Asphyxiant	2.2	Argon, carbon dioxide, compressed air, helium, nitrogen
	Oxidizing		Oxygen
4	Empty cylinders		

Figure 6.4 Vehicle labelling when carrying gases
Source: Based on British Compressed Gases Association, 2017

Figure 6.5 The U2 360° tour stage, Croke Park Dublin, 2009

Source: Strobech, 2009

crossing (imports and exports), whether they be transported with a specialist company as cargo or with an individual traveller as baggage.

The biggest investment in transporting equipment for international events belongs to the music industry. U2 currently hold the record for the most expensive stage in touring history that saw the show staged 110 times over 13 months in five continents and watched by over 7 million spectators (Wikipedia, n.d.). Figure 6.5 shows the stage in question with its integrated sound and lighting system.

Once an act becomes known for their live show, the effort and expense dedicated to providing a spectacular for the audience is almost unstoppable. These events tend to utilise sports stadia to maximise the capacity while at the same time ensuring the infrastructure required to host such large audiences is already in place. A number of major artists have individual stage designs contributing to some of the largest and most costly stages ever constructed. Table 6.2 lists the most recent top five.

6.6.3.1 ATA Carnets and other in-transit issues

Whichever means of travel is used, bureaucratic issues are arguably the most complicated to deal with when crossing borders, particularly as border controls take the process of imports and their contents very seriously. Mistakes in a consignment can be highlighted by customs officers creating delays to onward travel or preventing access to their release.

Customs difficulties and delays are considerably reduced by presenting an ATA Carnet at the border with the goods in transit. An ATA Carnet is an international customs document currently recognised in 78 countries. Virtually all types of goods can be transported under the ATA Carnet, from commercial

Table 6.2 Most expensive tour stages to date

	Artist	Tour Name	Cost
1	U2	360° Tour	US$23–31 million per set-up
2	Roger Waters	The Wall Tour	US$10 million per set-up
3	Madonna	Sticky And Sweet Tour	US$2 million per show
4	The Rolling Stones	A Bigger Bang Tour	US$1.6 million per set-up
5	Lady Gaga	Born This Way Ball	US$1 million per set-up

Source: Based on Drughi, 2014

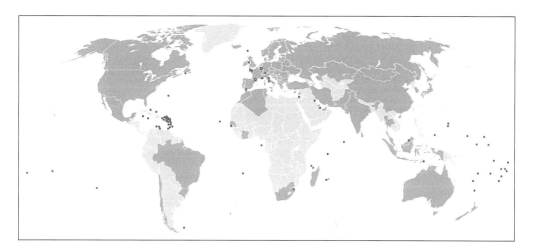

Figure 6.6 Member countries of the ATA Carnet system
Source: Acosta, 2019

samples, professional equipment to goods for exhibitions. Goods for exhibitions are often limited by some countries to a maximum travel time outside of the state of origin.

The ATA Carnet document is essentially a declaration of the goods or equipment being transported with the guarantee they are not for export and will be returned. Figure 6.6 shows the member countries of the ATA Carnet system in dark shading with a dot to highlight the smaller nations. It assists the likes of touring musicians, conference and exhibition attendees, designers, and manufacturers to speed through customs with free entry of commercial samples, professional equipment, and goods for exhibitions and fairs (Boomerang Carnets, n.d). It is essentially a temporary exportation licence for goods that circumvent customs payments and charges.

As can be seen from the data in Figure 6.6, the countries of the ATA Carnet system are spread across the world. Carnets apply to most non-perishable goods, providing the event organiser with an easier entry, exit, re-entry experience. The length of time for coverage may vary, but a standard length of time allows for 12 months' coverage across participating countries worldwide. The list of participating countries is detailed in Table 6.3.

Table 6.3 Member countries of the ATA Carnet system, 2019

Sint Maarten (The Netherlands)	European Union	Liechtenstein (Switzerland)	Reunion Island (France)
Albania	Faroe Islands (Denmark)	Lithuania*	Romania*
Algeria	Finland*	Luxembourg*	Russia
Andorra	France*	Macao, China	Saipan
Antarctica	French Guiana	Macedonia	Senegal
Aruba (The Netherlands)	French Polynesia – Tahiti	Madagascar	Serbia
Australia	Germany*	Madeira (Portugal)	Singapore
Austria*	Gibraltar	Malaysia	Slovakia*
Azores (Portugal)	Greece*	Malta*	Slovenia*
Bahrain, Kingdom of	Greenland (Denmark)	Martinique	South Africa
Balearic Islands (Spain)	Guadeloupe (France)	Mauritius	South Korea
Belarus	Guam	Mayotte (France)	Spain*
Belgium*	Guernsey (UK)	Melilla (Spain)	Sri Lanka
Bosnia & Herzegovina	Hong Kong	Mexico	St. Barthelemy (France)
Botswana	Hungary*	Miquelon (France)	St. Pierre (France)
Brazil	Iceland	Moldova	Swaziland (SACU)
Bulgaria*	India	Monaco (France)	Sweden*
Canada	Indonesia	Mongolia	Switzerland
Canary Islands	Iran	Montenegro	Tahiti (France)
Ceuta	Ireland*	Morocco	Taiwan
Chile	Isle of Man (UK)	Namibia (SACU)	Tasmania (Australia)
China	Israel	Netherlands*	Thailand
Corsica (France)	Italy*	New Caledonia (France)	Tunisia
Cote d'Ivoire	Ivory Coast	New Zealand	Turkey
Croatia*	Japan	Norway	Ukraine
Curacao	Jersey (UK)	Pakistan	United Arab Emirates
Cyprus*	Kazakhstan	Poland*	United Kingdom
Czech Republic*	Latvia*	Portugal*	United States
Denmark*	Lebanon	Puerto Rico (USA)	Wallis & Futuna (France)
Estonia*	Lesotho (SACU)	Qatar	

Source: boomerangcarnets.co.uk, 2019

Key

* Member state of the European Union (EU). No carnet is necessary for travelling within the EU countries. If goods are properly imported into one EU carnet country and re-exported from a different EU carnet country, the carnet holder is unlikely to encounter any claims fees.

** Taiwan requires a separate carnet called an EC-CPD-China-Taiwan-carnet.

Country names in brackets represent the responsible nation

SACU: South African Customs Union

Dealing with the transportation of goods for international events is complicated to begin with, but once the process is understood, it is possible to turn things around very quickly. A good example of this is international cruises. Cruise ships are a permanent source of international events and will deal with the complications of customs and border control paperwork every time they enter a port. With changeovers often governed by the tide, the procedure can begin at any time. A military style operation is needed to line up every vehicle to check, load, and sign off, in the region of 100 tonnes of food and drink to last an average-sized ship for a week.

6.6.3.2 Post border matters

Once the joys of border control have been completed, the event organisers should be through the worst of the challenges as communication from thereon in tends to be with other persons involved in the event. However, nothing should ever be taken for granted when on foreign soil and there may be a number of other surprises to contend with.

Some countries are very strict on the use of foreign nationals being used to carry out work. Workers unions may have to be dealt with and agreements made to allow the event to go ahead. Unions can be very strict on trades and skilled workers and want to know why a local skilled worker is not being employed. This has led to incidents of union representatives standing next to the camera operators at sporting events in order to allow them to film the event.

Visas have been discussed earlier in the chapter, but a common problem encountered by event organisers is salaried members of staff travelling abroad on a tourist visa whilst working for the company. It appears to be logical and less expensive to do, but working even when not taking money from the destination country has caused problems for the event organisers in many countries. For conference attendees and exhibitors, this situation should not arise as many countries today have separate entry regulations for these or waive the visa fees associated with the usual methods of trade.

In recent years, international events have had the added concern of contemporary piracy and armed robbery against ships. The threat of attack has severely affected these events as sailing into foreign water, particularly off the coast of Somalia, is very dangerous as it has been considered a no-go area for international shipping since around 1998 (Sterio, 2010). An area known as an anti-piracy 'stealth zone' now exists and all vessels navigating in the vicinity are advised to exercise extreme caution. Armed security patrols are known to be present to offer protection to international shipping, but considering the Arabian Sea's surface area is approximately 3,862,000km^2 (Morgan, Aleem and Verlaan, 2007), protecting the crew on a vessel that measures around 23m cannot be sufficiently achieved in any risk assessment.

One of the greatest problems for the organisers is the loss of income from some of the wealthiest nations who would normally be included as a stopping point in sailing competitions around the world. In 2012, the Volvo Round the World Yacht Race had to change the rules of the competition in order to avoid a clash with pirates.

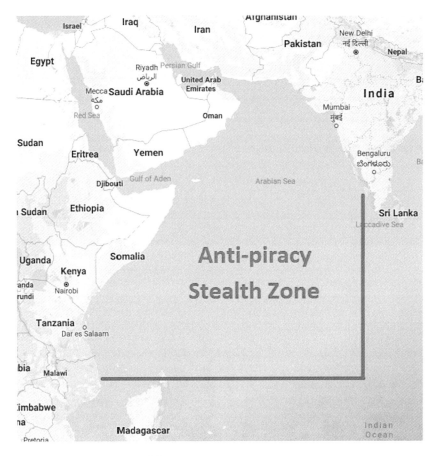

Figure 6.7 The anti-piracy Stealth Zone
Source: Author, using Google Maps

Abu Dhabi was one of the main sponsors for the race and a stopover at the city was central to the race itinerary. After leaving Cape Town for Abu Dhabi, the race organisers avoided the pirate issue by secretly changing the destination port to an island in the Maldives. Once all the yachts had arrived in port, they were loaded onto an armed ship and escorted into the Gulf of Oman for a sprint to Abu Dhabi (DNews, 2012).

Figure 6.7 shows the area of the Stealth Zone and highlights the size of the problem facing the security guards as well as the many nations who take part in sailing events. It also provides an indication of the nations who are most likely not to contribute to any international sailing event.

6.6.4 Transporting animals, animal bi-products and flora

Many international events require the transportation of animals, animal bi-products and flora. Many event businesses have live animal mascots who travel as part of events, while it is rare to see an international event that has not been decorated in live flora. Just like humans, animals will require a passport, health documents, insurance, and any documents demanded by the destination to travel overseas. Some organisations go further and insist on the animal being microchipped. There are a great deal of extra restrictions and care involved when transporting all of these products.

6.6.4.1 Animals and animal bi-products

The most common form of animal transport is equine, and, although banned from doing so in the UK, circuses elsewhere have collections of wild animals which they need to transport. International fishing competitors sometimes carry live bait which will need to be declared, museums transport taxidermy for exhibitions, and some events around the world still provide game trophies as prizes.

The act of mounting real bones, horns, hooves, claws, antlers, or teeth still exists as does the giving of prizes made out of animal hide. These need evidence to confirm sufficient processing has been undertaken to render them non-infectious and that they were legally killed. Trophies and taxidermy are subject to inspection for sanitary purposes. Even musical instruments come under these restrictions, particularly percussion instruments made from animal hide and other bi-products. The result of inspections may lead to quarantine, seizure or even the item being destroyed.

Whether the animal is dead or alive, it is a complicated subject from a global perspective and each country's laws and regulations should be considered prior to travel. Accepting a trophy acceptable in one country may cause the winner some problems at the border and at home. In the EU, regulations (EC) No. 1069/2009 and (EU) No. 142/2011 establish the requirements for the importation into the EU of game trophies of birds and ungulates that have not undergone a complete taxidermy treatment. This regulation sets out the health rules as regards animal bi-products and derived products not intended for human consumption (EU, 2009).

Every year, thousands of horses will travel all over the world for equine sports to get to their competition destination. These sports include: horse riding, show jumping, dressage, eventing, and polo. As the distance travelled has increased in recent years, many major airports are fitted out with specialised facilities for livestock transportation. Owners even have the opportunity to choose business or first class for the precious four-legged cargo (Rockefeller, 2018).

In the United States, passports are primarily intended for animals competing in International Federation for Equestrian Sports (FEI) events. It is a legal requirement in both Great Britain and Ireland for all equines to be issued with a passport. The legislation is different between the countries, but they share common principles (Weatherbys, n.d.).

One of the most common and important consequences that both animals and humans experience during transport is motion sickness (Santurtun and Phillips, 2015). Airlines have strict live animal regulations set by the International Air Transport Association (IATA). IATA's Live Animal Regulations constitute the worldwide standard for transporting live animals by commercial airlines. Whether it is a pet, an animal transported for zoological or agricultural purposes or for any other reason, the objective is to ensure all animals are transported safely and humanely by air (IATA, n.d.).

6.6.4.2 Flora

International events use plants, flowers, and all sorts of vegetation for design and presentation purposes. It is normal practice for these to be sourced locally, but there is often the need to source some products direct meaning some international transportation will be required. In the EU, many types of flora can be transported unrestricted, as long as they were grown in an EU country, and are visibly free of pests and diseases.

With the availability of many professional growers, the possibility of spreading disease is somewhat reduced. However, the disease itself is not capable of distinguishing between good, bad, professional or otherwise. Therefore, it is up to the professional growers to ensure their products remain disease-free and for the event organiser to ensure inspections are carried out and to ensure the proper paperwork is supplied for the transporting process.

It is impossible for many international event businesses to trade without travelling internationally. However, transportation is a real dilemma from a sustainability perspective, and the way the industry deals with this aspect of business is an example of the seriously underestimated sustainable targets (SUST) the industry must address. This and other sustainability issues are discussed in more detail in Chapter 10.

6.7 The aftershow party

Being involved with international events usually requires extremely long days and busy nights and being away from home demands an occupied mind when there is free time at one's disposal. Sightseeing and experiencing the local culture is a key part of life on the road, but once the event or gig is over, there is often a second wind of energy which requires some additional activity. It is usual to hold an aftershow party somewhere near to the event.

For some touring events, the aftershow is held after each gig while others prefer to have a single official event on the last night of the tour or at the end of a particular run. However, some international event organisers now see an aftershow party as a means of generating further revenue from fans happy to pay for tickets to attend and meet the cast and crew.

As a general rule, the aftershow party is largely a secret event within an event that is arranged for the cast and crew to have a bit of a blowout after the constant professionalism shown during the tour and for the band or cast to mingle socially with the rest of the team. A select number of others are invited along to create a more social and less formal gathering.

Conference and exhibition organisers, on the other hand, will usually invite delegates to their stand towards the end of the day and continue to do business in a much more relaxed and social manner. Free beer and snacks are standard, and sometimes some music is provided by a professional DJ or band. Figure 6.8 indicates just how much fun these gatherings can become.

Figure 6.8 The Norwegian stand after a long day at IMEX 2018

6.8 Summary

This chapter has discussed the various complications an event will come across when crossing borders and experiencing different cultures. It has discussed the ways in which cultures and borders can be plainly evident as well as remain invisible. The chapter also discussed how important it is for the organisers to prepare well in advance to ensure the event and all its elements are successfully transported to and from one culture to another as well as preparing for the changes the event and staff will have to adapt to when they are away from the customs of their usual habitat.

Case study 6.1 Navigating corruption on an international tour

As part of a promotional tour for a new album, a very famous UK band, Queen, were touring South America in early 1981 at the height of their career. The tour manager said likening it to an attempt to climb the north face of Mount Everest was putting it mildly; it was something of a challenge. The tour started in Buenos Aires, Argentina, where the initial meetings had to be with the then president and military dictator Roberto Eduardo Viola, who at the time was in prison. Naturally, the president's great worry was the mass gathering of people. What would happen if hundreds of thousands of people were to get together in a stadium? Having satisfied the president that the event was a much more contented gathering than he had envisioned, the gig was approved and the manager set about bringing things together to make it happen.

A number of the countries in South America were under military dictatorship at the time, and mob law ruled in many provinces. On another leg of the tour in Brazil, the head of security in Sao Paulo was said to have introduced himself by stating he had killed 206 people. The band had also learnt that the seizure of equipment in Brazil was a problem, as that of another band, Earth Wind & Fire, had been seized the year before – which Queen were then offered the use of upon arrival in the country! Having brought their own equipment, what were the crew going to do to get Queen's own, legitimate equipment back out of the country once it had been brought in?

Local promoters did not always do things as planned and re-negotiating a deal when someone is in possession of your most valuable equipment is a very unusual position to be in. However, an opportunity arose that would see the band and their valuable equipment safely out of the country.

The venue was next to the main airport and whilst the local promoter was busy stealing the artificial turf that had been brought in from America, the band's crew began loading up the equipment immediately after the gig. By 8am the following morning all of it had been safely removed and when the meeting took place the next morning to finally negotiate some kind of settlement and payment, the promoter suddenly realised that their major leverage – the band's equipment – had left whilst his people were busy stealing the fake grass.

Questions

1. Were the band's management too bold in their approach to completing the tour?
2. Should the tour have gone ahead in the first place?
3. Could the band's management team have done anything to improve the situation?
4. The record company usually plays a major role in the promotion of its artists. What role do you think they played in this situation?
5. How much do you think demand played in booking the tour?

Case study 6.2 Cultural oversight

Runcorn is an industrial town, an oil and cargo port, and the home of a large social network of canal barges that have been part of the local community for nearly 200 years. The canal and the barges are a quaint reflection of the town's previous industrial and cultural heritage. To some, the canal barges are considered an elite form of recreation due to the cost to purchase, maintain and moor a barge.

During a recent exchange between a delegation of civil servants from China who were due to visit this particular English town, a meeting was held by the local council to decide where the best accommodation would be to house the Chinese during their visit.

The councillors decided it would be a wonderful cultural experience to use the canal barges to house the visiting Chinese delegation. The decision was based on the local perception of a canal barge-stay as an indulgent luxury and the cost of hiring a canal barge for a week in comparison to the limited number of quality hotels in the city. The council overlooked the fact that many Chinese consider boat people as the lowest in society and saw the choice of accommodation as an insult.

Questions

1. What could the council have done to ensure the accommodation was culturally appropriate without insulting their guests?
2. Should the Chinese delegation have embraced the opportunity to experience the local culture and overlooked their own cultural misgivings?
3. If the visit was reversed, what might be the worst type of accommodation a Chinese authority could offer a European delegation?

6.9 Useful websites

List of ATA Carnet countries
https://iccwbo.org/resources-for-business/ata-carnet/ata-carnet-country/

Henley & Partners visa index
www.henleypassportindex.com/passport

WHO Emergencies preparedness, response
www.who.int/csr/en/

Guidance for the carriage of gas cylinders on vehicles
www.bcga.co.uk/assets/publications/GN27.pdf

US Customs and Border Protection: prohibited and restricted goods
www.cbp.gov/travel/us-citizens/know-before-you-go/prohibited-and-restricted-items

Fit to fly – Civil Aviation Authority guidance
www.caa.co.uk/Passengers/Before-you-fly/Am-I-fit-to-fly-/

References

Acosta, C. A. (2019). Mapa de los países que usan el cuaderno ATA. Retrieved from https://en.wikipedia.org/wiki/ATA_Carnet#/media/File:ATA-carnet_Map-World.svg Accessed 13th September 2019.

Armitage, D. (2007). *The Declaration of Independence a Global History.* Cambridge, MA: Harvard University Press.

Arnold, R., & Veth, K. M. (2018). Racism and Russian football supporters' culture: A case for concern? *Problems of Post-Communism, 65*(2), 88–100. doi:10.1080/10758216.2017.1414613

Arthur, A. (2018). Morrissey postpones all UK and Europe tour dates because of logistical problems, *The Independent.* Retrieved from www.independent.co.uk/arts-entertainment/music/morrissey-tour-cancel-manchester-uk-europe-postpone-a8423871.html Accessed 24th April 2019.

Boomerang Carnets (n.d). ATA Carnet Countries – Where Can An ATA Carnet Be Used? Retrieved rom: www.boomerangcarnets.co.uk/carnet-countries Accessed 17th September 2019.

British Compressed Gases Association (BCGA) (2017). *Guidance Note 27: Guidance for the Carriage of Gas Cylinders on Vehicles, Revision 2: 2017.* Retrieved from www.bcga.co.uk/assets/publications/GN27.pdf Accessed 20th September 2019.

Carder, K., & Machida, S. (2017). Does international travel boost one's interest in foreign policy? Attitude change among tourists. *Tourism Culture & Communication, 17*(3), 201–216.

Chan, G. (2017). Most indigenous Australians want date and name of Australia Day changed, poll finds. *The Guardian.* Retrieved from www.theguardian.com/australia-news/2017/jan/26/most-indigenous-australians-want-date-and-name-of-australia-day-changed-poll-finds Accessed 10th July 2017.

Davies, A., & Fitchett, J. A. (2004). 'Crossing culture': a multi-method enquiry into consumer behaviour and the experience of cultural transition. *Journal of Consumer Behaviour, 3*(4), 315–330. doi:10.1002/cb.145

DNews (2012). How to avoid pirates while sailing in a round-the-world race (no, seriously). Retrieved from www.seeker.com/how-to-avoid-pirates-while-sailing-in-a-round-the-world-race-no-seriou-1765618380.html Accessed 19th September 2019.

Doran, K. (2002). Lessons learned in cross-cultural research of Chinese and North American consumers. *Journal of Business Research, 55*(10), 823–829. doi:10.1016/s0148-2963(00)00222-8

Drughi, O. (2014). Rock on! The most expensive concert stages ever. Retrieved from www.therichest.com/most-expensive/rock-on-the-most-expensive-concert-stages-ever/ Accessed 13th September 2019.

European Union (EU) (2009). Document 32009R1069. Retrieved from https://eur-lex.europa.eu/legal-content/EN/ALL/?uri=CELEX%3A32009R1069 Accessed 19th September 2019.

Flannery, K. V. (1972). The cultural evolution of civilizations. *Annual Review of Ecology and Systematics, 3*, 399–426.

Georgiev, G. G. (2017). 'Soccer hooligans, ethnic nationalism and political economy in Bulgaria'. Culminating Project in Social Responsibility. St. Cloud State University, Bulgaria.

Happy (2016). Check out this list of bands that were banned in the Soviet Union during the 1980s. Retrieved from https://happymag.tv/check-out-this-list-of-bands-that-were-banned-in-the-soviet-union-during-the-1980s/ Accessed 21st September 2017.

Henley & Partners Passport Index (2019a). Access the world. Retrieved from www.henleypassportindex.com/access-the-world Accessed 18th September 2019.

Henley & Partners Passport Index (2019b). The Henley Passport Index Q3 Update July 2019. Retrieved from www.henleypassportindex.com/assets/2019/Q3/HPI%20 Report%20190701.pdf Accessed 18th September 2019.

Horobin, W. (2016). France moves to stem more soccer violence between Russia, England fans. *The Wall Street Journal*. https://www.wsj.com/articles/ france-prepares-for-more-soccer-violence-as-russia-england-fans-return-1465996157

Human Relations Area Files (HRAF) (2017). Outline of World Cultures List. Retrieved from http://hraf.yale.edu/resources/reference/outline-of-world-cultures-list/ Accessed 31st July 2017.

International Air Transport Association (IATA) (n.d.). Live animals. www.iata.org/ whatwedo/cargo/live-animals/Pages/index.aspx Accessed 20th August 2017.

Ivancevich, J. M., Konopaske, R., & Defrank, R. S. (2003). Business travel stress: A model, propositions and managerial implications. *Work and Stress, 17*(2), 138–157. doi:10.1080/0267837031000153572

Kwan, E. (2007). Celebrating Australia Day. www.australiaday.org.au/storage/ celebratingaustralia.pdf Accessed 17th July 2017.

Lal, B. B. (1995). Symbolic interaction theories. *American Behavioral Scientist, 38*(3), 421–441. doi:10.1177/0002764295038003005

Lengyel, A. (2014). Behind the Iron Curtain: Western music and the Soviet collapse. Retrieved from https://blogs.lt.vt.edu/aalrussia2014/2014/12/07/behind-the-iron-curtain-Western-music-and-the-soviet-collapse/ Accessed 20th Auguest 2018.

Loomis, G. (2012). The libretto that started a revolution. *The New York Times*. Retrieved from www.nytimes.com/2012/04/11/arts/11iht-loomis11.html Accessed 17th September 2019.

Mackaness, G. (1960). Australia Day. *Royal Australian Historical Society Journal, 45*(5).

McAlpine, F. (2018). 6 controversial gigs that broke cultural boycotts. Retrieved from www.bbc.co.uk/music/articles/8e3d9eb6-4d3d-4b76-8e54-dcf5bc188958 Accessed 17th September 2019.

McLaren, L. (2002). Public support for the European Union: Cost/benefit analysis or perceived cultural threat? *Journal of Politics, 64*(2), 551–566.

Morgan, J. R., Aleem, A. A., Verlaan, P. A. (2007). Arabian Sea. www.britannica.com/ place/Arabian-Sea Accessed 19th September 2019.

Murrmann, M. (2014). Burn your Beatles records! Retrieved from www.motherjones. com/politics/2014/08/burn-beatles-records-lennon-jesus/ Accessed 17th September 2019.

Ng, E. (2019). International events postponed as protests continue in Hong Kong. Retrieved from www.csmonitor.com/World/Asia-Pacific/2019/0913/International-events-postponed-as-protests-continue-in-Hong-Kong Accessed 14th September 2019.

Odello, M. (2012). Indigenous peoples' rights and cultural identity in the inter-American context. *The International Journal of Human Rights, 16*(1), 25–50. doi:10.1080/ 13642987.2011.597747

OED (2016). *Oxford English Dictionary online*. https://www-oed-com.ezproxy.wlv.ac.uk/ Accessed 12th December 2018.

Onuzo, C. (2016). Welcome to the world of restricted travel, British people, *The Guardian*. www.theguardian.com/commentisfree/2016/sep/13/restricted-travel-british-people-nigerian-visa-passports

Osman, N. (2019). Crazy for Eurovision? Madonna faces backlash over performance in Israel. Retrieved from www.middleeasteye.net/news/madonna-faces-backlash-over-eurovision-performance-israel-boycott Accessed 17th September 2019.

Pavia, W., & Bremner, C. (2019). Madonna to defy boycott of Tel Aviv Eurovision: Madonna's $1.3m to sing at Eurovision. *The Times*. Retrieved from www.thetimes.co.uk/article/ madonna-to-defy-boycott-of-tel-aviv-eurovision-cp6fff0jv Accessed 30th April 2019.

Perraudin, F. (2019). Southampton theatre cancels shows after actors in LGBT play attacked. *The Guardian*. Retrieved from www.theguardian.com/uk-news/2019/jun/09/southampton-theatre-cancels-lgbt-play-performances-after-actors-attacked Accessed 14th September 2019.

Philips, P., & Whannel, G. (2013). *The Trojan Horse*. London: Bloomsbury Academic.

Player, T., Skipper, H., & Lambert, J. (2002). A global definition of terrorism. *Risk Management, 49*(9), 60.

Rockefeller, A. (2018). When horses fly: The business of equine air travel. Retrieved from www.forbes.com/sites/arianarockefeller/2018/12/20/when-horses-fly-the-business-of-equine-air-travel/#3b7414fd3197 Accessed 19th September 2019.

Russell, G. (2019). He's a barbarian': Māori tribe bans replica of Captain Cook's ship from port. *The Guardian*. Retrieved from www.theguardian.com/world/2019/sep/17/hes-a-barbarian-maori-tribe-bans-replica-of-captain-cooks-ship-from-port?CMP=Share_AndroidApp_Email Accessed 17th September 2019.

Sabbagh, D. (2019). Human rights groups protest as world arms fair returns to London. *The Guardian*. www.theguardian.com/world/2019/sep/09/human-rights-groups-protest-as-world-arms-fair-returns-to-london

Santurtun, E., & Phillips, C. J. C. (2015). The impact of vehicle motion during transport on animal welfare. *Research in Veterinary Science, 100*, 303. doi:10.1016/j.rvsc.2015.03.018

Schengen Visa Information (n.d.). Schengen visa information. Retrieved from www.schengenvisainfo.com/ Accessed 24th November 2017.

Solomon, C. M. (2009). *Managing Across Cultures: The Seven Keys to Doing Business with a Global Mindset*. New York: McGraw-Hill.

Sterio, M. (2011). The Somali piracy problem: A global puzzle necessitating a global solution. *American University Law Review, 59*(5), 1449–1497.

Strobech, K. (2009). U2 360 Tour stage July 2009 Croke Park, Ireland. Retrieved from https://commons.wikimedia.org/wiki/File:U2_360_Tour_Croke_Park_2.jpg Accessed 13th September 2019.

Sweeney, M. (2020). Mobile World Congress axed after firms quit over coronavirus fears, *The Guardian*. Retrieved from www.theguardian.com/technology/2020/feb/12/mobile-world-congress-axed-coronavirus-fears?CMP=share_btn_link

Tippet, G. (2009). 90 years apart and bonded by a nation. Retrieved from www.theage.com.au/national/90-years-apart-and-bonded-by-a-nation-20090124-7p4i.html Accessed 10th July 2017.

Triandis, H. C. (1989). The self and social behavior in differing cultural contexts. *Psychological Review, 96*(3), 506–520. doi:10.1037/0033-295x.96.3.506

Trump, D. (2017). *Proclamation 9645-Enhancing Vetting Capabilities and Processes for Detecting Attempted Entry Into the United States by Terrorists or Other Public-Safety Threats*, 1–13. Washington, DC: Superintendent of Documents.

Tylor, E. B. (1871). *Primitive Culture: Researches into the Development of Mythology, Philosophy, Religion, Art, and Custom*. London: John Murray.

US Embassy & Consulates in the UK (n.d.). Criminal Records & Ineligibilities. Retrieved from https://uk.usembassy.gov/visas/visa-waiver-program/additional-requirements/ Accessed 18th September 2019.

Ward, C. A. (2001). The psychology of culture shock. In S. Bochner & A. Furnham (Eds.), *Culture shock* (2nd ed.). Hove: Routledge.

Weatherbys (n.d.). Horse passports information. Retrieved from www.weatherbys.co.uk/horses-racing/horse-passports/id-passports Accessed 19th September 2019.

White, N. (2014). Travelling while black: Brits share their experiences of racism in Europe. www.huffingtonpost.co.uk/ Accessed 14th September 2019.

Wikipedia (n.d.) U2 360 degree tour. Retrieved from https://en.wikipedia.org/wiki/U2_360%C2%B0_Tour Accessed 13th September 2019.

Willshire, K. (2013). Rite that caused riots: celebrating 100 years of 'The Rite of Spring'. *The Guardian*. www.theguardian.com/culture/2013/may/27/rite-of-spring-100-years-stravinsky Accessed 10th May 2020.

Wood, S. (2019). UN summit moves to Madrid after protest cancellations in Chile. *Conference & Meetings World*. Retrieved from www.c-mw.net/un-summit-moves-to-madrid-after-protest-cancellations-in-chile/ Accessed 14th November 2019.

World Health Organization (WHO) (2019). International travel and health: General precautions. Retrieved from www.who.int/ith/precautions/en/ Accessed 18th September 2019.

Zimmer, O. (2000). Competing memories of the nation: Liberal historians and the reconstruction of the Swiss past 1870–1900. *Past & Present*, 168, 194–226.

Part 3

EXTERNAL FORCES

Chapter 7

Access

Contents

7.1 Chapter overview

Access to international events, as this chapter will highlight, covers a multitude of topics. From simple considerations of who goes where in and around an event space, to the various ways of discrimination. Access, from an international event perspective, covers every aspect of the right of entry from getting to and about the event to how data is managed. Topical access issues include ticketing, data protection, gender, and how the event organisers can ensure the safety of all and legally monitor various aspects of the event. International events need to ensure all these different features of access are considered while shielding the event against unwanted entry.

7.2 Learning objectives

By the end of this chapter, the student will be expected to:

- Understand a number of ways of expressing access to an international event
- Recognise the different levels of management both inside and outside the event space
- Understand the differences between the primary and secondary ticketing market
- Understand the process in competing at different levels of sport
- Recognise the impact of protests and demonstrations.

7.3 Introduction

Access is an area of international events that in academic terms remains largely misunderstood and is disproportionately poor in practical terms, when often it remains unclear who is responsible for its different aspects. While access is largely concerned with gaining or denying the right of entry, the ability to manage, monitor, and provide adequate access to events is a highly complex responsibility. While technology has improved the way in which access is provided at events, it has also created many of the biggest problems surrounding legitimate and reasonable access.

Access covers many characteristics that have implications before, during and after the event. Access can include pre-event preparations, the safety of all participants (on and off site, particularly close to the event site itself), event design, site layout, and satisfaction. Data collected from the access process can improve the event experience, provide vital information for future planning and improve various features of subsequent events. Therefore, being able to deliver an event that is accessible for every potential attendee and participant is imperative. At the same time, it remains a challenging characteristic of international event delivery. From dealing with the whole range of special needs to being prepared for the risk and the threat of an unwanted incident during the event, the amount of time, effort, planning, and preparation can be overwhelming for the organisers as the demand for safeguarding the wellbeing of those who attend must not be compromised.

7.4 Who goes where?

There are a few key questions of access to certain areas in international events, which include:

1. Where can individuals go?
2. Is the access time-limited and, if so, for how long?
3. Do they need assistance or to be accompanied?
4. How will access be managed?
5. What is the impact on others of permitting access?

The type of international event will determine the set-up requirements on how access will be managed. However, all event spaces and venues follow the same basic site layout. This way, it is more manageable to provide and maintain safe working areas at all times. The welfare of all the contractors that the event engages with as well as the paying public will be incorporated into the site design and layout.

Outdoor and indoor events are designed on the same basic principles and will include two or three of the following areas as follows:

- Front of house (FOH)
- Backstage or back of house (BOH)
- Field of play/stage area/event space.

Once the event areas have been determined for the event, an access plan can be created. Indoor purpose-built venues tend to have stringent arrangements in place to separate the audience from the artists' areas, performance space or field of play. These spaces require very little added preparation or segregation planning as these boundaries form part of the venue design. However, this can change when venues built for a specific purpose are used for another type of event different from what they were built for. A typical example of this would be the now popular use of sports stadia doubling as a concert space. For example, racecourses and football venues are used for pop concerts. For racecourses, the concerts are often included as an added attraction to attend a race meeting. For venues such as football stadia, they are used during the closed season before the new turf is laid for the following season.

7.5 Access management

Once the type of venue has been chosen for the event, managing access is incorporated into the event design. Indoor, outdoor, and venues used for other purposes than what they were built for bring their own set of challenges. The use of sports stadia by event organisers for other types of events is done for very good reasons. They were built in the heart of large communities and access by public transport tends to be very good. The venues and their staff are well versed in delivering large-scale events, and all the necessary requirements for health and safety are in place. They can hold much bigger audiences than most other venues in the region. However, they were designed with the intention of having around 50 players and officials in and around the field of play. Modern concert promoters can put in excess of 50,000 partying spectators in the same space. Figure 7.1 shows how a field of play is converted into a concert venue. Notice how the field of play designed for 22 players and a referee becomes the standing space for tens of thousands of spectators.

Choosing a venue to host an international event is a technical challenge in itself. When it comes to global sporting events it is usually necessary for

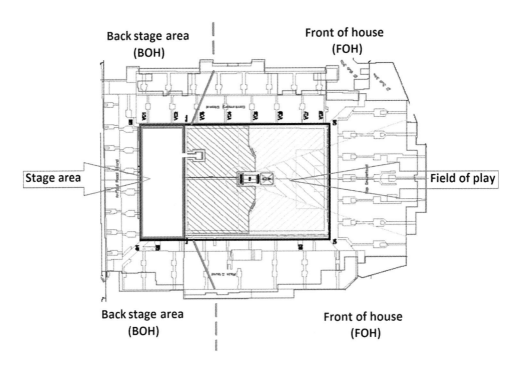

Figure 7.1 Site layout for a football stadium concert

many facilities, building and even stadia to be built for the event itself. Even relatively smaller events now require special access requirements. The modern football stadium is now used for internationally touring bands that have an audience of up to 70,000 using the field of play. Previously, the only other access requirement was for a large lawnmower and pitch-related equipment, making gated access to the field of play very limited. Because of international demands from FIFA and UEFA, many older stadia have updated their facilities in order to host the European and World Cup competition matches. The more recently built stadia provide improved facilities and amenities (Klepal and Tucker, 2015).

For large-scale international events that are delivered in sports and other similar outdoor stadia, access management will involve a number of organisations. These might include the venue owners, the promoter's security staff and stewards, as well as the local authority. Security and stewarding usually begin well outside the perimeter of the venue. The local authority will normally take care of access outside the wider footprint of the venue. Once within the venue's footprint, the venue's stewards and security staff may then take control of access.

Once inside the venue, venue security staff and stewards will also work in association with the promoter's team and crew. This is because security is more intense in certain areas. Professional teams who are either part of the touring party or employed by the act undertake much of the close monitoring. This includes the close care of equipment, spaces, and individuals.

7.5.1 Site plans

To assist with the access management, each international event will have its own site plan. A site plan will include everything within the designated event space. Site plans are made to assist everyone working on the event and will help the event organiser direct people to the correct part of the site when they arrive to set up. In some cases, site plans are distributed to the attendees to help plan how they will enter the site and move around it. The main areas on a site plan that will need to be shared will include:

- Any fencing or barriers
- Back stage and front of house
- Car parking
- Emergency exits and assembly points
- Entry and exit points
- First aid points
- Generators or power sources
- Lost children points
- Placement of all temporary structures
- Position and type of attractions
- Power supply runs
- Vehicle entry points
- VIP areas
- Any other site infrastructure or obstacles.

Figure 7.2 Examples showing the development of passes to events

For the majority of international events, in order for attendees to gain entry, tickets will be made available beforehand. However, assuming it is a ticketed event, everyone who has access will have either a ticket or a pass. To assist with queueing and general order, stewards, local police, and security staff will assist people as they arrive at the venue. The event organisers may also have people dealing with ticket touts, unofficial merchandise stalls, and breaches of sponsorship before, during and after the event. Figure 7.2 shows a variety of passes to different types of events from sticky-back paper passes to digitalised bar-coded passes with photographic ID.

Once inside the footprint of the venue, more support can be found, usually provided by regular venue security staff and stewards to help those with tickets and passes to the various areas or even the correct turnstile, door or access point. All access backstage or back of house (BOH) is gained with the use of a pass. Restrictions will still exist once backstage, and access to many areas will remain limited. The stage, catering area dressing rooms, and the venue organiser's offices are examples of specific areas that are further restricted even to those with access to the backstage area. Many VIPs and guests are issued with tickets to designated areas, while the general public will have designated spaces too.

Figure 7.3 highlights the various access control zones at a football stadium when it is used as a concert venue. The figure defines the zones from street level which is accessed by all, to the backstage area which is high security and requires special access.

As individuals amass to access the venue itself, security staff should now be dominating the access points. In today's high-security environment at events, an individual may typically experience three or four different levels of security checks at the point of entry. These might include a request to show you have a valid ticket to enter the event area and a pat-down body search to determine whether prohibited items or other threats are concealed on the person. Door security staff may then scan tickets before an inner guard will monitor general access activities such as direction and speed of the individual. Figure 7.4 shows the visible aspect of this type of security at a music event. The first level of security begins on the street, the second at the door and the third immediately inside the venue to both assist with directions and safety.

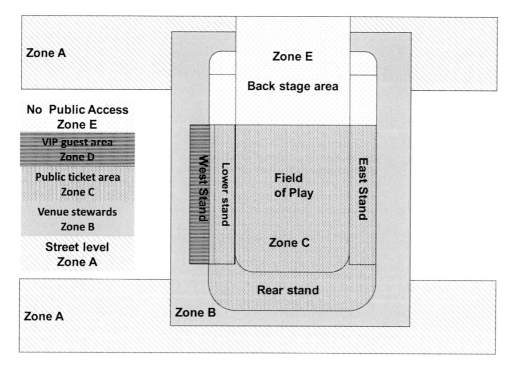

Figure 7.3 Different levels of access and management by zones in and around a football stadium being used as a concert venue

7.6 Access legislation

Many of what are considered the rudimentary and necessary circumstances of international events are protected by some kind of legislation which will vary from nation to nation. In particular, legislation will cover aspects of event certification, safety, permits, waivers, and visas. It is only possible to 'highlight' legislation issues in this text as the complexities are not only specific to regions, states, and territories, but they change and are amended on a regular basis. Added to the legal requirements are ethical guidelines that relate to corporate social responsibility (CSR) and accountability. These are discussed in more detail in Chapter 8. Again, ethical guidelines need to be reviewed with consideration for the laws and regulations of the individual nation where the event is to take place. Legal and responsible event management are the 'cornerstones of effective risk management' (Silvers, 2008, p. 76).

Another key aspect in the redevelopment and design of venues is access for all. It has been no longer acceptable for some time to assume that everyone in a potential audience is able-bodied. Good facilitation practices at international events can assist in creating an inclusive and supportive atmosphere for everyone. Event organisers must take into account accessibility due to reduced mobility of any kind from physical, mental visual or hearing impairment.

Figure 7.4 Current three-tier security checks provided at a major event

7.7 Accessibility

A key factor in dealing with access is the actual ability for people to attend. An individual's own physical constraints should not be a restriction on attendance, whether this is attending as an individual, with a friend or with support from the event organisers at the venue. International event organisers need to include reasonable adjustments for disabilities in the planning and delivery of events. Event organisers should also be cautious of policies, practices, or rules they introduce which apply to everybody in the same way, but still place certain groups or individuals at a disadvantage. This can be deemed indirect discrimination.

As event organisers, it is important to understand what is meant when an individual is restricted by a disability. Disabled World (2017) defines a disability as a condition or function judged to be significantly impaired relative to the usual standard of an individual or group. As events are delivered, it is important not to discriminate in any way either deliberately or inadvertently when planning them. All event organisers must consider access for those with any kind of special requirement. The range of disabilities that needs to be considered is very broad. Some require little change to the event plan, while others need to have very specific adjustments, clearly signposted, and integrated into the design of the event. Glastonbury, for example, has more than 600 deaf and disabled customers to each festival. To support accessibility, the organisers engage 100 deaf and disabled crew members to work on the event itself (Adams, 2018).

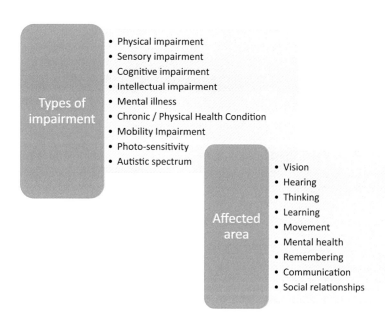

- Physical impairment
- Sensory impairment
- Cognitive impairment
- Intellectual impairment
- Mental illness
- Chronic / Physical Health Condition
- Mobility Impairment
- Photo-sensitivity
- Autistic spectrum

Types of impairment

- Vision
- Hearing
- Thinking
- Learning
- Movement
- Mental health
- Remembering
- Communication
- Social relationships

Affected area

Figure 7.5 Types of potentially disabling impairment and areas of activity affected

Disability is an important factor for international event organisers as figures from around the world suggest that around 20% of a nation's population has declared some kind of personal disability. According to another survey, 1 billion people experience some form of disability. The research also suggests that disability prevalence is higher for developing countries. One-fifth of the estimated global total, or between 110 million and 190 million people, experience significant disabilities (World Bank, 2019).

There are essentially six types of disability or impairment that can be grouped into a number of categories: physical, hearing, visual, learning, intellectual, and mental. Each of these categories and the level of impairment will vary and a disability can affect an individual in a number of ways. Figure 7.5 highlights the types of potentially disabling impairments and the various areas of activity they affect. Most of these impairments can be looked after during an event with little effort. Many impairments can be overcome individually or with one-to-one support. However, there are a number of disabilities that affect access that require considerable effort from the event organisers. With this in mind, international event organisers should provide opportunities for those with any kind of disability to communicate directly in the run-up to the event. This way, anyone turning up or participating can receive the necessary support.

Most venues will cater for all kinds of disabilities making issues of access largely a standard procedure. However, outdoor events such as music and street festivals need to be managed at a much higher level of care. Physical and mental disabilities create limitations that require support, including physical functioning, mobility, dexterity or stamina. It is important to remember that disabilities are both visible and invisible and issues such as dietary needs or care needs depending on age should not be overlooked. Similarly, there is also the need to consider the profile of those involved in the event. These can be all the more significant with touring events, particularly when medication is required.

The more international events are delivered, the better understanding event organisers have of the access requirements. Over the years, it has become apparent that customers with accessibility issues often require one or in some cases a combination of reasonable adjustments to satisfactorily attend and enjoy an event. Research on accessibility issues is limited compared to other areas related to access to events. However, in the UK, some in-depth research has been conducted by Attitude is Everything, a disability-led charity that supports non-profit and commercial organisations to make what they do more accessible and inclusive for those with accessibility issues.

A particular area of research was completed around access requirements when booking tickets and attending live music events. This research highlighted the many areas of events that have improved considerably over recent years, and areas that are in need of further improvement. What the research also highlighted was the widespread requirements events need to have in place. Table 7.1 indicates the percentage of demand for access requirements when 349 people completed a survey on the accessibility of booking procedures. While the research focused the typical access requirements at music events, these are just as important to the requirements at any type of international event in similar venues.

Disability or issues with accessibility count as one of a number of critical factors an international event organiser will need to recognise. The United Nations document (2016) on transforming our world asks nations to act in collaborative partnership to implement this plan. This includes realising the human rights of all and to achieve gender equality. Nations throughout the world have different laws and protections with different requirements with regards to race, colour, gender, language, religion, political opinion, national or social origin, and disability. Most importantly, there is the need for all nations to abide by

Table 7.1 Typical access requirements for live music events

Typical access demand/requirements at music events	Proportion of attendees who require each type (%)
Accessible seating or viewing platforms	77
Personal assistant / support worker / carer	76
Accessible toilets	64
Step-free access	54
Lowered bars / counters	23
Locations for hearing loop	7
Captioning of lyrics or audio-description	5
Sign language interpretation	4
Assistance dog user	2
Assistive technology to access websites	1

Source: Adams, 2018

international laws, human rights and to respect fundamental freedoms that exist for all. Event organisers must remember to contemplate each of these without distinction of any kind, when designing, and delivering international events.

7.8 Getting in and out

Access to almost every event, regardless of cost, is permitted with the presentation of either a ticket or a pass. As the event industry is heavily influenced by technology (see Chapter 11), it is in the midst of a major revolution taking us from a basic paper token to a mix of physical, chip and virtual tickets. Therefore, a broad range of ticketing options is available for use by the event organisers. Paper tickets, plastic wrist bands, plastic cards, wrist stamping, laminated cards on lanyards, barcodes and unique numbers are just a selection. However, regardless of the type of physical or virtual ticket used, they all require immense attention to detail in terms of creating ease of entry and exit, verifying validity, collection and monitoring (Wynn-Moylan, 2018). This means that ingress and to some extent egress controls will need to be in place.

When an international event is outdoors, restrictions on access need to be identified and monitored and in some cases built from scratch to protect the site from people intent on gaining access without paying, commonly known as 'gate crashers'. Probably the most well-known outdoor access management system is the temporary demountable structure (TDS) or perimeter fence at the Glastonbury Festival in Pilton, Somerset. It is a double fence measuring 4.5 miles (7.2km) around the perimeter and 12 feet (3.5m) high (BBC, 2002).

Even when an event is free, crowd management may need to be considered and implemented in order for the event to be safe and accessible for all residents, attendees, and participants. In fact, free events can be far more disruptive to local residents. The annual Tour de France can attract up to an estimated 12 million spectators lining the streets (ASO, 2019) and therefore requires considerable planning for setting up barriers, road closures, safety of the riders and spectators, and to ensure limited disruption to the usual daily activities of the local people.

7.8.1 Floorplans

International event organisers who are planning exhibitions will provide exhibitors with a floorplan to show the layout and access points for the event. This is important as the exhibitor will need to know where their allocated stand will be and how close or far from the main footfall, exits and entrances. The bigger the investment the exhibitor makes in their space in the show and the sooner they sign up, the bigger influence they can have on their final position. Exhibitors who sign up late may have less money to spend, or have a limited understanding of the importance of their position at the event vis-à-vis their competitors' stands. Less favourable positions tend to be away from the bigger exhibitors, in corners, or along the perimeter of the hall, away from the main footfall. Figure 7.6 is a typical example of a floorplan for a large international exhibition.

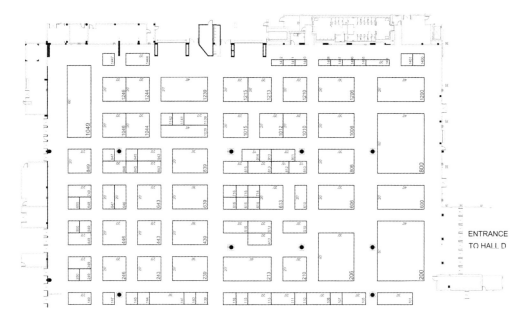

Figure 7.6 A typical example of a floorplan for a large international exhibition

7.9 Temporary demountable structures (TDS)

A key aspect of any international event that takes place outdoors will be the erection of temporary structures. These are universally known as temporary demountable structures (TDS) and cover a whole range of uses, sizes, categories, and fabrics. International events make use of a variety of TDS. These will include fencing, hoardings, and barriers for use both indoors and outdoors. Stages, lighting and rigging, security barriers, and grandstands can all be constructed on site. They can be constructed and become the venue itself and provide shelter in remote areas.

The design, erection and dismantling of TDS in the UK are all subject to the provisions of health and safety law including the Health and Safety at Work etc. Act 1974 and The Construction (Design and Management) Regulations 2015 (Hind, 2017). These can be related to the amount of stress the structure can undertake. Most TDS are built with a single specific use in mind and the stress tests are carried out during the manufacturing process. However, this means they will need to be set up by a qualified and competent team and require inspection with any relevant documentation signed off before they can be used.

There have been a number of fatal incidents involving TDS and the Institution of Structural Engineers produced useful advice in a document called 'Temporary Demountable Structures – Guidance on Procurement Design and Use'. This is currently in its fourth edition and provides detailed advice and best practice. With this in mind, it is important to get things right from the outset and the guide (Hind, 2017) advises that when procuring a structure the client should:

- Obtain written evidence that competent persons are employed to design, erect, inspect and dismantle the structure
- Agree the expected nature and character of spectator activity at the event
- Provide the contractor with a written technical specification of requirements (such requirements will be specific to the country in which the work is being undertaken)
- Make suitable arrangements for managing the project safely
- Obtain approvals from the relevant enforcing authority in good time
- Make sure that an event management plan is available, which includes a plan for dealing with adverse weather conditions — particularly strong winds and heavy rain.

Figure 7.7 shows two types of TDS that can be erected at the same international event. They are all specialist structures and fulfil an important part of the event. Each TDS can be brought to an empty space to create pretty much anything the event organisers want. Once the event is over, the TDS can be packed up, removed, and used again at another event.

7.10 Parking at international events

While it is advised that all international events promote the use of public transport and the transport links that exist in and around the venue, many international events will still have to provide access to parking for those arriving by road. This needs to be within a reasonable distance of the venue as it is central to the overall experience. Therefore, spaces for cars, vans, buses, coaches, including disabled access, will need to be provided. International events will also be delivered as part of a region's or venue's annual event programme and access to parking facilities will be absorbed by the general urban infrastructure. Large cities are well equipped to deal with the demand for parking for the majority of international events, although the increased pressure on already stressed facilities can be overwhelming. The level of management required in such circumstances comes down to guidance and advice on the cost, convenience, and availability of parking for all types of access within a reasonable distance.

For people attending as delegates, audience or spectators, the three foremost factors for those arriving by road are the driving time, parking cost, and the amount of time it takes to get from the parking space to the event. The cost of parking is often included or highlighted as an extra charge to the ticket price, while the driving time is taken into account by the transport provider or the individual. These two aspects can be much less of an issue for attendees when compared to the time it takes to walk from the parking facilities to the event.

First and foremost, when parking is provided as part of the event, the organisers must ensure the safety of the people using the parking space. This will come down to how the space is managed and how natural phenomena such as the weather and light affect the chosen space. For city-based events, multistorey parking facilities are widely available and have many safety features built in. However, open spaces provide their own sets of problems that will need to be considered and prepared for well in advance of the event. This might include the laying of access tracks to create a temporary roadway reinforcing

Figure 7.7 A range of temporary demountable structures (TDS) from picket fencing and catering marquees to a fully equipped raised stage with PA towers, lighting rigs and crowd control barriers

existing grassed areas to avoid vehicles becoming trapped in mud in the case of rain. A system will have to be devised to manage the traffic in and out of the designated area. Bearing in mind that tens of thousands of vehicles can descend on an event, this service should ideally be outsourced to a company who specialise in parking and traffic management.

The number of people expected to arrive by road at the event will affect a wide range of resources and facilities required. The type of facilities the event will provide will need to be carefully planned out with clear signage that is simple for all to understand. Fortunately, there is the Vienna Convention on Road Signs and Signals which is a multilateral treaty designed to aid international road traffic. Most traffic signs are understood by all drivers and can be used at events as they are in use internationally. Event organisers will want to avoid creating bottlenecks by positioning stewards to offer guidance and prevent bottlenecks turning into gridlock.

There may be a need for attendees to pre-book parking in many cities due to daily demand for space. Therefore, any procedures for booking such space will again need to be carried out in advance of the event to avoid potential problems at the event site. This is often done on the venue website at the point of purchasing the ticket.

When providing parking at an event on open ground, event organisers should not underestimate the hazards that exist. It is easy for parking to be overlooked as a simple process of providing space. However, even on open ground, surveys may need to be considered to ensure any buried services such as drains, gas, electric or communication cables are not buried underneath and potentially damaged. There may also be height restrictions for service vehicles if any overhead cables remain in situ. Safety at all times will be a priority and speed limits will have to be adequately displayed and implemented by staff during the event.

As well as providing parking for attendees, emergency access or muster points will need to be prearranged and be included in any planning documents. The key is to ensure they have more than enough space to hold the number of people attending the event.

7.11 Street closures

For many international events, it is necessary for the organisers to request the closure of major traffic routes and highways for a period of time. As this can cause disruption to the travel plans of some locals and delivery drivers, the event organisers should make every effort to guarantee road closures due to events are never a surprise to the road users. Some events are locally organised, while others are part of the much larger international sporting calendar that are parachuted in as one-off events for a region. The length of time needed for the closure will depend on the event itself, but usually the closure is anything from a couple of hours to most of the day.

Local events such as international markets are regular weekly or monthly events that the local community experiences as part of their normal life, the oldest examples being those developed in the market towns stretching throughout Europe to the Far East. These activities reflect the frequent economic and social interaction in a specific spatio-temporal context (Chan et al., 2015) and form part of the social fabric and identity of the region and community. Many of these market towns throughout the world have held events that are in fact older than the roads themselves.

Other mobile events such as street theatre, carnival parades, marching bands, processions, religious events, and some sporting events will have one-off annual closures that are planned well in advance of the event itself. Each type of event will spend a set amount of time in a specific place and this is managed with the use of a heat map to emphasise the accessibility of the road itself. A heat map allows each section of the procession or caravan to proceed with minimum delay or obstruction, while at the same time providing guidance on the opening, closing, and re-opening times. Figure 7.8 is an example of a heat map

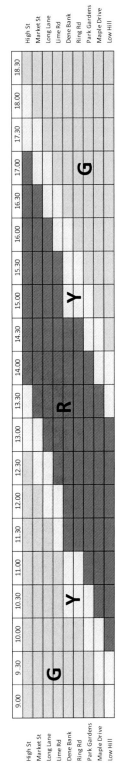

Figure 7.8 A road closure heat map – G – open, Y – closed, R – event live time

showing how the route has been planned for the day. For safety purposes, the road is closed in good time before the event arrives at the proposed location.

While events can take over a community, the organisers will always have to give full consideration to the local community and their day-to-day lives. This is because towns and cities will continue with their usual activities and other events still need to happen. Deliveries may be delayed, but a wedding that has been the centre of a family's life for many years cannot simply be re-organised to satisfy the demands of a major TV corporation. In these circumstances, events within events will occur and the various organisers involved with the disrupting event will need to communicate and be informed of such activities. However, a possibly unexpected environmental benefit when events have forced roads to be closed in major urban conurbations is the significant fall in pollution levels (Holder, 2014; Taylor, 2019b).

7.12 Sanitation facilities

Events have come a long way since the days of Woodstock in 1969 when 450,000 people turned up to an event to a pasture in Sullivan County with limited toilets and little or no access to running water. In today's hygienic event environment, audiences will retain many memories from a weekend spent at an event, but if there is one thing that is never forgotten, it's a bad toilet experience. Toilets may be considered an unusual addition to a chapter on access, but any kind of event today is restricted by the quality and quantity of its sanitation facilities.

Not only is the provision of toilets and taps a mathematical science for how to satisfy a variety of audiences, their numbers are a good indicator of how society has changed over the years. It is not the kind of research that is normally undertaken, but a review of developments in access to toilets and washing facilities reveals how event management and society has changed. Even towards the end of the 20th century, it remained difficult in some sports stadia to find toilets designated for women. At the same time, progress was being made and nations began to introduce laws to make it a requirement to have not only adequate numbers of toilets for women at sports stadia, but also wheelchair-accessible facilities in every new development.

Today, we are well-accustomed to using the term 'accessible' to describe facilities for those who require assistance or more space due to reduced mobility. In addition, many toilet facilities are becoming gender neutral. Figure 7.9 shows the sign for the toilets at a venue where the traditional female and male images have been removed and replaced with a symbol to denote their gender-neutrality. This is a typical example of how things have changed in recent years and the additional costs venues have to incur in order to satisfy the constantly evolving demands of 21st century regulations and audiences.

7.12.1 How many toilets?

There are a number of event suppliers who specialise in providing sanitation facilities for events of every size, and there are a number of considerations that

Figure 7.9 Unisex toilet sign

contribute to the calculations. The following are the basic requirements to calculate how many and what type of toilets are required:

- How many people are expected?
- How far is the event from any other facilities?
- What's the general age of the audience?
- Are children expected?
- Is alcohol, coffee, or tea available?

Once these basic considerations have been taken into account, a very good estimate of the number of toilets required can be made. It is not possible to provide a definitive figure as every event will be based on its own merits. However, Table 7.2 provides representative calculations for toilets for a set amount of people in a space for a set amount of time. Event organisers should take the lowest figure as a minimum requirement.

In the case of accessible toilets, it is really important to ensure that the emergency pull cord can be reached from the floor and, if these facilities can be locked, that there is clear information provided on how the public can access them in the event of an emergency.

Table 7.2 Estimated portable toilet numbers for an event

Event duration in hours		1	2	3	4	5	6	7
Audience size	Accessible toilets required	Minimum standard toilets required						
250	1	2	2	2	2	3	3	4
500	2	2	3	3	4	5	6	8
1000	4	3	4	5	6	8	9	10
2000	6	5	8	10	11	14	18	24
5000	10	-	20	24	27	32	45	50
8000	12	-	-	38	44	55	65	75
10000	15	-	-	50	60	70	85	100
20000	20	-	-	95	110	125	150	180

All venues today are built based on the highest calculations of capacity, so ordinarily it is the other types of space, in particular open spaces, that require much more attention and preparation for the event. The examples above in section 7.5 where a venue is being used for an alternative means may require additional sanitation facilities.

It is also important to remember that events targeted at families will require a number of additional facilities for parents and, consequently, more preparation from the organisers. Not only are extra facilities required for general hygiene factors, extra emergency facilities will be required for lost and found, a duty of care where alcohol is available, and safety checks when employing staff. Disclosure and Barring Service (DBS) checks will be required for staff as safeguarding children and young people at events is a high priority.

A welfare point should be set up with a safe area for any child who has been found or who wants to report themselves lost. Any report of a lost child should be logged with details being circulated to security staff by security management in order for the child to be identified and brought to the welfare point for return to the parent or carer. This should be conducted with great care with clear descriptions provided by both parties being matched and signed off beforehand.

Alcohol and drinks with caffeine such as tea and coffee are diuretic. Therefore, they naturally increase the amount of water and salt expelled from the body as urine. If an event has these drinks available, it can be expected that the demand for toilets will increase.

Many outdoor festivals require portable sanitation facilities to be positioned in a number of places throughout the event area to provide the best level of service to the audience. Where the facilities are positioned can only really be decided during the design phase. While it may be necessary to position them away from the stage or concession areas, consideration needs to be made for safety and security.

Toilet facilities have become a place for pranks at festivals when the event organisers position them in unmonitored spaces. Stories of deliberately locking people inside or transporting the unit whilst in use are not unusual. The craze of 'smurfing' has also spread throughout outdoor events and the cost of dealing with the problem can be substantial. Smurfing is when the unit containing the toilet is deliberately tipped on its side with somebody inside. The name comes from the blue detergent often used in portable toilets which is transferred along with any other contents onto the unfortunate occupant. (Smurfs are blue cartoon characters, originally created by a Belgian comic artist, Peyo, in 1958, and repopularised in a film by Disney in 2011). The problem and additional cost for the event organiser comes from cleaning up the contaminated area and potentially being responsible for any damages.

7.13 Access to the field of play

As a rule, access to the field of play is restricted to those who are about to use it. However, another aspect of international event management is managing the right to compete. Even the athletes themselves will have to go through some level of access management process. This ensures that teams and individuals who compete are doing so on the same level. To be able to participate in the top echelons of a sport, the organising bodies will have to manage the different levels of competition. Quite often, these processes are made more manageable with orders of merit. This allows for teams and individuals to regularly monitor their progress through the ranks. From qualifying events through to major finals, the same organising body will need to be the responsible agent.

Golf is a prime example of how the different levels of competition are managed and the managing organisations include the United States Golf Association (USGA) and the R&A. Strangely and despite deriving its name from the members' golf club, the Royal and Ancient Golf Club of St Andrews, the R&A is just the R&A. Together the USGA, and the R&A govern the sport of golf worldwide, operating in separate jurisdictions while sharing a commitment to a single code for the Rules of Golf, Rules of Amateur Status and Equipment Standards (R&A, n.d.).

Many sports, such as golf will hold international competitions on a weekly basis that are feeder events for those with higher demand and media interest, culminating in the globally recognised events that attract bidding venues and states. The demand to compete at the weekly events is created by the prize money that is provided by the event sponsors and customarily carries the name of the main sponsor. Once in the main competition, players will need to finish above a certain level to be sure of qualification for any future events at the same level.

As well as the weekly high-profile sponsored competitions, golf also has four annual golf majors and a variety of biannual team events, such as the Ryder Cup for men and the Solheim Cup for women. The annual golf majors include the Masters (March) which is always held at Augusta National in Georgia, the PGA (May) is primarily played in the eastern half of the United States, The US Open (June) is played throughout the USA and the Open (July) is held at a selection of venues in the UK and is golf's oldest and most international of the Major championships. Other sports such as cycling have regular monthly events with three major meetings or Grand Tours: the Giro d'Italia (May–June), the Tour de France (July) and the Vuelta a España (August–September). Each of these races are similar in format, with daily stages over an average of three weeks with occasional rest days.

7.14 Ticketing

Managing access for spectators to international events begins with some form of ticketing. Ticketing is not only a security measure to ensure eligible people have access to the event, it also provides important statistical information that can be used both before and after the event itself. Even in their simplest form, ticket sales can provide a predicted attendance figure with data collected at the event for an accurate attendance count (Berners, 2017).

A ticket is essentially the permit issued to the customer that is the proof of purchase and provides the necessary details of what has been purchased. In most cases, this is simply the details of the seating or standing position within the venue. A ticket, whether that is a physical item, a barcode or an image on a mobile device is something that is presented at the gate or point of access.

A 21st-century event needs to provide clear information about how those with accessibility needs can buy the necessary tickets. Alongside this, the event organiser needs to be clear about what facilities are available on site and how they can arrange for any necessary support in order to be able to attend.

7.14.1 Ticketing communication

Ticketing in its traditional form for events is fast becoming a thing of the past. Those once highly prized items, such as the season ticket booklet for the biggest football clubs that people cherish for years, have been reduced to a piece of plastic that is scanned on entry. Because of the increased demand for up-to-date information, most international events include digital marketing and greater control of their communication with spectators at live events. These facilities are provided by live engagement platforms and supplied by third-party organisations that are capable of delivering instant communication and information to the attendee's mobile device.

As discussed in Chapter 2, these online platforms provide an assortment of applications for each event and for its attendees to connect with before, during, and after the event. The main providers include Crowdpurr who focus on voting systems, Liveperson specialising in messaging, while others such as DoubleDutch provide a comprehensive set of applications, such as performance metrics that enable the organisers to more successfully orchestrate their live international events.

For the more community-based or charitable events, access to free online ticketing services has been made much simpler through companies such as Eventbrite, TicketSource, Bookitbee, Brown Paper Tickets, Tickettailor, Eventsmart and Capterra. However, monthly subscription fees are required by some service providers for the full programme of services.

At the same time as being a vital resource, ticketing events and managing how many people attend has become a major problem for some event providers, particularly the ones that create demand that is disproportionate to the event space. Moreover, judging the demand is central to safety and the broader event experience, both over- and under- estimating the audience creates problems for the organisers. Therefore, forecasting requires knowledge, expertise, and a considerable amount of care.

7.14.2 Putting tickets up for sale

Putting tickets on sale for an international event will depend on a number of circumstances. The most important things to consider are the size and the demand for the event itself. In most cases, the marketing and promotion of the event begins well in advance of the tickets going on sale. For others, the marketing, promotion, and sale of tickets begin at the same time.

For the venues that put the event on, tickets tend to be released at the same time as the marketing material, as details of events are sent out through mailing lists. These tend to be between three and six months before the event, but can be much earlier. Many venues that regularly sell their events out offer a subscription to a priority booking scheme. This allows customers the opportunity to avoid the rush for tickets online while often being the first to hear about new shows. For many events in high demand and highly anticipated, the initial information is supplied by word-of-mouth. Preparations for touring events require rehearsals or other planning activities that leak out and concealment from the general public is often impossible.

It is not unusual for a venue to announce an event and put tickets on sale more than a year beforehand. However, the reason to promote an event for this long would emphasise the venue's need to sell the event out. There are many famous artists touring the world whose popularity means they are taking bookings two years in advance. The cost to host these events requires a full house to see any reasonable return. Tickets for the 50th Anniversary Glastonbury Festival (24th–28th June 2020) went on sale in early October 2019, but required a registration deadline of 30th September 2019. These tickets eventually sold out in around 30 minutes, before much of the line-up was known, although the event was subsequently cancelled due to the COVID-19 pandemic.

Therefore, tickets can go on sale anything from 18 months to a few weeks before the event. However, leaving the release of tickets late requires good understanding of the necessary marketing and promotion needed to ensure enough people hear about the event to generate ticket sales and a full house.

7.15 Secondary ticketing

Secondary or 'peer to peer' ticketing has its origins in individuals selling the tickets they purchased for an event to other individuals they could not use. The complications that are known to exist with secondary ticketing are compounded by different legislation between state/country boundaries – if any is in existence at all. However, the act of re-selling tickets for events is not the problem. The problems begin when the price is either hiked beyond a perceived or acceptable level or, in the worst of cases, both the provider and ensuing ticket are found to be bogus.

If you buy a ticket for yourself direct from the seller, this is a primary ticket purchase. If a ticket has previously been purchased and is available again for sale, this is the secondary ticket market. Therefore, secondary ticketing refers to the practice of reselling or transferring tickets from the original purchaser to another person for an event. In recent years, secondary ticketing has caused serious problems for many of the most popular international events. In most cases, the practice has little if any impact and the exchange is more often than not based on the face value of the ticket or less. However, events with the highest demand and massive oversubscription such as sporting finals and pop concerts have seen tickets being sold for more than 100 times their face value.

Essentially, the secondary ticket market is based on a supply and demand problem and the ticket buying public's inability to differentiate between the official ticket handlers and the unofficial sites that appear to be genuine. The problem has been made all the worse by the major official ticket handlers opening their own satellite websites to sell tickets on the secondary market. International events that are likely to sell out within hours of release are the most vulnerable to the secondary ticketing market.

According to *The Telegraph* (2015), the consumer group Which highlighted the biggest issues with secondary ticketing when it spent eight weeks monitoring four of the biggest secondary ticketing websites of the time: Get Me In, Seatwave, StubHub and Viagogo. During the monitoring process, tickets for the most popular events would appear on these re-sale sites immediately and sometimes even before they went on sale to the general public.

The effect of secondary ticketing on international events has been so great that some countries have brought in legislation in an attempt to quash the problem. According to Conway (2017), in June 2016 the Competition and Markets Authority (CMA) began a separate compliance review of the secondary ticketing market in the UK. This was followed, on 19 December 2016, by the CMA opening an enforcement investigation into suspected breaches of consumer protection law in the online secondary tickets market. After considerable debate between the House of Commons and the House of Lords, a new clause in the UK's Digital Economy Bill made it an offence to use digital purchasing software (so-called 'bots') to harvest large numbers of tickets. The legislation itself has not actually managed to remove the problem and may even have contributed to the increase in bogus ticketing operations.

A *Telegraph* (2015) report also highlighted the power of these computer 'bots' when it found that 364 tickets were available for Rod Stewart's UK tour on Stubhub the day before presales began and 450 tickets for the same show were available on Get Me In the moment presales for the tickets began on the primary site. The number of available tickets on Stubhub increased to 2,305 two days later. However, a Stubhub account can be created by anyone and tickets may have been put up for sale by individual members before knowing their efforts were successful.

The law also contributes to the secondary ticket problem as during a landmark case against two people selling up to US$6 million worth of tickets on the secondary market, the jury was told there is nothing illegal about reselling tickets. The defending counsel stated:

> Some people may think the secondary ticket websites like Seatwave, StubHub, GetMeIn and Viagogo and sellers are parasitic. Others may think the market functions because it puts people who own a commodity that they are willing to sell together with others who wish to purchase it at an agreed price. Parliament has had the opportunity to remove the secondary ticket market. It has not done that. No one has ever banned it.
>
> (Davies, 2019b)

Some venues such as the O2 in North Greenwich, London, have attempted to evade 'bots' by introducing 'priority presale' for customers who must pre-register with the venue, download an app and enter the site through a secure log-in. However, Get Me In managed to ensure eight tickets went on sale for each of the 28 Riverdance tour dates within a minute of the O2 priority presale.

Many people who buy tickets on the secondary market are satisfied with the service provided even when they have paid a premium for the ticket which is well in excess of the face value. However, the less scrupulous companies involved have sold duplicated tickets that are worthless and create havoc at the venue and a great deal of distress for those unlucky enough to have been duped by the professional secondary ticket sites that the tickets were sourced from. In some cases, the tickets purchased from secondary ticketing sites never existed in the first place.

There are just a few online sites that take the blame for most of the secondary ticketing problem. The concert promoters and the official ticketing websites have just as much to answer to for the problem by not providing more secure purchasing practices and by confusing the market with satellite reselling websites that take advantage of the general public. Glastonbury has proven that it is possible to ensure the secondary ticketing market can have little or no effect on the event by insisting on the uploading of a photo as part of the ticketing process before tickets go on sale. Only individuals with a completed profile can then buy tickets on the day of sale. The bigger promoters blame the costs involved as to why they have not followed suit.

Currently, secondary ticketing websites are still able to create massive profits from the resale of tickets for many events. However, figures towards the end of 2019 suggest that the number of music, theatre and sports fans using tickets website Viagogo has plummeted after from 4.5 million visitors to 820,000 in a matter of months after its adverts were banned from Google (Davies, 2019b). Moreover, the continuous technological developments in the event industry could bring such activities pretty much to a close. Various forms of access are being trialled and if the latest facial recognition technology being developed is adopted more broadly by international events, the secondary ticketing market may struggle to find a customer.

7.16 Ticket distribution and allocation

All international events will have tickets that are set aside for one reason or another. These may be reserved for special guests or for promotional activities. The bigger the event, the higher the percentage of tickets there are that are reserved for VIPs, sponsors, family and friends or other similar 'important people'. Large-scale international events will have major sponsors who often if not always have priority access to a large number of tickets and include different levels of hospitality. There are those who believe that the real atmosphere of the event is being squeezed out by the distribution of tickets for promotional reasons. For example, the United States' 2014 Super Bowl distributed one quarter (25.2%) of all tickets to corporate partners. Based on the stadium capacity of 82,550, that is approximately 21,000 seats going directly to people with

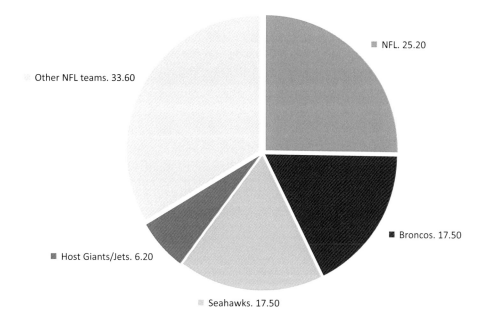

Other NFL teams. 33.60

NFL. 25.20

Broncos. 17.50

Host Giants/Jets. 6.20

Seahawks. 17.50

Figure 7.10 The distribution of tickets for Super Bowl XLVIII 2014

Source: Data from profootballtalk, 2014

no rooting interest but who are there through a business connection (Manfred, 2014). Figure 7.10 provides a chart for the overall allocation for tickets at Super Bowl 48.

Not only does ticket distribution affect the atmosphere at an event, the specific allocation of tickets for some events is central to the safety of those who attend. Events with opposing supporters will need segregation to avoid violent clashes before, during, and after the event. Similarly, ticket allocations might be separated into national teams and supporters in order to allow groups of fans to gather together in specific areas of a stadium, while some international events prefer the mixed approach and provide no seating allocation and allow spectators to choose their own seating arrangements.

7.16.1 Balloting

In cases where demand is high, ticket balloting has become a popular introduction for international events that are known to be oversubscribed. A ballot is meant to be the fairest way to distribute tickets at random without prejudice. Applicants must normally register an account via the official website and the ballots do not distribute tickets on a first come, first served basis. Instead, a ballot has an open and closing date between which those interested in attending must make their application.

Usually, the ballot can take any number of applications and the applicant simply chooses the type and amount of tickets required for the event. Only once the selection has been drawn does the applicant have to make payment. Some ballots will not re-open and any returned or unclaimed tickets are offered to those who were in the original ballot. Any remaining tickets will then go on general sale on a first come, first served basis. However, even a ballot can have different levels of access and many tickets are reserved for family, friends, club membership or sponsors of the event. During the application process, applicants can be asked to provide details of their relationship to the event to secure special access to another level of the ballot.

7.16.2 Getting paid

For some individuals, particularly for touring performers who make their living from live shows, the money generated from the event is sometimes collected by local promoters who in turn pay the tour manager. Depending on where the event is taking place, the promoter may need to deduct a Withholding Tax from the gross performance fee, which could amount to almost a third of the agreed amount. It is important for individuals to ascertain before travelling whether the agreed fee is gross or net of taxes (HM Revenue & Customs, 2017) or any other deductions for that matter.

In certain parts of the world, there remain a number of territories where the local culture can affect how (and in some cases whether or not), the visiting event will actually be remunerated for its efforts. Signed contracts that are the basis of all major events in the Western world become worthless pieces of paper and, in worst-case scenarios, the ability to negotiate can be the difference between leaving the visiting region with one's liberty and life.

Inexperience in the less stable territories requires the full attention and some very smart manoeuvring on the part of the event organisers when preparing the visit and on the ground during the event. In some cases, each individual in the travelling party will need to be aware of regulations on receiving payment abroad. While the majority of international events are successful, the event industry is littered with tales of non-payment and loss of equipment.

7.17 Data protection

Data protection is a global consideration for event organisers. In the USA, only a few states have laws on data privacy and there is currently no federal data privacy legislation. Unlike the USA, the EU has introduced laws for data privacy. As more personal information (data) is stored by companies about their customers or even those who just access a website, the General Data Protection Regulation (GDPR) was introduced in 2018 as the primary law regulating how companies protect EU citizens' personal data.

While GDPR legislation is an EU directive, if the event organisation is based outside of Europe, but targets customers in the EU by having the website in various European languages, the business will be subject to the requirements of the GDPR (Leslie, 2019). All organisations, from small businesses to large enterprises, must be aware of the GDPR principles. Failure to comply with the principles may leave companies open to substantial fines.

The GDPR regulation was agreed upon by the European Parliament and Council in April 2016 and replaced the Data Protection Directive (De Groot,

2019). Essentially, the law requires companies to implement reasonable data protection measures to protect consumers' personal data and privacy against loss or exposure. Considering most international event tickets are purchased online, a great deal of data is provided at the point of purchase. This means that the event organisers will need to ensure the data is securely managed and complies with the respective nation's data protection agency's regulations.

7.18 Cyberattacks

Most international events are now fully reliant on digital systems and technology. With so much information stored in an events database, cyberattacks have become increasingly common. These attacks can affect the confidentiality, integrity or availability of online systems and have a disruptive impact, resulting in financial and reputational damage.

It can be challenging to develop an accurate assessment of the threat to a specific event without undertaking an in-depth analysis. However, the National Cyber Security Centre (NCSC) (2019) has suggested a three step process for companies to follow to identify possible means of attack and to narrow down what must be protected. These steps are:

1. What are the digital technologies and systems that are critical to your event?
2. Who might attack them?
3. How they might be vulnerable?

A typical example of a cyberattack in computing is a denial-of-service attack (DoS). A DoS is a cyberattack in which the perpetrator seeks to make a machine or network resource unavailable to its intended users by temporarily or indefinitely disrupting services of a host connected to the internet. DoS is typically accomplished by flooding the targeted machine or resource with superfluous requests in an attempt to overload systems and prevent some or all legitimate requests from being fulfilled (NCCIC, 2009).

7.19 Surveillance

Surveillance is essentially a secretive process, but around the world its use is widespread, while being largely accepted as a part of modern-day living. The public knows it is constantly being watched. In the simplest of terms, surveillance is the tracking and monitoring of people's actions. It comes from the French words 'sur' – from above, and 'veiller' – to watch (Kirchner, 2014). In order to maintain a level of manageability at international events, a greater level of monitoring is required. It is well known that many international events have huge economic, political, and social significance and can attract both positive and negative forces. Positive responses can lead to overcrowding and the emergency services benefit from the rapid responses surveillance systems offer.

Due to the increased threat from those who want to deliberately disrupt events, surveillance teams are employed to monitor activities inside the event venue and within a certain radius outside based on the size and importance of the event itself. Events such as the Group of Seven (G7) summit (comprising leaders of Canada, France, Germany, Italy, Japan, the United Kingdom, and the United States), will have intensive surveillance, while the Boston Marathon on Patriot's Day 2013 had no direct surveillance related to the event. However, the city's surveillance cameras played a key role in the relatively quick apprehension of the bombers (IFSEC Global, 2014).

Surveillance on a global level by world governments raises many questions about civil liberties and the right to privacy in the 'digital age' (Hosenball and Whitesides, 2013). However, most venues and cities are equipped and appropriately use their surveillance capabilities to their maximum capabilities to ensure the safety of attendees and participants. While any kind of observation without permission continues to create a great deal of public foreboding, there is no doubting the safety value or level of assistance provided to event organisers.

International events are not only supported by surveillance procedures, they can also be the means of entry to a society by including specific measures within official bidding documentation. In certain cases, the implications of a winning bid for a major international event can mean heavy investment in a nation's wider and more permanent surveillance operations. Rojek (2014, p. 38) emphasised the London 2012 investment in 'securitisation' explaining how it contributed to the electronic wiring up of the city with a new range of number plates and facial recognition closed circuit television (CCTV) systems, checkpoints and new police control centres. The cost of 'super panopticon CCTV' security provision was approximately US$100,000 per competing athlete. Over 10,000 athletes from 204 National Olympic Committees (NOCs) participated (BBC, 2012). In Athens, the figure was even higher, at US$150,000 per competing athlete.

7.19.1 Blue zones

The cost of surveillance for international events can be substantial and for international state events, run into hundreds of millions. Some high-profile political events require specialist levels of security and surveillance and create what are known as 'blue zones'.

A blue zone is based on the United Nations (UN) flag. In certain circumstances when heads of state meet, the host nation will transfer control of sections of the inner event space over to the UN. This means the event space will become international territory and fall under international law. The area is then managed by the UN, including legislation. Local laws do not apply in the area designated as a blue zone.

7.20 A sense of security

At international events, one of the first effects participants will experience is the presence of security and stewarding. This is discussed in more detail in

Chapter 5. Regardless of the type of event, the reason for the deployment of security personnel should always be considered a positive experience and not one of restraint. The size of the event usually determines the level of presence although this can be a difficult balance, particularly when the event is a one off.

A sense of security and safety for both participants and spectators is provided on several levels. These include the visible presence of:

- Volunteers providing directions and advice
- Stewards in high-visibility gilets and jackets with specific knowledge of the venue
- Charitable organisations such as St John Ambulance
- The three main emergency services
- Security Advisory Groups (SAGs)
- Armed forces.

Some high-profile events will also include specialist security services including bodyguards and members of the secret service. As the size of the event and the level of celebrity increases, so does the level of security. In some cases, 24-hour security for participants can be necessary. Even safety for the event space itself has become a detailed aspect of delivery many weeks before the event arrives. The function is normally coordinated by specialist members of the law enforcement agency with officers and support teams conducting pre-event searches and maintaining a presence both inside and outside the venue.

The management of the space around the venue is often monitored with vehicle and pedestrian inspections and controls placed around the perimeter of the venue. The extent of the event itself is based on the whole footprint. For example, a political event that includes 20 international politicians is likely also to have heavy security restrictions and require far more resources than a major sporting event attracting 50,000 spectators. The G20 in Osaka in 2019 deployed 32,000 police officers in the streets with local officials warning visitors and residents of traffic delays, sealed rubbish bins and lockers in train stations, and restrictions on movement around major hotels (Johnston, 2019). The most heavily policed football matches in the UK have one officer present for every 50 fans, prompting calls for a review on over-policing (Homer, 2018).

When events extend the reach of security beyond their immediate footprint, it is important to advise the local community of what delays can be expected in order for them to prepare for the planned disruption. Not only does this allow local residents to make alternative plans, it assists in the overall communication between the event and the local community. For larger events, usual modes of transport and personal movement can become severely disrupted creating a nuisance for local residents. Such issues can add to the overall management of the event, particularly if disgruntled residents come together to object. The importance of forward-planning that involves the local community is crucial in planning the security for larger, potentially disruptive events.

Not only is it important to advise of road closures, inspection controls or any other kind of potential disruption, but also the fact that any movements related to the event will also be closely monitored, particularly around large gatherings in public spaces. Figure 7.11 shows how London Underground advised passengers about the potential disruption to their commute in the run-up to London 2012.

Figure 7.11 Posters positioned at stations in London during the Games 2012

Laws exist on the use of drones close to large gatherings and flying aircraft are monitored by air traffic control. Jockeys travelling between race meetings, canvassing politicians, and famous musicians are typical examples of those who have direct access to event spaces by helicopters. In such cases where the aircraft flies close to the general public, pilots must follow very strict guidelines when entering and leaving the event space. Helicopter operators will be well aware of the regulations governing their operations while the event organisers must ensure the organisational set-up and provision of ground facilities are adequate to ensure the safety of flights and the safety of people on the ground (CAA, 2012).

7.21 Facial recognition technology

Facial recognition is a relatively new form of surveillance technology that is able to quickly identify a person from a digital image. It is used at sporting events, in shopping centres, airports and on the high street. The technology can be fitted to every city's or business' CCTV security system. The debate over the widespread use of facial recognition technology at international events is very much split. On the one hand, the technology is said to meet the challenges of 21st century security (Coopersmith, 2009), for the prevention or detection of unlawful activities. On the other, it is unreliable, an invasion of privacy, has no code of conduct, and lacks any manageable legislative measures to regulate the distribution of and trade in people's data (Clifton, 2020).

In recent years, the use of facial recognition technology by police and private security companies has become much more prevalent and, because it is easy to integrate into existing security software, it can bring a number of benefits to audiences and international event organisers alike. Security is enhanced as individuals can be recognised quickly and before they reach the event. Facial recognition could reduce the chances of bottlenecks and crushes as the need to produce a ticket at the gate would no longer be required. The latest technology is incredibly accurate and can process data in milliseconds, making the speed at which intervention is made almost instantaneous.

However, as the technology is used in public spaces, the debate on its widespread use has intensified over breaches of personal privacy and the threat it could pose to marginalised groups such as those whose appearance suggests that they follow non-Western religions (Devlin, 2019). Civil rights groups believe the adoption of facial recognition technology amplifies existing prejudices and further entrenches existing power structures (Hopkins, 2019). Therefore, until an acceptable level of regulatory legislation is introduced, international events may be forced to delay their use of the technology.

Capturing and processing people's data without permission or knowledge is at the centre of a number of objections to its implementation in public spaces. In 2019, Manchester City Football Club were cautioned against the introduction of facial recognition technology, as it risked normalising a mass surveillance tool (Wolfe-Robinson, 2019).

Facial recognition software is thought by many to be used for serious purposes such as looking out for terrorists, and searching for other criminal suspects who are wanted by the police. This has made its use in a public space highly contentious (Perala, 2016; Kumar et al., 2018). However, international hallmark and mega events are most likely to be the catalyst for a change in legislation as safety and other security issues are used as the basis to overrule the civil rights objections.

London 2012 avoided problematic surveillance legislation by including the legislation as part of the event's broader delivery agreement (Rojek, 2014). In 2019, the organisers of the Tokyo Olympics announced that facial recognition technology would be used to improve security and to identify athletes, officials, staff and media at the Olympic and Paralympic Games then being planned for 2020 (Hall, 2019), though subsequently postponed due to COVID-19.

There remain opposing perspectives on the technology's reliability as some claims suggest that the technology is able to positively identify people walking by within half a second, even if they are not looking straight at a camera (Kastrenakes, 2018; Taylor, 2019a). However, Clifton (2020) suggests that the most recent trials show the technology is so unreliable, it regularly gets the gender wrong of the person it is attempting to recognise.

7.22 Terror attacks

While the issue of terrorism is largely the responsibility of the state, access to international events has become much more challenging in recent years for the organisers. All event organisers should take extra care when bringing people together for international events. Security and counterterrorism take up a considerable amount of effort in the planning of modern international events. For some events, counterterrorism strategies have become a routine part of the planning process, particularly in the staging of the major sporting events. However, the manner in which recent acts of terror in Nice and Manchester took place highlight how difficult such acts are to predict and for event organisers to protect their audience; this is discussed in more detail in Chapter 9.

International events attract large audiences and are therefore a target for terrorists. The sad truth is that the type of international events that are being targeted by terrorists and protestors are non-political in nature and instead are celebrating diversity and inclusion. The types of event targeted in recent years suggest a strategic objective of finding a weak spot and exploiting it. No event organiser would knowingly expose their audience to harm.

For the attackers, it is purely about the amount of exposure that can be gained from impacting on these events. But while fatal atrocities are rare in the grand scheme of international events, they are by no means new. History and biblical texts provide evidence of terrorist-style attacks dating back to the 1st century. Event organisers today have to plan, prepare and put in place appropriate levels of protection. Once this is done, the safety of the event is ultimately dependent upon the vigilance of the team at the time.

7.23 Demonstrations and violence

While most international events will pass without incident, there are some that generate a partisan response to either the host or the subject matter. Some sporting events have become notorious for the level of violence while global political events can bring protestors out onto the street in their tens of thousands. International soccer matches can attract highly coordinated gangs of supporters using the fixtures as an opportunity to damage property and inflict bodily harm on their opponent's supporters.

Demonstrations, on the other hand, are largely more peaceful in their approach but can create major problems for the organisers and the future of the event itself. Such activities politicise events and often to a level that is not understood by the event organisers. The issue international event organisers need to accept is that all events, process and practices which occur within the social sphere have the potential to be political (Hay, 2002, p. 3).

During the 2000 Olympics, Barkham (2000) reported Aborigines calling for an end to the genocidal 212-year war by white Australians against indigenous people, highlighting issues of social injustice and human rights violations. Waitt (2003) pointed out that even though a temporary Aboriginal Embassy had been set up in Victoria Park, Sydney, as a protest camp, protestors only managed to reach a few hundred and were completely dwarfed by the public presence of thousands at Olympics-inspired social activities.

To understand many of the access issues an international event will experience, it is important to understand the audience profile. A profile of the audience is created by reviewing the age, gender, and background of the fan base. This information can tell you a lot about the potential requirements for the event.

All major events that attract large audiences can also attract opposing opinions. Baker *et al.* (2017) suggest that many international events result in disorder with the need to deploy riot squads to protect delegates and participants and the possibility of arrests. In some serious cases, this can lead to the police introducing crowd control measures and the use of controversial tactics such as kettling.

7.23.1 Kettling

When a crowd (peaceful or otherwise) does not follow police supervision and guidance on the day, a process known as 'kettling' can ensue. Kettling is a police tactic whereby large numbers of protesters are effectively detained within a limited space. The tactic does not discriminate and everyone in the gathering, regardless of their intentions, is held and 'controlled' through pressure. There is a dichotomy of dilemmas when kettling is enforced as those being kettled feel the loss of their civil rights, which is usually related to the reason for the gathering in the first place.

It is possible for members of the public with no connection to the protest to become involved by being in the wrong place at the wrong time. The method has a tendency to spread fear and frustration amongst the innocent and vulnerable who become contained, with the potential of causing further reactions from the crowd, so making a bad situation worse.

7.24 Social inequality

It would not be right to have a chapter on access and not include a section on social inequality. Throughout the world, the effects of social inequality are under-reported while the burgeoning world of events is the centre of many people's lives. Many of the people international events are targeted at are stuck in a cycle of poverty.

To put social inequality into context, 21% of the UK's population live in poverty. Moreover, those living in families with a disabled member are more likely to be on low income (Department for Work & Pensions, 2016). The market value of the English Premier League is estimated to be over US$10.13 billion (Transfermarkt, n.d.). The transfer window of 2017 took spending by English clubs up to US$1.73 billion (Davies, 2019a). The wages of English Premier League players from its twenty teams have continued to rise, regardless of a global economic downturn and freezes on many benefits and working-class wages. In 2019, the BBC (2019) reported that the annual wage bill was at US$3.5 billion, while the revenue generated was at US$5.79 billion. Figure 7.12 shows the figures in sterling and the continued rise in both wages and revenue.

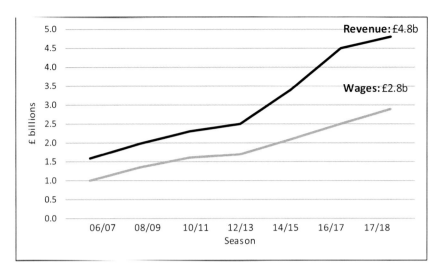

Figure 7.12 The continued rise in wages and revenue English Premier League, 2006/07–2017/18

Source: Based on data from Parrett and Tantam, 2019

The key effect from this example is that a working-class sport that has previously been the focal point of a local community is totally pricing out of the game the very people who it was made for. Association football is part of working-class life and local people arguably rely on it the most. Season ticket prices have seen continued increases: even at the lower end of the Premier League, newly promoted clubs for 2019 Aston Villa and Sheffield United saw their season ticket prices rise by 15% and 11% respectively compared with the previous season. What has long been considered the great escape for the working class has driven them back to the bars or the armchair of a friend who can afford to pay the subscription on the satellite TV. Moreover, alcohol consumption in the poorest communities is both a major health and social problem, but it is now cheaper for an individual to spend the afternoon drinking than it is to attend the game.

When it comes to participation, access to sport is often based on social division. The sports people play in school are commonly determined by their social class. The budget for a working-class school does not normally extend to 22 tennis racquets, but it can afford a football. Jarvie (2011) believes that the potential coherence of social divisions lies in the notions of hierarchy, social inequality and social injustice that permeate sport.

7.25 Summary

Access to events is a much deeper subject than one might suspect. This chapter has taught us that as one access topic is discussed, another is revealed, and it becomes difficult to avoid raising more and more issues that relate to accessing international events. We have learned that many of the issues to do with access relate to safety and fairness – not only through attendance, but also through participation. There remains much to be done to provide the appropriate levels of access, but there is also solid evidence that international events have developed considerably in recent years and meet the many demands to warrant our events are safe and ensure the needs of the minority and less represented groups are met.

Case study 7.1 Fantasy case of ticket sales for an Ed Sheeran concert

Ed Sheeran has announced a tour of Europe with tickets going on sale next month. His latest idea to avoid his fans being ripped off by the secondary ticketing sites is for his promoter to charge £500 for a ticket and to reimburse the purchaser £475 through online banking the moment they are scanned into the venue.

Questions

1. What do you consider to be the most notable problems this approach might create for the event organisers?
2. Is the approach feasible, considering that most of his fans are teenagers and rely on the bank of mum and dad?
3. What other safety precautions could Ed and his promoters include to avoid secondary ticket sales?

7.26 Useful websites

Live music is for everyone
www.attitudeiseverything.org.uk/

Event checklist for disability and access
www.lahf.org.uk/sites/default/files/Briefing_128_-_Events_Checklist_-_Disability_
   and_Access.pdf

Transforming our world: the 2030 Agenda for Sustainable Development
https://sustainabledevelopment.un.org/post2015/transformingourworld

Temporary demountable structures (TDS)
www.hse.gov.uk/event-safety/temporary-demountable-structures.htm

Cyber security for major events. Assessing the cyber security needs of major events.
www.ncsc.gov.uk/guidance/cyber-security-for-major-events

External forces

GDPR: The principles
https://ico.org.uk/for-organisations/guide-to-data-protection/guide-to-the-general-
    data-protection-regulation-gdpr/principles/

Managing temporary carparks
www.rightguard.co.uk/services/parking-services/

References

Adams, J. (2018). State of access report 2018: Ticketing without barriers. Retrieved
    from   www.attitudeiseverything.org.uk/uploads/general/State_of_Access_Report_
    2018.pdf Accessed 27th June 2019.
Amaury Sport Organisation (ASO) (2019). The publicity caravan of the 2019 Tour de
    France. www.aso.fr/en/
Baker, D., Bronitt, S., & Stenning, P. (2017). Policing protest, security and freedom: The
    2014 G20 experience. *Police Practice and Research, 18*(5), 425–448. doi:10.1080/
    15614263.2017.1280674
Barkham, P. (2000). Divided we fall. *The Guardian*. Retrieved from www.theguardian.
    com/sydney/story/0,7369,367879,00.html Accessed 26th June 2017.
BBC (2002). Glastonbury reveals 'super-fence'. Retrieved from http://news.bbc.co.uk/1/
    hi/entertainment/2002549.stm Accessed 19th December 2017.
BBC (2012). London 2012 Olympics close with spectacular ceremony. Retrieved from
    www.bbc.co.uk/news/uk-19236754 Accessed 14th June 2018.
BBC (2019). Premier League wage bill surges to £2.9bn. Retrieved from www.bbc.co.uk/
    news/business-48042814 Accessed 13th August 2019.
Berners, P. (2017). *The Practical Guide to Organising Events*. London: Routledge.
Chan, T.-C., Pai, P.-L., Shaw, S.-L., & Fan, I. C. (2015). Spatiotemporal evolution of market
    towns in the Jiangnan area during the Ming-Qing dynasties of China. *Historical
    Methods: A Journal of Quantitative and Interdisciplinary History, 48*(2), 90–102.
    doi:10.1080/01615440.2014.995783
Civil Aviation Authority (CAA) (2012). Guidance for event organisers and heli-
    copter operators at special events. Retrieved from www.caa.co.uk/WorkArea/
    DownloadAsset.aspx?id=4294975100 Accessed 12th August 2019.
Clifton, H. (Producer), White, G. (Reporter) (2020). Facial recognition. In *File on Four*.
    London: BBC Radio 4. [:]
Conway, L. (2020). *Briefing Paper Number 4715, 2 March 2020: Secondary ticketing*.
    London: House of Commons Library.
Coopersmith, J. C. (2009). The history of information security: A comprehensive hand-
    book. *Technology and Culture, 50*(1), 262.
Cybersecurity & Infrastructure Security Agency (CISA) (2009). Understanding denial-
    of-service attacks. Retrieved from www.us-cert.gov/ncas/tips/ST04-015 Accessed 8th
    July 2019.
Davies, L. (2019a). How much money every Premier League club has spent in the
    2019 transfer window. Retrieved from https://talksport.com/football/572055/every-
    premier-league-club-spent-summer-transfer-window-2019–2020/   Accessed   13th
    August 2019.
Davies, R. (2019b). Nothing illegal about reselling tickets', jury at fraud trial told. *The
    Guardian*. Retrieved from www.theguardian.com/business/2019/nov/20/nothing-
    illegal-about-reselling-tickets-jury-at-trial-told Accessed 19th November 2019.
De Groot, J. (2019). What is the General Data Protection Regulation? Understanding
    & complying with GDPR requirements in 2019. *Digital Guardian*. Retrieved from

https://digitalguardian.com/blog/what-gdpr-general-data-protection-regulation-understanding-and-complying-gdpr-data-protection Accessed 9th July 2019.

Devlin, H. (2019). 'We are hurtling towards a surveillance state': the rise of facial recognition technology. *The Guardian*. Retrieved from www.theguardian.com/technology/2019/oct/05/facial-recognition-technology-hurtling-towards-surveillance-state Accessed 10th October 2019.

Department for Work & Pensions (DWP) (2016). *Households Below Average Income: An analysis of the UK income distribution: 1994/95–2014/15*. Retrieved from https://assets.publishing.service.gov.uk/government/uploads/system/uploads/attachment_data/file/532416/households-below-average-income-1994-1995-2014-2015.pdf Accessed 13th August 2019.

Disabled World (2017). Disabilities: Definition, types and models of disability. Retrieved from www.disabled-world.com/disability/types/ Accessed 27th June 2019.

Hall, T. (2019). Giant itab's top 4 tech trends in 2019. Retrieved from https://accessaa.co.uk/giant-itabs-top-4-tech-trends-in-2019/ Accessed 10th October 2019.

Hay, C. (2002). *Political Analysis: A Critical Introduction*. Basingstoke: Palgrave.

Hind, P. M. (2017). *Temporary Demountable Structures – Guidance on Procurement Design and Use* (4th Ed.). London: Institution of Structural Engineers.

HM Revenue & Customs (HMRC) (2017). Pay tax on payments to foreign entertainers and sportspersons. Retrieved from www.gov.uk/guidance/pay-tax-on-payments-to-foreign-performers Accessed 23rd March 2018.

Holder, M. (2014). Tour de France boosts Huddersfield air quality. Retrieved from https://airqualitynews.com/2014/08/15/tour-de-france-boosts-huddersfield-air-quality/ Accessed 13th August 2019.

Homer, A. (2018). Premier League and EFL football matches 'over-policed'. Retrieved from www.bbc.co.uk/news/uk-england-44871578 Accessed 15th November 2019.

Hopkins, O. (2019). Facial recognition is a fundamental threat to society. Retrieved from www.dezeen.com/2019/10/09/facial-recognition-hong-kong-threat/ Accessed 10th October 2019.

Hosenball, M., & Whitesides, J. (2013). Reports on surveillance of Americans fuel debate over privacy, security. Retrieved from www.reuters.com/article/us-usa-wiretaps-verizon/reports-on-surveillance-of-americans-fuel-debate-over-privacy-security-idUSBRE95502920130607 Accessed 12th August 2019.

IFSEC Global (2014). Role of CCTV cameras: Public, privacy and protection. Retrieved from www.ifsecglobal.com/video-surveillance/role-cctv-cameras-public-privacy-protection/ Accessed 20th March 2018.

Jarvie, G. (2011). Sport, social division and social inequality. *Sport Science Review, 20*(1–2), 95–109. doi:10.2478/v10237-011-0049-0

Johnston, A. (2019). Osaka braces for unprecedented security measures ahead of G20 summit. *Japan Times*. Retrieved from www.japantimes.co.jp/news/2019/06/23/national/osaka-braces-unprecedented-security-measures-ahead-g20-summit/#.XdTx11f7TIU Accessed 15th November 2019.

Kastrenakes, J. (2018). Ticketmaster could replace tickets with facial recognition. Retrieved from www.theverge.com/2018/5/7/17329196/ticketmaster-facial-recognition-tickets-investment-blink-identity Accessed 9th July 2019.

Kirchner, R. (2014). *Surveillance and Threat Detection: Prevention Versus Mitigation*. Waltham, MA: Butterworth-Heinemann.

Klepal, D., & Tucker, T. (2015). Skyrocketing stadium costs: Dallas Cowboys' new home has led way for other $1 billion NFL facilities. *The Atlanta Journal-Constitution,* 22nd February 2015.

Kumar, V., Malathi, S., Vengatesan, K., & Ramakrishnan, M. (2018). Facial recognition system for suspect identification using a surveillance camera. *Pattern Recognition and Image Analysis, 28*(3), 410–420. doi:10.1134/s1054661818030136

Leslie, J. (2019). The EU will start enforcing the GDPR Soon—is your business ready? Retrieved from https://keap.com/product-updates/how-to-prepare-for-gdpr Accessed 9th July 2019.

Manfred, T. (2014). Why real fans can't go to the Super Bowl. Retrieved from www.businessinsider.com/super-bowl-48-tickets-seahawks-broncos-2014-1?r=US&IR=T Accessed 13th August 2019.

National Cyber Security Centre (NCSC) (2019). Cyber security for major events: Assessing the cyber security needs of major events. Retrieved from:www.ncsc.gov.uk/guidance/cyber-security-for-major-events Accessed 9th July 2019.

Parrett, G., & Tantam, L. (2019). Premier League clubs' revenues reach a record £4.8 billion, but profitability is dampened by rising wage spend. https://www2.deloitte.com/uk/en/pages/press-releases/articles/premier-league-clubs-revenues-reach-a-record.html Accessed 24th June 2019.

Perala, A. (2016). New York to test facial recognition software at bridge, tunnel crossings. Retrieved from https://findbiometrics.com/new-york-facial-recognition-bridge-tunnel-310073/ Accessed 21st May 2020.

Profootballtalk (2014) Super Bowl XLVIII sets record for largest audience. Retrieved from https://profootballtalk.nbcsports.com/2014/02/03/fox-super-bowl-xlviii-sets-record-for-largest-audience-on-average/ Accessed 24th June 2019.

R&A (n.d.). About Us. Retrieved from www.randa.org/en/about-us Accessed 12th August 2019.

Rojek, C. (2014). Global Event Management: A critique. *Leisure Studies, 33*(1), 32–47. doi:10.1080/02614367.2012.716077

Silvers, J. R. (2008). *Risk Management for Meetings and Events*. London: Butterworth-Heinemann.

Taylor, A. (2019a). Startup aims to replace concert tickets with facial recognition technology. Retrieved from:www.abcactionnews.com/news/national/startup-aims-to-replace-concert-tickets-with-facial-recognition-technology Accessed 9th July 2019.

Taylor, M. (2019b). Sadiq Khan announces car-free day in London to tackle air pollution. *The Guardian*. Retrieved from www.theguardian.com/environment/2019/jun/20/sadiq-khan-announces-car-free-day-in-london-to-tackle-air-pollution

Telegraph, The (2015). Watchdog reveals secondary ticketing 'stitch up' as event tickets go on sale before official release. www.telegraph.co.uk/news/shopping-and-consumer-news/11993056/Watchdog-reveals-secondary-ticketing-stitch-up-as-event-tickets-go-on-sale-before-official-release.html Accessed 20th June 2017.

Transfermarkt (n.d.). Premier League. Retrieved from www.transfermarkt.co.uk/premier-league/transfers/wettbewerb/GB1 Accessed 13th August 2019.

United Nations (2016). *Transforming Our World: 2030 Agenda for Sustainable Development.* Available at sustainabledevelopment.un.org

Waitt, G. (2003). Social impacts of the Sydney Olympics. *Annals of Tourism Research, 30*(1), 194–215. doi:10.1016/s0160-7383(02)00050-6

Wolfe-Robinson, M. (2019). Manchester City face calls to reconsider facial recognition tech: Campaigners say decision to grant fans access by facial scan 'intrusive' and 'disturbing. *The Guardian.* Retrieved from www.theguardian.com/technology/2019/aug/18/manchester-city-face-calls-to-reconsider-facial-recognition-tech Accessed 20th August 2019.

World Bank (2019). Disability Inclusion. Retrieved from www.worldbank.org/en/topic/disability Accessed 27th June 2019.

Wynn-Moylan, P. (2018). *Risk and Hazard Management for Festivals and Events*. London: Routledge.

Chapter 8

Key stakeholder implications

Contents

8.1 Chapter overview

This chapter discusses the implications of stakeholder management from the perspective of international events and the consequential effects these can have on an event. All international events have a whole host of stakeholders that will have their own objectives that on occasion may be at odds with another. For clarification purposes, the chapter will begin by setting out the concept of stakeholder management within international events. It will then cover the responsibilities of stakeholders including ethical considerations and the ever-present possibilities of corruption in international events.

8.2 Learning objectives

By the end of this chapter, the student will be expected to:

- Understand the significance of stakeholders in an international event context
- Appreciate the difference between internal and external stakeholders
- Recognise the importance of maintaining good stakeholder relationships.

8.3 Introduction

International events are dynamic, precarious in nature, and will challenge even the most experienced of organisers. They cannot be accomplished without the cooperation of a number of participants who undertake key stakeholder roles in the delivery process. Every international event will encounter some kind of stakeholder complications along the way. Individual priorities from stakeholders can dramatically increase the possibility of conflict and add to the complexity of the delivery process. This means that identifying the event's key stakeholders is imperative for two reasons:

1. It is not possible to satisfy the needs of every stakeholder at every stage of the event
2. Without executive decisions, conflict management would take over the planning process.

Deciding where the stakeholder level ends for each stage of the event and how much influence is afforded to each stakeholder is what makes delivering an international event an achievable task. If not, the consultation stage would still be in full swing on the date the event was meant to start.

8.4 Defining stakeholders in an international event setting

Effective management in international events is based upon understanding the often complex relationships with, and amongst stakeholders (Todd *et al.*, 2017). An international event has the potential to include a large number of stakeholders making it important to understand their involvement, stake or influence. Key stakeholders are by definition those essential to the success of the event, but determining who the key stakeholders are is a challenge in itself as the definition can be interpreted as broadly inclusive. A stakeholder, according to the Oxford English Dictionary, is defined as a person, company, etc., with a concern or interest in ensuring the success of an organisation, business, or system (OED, 1989). Freeman (1984) classified the function of stakeholders as owners, consumer advocates, customers, competitors, media, employees, special interest groups, environmentalists, suppliers, governments, and the local community organisations. Based on these definitions, everyone and everything is a stakeholder. If presented correctly, insects, invertebrates, or any kind of wildlife could be considered a key stakeholder in an international event as they can have a significant influence. How key each is to the event will depend on how well their case is presented as to their level of stakeholder value.

This is not a flippant suggestion as more serious claims may have been considered flippant until they lead to the cancellation of a number of music festivals. T in the Park was a long-running music festival that was held annually from 1994 to 2016. Attracting an audience of over 250,000 it became one of the best known, biggest and best-loved festivals in the world (T in the Park, 2016). The event was cancelled in 2016. The presence of an osprey's nest on the site in Perthshire had led to a change in planning requirements, making the event unworkable (Boult, 2016). Ospreys are a protected species and it is against the law to disturb them during breeding season.

A Chicago festival was cancelled due to the presence of the Great Lakes' piping plover shorebirds, a federally protected species. Noise disturbs piping plovers, and the US Fish and Wildlife Service mandates that no loud activities take place within six-tenths of a mile of a piping plover nest (Hermann, 2019). The event organisers cited circumstances beyond their control which included significantly higher than average waters of Lake Michigan eliminating the beach portion of the intended site (Skinner, 2019)

Therefore, key stakeholders in international events are a combination of those who are selected by the organisers as part of the delivery process for the event and whoever or whatever is able to impact on the delivery process. It does not matter if this is an individual, a group of people or an organisation. They become key stakeholders because of the influence created by their stake in the event.

Each stakeholder influencing the event will naturally have their own interest. For the most part, stakeholders are all engaged in making things happen, working towards the same goal, and keeping focused on deadlines and their contribution towards the success of the event.

Figure 8.1 A selection of internal stakeholder examples for an international event

8.4.1 Internal and external stakeholders

The breadth of stakeholders involved in an international event can go a long way beyond any apparent margin for the event. While every international event will include a local stakeholder community, they can include government departments from various nations affecting whole continents with each stage of the event being closely observed by the media.

Within the delivery of an international event, internal and external stakeholders will exist. Internal stakeholders are best defined as those who are involved with the actual delivery of the event. External stakeholders are those who are necessary contributors, may also benefit, but have no direct contribution to the delivery process. For example, a local business may have increased sales due to the event, but have little involvement in the delivery process. Similarly, local residents will be affected by the event but have no involvement in the delivery process. These are external stakeholders. The local emergency services have no direct benefit from the event, but are an internal stakeholder as they will play a crucial role in the delivery process. Some crossover will always exist, but the internal and external stakeholders can usually be defined by considering which stakeholder is involved with the delivery process. Figures 8.1 and 8.2 provide a number of examples of internal and external stakeholders.

With interest from and impacts on local communities and in some cases whole nations, the stakes can be very high. The event organisers are tasked with delivering excellent project outcomes at every stage of the event.

8.5 Identifying key stakeholders

Identifying the key stakeholders for an international event is one of the foremost tasks of the main organisers. It is a complicated process and requires due consideration of the event as a whole. This includes event organisers being in a position to evaluate the tangible economic and marketing impacts of an event, while attempting to gain an understanding of its symbolic influence upon the host destination (Getz and Page, 2016). For profit-seeking corporate events, the

Figure 8.2 A selection of external stakeholder examples for an international event

strategy may be to focus on how cost-effective or profitable the event can be. This would naturally be in the interest to stakeholders whose objective is financial gain. However, while this may be how the identification process begins or even be a key consideration, a great deal of moral and ethical scrutiny from external stakeholders will be placed on the profit-seeking stakeholders.

The identification of all stakeholders and a review of their agendas will assist event managers in balancing the competing needs, tensions and expectations (Reid, 2011). Moral and ethical considerations (discussed below), will play a major role in the identification process, as will revenue, customer satisfaction, and abiding by the law. This shows how strategic key stakeholder identification is; it therefore requires time to allow for serious deliberation.

Bryson (2004) presented 15 stakeholder identification and analysis techniques that were grouped into four categories:

- Organising participation
- Creating ideas for strategic interventions
- Building a winning coalition, and
- Implementing strategic proposals.

Stakeholder analysis methods such as those above are used to facilitate the approaches a company will use for its stakeholder management. This approach allows the organisers to predict who the key stakeholders may be at any given time in the delivery process. This is because the importance of stakeholder power will vary throughout the process. One stakeholder who plays a key role at the start of the event may play a less important role towards the end of the event. Equally, a stakeholder established as being less significant could develop into a key player. Local residents are leading examples of stakeholders who are elevated in this way, particularly when an application to hold the event is challenged.

It is not possible to discuss stakeholder management of any kind without referring to the work of Eden and Ackermann (1998). Their development of the 'stakeholder grid' allows event organisers to conceptualise the relationship

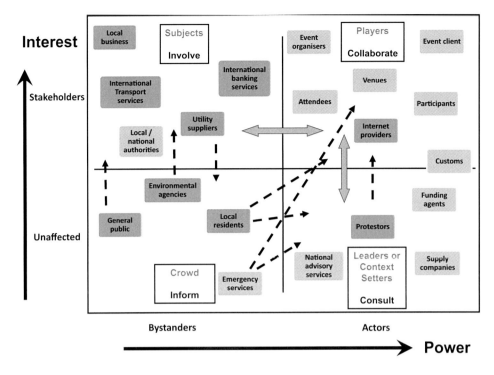

Figure 8.3 International event stakeholder Power Interest Grid

Source: Based on Eden and Ackermann, 2011

between the event and the stakeholder at any point in the life cycle of the event in two dimensions – the stakeholder's interests and their power. It creates a framework for understanding the changing nature [of the event] over time (Eden and Ackermann, 1998, p. 123).

By plotting stakeholders into four different categories – crowd, subjects, strategy content setter and players – their influence on the event and the level of communication necessary becomes visible. Some stakeholders may only need to be informed about certain activities, while others require collaboration. Figure 8.3 based on the Eden and Ackermann grid shows how the internal and external stakeholders suggested in Figures 8.1 and 8.2 could be treated at a given point in the event life cycle. The dotted arrows represent the extent and nature of instability and the solid arrows suggest the direction of likely management of the power or interest of stakeholders (Eden and Ackermann, 2011).

In this example, the level of communication is expressed as inform, consult, involve or collaborate. By plotting stakeholders in this way, the amount of effort in managing each stakeholder becomes clearer. Key stakeholder identification is a critical component of the initial scoping phase of an international event and should occur before any engagement or planning is formulated and consultations begin. Based on the Bryson (2004) method, MacDonald (2016) suggests organisers begin by holding brainstorming sessions to answer a number of questions to make sure all the potential stakeholders are included in the deliberations. Questions organisers should consider include:

- Who is affected positively and negatively by the project?
- Who has the power to make it succeed (or fail)?
- Who makes the decisions about money?
- Who are the suppliers?
- Who are the end users?
- Who has influence over other stakeholders?
- Who could solve potential problems with the project?
- Who is in charge of assigning or procuring resources or facilities?
- Who has specialist skills which are crucial to the project?

Once the key stakeholders have been identified along with the varying levels of communication, the manner and means of communication become the next important part of the process. International events are often vulnerable to the will or decisions of others. Less integrity leads to more conflict. Therefore the manner in which the will or decision is communicated as well as the integrity of the content will essentially be deciding factors in the strength of the relationship that is built between stakeholders.

The consequences of poor stakeholder communication were in many ways played out during the IAAF World Championships in Athletics in Doha 2019. The opening three days of competition were marked by swathes of empty seats at the Khalifa Stadium. The venue's normal capacity of 48,000 had been reduced to a modest 21,000 (Sportstar.com, 2019). Eventually, large numbers of soldiers attended in plain clothes and free tickets were distributed to embassies, employees, schools and higher education institutions (The Independent, 2019).

The empty seats sent a very negative signal as to Doha's ability to host any major event (Morgan, 2019). The poor management of such an important international event can affect the sport itself as the impression given on TV was one of a complete lack of interest in the event. Such impressions can lead to reduced global media figures which in turn lead to an eventual global downturn in public interest and attendance.

8.6 Ethics and stakeholder issues

To understand the stakeholder relationships as both strategic and ethical, the focus of analysis should be shifted from stakeholder attributes to the dimensions of stakeholder relationships (Kujala *et al.*, 2012). Successful stakeholder management is an achievement in itself and will make use of all the skills an event organiser has learned. To find and sustain a permanent niche, the event organisation must be expert in developing a supportive network and in managing its many, diverse stakeholder relationships (Andersson and Getz, 2008).

Considering international events will have multiple stakeholders, the last thing an organiser needs is a transition from stakeholder management to conflict management. Any kind of conflict with or between the stakeholders only increases pressure on the event and will impact on the planning process. Interests, values, and expectations can be at odds and how each stakeholder is managed in order to satisfy their needs will vary. Therefore, serving the needs of one stakeholder over another is likely to guarantee conflict and may influence other stakeholders, potentially putting the success of the event at risk. The only real way to avoid such encounters is to adopt an ethical approach to the communication process.

Business ethics asks what is good and bad, right and wrong, harmful and beneficial in business decisions and actions in organisational transactions (Weiss, 2014). Therefore, doing business in an ethical manner is essentially doing what is ethically correct. When working on an international stage, it can be easy to overlook local ethical responsibilities and differences that exist in each individual nation. International events have a responsibility to continue to honour ethics and global justice based on respect and consideration from both moral and political perspectives.

Many of the arrangements between international event stakeholders are covered by agreements and contracts. Therefore, it can be important for the event organisers to have some knowledge of the areas their event is travelling to and make sure any questionable issues are researched and if necessary included in the contract. These might include safe transport between venues when there are security issues or access to bottled water when there are sanitation issues, By including such issues in the contract, the responsibility is set out and clearly understood before you travel. Beyond a legal contract, all partnerships involve moral responsibilities such as the obligation to treat partners with respect and decency, as well as the right for correct information and the duty not to harm (Minoja, 2012). However, entering some international states is a risk in itself and moral responsibilities cannot always be guaranteed in overseas states.

Ethical decisions will have to be addressed regardless of the size of the international event. For example, merchandise will be a contributor to the profits of the event and the organisers will have to choose a partner organisation to provide this service. It is quite common for an event organiser to overlook where merchandise for an event is produced. The supply chain is often not properly considered at the point of purchase when the deciding factor is based on cost and profit margins.

From an audience stakeholder perspective, Henderson and Musgrave (2014) suggest that the level of waste from an outdoor festival is a particularly serious problem whether viewed simply as an issue of environmental damage or, pragmatically, as an increase in the charges incurred with landfill. It is essential for international events to have a plan in place to manage waste on site. Festival goers may not consider the ethical implications of leaving their tent and other waste on the festival site or that their behaviour should be ethically questioned when it seems everybody is doing it.

Festival organisers who have not previously been able to properly address the problem of waste management are slowly introducing alternatives to the mass bringing and dumping of camping equipment by providing it on site. Renting set areas of a festival site to companies who provide all the camping equipment is one approach. The festival goer hires their equipment online prior to the event. However, the reality is that providing individual occupancy dwellings (for up to four people), will not totally remove the problem, but simply pass it on to other stakeholders. However, a chain of responsibility for such activities when such plans are in place is easier to manage. Ethical questions may well then be asked of the event organisers when festival camping equipment continues to go to landfill. It could be argued that a much more beneficial development would be to provide robust multi-occupancy temporary demountable structures based on a marquee that can house hundreds of people along with other facilities built in and use these year-on-year.

8.7 Corporate social responsibility (CSR)

On a global scale there are 5–6 million regularly occurring festivals and events held throughout the world each year which can cause long-term extensive damage and degradation (Hanrahan and Maguire, 2016). Considering the number of major stakeholders in each of these events, the subject of corporate social responsibility (CSR) becomes an important factor. So much so that Carlsen *et al.* (2007) suggests that while the attention of stakeholders has been on economic benefits, the very important cultural, community, and social benefits have been overlooked.

CSR is a broad and much developed concept that can take many forms depending on the kind of company and industry it engages with. Carroll (1991) proposed a pyramid of corporate social responsibility which included four domains. Modern interpretations refer to a three-domain approach that includes economic, legal, and ethical responsibilities (Schwartz and Carroll, 2003). Modern international events tend to include environmental, economic and sociocultural aspects of event development, and a suitable balance must be established between these three dimensions to guarantee an event's long-term sustainability and legacy (Raj and Musgrave, 2009).

The ultimate in stakeholder management practice has to be looking after ourselves and the planet we live on. Whether this is considered as a CSR responsibility will depend on the company itself. The international event industry's approach to sustainability may be changing, but by adopting a sustainable stakeholder approach to every detail, more of the hidden environmental impacts can be managed. Sustainability at international events is discussed in more detail in Chapter 10, but when we consider how wasteful the international event industry is, every decision should be making adjustments aimed at reducing the negative environmental impacts.

Apart from a number of external contributions of recycling, the current supply chain model of most events is linear. That is, much of what comes in is not recycled, but thrown away after use. Recent reports have revealed that stakeholders in the event process are not upholding their responsibilities. In the UK, much of the mixed recyclate is shipped to the Far East for processing (McIntosh, 2013) only then to end up in landfill (Beard, 2019).

The reality is that many event organisers throughout the world cannot be certain their waste is being properly disposed of. Shiploads of unwanted rubbish from the West accumulates in the ports of the Philippines, Indonesia and Vietnam while vast toxic wastelands of plastics imported from Australia, Europe and the US have built up across Malaysia (Ellis-Petersen, 2019). Waste transported from international events is almost certainly included in these shipments.

The conscious decision to ship the waste is made by councils and governments in full knowledge of the kind of impact they are having on all aspects of society, including economic, social, and environmental. Therefore, the ethical principles of CSR are being abandoned. The local authority or national government may not be breaking any laws in dealing with the waste in this way, but the integrity of the agreed responsibility as a stakeholder in the event is ruined as no recycling is taking place.

Such instances bring into question the numerous examples of best practice in CSR that are available on the internet. How can one stakeholder be certain that the various other stakeholders in any given operation are genuinely seeing through their responsibilities in an ethical and honourable manner? There will be numerous companies making genuine efforts to maintain their corporate and social responsibilities. Others regularly associated with international events such as, Coca Cola, Pfizer, Walt Disney, Johnson & Johnson, Starbucks, and Wells Fargo strongly market their CSR efforts promoting the contribution to CSR good practice (O'Brien, 2019). On the surface, this may suggest they are all being socially and corporately responsible. However, these are the same corporations who are alleged to be the biggest regulatory violators (Good Jobs First, n.d.).

Progress in exposing failings is CSR in international events and business in general is much more widespread these days, but much still needs to be achieved in order to see CSR as a genuine and ethical contribution rather than being used as a promotional activity just to appear corporately and socially responsible. With greater emphasis being placed on sustainability, carbon footprints, and the knock-on effects to innocent communities, the actions of the larger corporations are raising the level of scrutiny.

8.8 Stakeholder dishonesty and corruption

We have discussed the importance of power in international events in Chapters 4 and 5. Along with power comes a great deal of moral responsibility. Power and responsibility imply access to superior knowledge and those stakeholders with knowledge and power can take advantage of their position and pervert the integrity of their duties with acts that can be considered dishonest or corrupt. Considering many international events are funded through public funds with major contracts awarded and funds processed through unique channels, many opportunities exist for individuals or groups to bend rules into acts that on one level are more than just questionable and on another considered dishonest. However, in reality, corruption is collective rather than simply individual, going beyond private gain to encompass broader interests and benefits within political systems (DfID, 2015). The awarding of major events is meant to be totally transparent.

When considering the unique nature of some international events, the United Nations Convention against Corruption 2013 clearly defines the unusual circumstances that can be advantageously manipulated leading to dishonest practices. The convention states:

> The exceptional nature of events increases the likelihood that regulations and standard procedures might be relaxed or set aside during the special situation as many different actors are involved and resources arrive from less familiar sources, often travelling through unfamiliar channels. The shortness of time may make it difficult for existing monitoring, auditing and accountability mechanisms to effectively perform their functions and have the desired impact. As a result, the necessary independent oversight of activities might be

lacking and the allocation of public funds may not be transparent or subject to adequate controls.

(United Nations, 2019)

The awarding of major international events is a procedure that has over time attracted numerous claims and proven acts of dishonesty and corruption. Year-on-year, large-scale international events that require public funding have been criticised for unusual activities related to the integrity of the bidding and awarding process. These include bribery scandals resulting from event bidding process, dubious contract arrangements, and fantasy budgeting (Dodds, 2016; Harding, 2010; Rawling, 2005). Rusbridger (2014) suggested that FIFA's secret ballots and unaccountable, barely scrutinised machinations make it at best an out-of-touch anachronism in the modern commercial world.

During these unusual and regularly secretive undertakings, opportunities to take advantage of a situation are real. Such situations have tempted and continue to tempt many event organisers into dishonest actions. From the highest levels of international event management including local organising committees, IAAF, FIFA and the IOC to local councils and support organisers, questions of dishonesty have been uncovered on a regular basis. In fact, the questionable nature of winning international event bids seems to have become more predictable in recent years than the process itself. Coincidences and illogical decisions have fuelled journalistic interest in bidding processes and award decisions (Almeida et al., 2014; Calvert, 2019; Kassens-Noor and Lauermann, 2018; Macaloon, 2011; Maguire, 2011; Tufts, 2004; Wamsley, 2002; Witherow, 2019).

While not considered corrupt, there have been questions over the recent decision to hold the 2021 IAAF world championships in Eugene, Oregon. A place notable in terms of world athletics only for being the town where Nike was founded and has its world headquarters (Williams, 2019). At the time of the bidding process, IAAF President Sebastian Coe had to give up his role as a special advisor to Nike Inc. after receiving accusations that he had personally lobbied the city and his role was a conflict of interest. Coe had held the ambassadorial role with Nike for nearly 40 years (Dutch, 2015). Moreover, Eugene, Oregon, was given the event without the usual bidding process, despite interest from the Swedish city of Gothenburg (Daly and McKay, 2015).

Similarly, the decision in 2010 to make two FIFA World Cup awards at the same time to Russia and Qatar respectively was met with controversy from the outset. In Qatar, logistical challenges included how football was to be played in Qatar's scorching heat and whether beer would be available at the conservative Muslim emirate's stadiums that were yet to be built (Flynn, 2015). These announcements came not long after the world football body, FIFA, saw the arrest of several senior officials on corruption charges in Switzerland (Britner, 2015).

These international event scandals and revelations of corruption are nothing new. Junichi Yamaguchi, a senior committee member for the 1998 Winter Olympics in Nagano admitted ordering the burning of 90 volumes of accounting documents in 1992 because they took up too much space and held information not intended for the public (Baade and Matheson, 2016; Bruer and Forrest, 2018; Whymant, 1999). The 2002 Winter Games in Salt Lake City corruption scandal lead to the resignation of ten members of the IOC (Bruer and Forrest, 2018) along with two members of the Salt Lake City Organizing Committee (SLOC) facing 15 criminal charges for providing more than US$1.2 million in cash and gifts to entice IOC members to support its bid. In the end, both SLOC members were acquitted of all charges (Mark, 2016).

If it is not the bid that comes under scrutiny, the budget to host is regularly revised soon after the bid has been won (The Economist, 2015). Montreal 1976, Sarajevo in 1984, Athens 2004, and London 2012 all had their projected Games budgets massively revised upwards (Pagels, 2016; Peck, 2012). There are also the corrupt processes with the awarding of contracts. On one side of the world, Sochi Olympics construction contract investigators found evidence of contracts being awarded without a bidding process or authorisation, often for inflated prices (Khazov-Cassia, 2016) On the other, a US probe focused on alleged vote-buying and possible corruption in contracting for the 2016 Rio de Janeiro Olympics, including for lucrative media and marketing rights (Kiernan and Davis-O'Brien, 2017).

Müller (2015) suggests that while international event organisers seek public support during the bidding process, the participation of the public is often considered expendable or is reduced once a city [or nation] has won. However, the evidence above suggests that while public support may be an important part of a bid, the bid itself can have very little to do with winning.

As event organisers seek to deliver international events in foreign states, it would be advisable to understand the level of corruption in each given state prior to making agreements or exchanging monies. To give an indication of the level of perceived corruption, Transparency International created the Corruption Perceptions Index (CPI) which ranks 180 countries and territories by their perceived levels of public sector corruption. While not a definitive indication of the way all business is conducted, it is a clear warning of certain values that exist. The CPI table uses a scale of 0 to 100 where 0 is highly corrupt and 100 is very clean. More than two-thirds of countries have scored below 50 in recent years, with an average score of just 43 (transparency.org, 2018). Table 8.1 provides a selection of the lowest ranking nations of the 180 scored along with their CPI index.

Transparency International suggests the figures reveal that the continued failure of most countries to significantly control corruption is contributing to a crisis in democracy around the world. While there are exceptions, the data shows that, despite some progress, most countries are failing to make serious inroads against corruption (Transparency International, 2018).

8.9 Summary

This chapter has considered the key stakeholder implications at international events. It has explained how stakeholders can place influence on the event from a number of sources. Not all stakeholders are human beings. They can be organisations and other living things. We have learned that organisations also have a great deal of responsibility economically, legally, and ethically towards events and their stakeholders and these responsibilities are often abused by the most powerful of international event organisations.

Table 8.1 A selection of low-ranking nations on the Corruption Perceptions Index, 2018

Country	ISO3	CPI Score 2018	Rank	Country	ISO3	CPI Score 2018	Rank
Denmark	DNK	88	1	Saudi Arabia	SAU	49	58
New Zealand	NZL	87	2	Croatia	HRV	48	60
Finland	FIN	85	3	Malaysia	MYS	47	61
Singapore	SGP	85	3	Hungary	HUN	46	64
Sweden	SWE	85	3	Greece	GRC	45	67
Switzerland	CHE	85	3	Jamaica	JAM	44	70
Norway	NOR	84	7	South Africa	ZAF	43	73
Netherlands	NLD	82	8	Tunisia	TUN	43	73
Canada	CAN	81	9	Bulgaria	BGR	42	77
Luxembourg	LUX	81	9	India	IND	41	78
Germany	DEU	80	11	Turkey	TUR	41	78
United Kingdom	GBR	80	11	China	CHN	39	87
Australia	AUS	77	13	Indonesia	IDN	38	89
Hong Kong	HKG	76	14	Bahrain	BHR	36	99
Iceland	ISL	76	14	Thailand	THA	36	99
Belgium	BEL	75	17	Brazil	BRA	35	105
Ireland	IRL	73	18	Egypt	EGY	35	105
Japan	JPN	73	18	Peru	PER	35	105
France	FRA	72	21	Pakistan	PAK	33	117
USA	USA	71	22	Vietnam	VNM	33	117
UAE	ARE	70	23	Ukraine	UKR	32	120
Barbados	BRB	68	25	Nepal	NPL	31	124
Chile	CHL	67	27	Iran	IRN	28	138
Bahamas	BHS	65	29	Lebanon	LBN	28	138
Portugal	PRT	64	30	Mexico	MEX	28	138
Taiwan	TWN	63	31	Russia	RUS	28	138
Qatar	QAT	62	33	Kenya	KEN	27	144
Israel	ISR	61	34	Nigeria	NGA	27	144
Poland	POL	60	36	Bangladesh	BGD	26	149
Czech Republic	CZE	59	38	Mozambique	MOZ	23	158
Spain	ESP	58	41	Zimbabwe	ZWE	22	160
Korea, South	KOR	57	45	Iraq	IRQ	18	168
Malta	MLT	54	51	Afghanistan	AFG	16	172
Italy	ITA	52	53	Yemen	YEM	14	176
Jordan	JOR	49	58	South Sudan	SSD	13	178

Source: Transparency International, 2018

Case study 8.1 Rule 22 of the Olympic Charter, IOC Ethics Commission

The IOC Ethics Commission is a self-monitoring body charged with defining and updating a framework of ethical principles, including a Code of Ethics, based upon the values and principles enshrined in the Olympic Charter of which the said Code forms an integral part. In addition, it investigates complaints raised in relation to the non-respect of such ethical principles, including breaches of the Code of Ethics, and, if necessary, proposes sanctions to the IOC Executive Board.

The chair and members of the IOC Ethics Commission are elected by the IOC Session, in a secret ballot, by a majority of the votes cast.

Questions

1. Is the current process of self-monitoring complaints and breaches of the code on points of ethical principles suitable in the 21st century?
   a. If no, what other process would be better suited and why?
2. Is a secret ballot to appoint the chair and the members of the IOC Ethics Commission the best way to ensure fairness and impartiality?
3. Should all the major sports bodies such as the IOC, FIFA, IAAF, etc. be monitored by an independent regulator?
   a. If yes, what do you think would change?
   b. If no, what are the reasons for maintaining the current method?

8.10 Useful websites

Effective stakeholder management blog
www.cuckoo.ie/blog/event-related/effective-stakeholder-management.html

Circular economy
www.ellenmacarthurfoundation.org

Tracking Subsidies, Promoting Accountability in Economic Development
goodjobsfirst.org

Olympic Games documents
www.olympic.org/documents

The Anti-Corruption Evidence (ACE) research consortium
https://ace.soas.ac.uk/

References

Almeida, B. S. d., Marchi Júnior, W., & Pike, E. (2014). The 2016 Olympic and Paralympic Games and Brazil's soft power. *Contemporary Social Science, 9*(2), 271–283. doi:10.1080/21582041.2013.838291

Andersson, T. D., & Getz, D. (2008). Stakeholder management strategies of festivals. *Journal of Convention & Event Tourism, 9*(3), 199–220. doi:10.1080/15470140802323801

Baade, R., & Matheson, V. (2016). Going for the Gold: The Economics of the Olympics. *The Journal of Economic Perspectives, 30*(2), 201. doi:10.1257/jep.30.2.201

Beard, T. (Director) (2019). War on plastic with Hugh and Anita. Sloane, J. (Producer). First broadcast, 19th June 2019. BBC1. Retrieved from www.bbc.co.uk/programmes/m0006347 Accessed 4th October 2019.

Boult, A. (2016). T in the Park music festival cancelled next year – thanks to ospreys, *The Telegraph*. Retrieved from www.telegraph.co.uk/music/news/t-park-2017-cancelled-thanks-ospreys/ Accessed 23rd March 2018.

Britner, L. (2015). Coca-Cola Co, Anheuser-Busch InBev express concern over FIFA scandal. Retrieved from www.just-drinks.com/analysis/anheuser-busch-inbev-q1-2018-results-data_id125836.aspx

Bruer, M., & Forrest, D. (2018). *The Palgrave Handbook on the Economics of Manipulation in Sport*. Cham: Palgrave.

Bryson, J. (2004). What to do when stakeholders matter: Stakeholder identification and analysis techniques. *Public Management Review, 6*(1), 21–53.

Calvert, J. (2019). Jigsaw of evidence slowly built up picture of bribery and dirty tricks. Retrieved from www.thetimes.co.uk/article/jigsaw-of-evidence-slowly-built-up-picture-of-bribery-and-dirty-tricks-hw793957n Accessed 6th November 2019.

Carlsen, J., Ali – Knight, J., & Robertson, M. (2007). Access-A research agenda for Edinburgh festivals. *Event Management, 11*, 3–11.

Carroll, A. B. (1991). The pyramid of corporate social responsibility: Toward the moral management of organizational stakeholders. *Business Horizons, 34*(4), 39–48. doi:10.1016/0007-6813(91)90005-g

Daly, M., & McKay, C. (2015). Lord Coe role in Eugene 2021 Worlds decision questioned. Retrieved from:www.bbc.co.uk/sport/athletics/34908237 Accessed 3rd October 2019.

Department for International Development (DfID) (2015). Why corruption matters: Understanding causes, effects and how to address them. Retrieved from https://assets.publishing.service.gov.uk/government/uploads/system/uploads/attachment_data/file/406346/corruption-evidence-paper-why-corruption-matters.pdf Accessed 31st August 2019.

Dodds, M. (2016). Revisiting the Salt Lake City Olympic scandal: Would the outcome be different today? *Choregia, 12*(1), 1–14. doi:10.4127/ch.2016.0104

Dutch, T. (2015). Sebastian Coe gives up role with Nike in response to accusations. Retrieved from www.flotrack.org/articles/5047638-sebastian-coe-gives-up-role-with-nike-in-response-to-accusations Accessed 3rd October 2019.

Economist, The (2015). Going for bronze: The Olympic Park. *The Economist, 416*(8948), 27.

Eden, C., & Ackermann, F. (1998). *Making Strategy: The Journey of Strategic Management*. London: Sage.

Eden, C., & Ackermann, F. (2011). *Making Strategy: Mapping Out Strategic Success.* London: Sage.

Ellis-Petersen, H. (2019). Treated like trash: south-east Asia vows to return mountains of rubbish from west. *The Guardian*. Retrieved from www.theguardian.com/environment/2019/may/28/treated-like-trash-south-east-asia-vows-to-return-mountains-of-rubbish-from-west Accessed 4th October 2019.

Flynn, A. (2015). FIFA Won't Switch World Cup Venues Despite Pitched Debate. *Wall Street Journal*. Retrieved from www.wsj.com/articles/fifa-wont-switch-cup-venues-despite-pitched-debate-1432756343 Accessed 23rd May 2018.

Freeman, R. (1984). *Strategic management: A stakeholder approach*. Boston: Pitman Books.

Getz, D., & Page, S. J. (2016). Progress and prospects for event tourism research. *Tourism Management, 52*(C), 593–631. doi:10.1016/j.tourman.2015.03.007

Good Jobs First (n.d.). Violation tracker. Retrieved from www.goodjobsfirst.org/violation-tracker Accessed 4th October 2019.

Hanrahan, J., & Maguire, K. (2016). Local authority provision of environmental planning guidelines for event management in Ireland. *European Journal of Tourism Research, 12*, 54–81.

Harding, J. (2010). A World Cup tainted by corruption, *The Times,* p. 24. Retrieved from www.thetimes.co.uk/article/a-world-cup-tainted-by-corruption-9k396hb89x8 Accessed 12th June 2018.

Henderson, S., & Musgrave, J. (2014). Changing audience behaviour: Festival goers and throwaway tents. *International Journal of Event and Festival Management, 5*(3), 247–262. doi:10.1108/ijefm-11-2013-0031

Hermann, A. (2019). Jersey Shore concert series canceled to protect endangered piping plover birds. *PhillyVoice*. Retrieved from www.phillyvoice.com/piping-plover-bird-nest-sandy-hook-beach-concert-canceled-jersey-shore-live-music/ Accessed 30th October 2019.

Independent, The. (2019). World Athletics Championships 2019: Free tickets handed out in desperate bid to fill empty stadium in Doha. *The Independent*. Retrieved from www.independent.co.uk/sport/general/athletics/world-athletics-championships-2019-doha-tickets-stadium-a9144821.html Accessed 7th October 2019.

Kassens-Noor, E., & Lauermann, J. (2018). Mechanisms of policy failure: Boston's 2024 Olympic bid. *Urban Studies, 55*(15), 3369–3384. doi:10.1177/0042098017740286

Khazov-Cassia, S. (2016). Russian whistle-blower pulls back cover on railways corruption. *Radio Free Europe/Radio Liberty*. Retrieved from www.rferl.org/a/russia-railways-yakunin-whistle-blowercorruption/28042893.html Accessed 23rd October 2019.

Kiernan, P., & Davis-O'Brien, R. (2017). U.S. Officials Probe Awarding of 2016 Olympics to Brazil. *The Wall Street Journal.* www.wsj.com/articles/u-s-officials-probing-the-awarding-of-2016-olympics-to-brazil-1513117551 Accessed 12th May 2020

Kujala, J., Heikkinen, A., & Lehtimäki, H. (2012). Understanding the nature of stakeholder relationships: An empirical examination of a conflict situation. *Journal of Business Ethics, 109*(1), 53–65. doi:10.1007/s10551-012-1379-2

Macaloon, J. J. (2011). Scandal and governance: inside and outside the IOC 2000 Commission. *Sport in Society, 14*(3), 292–308. doi:10.1080/17430437.2011.557265

MacDonald, J. (2016). Stakeholder identification and analysis made easy for project managers. Retrieved from www.business2community.com/strategy/stakeholder-identification-analysis-made-easy-project-managers-01440041 Accessed 9th September 2019.

Maguire, J. A. (2011). 'Civilised Games'? Beijing 2008, power politics, and cultural struggles. *Sport in Society, 14*(7–8), 1027–1039. doi:10.1080/17430437.2011.603556

Mark, D. (2016). Revisiting the Salt Lake City Olympic scandal: Would the outcome be different today? *Choregia, 12*(1), 1–14. doi:10.4127/ch.2016.0104

McIntosh, S. (2013). Disposable rules set to impact businesses. *Scottish Business Insider*, 1st September 2013, 33.

Minoja, M. (2012). Stakeholder Management Theory, Firm Strategy, and Ambidexterity. *Journal of Business Ethics, 109*(1), 67–82. doi:10.1007/s10551-012-1380-9

Morgan, T. (2019). Poor Doha World Athletics Championships attendances a 'disaster' for Qatar's chances of hosting Olympics. *The Telegraph*. Retrieved from www.telegraph.co.uk/athletics/2019/09/30/poor-doha-world-athletics-championships-attendances-disaster/ Accessed 17th October 2019.

Müller, M. (2015). The mega-event syndrome: Why so much goes wrong in mega-event planning and what to do about it. *Journal of the American Planning Association, 81*(1), 6–17. doi:10.1080/01944363.2015.1038292

O'Brien, C. (2019). 16 brands doing corporate social responsibility successfully. Retrieved from https://digitalmarketinginstitute.com/en-gb/blog/corporate-16-brands-doing-corporate-social-responsibility-successfully Accessed 4th October 2019.

OED (1989). *The Oxford English Dictionary*. Oxford: Clarendon Press.

Pagels, J. (2016). Olympic ruins. *Reason, 48*(4), 44–49.

Peck, T. (2012). Olympic Games run £2bn over budget: From £2.4bn to £11bn: report savages soaring costs as Olympian-scale overspend is laid bare. *The Independent*. Retrieved from www.independent.co.uk/sport/olympics/olympic-games-run-2bn-over-budget-7546201.html Accessed 3rd October 2019.

Raj, R., & Musgrave, J. (2009). *Event management and sustainability*. Wallingford: CABI.

Rawling, J. (2005). London's financial sweetener was an avoidable gaffe. *The Guardian*. Retrieved from:www.theguardian.com/sport/2005/apr/25/Olympics2012.politics Accessed 6th November 2019

Reid, S. (2011). Event stakeholder management: developing sustainable rural event practices. *International Journal of Event and Festival Management, 2*(1), 20–36. doi:10.1108/17582951111116597

Rusbridger, A. (2014). Fifa's shady practices taint the joy and glory of a World Cup, *The Guardian*. Retrieved from www.theguardian.com/commentisfree/2014/jun/07/fifa-shady-practices-taint-world-cup Accessed 6th November 2019.

Schwartz, M., & Carroll, A. (2003). Corporate social responsibility: A three-domain approach. *Business Ethics Quarterly, 13*(4), 503–530. doi:10.5840/beq200313435

Skinner, T. (2019). Chicago festival cancelled due to presence of endangered birds *NME*. Retrieved from www.nme.com/news/music/chicago-festival-cancelled-due-to-presence-of-endangered-birds-2531169#peJ8uxUxsmDbTxBJ.99 Accessed 30th October 2019.

Sportstar (2019). IAAF World Athletics Championships: Coe plays down empty seats. Retrieved from https://sportstar.thehindu.com/athletics/sebastian-coe-plays-down-empty-seats-at-khalifa-stadium-iaaf-world-athletics-championships-doha-qatar/article29577621.ece# Accessed 4th October 2019

T in the Park (2016). Thank You. Retrieved from:www.tinthepark.com/ Accessed 6th Sepember 2019.

Todd, L., Leask, A., & Ensor, J. (2017). Understanding primary stakeholders' multiple roles in hallmark event tourism management. *Tourism Management, 59*, 494–509.

Transparency International (2018). Corruption Perceptions Index 2018. Retrieved from www.transparency.org/cpi2018 Accessed 23rd November 2019.

Tufts, S. (2004). Building the 'competitive city': Labour and Toronto's bid to host the Olympic games. *Geoforum, 35*(1), 47–58. doi:10.1016/j.geoforum.2003.01.001

United Nations (2005). *United Nations Convention against Corruption*. Retrieved from www.unodc.org/unodc/en/treaties/CAC/ Accessed 3rd October 2019.

Wamsley, K. (2002). The global sport monopoly: a synopsis of 20th century Olympic politics. *International Journal, 57*(3), 395–410. doi:10.2307/40203675

Weiss, J. W. (2014). *Business Ethics: A Stakeholder and Issues Management Approach* (6th ed.). San Francisco, CA: Berrett-Koehler Publishers.

Whymant, R. (1999). Train was laid on for Olympic chief. Corruption and the Olympics. *The Times,* 4th February 1999, p. 12.

External forces

Williams, R. (2019). Doha's empty seats tell tale of corruption, warped priorities and vested interests. *The Guardian*. Retrieved from www.theguardian.com/sport/blog/2019/sep/30/doha-empty-seats-iaaf-sellout-world-athletics-championships

Witherow, J. (2019). Exclusive investigation: Qatar's secret $880m World Cup payments to Fifa, *The Times,* p. 1. Retrieved from www.thetimes.co.uk/article/revealed-qatars-secret-880m-world-cup-payments-to-fifa-p3r5rvw9x Accessed 6th November 2019.

Chapter 9

Globalisation and international events

Contents

9.1 Chapter overview

This chapter discusses how international events and the spread of globalisation are inextricably linked. It considers both the positive and negative effects brought to communities and the various implications for international events such as widening access to distant states, the new and emerging markets created through the forces of globalisation, the impact of digital communication, the rise of extremism and terrorism, and disparities of wealth distribution.

9.2 Learning objectives

By the end of this chapter, the student will be expected to:

- Appreciate the link between globalisation and international events
- Understand how the forces of globalisation impact upon international events
- Appreciate the unintentional consequences of globalisation
- Recognise the different perspectives on the spread of globalisation and its main forces and how these play out in international events.

9.3 Introduction

Globalisation is essentially the process by which economies and cultures are drawn closer together. As travelling long distances has been made easier and quicker, and our ability to communicate has become instant, far off nations and the people who live in them have become more inter-connected through global networks and communication channels. This has led to greater levels of integration in trade, capital flows, cultures, and people. The OED (1989) defines globalisation as:

> The action, process, or fact of making global; esp. (in later use) the process by which businesses or other organisations develop international influence or start operating on an international scale, widely considered to be at the expense of national identity.

Perelman (2015) believes that the problem with globalisation is how it is framed according to two conflicting ideological perspectives. He suggests that:

> On the one hand, the anti-Globalisation side emphasizes the effects of self-interested intentionality, in which major powers want to extend their access to markets or resources. The opposing story of Globalisation emphasizes a complete absence of intentionality in which people merely respond to presumably efficient, impersonal market forces in a way that supposedly allows the invisible hand to spread shared prosperity throughout the globe.
>
> (Perelman, 2015)

More recently, globalisation is considered more as a process that focuses on the economic integration between countries and regions of the world. However, with economic integration come a number of other forces that have just as great an impact. As we entered the 21st century, the International Monetary Fund (IMF) identified four basic forces that make up the principle of globalisation (IMF, 2000). These comprise:

1. Trade
2. Capital (financial) movements
3. Movement of people
4. The spread of knowledge and digital communication.

For the international event manager, it is essential to appreciate the close relationship between international events and globalisation. At the same time, it is just as important to appreciate how the effects of globalisation reach deep into local communities, changes people's perceptions of their lives, and how the various markets react to this opportunity of change. The increase in international events around the world and the march of what is now understood as globalisation are inextricably linked. To use an events term, international events are the proverbial '+1' on the guest list with globalisation. In other words, they enter a region together with globalisation. However, it could just as well be argued that international events are used as a means of opening previously closed states through gatherings such as international sport and business events.

The appeal of potential investment and reports of better living conditions from the financially richer nations to the poorer states can be difficult to reject. In the largely Westernised nations, the effects can be seen as an acceleration of what would be natural progress. At the extreme end of the scale, the gains for some within the local population are welcome. However, the losses can also be serious, threatening indigenous values, cultures, and beliefs as well as having serious implications for the environment and social cohesion. The knock-on effects of globalisation can be far-reaching and while globalisation can be beneficial to the event industry, it also offers up some serious challenges.

9.4 Understanding globalisation and international events

With increasing globalisation, growing international markets present potentially significant and increasing market opportunities for cultural events throughout the world (Kay, 2004). Globalisation is the term used to express international integration and how humanity is progressing politically, culturally, and economically. In Chapter 1, we discussed the origins of international events and how the development of trade roots and shifting cultures led to the integration of people, culture, and goods. It should therefore be remembered that originally, the only limitation to trade was how far people were capable of travelling. The first industrial revolution and the 19th century instigated a new breed of globalisation. While the era remained largely a time of open global trade (Giddens,

2002), a new influence began that was, as the OED (1989) definition explains above, widely considered to be at the expense of national identity.

A modern definition of globalisation explains the emergence of a single world market, dominated by multinational companies and characterised by the free flow of private capital across borders (Ghauri and Powell, 2008). This kind of definition is comprehensively established around economic values and overlooks the broader effects, consequences, ideals, and changes globalisation brings about. Many large-scale international events are very much aligned with this characterization of globalisation. However, not all international events strive for such dominance and many are more respectful to what already exists in the places they visit or represent.

Even though respect occurs within international events, contrary to previous eras, the kind of globalisation observed during the past few decades is a process impacting on the whole world (Göll and Evers-Wölk, 2014). Even the most remote of civilisations are affected.

The term in its current usage emerged during the 1970s (James and Steger, 2014). Rüttimann (2006) describes globalisation as:

> The phenotypical manifestation of transnational business within the causal systemic world of borderless economy. i.e. the effects of a worldwide systemic behaviour of individuals who are part of a complex economic system… a kind of deterministic chaos: chaos not commonly intended as non-linear order. Despite having order, a deterministic chaos is not clearly predictable.
>
> (Rüttimann, 2006, 25–26)

The process of globalisation is becoming increasingly interconnected as a result of massively increased trade and cultural exchange (BBC, 2019). There is no doubt that globalisation is one of the key drivers of international events and likewise international events have contributed to the progress of globalisation over the last 75 years. The large-scale international events such as the Olympics Games and the FIFA World Cup along with the biggest conferences and expos all have served as a platform for promoting national and international potential, and the expansion of capitalist methods of business.

Cities develop around the possibility of trade. International airports, roads, public transport, and the building of hotels, convention centres, and exhibition spaces are all key attributes of a modern city in a globalised world. It has become such an important aspect of the international event industry that an annual Global Meetings and Events Forecast is produced each year. In Chapter 4 we discussed how cities compete to strengthen their global status. Table 9.1 illustrates this competition with the global forecast of the ten most popular destinations for meetings, conferences, and exhibitions in each territory.

One of the key drivers of international events is the meetings, incentives, conventions, and exhibitions (MICE) industry. The MICE sector is essentially business events and represents a major element of the events portfolio of many destinations (Celuch and Davidson, 2008). As the forces of globalisation impact around the world, the MICE industry contributes as a significant component of the modern-day developing or aspiring global city. Sporting and other cultural festivals and events represent particularly attractive communication vehicles as

Table 9.1 The top global meeting destinations

United States	South America	Canada	Asia Pacific	Europe
Orlando, FLA	Rio de Janeiro, Brazil	Toronto, Ontario	Singapore	London, England
Las Vegas, NEV	Cancun/Riviera Maya, Mexico	Vancouver, British Columbia	Sydney, Australia	Barcelona, Spain
Chicago, ILL	Mexico City, Mexico	Montreal, Quebec	Bangkok, Thailand	Berlin, Germany
San Diego, CA	São Paulo, Brazil	Calgary, Alberta	Kuala Lumpur, Malaysia	Amsterdam, Netherlands
Atlanta, GA	Cartagena, Colombia	Ottawa, Ontario	Hong Kong	Madrid, Spain
Dallas, TX	Panama City, Panama	Mississauga, Ontario	Shanghai, China	Paris, France
Nashville, TENN	Punta Cana, Dominican Republic	Banff, Alberta	Melbourne, Australia	Frankfurt, Germany
New York, NY	Buenos Aires, Argentina	Edmonton, Alberta	New Delhi, India	Rome, Italy
Washington, DC	Lima, Peru	Whistler, British Columbia	Tokyo, Japan	Munich, Germany
San Francisco, CA	Santo Domingo, Dominican Republic	Quebec City, Quebec	Mumbai, India	Lisbon, Portugal

Source: Adapted from Cvent, 2018

cities become driven by the need to create a favourable image to encourage tourism, migration and business (Foley et al., 2008).

International event tourists attending conferences and exhibitions will seek to experience a balance of new horizons or destinations, new cultural experiences and widespread access to technology. As new hotels are built, more meeting spaces become available. When multinational companies reward their staff, destination experiences form part of the incentive. Forward-facing cities build new conference and exhibition spaces which in turn attracts the international event organiser. For these developments to work for the international event traveller, the destination requires good international access, a quality transport infrastructure, places to eat, and quality hotels and accommodation space.

In order to appreciate the full financial value of international events, we have to consider the significance of each sector. UFI (2019) put the exhibitions industry on a par with sectors such as machine tools or medical and surgical equipment. The figures rank the sector as the 56th largest economy in the world, larger than Hungary, Kuwait, Sri Lanka, and Ecuador. In 2019, the key figures were as follows:

- Exhibitions generate US$325 billion in total output globally
- Exhibitions contribute US$198 billion to global gross domestic product (GDP)

- Exhibitions support 3.2 million jobs around the world.

Considering this is just one sector of international events, we need to add other sectors to get the full extent of global influence from international events on the four IMF forces of globalisation. The music industry was estimated to be worth US$43 billion in 2018 (McDermot, 2018) with electronic music alone estimated to be worth US$7.2 billion for the period 2018/19 (Watson, 2019). Other contributions are more difficult to get figures on, for example the value of global political, religious, and private events.

If we take the preliminary findings of the Event industry Council (IEC), the depth and reach of the business events sector puts the global significance of international events into perspective. Business events (including the exhibitions industry) have some impressive figures, including:

- Generating US$621.4 billion of direct gross domestic product(GDP) impact
- Creating US$2.5 trillion of output (business sales)
- Creating 26 million jobs
- Contributing a total global GDP of US$1.5 trillion.

The final GDP figures would rank the business events sector as the 14th largest economy in the world, ahead of the GDPs of Australia, Spain, Mexico, Indonesia and Saudi Arabia (IEC, 2018).

These figures underline the indisputable connection between globalisation and international events. The presence of international events exposes the appearance and development of globalisation in real time. As destinations embrace the four forces of globalisation, international events increase in size and quantity. Established destinations listed in the various popularity charts continue to compete to maintain position and attraction. Developing destinations being affected by the forces of globalisation now appear in other research as new and emerging markets.

9.5 New and emerging markets

One of the main opportunities for business in a globalised world is to look elsewhere for business. As markets become saturated, i.e. when many competitors in one market compete for the same trade, the more experienced businesses will seek to obtain a sense of the future and identify new trends and opportunities in their sector elsewhere. This means looking to new markets to trade. Considerable research is then carried out in order to understand what implications exist for trading in these new markets. While established businesses in one market can look to emerging markets, it is a two-way process and it is not just the more powerful nations building a presence in the developing markets. Providers from emerging markets can deliver similar levels of experience and quality, but for half the price. The reason why these are developing markets is due to growth emitting from them. For the international event industry, these nations provide new opportunities in both directions, internally and externally, for international events as the platform for international networking processes increases (Hoersch, 2019).

Table 9.2 The various acronyms and groupings used to understand emerging markets

BRIC	Brazil, Russia, India, China
BRICS	Brazil, Russia, India, China, South Africa
MIST	Mexico, Indonesia, South Korea, Turkey
MINT	Mexico, Indonesia, Nigeria, Turkey
Next 11	Bangladesh, Egypt, Indonesia, Iran, Mexico, Nigeria, Pakistan, Philippines, Turkey, South Korea, Vietnam
EAGLEs	Brazil, China, Egypt, India, Indonesia, South Korea, Mexico, Russia, Taiwan, and Turkey
CIVETS	Colombia, Indonesia, Vietnam, Egypt, Turkey, South Africa
SANE	South Africa, Algeria, Nigeria, Egypt
TIMPs	Turkey, Indonesia, Mexico, Philippines

Table 9.3 The various acronyms used to understand struggling markets

Fragile Five/BIITS	Brazil, Indonesia, India, Turkey, South Africa
PIIGS	Portugal, Italy, Ireland, Greece, Spain
STUCK	South Africa, Turkey, Ukraine, Colombia, UK

In this sense, markets (or nations) increasing their engagement with the IMF's four forces above have become classified by their future value for investment. Another popular classification is to consider the views and practices of the international investment community based on three criteria: economic development, size, and liquidity, as well as market accessibility (MSCI Inc., 2014). Since the turn of the century, new and advanced economic development in emerging markets has led to a growth in the grouping of a number of territories into a related acronym. It was the former Goldman Sachs economist, Jim O'Neill, who essentially started and developed the trend. However, over time, many of the predictions have proved to be flawed (Wright, 2014). Terms such as BRIC and MIST became buzz words in business management discussions. Table 9.2 lists the most popular acronyms and groupings associated with emerging markets.

For the international event industry, these new and emerging markets are sources of continuing and new trade. As new and emerging markets become accessible, more international trade visits and events occur. National governments set up trade links and the demand for specialist knowledge and expertise intensifies. Established trade events receive increased international attendance and government intervention provides financial support and advice for businesses ideally positioned to fill the demand.

While some business leaders were keen to highlight the emerging markets, others were working on expressing what appeared to be less investable markets with more disparaging acronyms. Table 9.3 lists the common descriptions. It is significant to note how many emerging markets are also grouped in the less attractive markets.

9.6 Megatrends

One of the most significant challenges confronting global corporations is understanding the emerging issues in an increasingly interconnected and culturally complex world (Bhagat, 2004). As the forces of globalisation continue to spread, effects of the changes are evidenced on a global scale as megatrends. The term 'megatrends' was originally coined by John Naisbitt in the early 1980s and is used to describe a series of global changes (Slaughter, 1993). Megatrends today are macroeconomic and geostrategic forces that are shaping the world. They are factual and backed by verifiable data. By definition, they are big and include some of society's biggest challenges and opportunities (PwC, 2016). A megatrend is a prominent feature of global politico-economic change brought about by the recent thrust of capitalist globalisation (Alam Choudhury, 1999). Research into what are known as megatrends provides insight into the future of different aspects of the business sector and has been conducted across a number of international event-related subject areas (Buckley *et al.*, 2015; Retief, 2016; Stank, 2015; Hajkowicz, *et al.*, 2016).

Megatrends can be applied to almost any future scenario, but tend to focus on aspects of PESTEL impact studies. A PESTEL analysis is normally applied to understand the external influences on an organisation. Such impact studies from a megatrend perspective focus on the prominent contemporary political, economic, social, technological, environmental, and legal changes on global business.

Forecasting how the international event industry is progressing is a very risky strategy, but most would agree that globalisation will have a major effect on the future of the international event industry. According to the Zukunfts Institute (Future Institute), there are currently twelve megatrends of our time. These include, Gender Shift, New Work, Neo-Ecology, Silver Society, Individualisation, Health, Globalisation, Security, Urbanisation, Mobility, Knowledge Culture, and Connectivity (Zukunfts Institute, n.d). Each of these megatrends interacts with one another almost as a modern-day reaction to the growing and emerging markets and developing economies, and the ability to communicate across borders and cultures. New alliances and networks are formed, as megatrends steer a path to the future.

As one of these twelve megatrends, globalisation is one of the key drivers of change and has a direct relationship with the other megatrends. Figure 9.1 shows the megatrend map which depicts the correlation between the twelve megatrends based on a Beck (1933) style underground map. It illustrates how megatrends are related and how each sub-category influences another with parallels and overlaps. The individual stations illustrate the different dimensions and complexity of a megatrend along with the various influencing factors. A link to a more detailed version of the megatrend map is provided at the end of the chapter in the 'Useful websites' section.

The significance of megatrends for the international event industry is multifaceted. As discussed in Chapter 6, the awareness of local cultures must be appreciated at all times. The international event industry may become more streamlined through the forces of globalisation, but these are not always considered positive impacts in less powerful countries and include a number

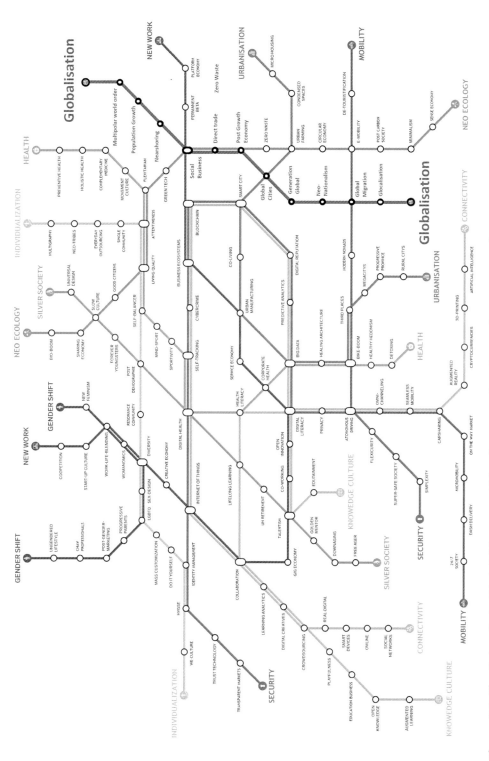

Figure 9.1 The Zukunfts Institute's Megatrend Map incorporating the twelve megatrends

Source: zukunftsinstitut.de, n.d.

of the Zukunfts Institute's twelve megatrends, such as security, health, and the silver society. However the most significant impact of globalisation is most likely to be the increase in the internationalisation of events or the re-orientation from local to international and the corresponding international activities. This internationalisation is occurring in both the core and support activities along the various stages of the supply chain (Etemad and Motaghi, 2018).

Not all future predictions for globalisation are positive. As some economies struggle in view of economic crises, competition between destinations has the potential to become more localised. Destinations in the conference and events sector in distant places might decrease because of the time needed and the associated costs and efforts (Göll and Evers-Wölk, 2014). Moreover, sustainability issues discussed in Chapter 10 may have an even bigger impact on long-haul travel to conferences and events.

9.7 Glocalisation

One of the essential aspects of international events is the celebration of different cultures. The importance of this is discussed in Chapter 6. Regions, countries and continents develop over many centuries and in so doing create distinctive cultural and localised values. Globalisation brings with it both a number of challenges and opportunities for these long-established values. Globalisation, it is suggested, does not erase local cultures, but it does undermine their original form (Nijman, 1999).

While this chapter focuses largely upon the impact of globalising influences on international events, the concept and corresponding effects of glocalisation should also be reflected upon. The term combines the words 'globalisation' and 'localisation' and is said to have developed in late 1980s'Japanese business methods (Foley et al., 2006; Robertson, 2012) as an explanation as to how a company trading internationally meets the demands of a local market. It is the link between the global and the local. In its most basic form, glocalisation is anything from the availability of beer at McDonald's in mainland Europe, the change in flavoured crisps (or chips depending on the local term used) for consumption in overseas markets, to the development of left-hand drive vehicles from a manufacturer originating in a right-hand drive country (or vice versa).

For many international events, particularly conferencing, meetings, and the creative industries, local protocols and traditions have to be observed as part of the delivery process. Ceremonial activities, political, economic, and cultural circumstances will all impact on the event, with detailed knowledge being required in order to satisfy local requirements. In some cases, this can mean businesses setting up a territorial base with local employees to ensure local customs are routinely observed. This is particularly important in new and emerging markets where customs and protocols are not widely understood by outsiders.

The territorial base would go some way towards safeguarding international relations while avoiding the clocking up of unnecessary carbon miles (Banks, 2010). In view of the continued growth of international events throughout the world, many leading events businesses are maintaining and extending this 'glocal' approach to their trading activities, resulting in greater numbers of international event businesses trading multi-nationally.

9.8 Globalisation and automated technology

We discuss digital communication and its more general use in Chapter 11, but the use of automated technology in international events is just as significant on a global level. While globalisation offers opportunities for international events to be held, the actual delivery of international events may not on the surface appear to be particularly affected by the spread of globalisation. It is only when we look closely that we can see how advances in global business and automated technology are directly linked to how international events are delivered. Primarily, the automation of tasks, which is a key feature of globalisation, can increase the productivity of an event, but at the same time it has the potential to reduce employment.

The way international events use digital communication as part of their day-to-day activities (such as the web, artificial intelligence, big data, and improved analytics to monitor delegate engagement) is all made possible by the ever increasing availability of cheap computing power and storage capacity (Rotman, 2013). Furthermore, large-scale international events rely on doing much of their trade and communication online. Everything from transferring funds through international banking to purchasing equipment through e-commerce sites delivered in hours to the event are essential to the smooth running of international events today.

We may not yet see the general integration of robots replacing international event employees in the way they have in manufacturing assembly lines, but anyone who has attended a conference or exhibition recently may well have interacted with greeting robots such as 'Pepper' at the Festival of Enterprise in Birmingham or 'Amy' at the IMEX conference in Frankfurt (both in 2019 – see Figure 9.2). Pepper, for example, was part of the developments from Amadeus and TUI Germany and the experimental and innovative project centred on a humanoid robot. Together, the companies sought to explore the value a robot could bring to retail travel agencies (Monhof, 2018). Robots may currently be treated as a gimmick at international events, but that was also the case for a whole host of other technologies we take for granted today.

Robots in general, and social robots in particular, tend to be very focused on functionality (Ackerman, 2019). However, an ever recurring question is whether the robots can function better than a human. From an international event delivery perspective, it is important for the organisers to understand what human characteristics can be absent from the experience in order to improve efficiency.

When engaging with or travelling to events, most delegates have experienced a multitude of automated activities that include assistance on websites (chatbots), to check-in at airports. In fact, nearly all of the processes involved in travel are completed by machines and robots with the now occasional assistance of a human operative.

With the development of human-to-machine voice interaction, the relationship between international events and robots is set to increase. The Hilton group of hotels has installed 'Connie', named after company founder Conrad Hilton, at the hotels' front desk as a mechanical concierge (Mest, 2016). For improved security, Knightscope, Inc has developed the K5, an outdoor machine

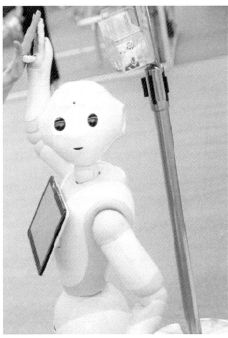

Figure 9.2 Amy and Pepper interacting with delegates at conferences

which runs 24/7 on its own and can autonomously recharge itself without any human intervention. It is best suited for securing large outdoor spaces. Using K5 in combination with other surveillance systems, security managers are better equipped to keep all areas of an international event, including car parks and corporate campuses, safe (Knightscope Inc., n.d.).

9.9 Globalisation and wealth distribution

To expand on the IMF's four forces of globalisation discussed above, the corporate understanding of globalisation covers increased international trade, enhanced technology and communication, easing of travel restrictions, increased political movement, and the opportunity for individual and mass mobility (Button, 2008). The main argument supporting corporate globalisation is that these factors bring about increased levels of wealth. The figures in section 9.4 indicate how wealthy the sector is. However, while incomes have increased in some Asian countries (Milanovic, 2016), the 21st century has also seen a rise in economic inequality bringing into question the level to which the forces of globalisation trickle wealth down. These circumstances will have a direct effect on a territory's ability to attract international events and the living conditions of those in places where international events are hosted.

Complex procedures such as hosting international events can have major initial cost implications. While discussing the confounding paradox of mega projects, Jennings (2012) observed:

vast and complex undertaking(s) of this sort remain popular with governments and planners in view of their inherent riskiness, both in manufacturing societal risks (such as hazards related to pollution or transport accidents and threats from terrorism) and risks to institutions (for example, suffering from poor track records in terms of cost over-runs and shortfalls in their completion times, financial revenues and economic impacts).

(Jennings, 2012)

Aside from the mega events, many international events require evidence of financial resources to support the revenue and capital costs of hosting some international conferences, and other cultural and sporting events. These demands effectively exclude many nations from participation, although the vision of lucrative financial returns from mega events has seen many nations bid and lose from hosting them (Scherer and Shi, 2016). Ironically, it is the countries with the biggest wealth distribution inequalities that tend to bid and eventually host the mega events of the world.

According to the World Inequality Report (Alvaredo et al., 2018), income inequality has increased more rapidly in North America, China, India, and Russia than anywhere else in the world, while South Africa is rated as the country with the worst levels of inequality (Barr, 2017). Each of these nations, has in recent years, bid, hosted or is about to host a number of the biggest international sporting events in the world including the Summer Olympics, Winter Olympics, FIFA World Cup, Commonwealth Games, Cricket World Cup, and meetings for the Formula 1 Grand Prix.

While the data in this chapter largely suggests increased wealth from the spread of globalisation, this is not the case for all due to high and rising inequality throughout the world (Badolo and Traoré, 2015; Beer and Boswell, 2015). There is growing evidence that the gap between the rich and poor has increased year-on-year (Peachey, 2019; Alvaredo et al., 2018; Roser and Ortiz-Ospina, 2017), and the hosting of international events can take a toll on the host countries' and host cities' ways of life, including their economic development policy (Desmangles, 2013).

Once a bid for a large-scale event has been successful there is generally the building of sports stadia and hotels, roads and other transport infrastructure. These activities often require the eviction of inner-city populations and the destruction of areas of outstanding natural beauty (Rojek, 2013). The effect on these communities is a further reflection of the inequalities created due to the relationship between globalisation and international events. Mass evictions have been increasingly linked to large international events, and families who have lived in an area all their life are forced to relocate (Becerril, 2017; Davis, 2011; Greene, 2003).

These are quite significant factors for international events as the winning bids are often secured on the promise of reducing inequality. The designers of mega international events have been questioned on their ability to fully grasp the social and environmental implications of the spatial decisions they take (Burdett, 2016). The explanation for these extensive changes has been linked to slum clearance. However, much still appears to be due to political approval processes and accelerated financing mechanisms that make large urban infrastructure projects attractive to investors (Altshuler and Luberoff, 2003)

Civic leaders along with private entrepreneurs have long exploited poorer communities through the event-related sense of urgency, mobilisation, and consensus in order to remake a city in their own image (Sánchez and Broudehoux, 2013). By the same token, opportunities have been lost to use mega events such as the FIFA World Cup as a catalyst for urban development (Pillay and Bass, 2008).

9.10 Negative reaction to globalisation

Jovanovic (2010) suggests that there were once hopes that globalisation would benefit everyone everywhere, but as time passes, globalisation's downside becomes more and more apparent. More recently, events such as large-scale demonstrations against globalisation have been used by a population as a means of removing political barriers or, in the case of political discontent, to secure the support of the public to come together to bring about change.

Aside from the international trade events such as conferences and exhibitions that come about through the spread of globalisation, the other most noticeable and arguably more newsworthy connection between globalisation and international events are the protests and demonstrations carried out throughout the world. We discussed in Chapter 4 how social movements can use the media at major events to draw attention to issues they deem important by organising public demonstrations near the event site. Significant geopolitical problems remain and through the power of connectivity and social media, the downside of globalisation is beginning to impact more in the minds of ordinary people.

There are many opponents of globalisation, who include environmentalists, anti-poverty campaigners and trade unions. There is huge variation both in their agendas and in how those agendas are pursued, from vociferous, often violent confrontation through to more reformist movements (Dicken, 2011). More broadly, George and Wilding (2002) believe the theoretical and ideological debate itself is very much confused. However, all international events are vulnerable to a variety of external negative activities because of the high media exposure many international events receive. Some international events attract protests and demonstrations when certain subjects are considered to be receiving little action or limited coverage in the media.

In previous centuries, a global protest of any kind would be considered a rare event, but with relatively inexpensive access to global networks, the 21st century has seen a marked increase in global protests, largely against the forces of globalisation. For example, the strategies used by some groups promoting climate change mitigation, conservation, and environmental protection will disrupt the daily lives of ordinary people in order to force the subject into the news. Other movements, such as gender equality, have received increased global support and media coverage. As well as environmental and gender issues, politics and health are also key themes that motivate ordinary people into action, bringing people together to generate mass peaceful demonstrations throughout the world.

Interestingly, globalisation is both the reason for and the result of these mass international event movements. As the forces and actions of globalisation appear to impact in a negative way on the less wealthy members of society, greater dissatisfaction with globalisation has developed into a global movement. According to George and Wilding (2002), globalisation demands that labour costs remain low, management styles remain lean and mean, and state expenditure be reduced. Such strategies can create greater divisions among populations, institutions or even within the state itself. However, as suggested above, globalisation improves the spread of knowledge and technology, which in turn informs societies on the injustices and weaknesses of the other three forces of globalisation.

According to Jovanovic (2010), the strategy of the anti-globalisation movement is to address four weaknesses of the globalisation process:

- A lack of legitimacy
- A lack of accountability
- A lack of organization, and
- A lack of transparency.

There is an acceptance by anti-globalisation supporters that favourable forces exist that contribute to economic activity, creating necessary resources to achieve valuable social goals. However, by restraining the forces of globalisation, a more inclusive set of consequences can be achieved. The suggestion is that if the forces of globalisation are not restrained, local cultural values will be erased.

9.11 Globalisation, terrorism, and extremism

While most international events are about unifying people, celebrating life and pursuing enlightenment, a much starker aspect that emanates from the march of globalisation can deliver devastating effects on innocent gatherings of people. Terrorism itself is nothing new. The Gunpowder Plot and Guy Fawkes' attempt to blow up the UK parliament in 1605 is largely considered as a terrorist act, even though the term did not exist at the time. However, the modern sense of terrorism emerged in the mid-19th century when a small band of Russian revolutionaries used the word 'terrorist' to describe themselves and their actions. They developed certain ideas that were to become the hallmark of subsequent terrorism around the world (Roberts, 2002).

Extremism is even more complicated to understand as it is not seen as a tactic or an ideology, but as a pathological illness which feeds on the destruction of life (Coleman and Bartoli, 2004). With the need to deal with the potential of terrorists or extremists targeting an event, international event organisers are forced to prepare for worst-case scenarios and include the necessary preparations to protect the event from these unknown probabilities. However, the actions of extremists are sometimes impossible to anticipate, making the eventual attack all the more shocking. For example, preparing for the probability of someone firing indiscriminately from 500 metres at a festival audience from a hotel room would previously have been unimaginable. Figure 9.3 depicts how one local extremist in the United States managed to attack the audience at the Route 91 Harvest Music Festival in Las Vegas in 2017, killing 58 and injuring 422.

In any emergency situation at an event, it is the organiser's responsibility to either safely evacuate or secure the premises. Acts of terror present a further dimension to the usual plans if access is obtained. If it is not possible to secure or evacuate the premises, the organisers are restricted to attempting to minimise

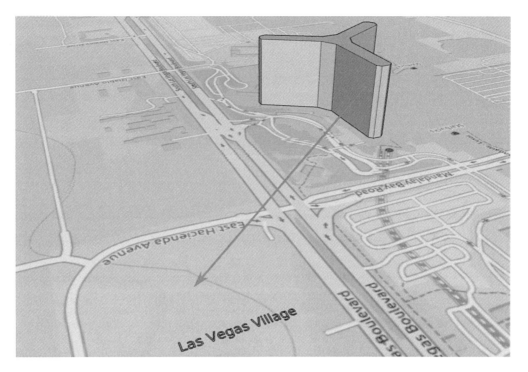

Figure 9.3 Diagram showing the means of attack on the Route 91 Harvest Music Festival on the Las Vegas Strip, 2017

Source: Wikipedia, n.d.

the attack until professional response teams arrive on the scene. The Route 91 Harvest Music Festival attack created pandemonium in the audience because at first it was not possible to make out where the attack was coming from, nor was it possible for the audience to take cover.

The label terrorism has become a pejorative term in itself. The term is used in political discourse to delegitimise political enemies. The groups themselves avoid the term to describe their activities, preferring other more positive labels such as revolutionary cells, urban guerrillas, and Islamic fighters (or mujahidin). (Lia, 2005). However, while the political perspective may be changeable, it is the act of terrorism or extremism, regardless of its origins, that has the direct effect on international events.

In the aftermath of the terrorist attacks in Paris in 2015, which included a football stadium, a number of sports events were cancelled. Some were rearranged and others never took place. In each of these cases, sports organisations are likely to have suffered either an increase in expenses related to re-scheduling the event or a loss of revenue that was attached to the sports event (Tolley, 2016). If it was not for the efforts of the security staff at the Stade de France where 79,000 spectators were gathered to watch a football game between France and Germany, the consequences, devastating as they were, would certainly have been much worse.

Political and economic integration, two pillars of globalisation, have created a new field of operations for international terrorists and extremists. In effect, globalisation accommodates the operational choices of committed extremists (Martin, 2016). Almost as a response to the values of globalisation, a worldwide resurgence of local ethnic and religious identity has led to numerous conflicts locally, and globally, since the end of the Cold War (Reuter, 2009). Globalisation is said to be a facilitator of poverty, increased inequality, and social breakdown (three of the foundations of extreme violence) because of the resistance shown by those who become oppressed by its effects (Chisadza and Bittencourt, 2018). When some states suffer from political and economic repression, globalisation can provide external intervention which is often quoted as one of the main sources of violent revolts in the developed world (Onwudiwe, 2001).

The last 20 years have seen a marked increase in terrorist activity targeting international events. In fact, it would be fair to suggest that international events have always been one of the easy targets as so many international events are free, outdoors, and have limited access restrictions to large gatherings of people in one place. This has essentially defined the increasing importance of safety and security management as an integral part of the international event industry's operations.

As well as the influence of globalisation on the ground, advances in technology and communication have intensified the pace of globalisation in recent years. At the same time, the same advances have increased the ability to bring about acts of terrorism. There are claims that globalisation may be one of the main causes of the spread of terrorism because it assists terrorist groups to distribute literature through communication technologies and enforce their views on like-minded people or those who can be radicalised in other parts of the globe (Khan and Estrada, 2017). More recently, Alex (2014) observed a rise of home-grown terrorism in international events in several Western countries. Often, the actions are carried out by lone wolf-type individuals reacting to local/global politics and changes in society, looking for a cause to identify with – but, most notably, by *local* residents.

The ease of access to extreme or fake material available via the internet increases the ability to influence susceptible individuals who live in well-established Western democracies. It can also overly influence individuals that hold extremist views as they appear to deem international events and attendees as easy targets.

The Council of Europe (COE, n.d.) observes that propaganda, misinformation, and fake news also have the potential to promote violent extremism and hate to undermine democracies and reduce trust in the democratic processes. These democratic processes are a central contributor to access for international events as they are more conducive to foreign engagement. Moreover, any kind of instability in the governing process creates uncertainty which can be devastating to any international event, whether it is home-grown or visiting. While early terrorists had to rely on face-to-face communication or printed material that requires time and costly dissemination, modern extremists have quick and reliable communication channels at their disposal that allow them to communicate instantaneously to thousands at negligible cost (Zanini and Edwards, 2001). Obviously, conducting communication in this way allows for traceable activities and may ultimately expose radical groups and individuals.

The links between globalisation, extreme views, and terrorism, particularly since 9/11, have made the subjects much more widely researched. From terrorism at sports events (Hassan *et al.*, 2012) and public events (Kaszeta, 2013), to tourism (Bowen *et al.*, 2014; Dean, 2002; Korstanje and Clayton, 2012) and sociology (Buchalter and Curtis, 2003; Crijns *et al.*, 2017; Holgersson *et al.*, 2016), greater effort is being made in the research community to understand the extensive effects of terrorism on humanity.

From an international event management perspective on terrorism, it is normal to liaise with the emergency services. However, the increased likelihood of terrorist acts means the added potential of liaison with the armed and specialist security forces. Where crisis management and continuity plans in the event of a disaster have largely been based on the risk of fire, the weather, and other potential accidents, targeted interference is affecting the cost of hosting international events with the need for extra security measures and the potential requirement for a terrorist attack to be included in the international event's insurance policy. The increased costs may be significant, but in most cases, these are passed back to the customer by simply being included in the ticket price.

Despite the fact that terrorism has raised great difficulties for international events, the international event industry has led the way in addressing the problem. Advances in technology and digital communication, which are discussed in Chapters 7 and 11, have greatly improved the safety of audiences around the world. It is a common trait for international events to be used as the catalyst for change and the development of increased security measures in cities around the world.

9.12 Summary

Globalisation is a powerful ally of international events. It provides many opportunities for international events to expand into new territories as well as supporting the spread of globalisation itself. However, some of the effects of globalisation have serious negative impacts on international event stakeholders and these have created some of the biggest problems event organisers now have to take into consideration. The chapter has provided a deep review of the contradictions an international event organiser must be able to balance and qualify when engaging with the larger international events and their contribution to the local communities they encounter along the way.

Case study 9.1 Singapore

It is over 200 years since Sir Stamford Raffles landed in Singapore setting up a trading post for the British East India Company. Today, Singapore is a sovereign Island, the archetypal modern country. It is an economy built on international trade and provides a series of offerings for the international event traveller including cultural and gastronomic experiences and ancient religious traditions. It has been consistently rated as the top destination for meetings and incentives, winning numerous awards since 2015, including the accolade of 'top convention city in Asia' (Jain, 2019).

Singapore is placed highly for a number of key social indicators including education, healthcare, quality of life, personal safety, and housing, with a home ownership rate of 90% (Statistics Singapore, 2019). However, for the last five years, it has also been rated as the most expensive city in the world (Economist Intelligence Unit, 2020).

The two international airports have direct links to almost 300 cities with around 7,000 flights a week. People who live and work in Singapore can wake up every morning to a British news channel, sip on an American brand of coffee, wear a Swiss watch, drive a German car to work, and have Italian food for lunch (AsiaBiz, n.d).

Questions

1. What might be the main factors that would guide a decision to host an international event in Singapore?
2. What influence have the four main forces of globalisation contributed to the rise of international events in Singapore?
3. What glocalisation potential exists to be attached to international events in Singapore?

9.13 Useful websites

Megatrends map (English version)
https://medium.com/@jwokittel/the-megatrend-map-a-great-method-to-improve-your-workshop-participants-visionary-thinking-to-d1f61c0eb375

Globalisation: threat or opportunity?
www.imf.org/external/np/exr/ib/2000/041200to.htm

List of country groupings
https://en.wikipedia.org/wiki/List_of_country_groupings

BBC Bitesize: Globalisation
www.bbc.co.uk/bitesize/guides/zxpn2p3/revision/5

Meetings made in Germany
www.gcb.de/

The myth of globalisation | Peter Alfandary | TEDxAix
www.youtube.com/watch?time_continue=29&v=xUYNB4a8d2U

Amex global business travel
www.amexglobalbusinesstravel.com/

References

Ackerman, E. (2019). Greeting machine explores extreme minimalism in social robots. Retrieved from https://spectrum.ieee.org/automaton/robotics/home-robots/greeting-machine-explores-extreme-minimalism-in-social-robots Accessed 16th October 2019.

Alam Choudhury, M. (1999). Global megatrends and the community. *Humanomics, 15*(2), 16–41. doi:10.1108/eb018826

Alex, P. S. (2014). Violent and non-violent extremism: Two sides of the same coin? *ICCT Research Papers, 5*(5), 1–29. doi:10.19165/2014.1.05

Altshuler, A., & Luberoff, D. (2003). *Mega-Projects: The Changing Politics of Urban Public Investment*. Washington DC: Brookings Institution.

Alvaredo, F., Chancel, L., Piketty, T., Saez, E., & Zucman, G. (2018). *World Inequality Report*. Paris: World Inequality Lab. Retrieved from https://wir2018.wid.world/files/download/wir2018-full-report-english.pdf Accessed 16th October 2019.

AsiaBiz (n.d.) How globalisation has affected Singapore's development. Retrieved from www.asiabiz.sg/blog/globalisation-and-singapore-development/ Accessed 6th November 2019.

Badolo, F., & Traoré, F. (2015). Impact of rising world rice prices on poverty and inequality in Burkina Faso. *Development Policy Review, 33*(2), 221–244. doi:10.1111/dpr.12099

Banks, T. (2010). Hotel conference addresses the next decade's challenges. *Design Week, 25*(21), 7.

Barr, C. (2017). Inequality index: where are the world's most unequal countries? *The Guardian*. Retrieved from www.theguardian.com/inequality/datablog/2017/apr/26/inequality-index-where-are-the-worlds-most-unequal-countries Accessed 26th May 2018.

BBC (2019). Globalisation. Retrieved from www.bbc.com/bitesize/guides/zxpn2p3/revision/1 Accessed 13th May 2019.

Becerril, H. (2017). Evictions and housing policy evolution in Rio de Janeiro: An ANT perspective. *Journal of Urban Affairs, 39*(7), 939–952. doi:10.1080/07352166.2017.1328975

Beck, H. (1933). London Underground Map.

Beer, L., & Boswell, T. (2015). The Resilience of dependency effects in explaining income inequality in the global economy: A cross national analysis, 1975–1995. *Journal of World-Systems Research, 8*(1), 30–59. doi:10.5195/jwsr.2002.273

Bhagat, R. S. (2004). Megatrends in world cultures and globalisation. *Journal of International Management, 10*(4), 515–516. doi:10.1016/j.intman.2004.08.005

Bowen, C., Fidgeon, P., & Page, S. J. (2014). Maritime tourism and terrorism: Customer perceptions of the potential terrorist threat to cruise shipping. *Current Issues in Tourism, 17*(7), 610–639. doi:10.1080/13683500.2012.743973

Buchalter, A. R., & Curtis, G. E. (2003). *Inventory and Assessment of Databases Relevant for Social Science Research on Terrorism*. Federal Research Division, Library of Congress. Retrieved from www.loc.gov/rr/frd/ Accessed 30th April 2017.

Buckley, R., Gretzel, U., Scott, D., Weaver, D., & Becken, S. (2015). Tourism megatrends. *Tourism Recreation Research, 40*(1), 59–70. doi:10.1080/02508281.2015.1005942

Burdett, R. (2016). Designing inequality? *Architectural Design, 86*(3), 136–141. doi:10.1002/ad.2056

Button, K. (2008). 'The Impacts of Globalisation on International Air Transport Activity: Past trends and future perspectives'. Paper presented at the Global Forum on Transport and Environment in a Globalising World, Guadalajara, Mexico, November 2008.

Celuch, K., & Davidson, R. (2008). Human resources in the business event industry. In J. Ali – Knight, M. Robertson, A. Fyall & A. Ladkin (Eds.), *International Perspectives of Festivals and Events,* 241–252. Oxford: Butterworth Heinemann.

Chisadza, C., & Bittencourt, M. (2018). Globalisation and conflict: Evidence from sub-Saharan Africa. *Revue Internationale de Politique de Développement, 10*(1), 1–23. doi:10.4000/poldev.2706

Coleman, P. T., & Bartoli, A. (2004). Addressing extremism. White Paper. The International Center for Cooperation and Conflict Resolution, Colombia University, New York. Retrieved from www.tc.columbia.edu/i/a/document/9386_WhitePaper_2_Extremism_030809.pdf Accessed 22nd October 2019.

Council of Europe (COE) (n.d.). Dealing with propaganda, misinformation and fake news. Retrieved from www.coe.int/en/web/campaign-free-to-speak-safe-to-learn/dealing-with-propaganda-misinformation-and-fake-news Accessed 22nd October 2019.

Crijns, H., Cauberghe, V., & Hudders, L. (2017). Terrorism threat in Belgium: The resilience of Belgian citizens and the protection of governmental reputation by means of communication. *Public Relations Review, 43*(1), 219–234. doi:10.1016/j.pubrev.2016.10.006

Davis, L. K. (2011). International events and mass evictions: A longer view. *International Journal of Urban and Regional Research, 35*(3), 582–599. doi:10.1111/j.1468-2427.2010.00970.x

Dean, A. P. (2002). Tourism and terrorism. *International Journal of Hospitality Management, 21*(1), 1–3. doi:10.1016/s0278-4319(01)00037-8

Desmangles, L. K. (2013). Other side of sporting events: How they affect development. Retrieved from https://borgenproject.org/side-mega-sporting-events-affect-development/ Accessed 16th October 2019.

Dicken, P. (2011). *Global Shift Mapping the Changing Contours of the World Economy* (6th ed.). New York: Guilford Press.

Economist Intelligence Unit (n.d.) Worldwide Cost of Living Summary Report. Retrieved from www.eiu.com/n/campaigns/worldwide-cost-of-living-2020 Accessed 23rd May 2020.

Etemad, H., & Motaghi, H. (2018). Internationalization pattern of creative-cultural events: Two cases from Canada. *International Business Review, 27*(5), 1033–1044. doi:10.1016/j.ibusrev.2018.03.003

Foley, M., McPherson, G., & Matheson, C. (2006). Glocalisation and Singapore festivals. *International Journal of Event Management Research, 2*(1).

Foley, M., McPherson, G., & McGillivray, D. (2008). Establishing Singapore as the events and entertainment capital of Asia: Strategic brand diversification. In J. Ali-Knight, M. Robertson, A. Fyall & A. Ladkin (Eds.), *International Perspectives of Festivals and Events: Paradigms of Analysis*, 53–64. Oxford: Butterworth Heinemann.

George, V., & Wilding, P. (2002). *Globalisation and Human Welfare*. London: Macmillan Education.

Ghauri, P., & Powell, S. (2008). *Globalization* (1st ed.). London: Dorling Kindersley Limited.

Giddens, A. (2002). *Runaway World: How Globalisation is Reshaping Our Lives* (2nd ed.). London: Profile.

Göll, E., & Evers-Wölk, M. (2014). *Meetings and Conventions 2030: A Study of Megatrends Shaping Our Industry*. Frankfurt: Institute for Futures Studies and Technology Assessment.

Greene, S. J. (2003). Staged cities: Mega-events, slum clearance, and global capital. *Yale Human Rights and Development Law Journal*, 161.

Hajkowicz, S., Reeson, A., Rudd, L., Bratanova, A., Hodges, L., Mason, C., & Boughen, N. (2016). Tomorrow's digitally enabled workforce: Megatrends and scenarios for jobs and employment in Australia over the coming twenty years. Brisbane: CSIRO.

Hassan, D., Giulianotti, R., & Klauser, F. (2012). Sport mega-events and 'terrorism': A critical analysis. *International Review for the Sociology of Sport, 47*(3), 307–323. doi:10.1177/1012690211433454

Hoersch, S. (2019). Globalization: How it influences and challenges the event industry. Retrieved from https://ungerboeck.com/resources/Globalization-how-it-influences-and-challenges-the-event-industry Accessed 8th October 2019.

Holgersson, A., Sahovic, D., Saveman, B.-I., & Björnstig, U. (2016). Factors influencing responders' perceptions of preparedness for terrorism. *Disaster Prevention and Management, 25*(4), 520–533. doi:10.1108/dpm-12-2015-0280

Insights Events Council (IEC) (2018). Global economic significance of business events. Retrieved from: https://insights.eventscouncil.org/Portals/0/OE-EIC%20Global%20Meetings%20Significance%20%28FINAL%29%202018-11-09-2018.pdf Accessed 15th October 2019.

International Monetary Fund (IMF) (2000). Globalization: Threat or opportunity? Retrieved from www.imf.org/external/np/exr/ib/2000/041200to.htm Accessed 9th October 2019.

Jain, A. (2019). Singapore is top meeting destinations in Asia for 2019. *Cvent blog.* Retrieved from https://blog.cvent.com/au/hospitality-cloud/cvents-top-meeting-destinations-asia-2019/ Accessed 6th November 2019.

James, P. & Steger, M. B. (2014) A genealogy of globalization: A career of a concept. *Globalizations,* 11(4), 417–434. doi:10.1080/14747731.2014.951186

Jennings, W. (2012). Mega-events and risk colonisation: Risk management and the Olympics. *Centre for Analysis of Risk and Regulation Discussion Paper 71.* London: Carr, London School of Economics and Political Science.

Jovanovic, M. N. (2010). Is globalisation taking us for a ride? *Journal of Economic Integration, 25*(3), 501–549. doi:10.11130/jei.2010.25.3.501

Kaszeta, D. (2013). *CBRN and Hazmat Incidents at Major Public Events Planning and response.* Hoboken, N.J: John Wiley & Sons.

Kay, P. (2004). Cross-cultural research issues in developing international tourist markets for cultural events *Event Management, 8*(4), 191–202.

Khan, A., & Estrada, M. A. R. (2017). Globalisation and terrorism: An overview. *Quality & Quantity, 51*(4), 1811–1819.

Knightscope, Inc. (n.d.). Autonomous security. Retrieved from www.knightscope.com/ Accessed 16th October 2019.

Korstanje, M. E., & Clayton, A. (2012). Tourism and terrorism: conflicts and commonalities. *Worldwide Hospitality and Tourism Themes, 4*(1), 8–25. doi:10.1108/17554211211198552

Lia, B. (2005). *Globalisation and the Future of Terrorism: Patterns and Predictions.* London: Routledge.

Martin, G. (2016). *Understanding Terrorism* (5th ed.). London: Sage.

McDermot, M. (2018). The music industry is booming, but artists are losing big with just 12% of the revenue, report claims, *USA Today.* Retrieved from https://eu.usatoday.com/story/life/music/2018/08/08/music-industry-booming-but-artists-only-get-12-percent-revenue/936711002/ Accessed 3rd January 2020.

Mest, C. E. (2016). Tech goals: efficiency, synergy. (FRONT-DESK OPERATIONS). *Hotel Management, 231*(6), 24.

Milanovic, B. (2016). *Global Inequality: A New Approach for the Age of Globalization.* Cambridge, MA: The Belknap Press of Harvard University Press.

Monhof, D. (2018). Humanoid robot teams up with TUI Germany. Retrieved from https://amadeus.com/en/insights/blog/humanoid-robot-teams-tui-germany Accessed 16th October 2019.

MSCI Inc. (2014). MSCI market classification framework. Retrieved from www.msci.com/documents/1296102/1330218/MSCI_Market_Classification_Framework.pdf/d93e536f-cee1-4e12-9b69-ec3886ab8cc8 Accessed 8th October 2019.

Nijman, J. (1999). Cultural globalization and the identity of place: The reconstruction of Amsterdam. *Ecumene, 6*(2), 146–164. doi:10.1191/096746099701556141

OED (1989). *The Oxford English Dictionary*. Oxford: Clarendon Press.

Onwudiwe, B. D. (2001). *The Globalization of Terrorism*. London: Routledge.

Peachey, K. (2019). Gap between rich and poor starts to widen. Retrieved from www.bbc.co.uk/news/business-47370739 Accessed 13th May 2019.

Perelman, P. (2015). The anarchy of globalization: Local and global, intended and unintended consequences. *World Review of Political Economy, 6*(3), 352–374. doi:10.13169/worlrevipoliecon.6.3.0352

Pillay, U., & Bass, O. (2008). Mega-events as a response to poverty reduction: The 2010 FIFA World Cup and its urban development implications. *Urban Forum, 19*(3), 329–346. doi:10.1007/s12132-008-9034-9

Price Waterhouse Coopers (PwC) (2016). Five megatrends and their implications for global defense & security. Retrieved from www.pwc.com/gx/en/government-public-services/assets/five-megatrends-implications.pdf Accessed 15th October 2019.

Retief, F., Bond, A., Pope, J., Morrison-Saunders, A., & King, N. (2016). Global megatrends and their implications for environmental assessment practice. *Environmental Impact Assessment Review, 61*(C), 52–60. doi: doi:10.1016/j.eiar.2016.07.002

Reuter, T. (2009). Globalisation and local identities: The rise of new ethnic and religious movements in post-Suharto Indonesia. *Asian Journal of Social Science, 37*(6), 857–871. doi:10.1163/156848409x12526657425181

Roberts, A. (2002). The changing faces of terrorism. Retrieved from www.bbc.co.uk/history/recent/sept_11/changing_faces_02.shtml Accessed 22nd October 2019.

Robertson, R. (2012). Globalisation or glocalisation? *The Journal of International Communication, 18*(2), 191–208. doi:10.1080/13216597.2012.709925

Rojek, C. (2013). *Event Power: How Global Events Manage and Manipulate*. London: Sage.

Roser, M., & Ortiz-Ospina, E. (2017). Global extreme poverty. Retrieved from https://ourworldindata.org/extreme-poverty Accessed 13th May 2019.

Rotman, D. (2013). How technology is destroying jobs. *MIT Technology Review, 116*(4), 27–35.

Rüttimann, B. (2006). *Modeling Economic* Globalisation. *A Post-Neoclassic View on Foreign Trade and Competition*. Münster: Verlagshaus Monsenstein und Vannerdat.

Sánchez, F., & Broudehoux, A.-M. (2013). Mega-events and urban regeneration in Rio de Janeiro: Planning in a state of emergency. *International Journal of Urban Sustainable Development, 5*(2), 132–153. doi:10.1080/19463138.2013.839450

Scherer, J., & Shi, A. (2016). Here are the 7 biggest financial disasters in modern Olympic history. Retrieved from https://fortune.com/2016/08/10/olympics-financial-disasters/ Accessed 16th October 2019.

Slaughter, R. A. (1993). Looking for the real 'megatrends'. *Futures, 25*(8), 827–849. doi:10.1016/0016-3287(93)90033-P

Stank, T., Autry, C., Daugherty, P., Closs, D. (2015). Reimagining the 10 megatrends that will revolutionize supply chain logistics. *Transportation Journal, 54*(1), 7–32.

Statistics Singapore (2019) *Singapore in Figures 2019.* Retrieved from www.singstat.gov.sg/-/media/files/publications/reference/sif2019.pdf

Tolley, R. (2016). Managing increasing terror risk within the sports and event industry. *Global Sports and Events Practice,* September 2016, 1, 1–6.

UFI (2019). UFI releases figures showing global economic impact of exhibitions. www.ufi.org/wp-content/uploads/2019/04/23_04_19-UFI-releases-figures-showing-global-economic-impact-of-exhibitions.pdf Accessed 9th October 2019.

Watson, K. (2019). IMS Business Report 2019. Retrieved from www.internationalmusicsummit.com/wp-content/uploads/2019/05/IMS-Business-Report-2019-vFinal.pdf Accessed 9th October 2019.

Wikipedia (n.d.). Las Vegas Strip shooting. Retrieved from https://commons.wikimedia.org/wiki/File:Las_Vegas_Strip_shooting.svg#filelinks Accessed 23rd October 2019.

External forces

Wright, C. (2014). After the BRICS are the MINTs, but can you make any money from them? Retrieved from www.forbes.com/sites/chriswright/2014/01/06/after-the-brics-the-mints-catchy-acronym-but-can-you-make-any-money-from-it/#6381f34329a6 Accessed 8th October 2019.

Zanini, M., & Edwards, S. J. (2001). The networking of terror in the information age. In J. Arquilla & D. Ronfeldt (Eds.), *Networks and Netwars: The future of Terror, Crime, and Militancy*. E-book. Retrieved from www.rand.org/pubs/monograph_reports/MR1382.html.

Zukunfts Institute (n.d). The Megatrend Map. Retrieved from www.zukunftsinstitut.de/artikel/die-megatrend-map/ Accessed 15th Ocober 2019.

Chapter 10

Sustainable international events – an oxymoron?

Contents

10.1 Chapter overview

In light of the now intense global focus on sustainability and the future of planet earth, the first consideration for all event organisers when discussing international events and sustainability is not so much knowing where to start, but deciding where to stop. This in itself is a sustainability question for the hosting of international events. It is not possible for international events to avoid creating an impact on the environment, so the organisers should include measures to reduce the impact at every stage. With international events being one of the best ways to communicate a sustainability message, individuals and companies should make every effort to demonstrate their event contributes to being as green as possible.

There are a number of environmental concerns that international events will have a greater or lesser impact upon, including global warming, pollution, and deforestation. To cover all of these topics in relation to international events in any reasonable depth is way beyond the capabilities of this chapter. With this in mind, this chapter will discuss some of the main themes related to sustainability, particularly around an area where the available science is most robust, greenhouse gas (GHG) emissions. This will contribute to understanding sustainability and the management of international events and what international event organisers should consider in the delivery process.

10.2 Learning objectives

By the end of this chapter, the student will be expected to:

- Understand the broader effects of international events and the environment
- Appreciate the value in measuring carbon footprint impacts
- Recognise the events/sustainability oxymoron
- Understand the importance of international events and global sustainability issues.

10.3 Introduction

Scientific research is yet to prove with absolute certainty why the world is going through the changes it is. What is proven is that humanity is contributing to issues of sustainability. From air pollution to plastics, there is considerable visible evidence to justify a number of concerns. Some areas of research, particularly in areas of microplastic pollution, may prove to be even more devastating than the ones we are aware of currently; further research is still required to understand the implications of these relatively new discoveries in our air, land, and seas (Carrington, 2019). However, based on what is already happening in the event industry, the next ten years (or possibly even less) will see demonstrable environmental modifications to the way international events are delivered.

Considering the size and importance of international events, the global event industry, and their contribution to the world economy, the impact on the environment cannot be overestimated. Greta Thunberg's speech to the International Sustainability Council, where she now famously protested 'You come to us young people for hope. How dare you?', emphasised the younger generation's dissatisfaction with world leaders' response to climate change (Thunberg, 2019). The world's largest international event organisations can be just as deservedly chastised for their response to date on the issue.

Events and the environment are two subjects that, when mentioned in the same breath, it is either to promote the encouraging efforts being made around the world to reduce the damaging effects on the environment (Caratti and Ferraguto, 2011; De Brito, 2018; Powell, 2019), or to emphasise the size of the problem caused by and within the international event industry (Bonilla-Priego et al., 2014; Case, 2013). Energy consumption from international events contributes to pollution, environmental deterioration, and GHG emissions. As both a major contributor to the problem and as one of the principal means of disseminating information about it, international events are in the most unusual of situations.

In Chapter 3, the triple bottom line was introduced. In this chapter we discuss aspects of that concept in much more detail. With serious environmental impacts being created by the event industry's transportation, stadia construction, infrastructure, energy and water use, along with excessively high levels of waste, it is surprising that international events are not condemned much more widely for their GHG emissions and their contribution to the world's sustainability problem. Such criticisms tend to be addressed to the aviation industry, companies who extract fossil fuel, and individual nations such as the USA, China and Brazil (Friedrich et al., 2017). However, sustainability is a key aspect of every major event's bidding process, international event environmental legacies, and national and international clean-up events. Therefore, there are many positive as well as negative contributions to the conundrum of sustainability and international events.

International events undoubtedly make some of the most significant contributions to highlighting the issues of sustainability, but with so many damaging contributions being created that remain unacknowledged, the negative impacts far outweigh the positive.

10.4 Sustainability and international events

It is important to put sustainability into perspective in order to address some of the issues at stake for the international events sector. Therefore, some background information is necessary.

There are three pillars of sustainability. These pillars are economic, social, and environmental (Gibson et al., 2012). Achieving a balance between the environment, society, and the economy is considered essential to meet the needs of the present without compromising the ability of future generations to meet their needs. Sustainable development as a goal is achieved by balancing the three pillars of sustainability (Haider, 2011). Therefore, sustainability in this context is simply a balance for the long-term future existence through the use and replenishment of anything from the earth. One of the main contributions from human activity to the sustainability conundrum (that international event organisers should have at least a general knowledge of), is the effect of greenhouse gas (GHG) emissions.

Human activities are responsible for almost all of the increase in greenhouse gases in the atmosphere over the last 150 years (IPCC, 2007). The complication is how we attribute the contribution from international events. We will learn in this chapter that international events contribute more than is necessary to the imbalance by removing, using or burning more of the earth's vital resources that are required to maintain a sustainable balance.

10.4.1 Agenda for sustainable development

In 2016, the 2030 Agenda for Sustainable Development was released. This is the plan of action for people, planet and prosperity released by the United Nations (UN), made up of 17 optimistic Sustainable Development Goals (SDGs) covering poverty, fighting inequalities and tackling climate change. While these remain the UN's shared vision of humanity and a social contract between world leaders and the people, they have already admitted that meeting the 2030 target is not possible. Even before the agenda's official release, various commentators disputed the use of the targets, dismissing them as sprawling and misconceived, with the entire enterprise being set up to fail (The Economist, 2015). Dearden (2015) observed that the real problem was that 'the wish-list came with no historical background of how we got here, and no political strategy for how we get out'.

The 17 SDGs to transform the world consist of:

1. No Poverty
2. Zero Hunger
3. Good Health and Wellbeing
4. Quality Education
5. Gender Equality
6. Clean Water and Sanitation
7. Affordable and Clean Energy
8. Decent Work and Economic Growth
9. Industry, Innovation and Infrastructure
10. Reduced Inequality
11. Sustainable Cities and Communities
12. Responsible Consumption and Production
13. Climate Action
14. Life Below Water
15. Life on Land
16. Peace and Justice Strong Institutions
17. Partnerships to achieve the Goal.

While it remains critical for event businesses to continue to turn a profit while contributing to the cost of improving their sustainability efforts, sustainability targets of any kind will remain idealistic when the foremost efforts on the ground are cancelled out by values of profit over sustainability. Money is continuing to take precedence over the environment and when it comes to investments, there would appear to be a number of shades of being green. This was put into context when, in December 2019, the company with the biggest carbon footprint ever, Saudi Aramco, arrived on the stock market as the world's biggest listed company. Interest in Aramco's first day of trading was reflected in the value reaching the 10% rise restriction level with ease (Pratley, 2019).

10.5 The carbon footprint

The 1992 United Nations Framework Convention on Climate Change (UNFCCC) calls for the stabilisation of GHG concentrations in the atmosphere at a level that would prevent dangerous anthropogenic (human) interference with the climate system (Rao and Riahi, 2019). Measuring the carbon footprint of an international event company is a complicated and difficult process as it includes a lot of complicated science and symbols that many people simply do not understand. Furthermore, accurate figures are difficult to calculate because of the many variables that exist in the calculations and how the carbon is burned. For example, a small office-based international event company's energy use will most probably be dwarfed by its GHG emissions through its travel activities.

To begin to understand the difficulties involved in calculating a carbon footprint, it is necessary to understand that gases that trap heat in the atmosphere are called greenhouse gases (GHG) and that a carbon footprint is measured in tonnes of carbon dioxide equivalent (tCO_2e). The carbon dioxide equivalent (CO_2e) allows the different GHGs to be compared on a like-for-like basis relative to one unit of carbon dioxide (CO_2). This carbon dioxide equivalent (CO_2e) is calculated by multiplying the emissions of each of the six main contributing greenhouse gases by its 100-year global warming potential (GWP) (Carbon Trust, 2018). The six main greenhouse gases are: carbon dioxide (CO_2), methane (CH_4), nitrous oxide (N_2O), hydrofluorocarbons (HFCs), perfluorocarbons (PFCs), and sulfur hexafluoride (SF6).

As the data above suggests, acronyms and numbers make the process of understanding the impact of a company's carbon footprint difficult to appreciate. A ten tonne footprint could be considered either good or bad depending on the activities of the company. This is made all the more difficult when there is nothing immediately obvious to highlight how bad the impact really is. Furthermore, if the impact is creating a detrimental effect, nobody really knows until data has been collected and analysed, which can take years.

Consequences such as the effects on the weather and people's health begin to appear later in the process. Therefore, predictions have been used to highlight the potential ongoing impact. The problem with predictions has been the ease with which they can be disregarded in present day plans. However, recent studies suggest previous model simulations published between 1970 and 2007 have proved to be accurate in their predictions on global warming (Hausfather *et al.*, 2019). The point is that the earth is warming and human activity is a major contributory factor. The simulations further suggest that any future projections using the same models should also be accurate.

To assist international event companies in achieving reductions over the last 20 years, all nations have been guided on reducing GHG emissions through the 1997 Kyoto Protocol, the 2015 United Nations Climate Change Conference (COP 21) and the 2016 Paris Climate Agreement. Yet, difficulties exist in nations meeting their own targets while the major polluters are making little effort to meet their goals. This is further complicated by the scale of shipping emissions from both container and cruise ships that are not part of emissions reduction targets made by countries as part of the Paris agreement (Laville, 2019). This omission relates directly to the contributions from international events. According to Abbasov (2019), in absolute terms, the shipping sector emitted about 139 million tonnes of CO_2 in 2018 – equal to CO_2 from a quarter of Europe's total passenger car fleet or 68 million cars.

Unfortunately, these climate agreements have become better known for countries withdrawing from them rather than committing to the challenge. Of all the countries involved in the Paris agreement, only seven have made commitments that would achieve its goal (Erickson, 2018). Without nation states adhering to these agreements, event companies are less inclined to implement the substantive changes required.

10.5.1 Calculating the carbon impact

Because of the difficulty most event organisers will have in understanding how to calculate a carbon footprint, a simple equation is needed. This is not a scientific or proven mathematical procedure, but rather a means to appreciate the extreme levels events contribute to GHG emissions.

If we take a number based on the average individual CO_2 emissions as being an absolute maximum for each individual to live a sustainable life in a given year, then every event would be able to calculate a representable allowable carbon footprint by applying this to the number of people attending.

For example, the most recent data for the average CO_2 emissions per person in metric tonnes (tCO_2e) for a year in the UK were estimated to be 5.6 tCO_2e (Wikipedia, 2019). The Rio Olympics and Paralympic Games 2016 made available 7.5 million tickets (Settimi, 2016). The overall carbon impact of the 2016 Olympic and Paralympic Games (excluding any above mentioned shipping emissions, of course), is estimated to be around 3.6 million tonnes of carbon dioxide equivalent ($mtCO_2e$) (Edie, 2016). Therefore, if the carbon cost of a ticket was to be shared between attendees, it would cost an individual from the UK (if they were observing the average of 5.6 tCO_2e per year), over 37% of their annual carbon budget. However, this would not include the other carbon cost of getting to Rio and the supplementary costs of daily sustenance, accommodation, and entertainment.

The emissions generated just from the two-week Games period itself in Rio were estimated to be 724,000 tCO_2e. This is equivalent to the annual carbon footprint of around 130,000 people from the UK. This figure contains within it emissions from the use of temporary structures, catering, athlete's travel grants, and so on. More detail is provided in Figure 10.1.

It is important to consider the per person (per capita) figures as these provide an indication of emissions with respect to the population of the polluting country. For example, the biggest absolute emissions come from China and the United States. However, in terms of CO_2 emissions per capita, China is ranked only ranked

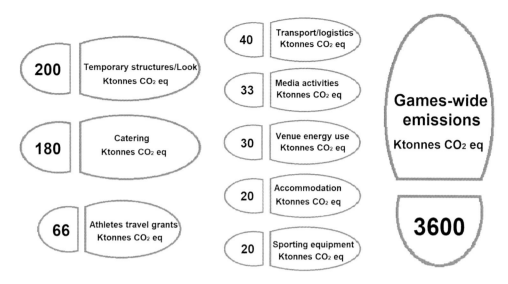

Figure 10.1 The estimated carbon footprint of the 2016 Olympic and Paralympic Games

Source: Edie, 2016

47th, at 7.5 metric tonnes (tCO$_2$e) per capita. The US is ranked 11th at 16.5 metric tonnes (tCO$_2$e) per capita. Amongst countries with sizeable populations, the USA has the highest CO$_2$ emissions per capita. India is the third highest country in terms of absolute emissions, but only 158th in terms of per capita output with 1.7 metric tonnes (tCO$_2$e) per capita (Pettinger, 2019). Figure 10.2 provides data from 2017 on the CO$_2$ emissions per capita from 15 selected countries.

A simple, but effective method to address carbon emissions would be for countries to limit an individual's carbon allowance to a maximum of the country's own average, and then impose stringent carbon taxes to offset any excess on any further usage. If so, the likelihood would be that emissions would reduce significantly. However, it would be impossible to include everything, as much of an individual's daily usage comes from general consumption. To achieve sustainable production and consumption, all food products and manufactured goods would need to carry carbon footprint labelling, and a process of allotting these to individual purchases would be required. White goods such as washing machines, for example, already come with energy ratings, but provide no information on the carbon cost from the production and global transportation process.

Developments such as these may be achievable sometime in the future as advances in technology increase communication through the Internet of Things (Ryan *et al.*, 2020). This is discussed in more detail in Chapter 11. The value today would be from assisting consumers in making decisions on the goods they purchase based on these figures. A number of methodologies are under development for the carbon footprinting of products around the world. Some of these initiatives aim to develop the measurement of carbon footprinting into labelling schemes, while others focus on the efficiency benefits companies can gain from undertaking a carbon analysis of their products (Mugnier *et al.*, 2010).

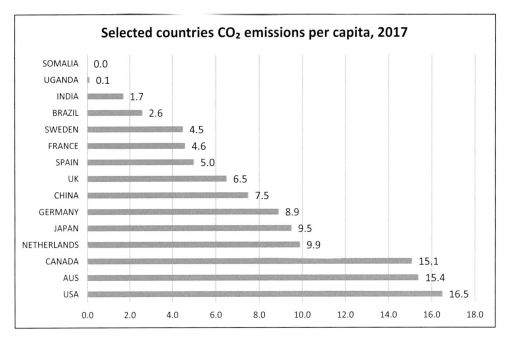

Figure 10.2 Selected countries' CO_2 emissions per capita

Source: Based on World Bank data, 2018; Pettinger, 2019

10.6 Contributing factors

The international event industry is an industrial polluter. However, instead of witnessing and quantifying the harmful emissions that can be measured and attributed to a single company or nation, the international event industry's contribution is obscured by other factors such as external manufacturers, travel companies, and other suppliers. The realisation of this emphasises the importance of each individual's contribution to the international event's CO_2 emissions, particularly from attending events.

The international event industry's CO_2 emissions can be viewed as being created on three main levels. These are:

1. As a direct result of hosting and attending major and mega events
2. As a direct result of the developments involved in delivering international events, such as buildings, infrastructure, and waste management
3. As a direct result of the individual attendees, e.g. sports fans and business delegates who travel to attend public/private events (APEs) such as sporting events, meetings, conferences, and exhibitions.

All of these impact levels are included in mega events, while smaller events will have lesser impacts. In 2009, the United Nations Environment Programme produced an independent environmental assessment of the 2008 Beijing Olympic Games. The report highlighted the broader impact mega events have on the environment with carbon emissions exceeding 1 million tonnes. Table 10.1 breaks down the various areas of impact to show the sources of carbon emissions.

Table 10.1 Greenhouse gas (GHG) emissions from Beijing 2008

Sources		GHG emissions (1,000 tonnes)	Proportion of total (%)
Construction of venues		24.0	2.00
Operation of venues		77.0	6.50
International flight trips	International spectators	680.0	57.50
	Media and others	44.5	3.80
	Athletes, Olympic family	33.6	2.80
Domestic flight trips		139.0	11.80
Other domestic trip and in-city trips		29.0	2.50
Operation of BOCOG*		0.4	0.03
Accommodation		144.0	12.20
Waste treatment		1.5	0.10
Torch relay		8.9	0.80
Total		**11,819**	**100****

*Beijing Organizing Committee for the Olympic Games

**In fact, the total is 100.03 - but they are the figures in the official report! There is a note that states: 'The study presented above was commissioned by the Beijing Environment Protection Bureau. However, the EPB has not fully endorsed the findings of the study.'

Source: Carmichael et al., 2009

The hosting of mega events and sustainability is a much discussed subject in academia (Caratti and Ferraguto, 2011; Case, 2013; Dolles and Söderman, 2010; Hall, 2012; Vanwynsberghe, 2015), with each article highlighting the continued efforts to address the four main areas of sustainability: water, waste, energy, and transportation. These four areas include considerable sustainability consequences for the host city. The broader conclusion is that policies to control the impact of mega events are not in place.

The more that is learned about the state of the global sustainability problem, the greater the impact of mega events becomes. This increases the oxymoronic nature of mega events and sustainability: a sustainable mega event is a contradiction in terms. However, the problem has become a behemoth that manages to avoid all attempts to bring it under control. Hall (2012) concluded that:

> The combined external pressures of biodiversity loss, climate change and peak oil, as well as financial and economic crisis and lack of equity might be the most significant contributors to a policy paradigm change with respect to sustainable tourism/events. Trouble is, for far too many people and places, hosting a mega-event so as to remain competitive in a declining global economy and environment has become the solution rather than a symptom of the problem.
>
> (Hall, 2012)

In fact, many of the activities that make up an international event do zero-harm and can be sustainable. Much of the equipment required has more than a single use and some of it can last a lifetime; local inputs include processes and goods that are reused year-on-year including, for example, an established venue, local workforce, public transport, local suppliers, and the necessary equipment and apparatus. As international events grow in size and financial value, more is spent on activities that increase the carbon footprint, most notably, the production of materials, waste management, and travel. Investment in supporting infrastructure, such as improved airport capacity, hotel accommodation, public transport, water and sewage systems, and urban landscaping, becomes necessary to ensure the effective operation and the best possible image of the host city to be presented to the international audience (Chalkley and Essex, 1999).

As we will discuss in Chapter 11, each major international event will seek to utilise the most up-to-date technology and digital communications to improve the experience of the event. Tokyo 2020 – now scheduled to take place in 2021 due to the COVID-19 pandemic – has taken this idea of image and breaking boundaries to a much greater level with plans for the first satellite to orbit the earth to celebrate the Games and an opening ceremony artificial meteor shower.

The miniature G-Satellite is set up to house Gundam and Zaku, two of Japan's favourite cartoon characters, in a cubicle with a number of small cameras installed to record and transmit their images back to earth. There will also be an electric bulletin board displaying messages in English, French and Japanese which will be deployed once the satellite is in orbit (Tokyo2020, 2019). Project Sky Canvas goes beyond even the massive investment made by China in the Beijing Olympics fireworks display. Japan's proposal involves launching a satellite into space loaded with around 1,000 source particles that become ingredients for a shooting star (Cooper, 2016). The sustainability report from the event may also break new ground providing it includes the impact of manufacturing the goods and getting the items into space.

Mega events still require the support of the local population, particularly when the cost to host is collected through taxation and the impact of increased levels of GHG emissions on local residents' health. O'Brien and Gardiner (2006) suggest one solution to making events more viable is to enhance the breadth and sustainability of their impacts through relationship development. However, much ambiguity surrounds the relationship between the overall attitude of residents close to mega event sites and support for the event (Andereck and Vogt, 2000). Prayag et al. (2013) recommend the importance of using a triple bottom line approach when assessing residents' perceptions of the various impacts mega events bring.

Considering that the carbon footprint of the Beijing 2008 Olympics was estimated to be 1.2 million tonnes of emissions, with international flights accounting for more than 60% of the total, and competition venues and accommodation accounting for around 20%, the organisers would have to rely considerably on compensation measures for the event to become carbon neutral.

10.6.1 Attending public/private events (APEs)

In 2018, approximately 32,000 exhibitions were held which directly involved 303 million visitors and over 4.5 million exhibitors across more than 180 countries (UFI, 2019). The top ten best-attended domestic sports leagues in the world attract an audience of around 171 million (Sporting Intelligence, 2017). When compared to national populations, these two figures alone place the international event industry as the third biggest population in the world. Table 10.2 shows the number of event attendees in comparison to national populations.

These figures are very conservative, as many other sporting events such as Formula 1 and the world cycling tours are not included. However, while the numbers are important to ascertain the impact of international events on the environment, without further research, it is not possible to confirm if the figures would take them above the populations of both India and China. However, it is probably inevitable if international political and religious events were to be included in the total.

Understanding the actual impact attendance at international events has on the environment remains a complicated calculation. A great deal of data is required to accurately measure such activities. Ballpark or estimated figures based on similar activities are currently as good as can be created. Therefore, if the conservative population data in Figure 10.2 were compared to the number of domestic flight trips for the Beijing Olympics in Table 10.1, a sense of the impact can be created. For example, the Beijing Olympics was said to have sold 7 million tickets. This is around 67 times fewer than the amount of APEs in Table 10.2. This would make APEs' annual contribution in the region of 9,313 million equivalent tonnes of carbon (mtCO$_2$e).

10.6.2 Carbon neutrality

For an international event to suggest it has achieved carbon neutrality is to imply the problem of carbon emissions does not exist as a result of the event taking place. For an international event to be carbon neutral, it must either have a zero contribution rate or balance its contribution to carbon emissions with carbon removal. Because of the basic nature of events and the need to burn fossil fuels throughout the process, a zero contribution rate event is not actually possible. This means neutrality may only be achieved by offsetting many of the emissions created. The demand for offsetting carbon emissions has morphed into an environmental commodity market (Dhanda and Hartman, 2011).

In order to offset the carbon footprint of an event, the organisation will first need to have a strategy to address the impact being created. This means conducting an audit of activities over a period of time (usually a year) to fully understand the impact and where to manage and reduce GHG emissions. Once a

Table 10.2 The number of people attending public/private events (APEs) compared to the world's most populous nation states

Country	Population 2019
China	1,435,238,808
India	1,369,792,995
APEs	**473,692,298**
United States	329,553,894
Indonesia	271,352,010

Source: Based on World Population Review, 2019

figure has been calculated, the organisation is in a position to demonstrate how carbon neutrality is being achieved by offsetting the impact through investments in other environmental projects. Environmental projects are designed to reduce future emissions and involve rolling out clean energy technologies or purchasing carbon credits from an emissions trading scheme. Other schemes work by soaking up CO_2 directly from the air through the planting of trees (Clark, 2011).

There are currently no fixed industry-wide rules or governing bodies for GHG emissions for international events. Therefore, without any fixed rules, opportunities exist for the event organisers to mislead or be misled. Buyers of carbon credits should undertake full research of carbon credit programmes in order to ascertain the quality of the credits on offer. Worthless credits have been sold that do not yield any reductions in carbon emissions. To address such actions, a code advising buyers to buy credits that have been certified by the United Nations was introduced. Most are issued by the UN, under the Kyoto protocol, which allows richer countries to meet their carbon-cutting targets by purchasing credits from poorer countries (Harvey, 2008).

International event organisations can sign up to specification standards detailing how to demonstrate carbon neutrality. Organisations such as ISO 14064 (international), PAS 2060 (UK) and the National Carbon Offset Standard (Australia) all offer principles to follow when carrying out a carbon audit (Rapier Group, 2019).

10.7 Balanced sustainable development

To improve the understanding of how international events contribute to the sustainability question, a review of how many of the earth's resources are used by humankind in any given year should improve this understanding. This is what is known as balanced sustainable development.

Balanced sustainable development will occur when the production of the earth's resources is the same as those that are used. Since the 1960s, the Global Footprint Network has pointed out the date each year by when the annual available environmental budget will be consumed. It is only natural to assume that an intelligent race that appreciates complicated budgeting systems would not allow the over-use any of the earth's resources. However, since the early 1970s humanity has gone way beyond its environmental budget. This means that for the last 50 years, we have been increasingly over consuming. Figure 10.3 shows the progressive increase in the over-use of the world's resources. The data has been compiled from the National Footprint and Biocapacity Accounts that measure the ecological resource use and resource regeneration capacity of countries over time. Based on approximately 15,000 data points per country per year, the accounts contain the ecological footprints of over 200 countries, territories, regions, and the world from 1961 to 2016, providing the core data needed for all ecological footprint analyses worldwide. According to Global Footprint Network, in 2018 humankind had used nature's resource budget for the entire year by 1st August (Earth Overshoot Day, 2018). International events are dependent on all six of the resources in Figure 10.3 and provide at best limited data on how much they over-use. The major and mega international events are some of the biggest contributors to the over-use problem and every event organiser should encourage greater clarity on how much demand an

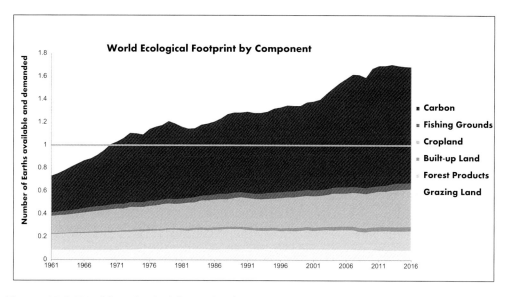

Figure 10.3 World ecological footprint by component and the number of earths required to sustain their use

Source: Global Footprint Network, 2019

event makes on biologically productive surfaces and the efforts being made to ensure any imbalance is eradicated.

There is an abundance of data to suggest a metaphorical crystal ball exists to guide the future of international events. There is certainly a wealth of scientific information. Organisations, business leaders, politicians, academics, and current students engaged in the delivery of future international events need to consider what actionable options exist to them. We have discussed in other chapters what many consider to be the key themes that will eventually shape the future, including globalisation, legislation, environmental issues, health, and technological advances. The task now is to address the international event industry's contribution to each of these problems.

It is not an option to completely stop the impact events have on the environment, but it is possible to reduce them substantially and even flip the usual approach to lobbying politicians by proactively demanding that legislation be applied instead of lobbying for it to be waived. On the other hand, governments could take the problem out of the industry's hands by applying stringent carbon tariffs to businesses. As of early 2018, more than 25 national or subnational carbon tax systems had been implemented or were scheduled to be implemented around the world (Metcalf, 2019). This concept could even be extended to individual carbon use.

10.7.1 Negative production externalities

Negative production externalities relate to the wider production costs that are created by an event. A term normally used in economics, negative externalities focus on factors that exist outside of the directly related costs and are known as the 'spill-over effects' (Riley, 2019). Externalities can arise from both production and consumption associated with international events. For example, facilities have to be built and people have to travel to the event. An external cost such as the cost of pollution from the putting-on of an international event is a typical example of a negative production externality and can be considered a secondary impact. In such a situation, the effect of the event on the environment makes the social cost higher than the private cost. Therefore a negative production externality is created when the secondary impacts are included in the data.

10.8 Greenwashing

In international events, the process of greenwashing data in reports can prove to be misleading about an event's environmental features and can distort perceptions. 'Greenwashing' is a term used when any business makes unsubstantiated or misleading claims about its environmental impact (Pernecky and Lück, 2013). Greenwashing makes an international event appear to be environmentally greener than it really is. Impacts such as the negative production externalities discussed above are either completely ignored or lost in the detail of reports that cover the large-scale international events. The data creating the impact may be mentioned in reports, but the actual impact can be omitted by suggesting that data will take years to collect and therefore not being readily available, or further research being required outside of the remit of the report.

The whole event industry is in the midst of a massive conundrum. International event managers need to proactively look forward to determine the future of the industry. It should no longer be acceptable to ignore the secondary impacts caused by international events. In fact, they should not be considered secondary impacts; they need to be accounted for as part of the reporting process.

Planning international events must go much further than just having sustainable plans. They should be much clearer on the size of carbon footprint and seek to avoid extreme reliance on fossil fuels, the majority of which are used in building new infrastructure and getting to the event. The transformation of the industry will only succeed if we apply foresight, innovation, and a genuine care for the future of the planet instead of the profit margins. The event industry is also in the midst of a transformation from the technological possibilities. We need to apply this knowledge with common sense decision making to contribute to the future of international event reporting.

10.8.1 Purpose and profit

International events have proved to provide a lot more than just profit. The values expressed in legacy documents often prioritise other values that bring good to communities. Because of this focus on the very heart of society, international events have the necessary influence and power to lead the changes required in capitalist culture to meet the world's sustainability challenge. The broader values must remove the act of greenwashing and go beyond the importance of profit to prioritise purpose. This is not to undermine profit per se, but rather to undermine the maximising of profit to the detriment of maintaining sustainable practices.

10.9 Seriously underestimated sustainability targets (SUST)

International events are now a central factor of modern society and many of the environmental impacts international events create are inescapable. This can to some degree be acknowledged because sustainability is about a balance between the use of the earth's resources and their replenishment or availability (O' Shea et al., 2013). However, failures in the managing of an international event's sustainability data are surprisingly easy to detect when important factors are simply disregarded from the equation. To measure the success of a meeting in terms of the number of delegates in attendance while ignoring the amount of CO_2 their flights pumped into the atmosphere is to show a reckless disregard for reality (Lancaster, 2019). This is a typical example of a seriously underestimated sustainability target (SUST) being employed.

Many company policies on sustainability have improved somewhat since their previously modest reductions. Actions such as using 100% recycled paper (Groves, 2008) or the reduction of building-project expenses (Schnitzer, 2011) have given way to much more substantial efforts. Any contributions to reducing the effects international events have on the environment are of course commendable. However, it is usually the case that the activities with the biggest impact, such as international travel, transportation of goods, waste, or the contributions generated in the production of promotional and single use material, are either overlooked or passed off as being unavoidable. This should no longer be acceptable if the industry is to be genuinely responsible for its contribution to the sustainability problem.

It cannot be overstated that the international event industry does go to considerable lengths to address issues of sustainability. However, working sustainably in international events is not an optional or infrequent activity, it is something that must be applied to each and every activity that is not carbon-free. Every action must be assessed according to its environmental impact. Many of these actions are relatively simple to monitor and fall into an individual's everyday awareness of recycling, eliminating the use of single-use plastics, avoiding waste, and reducing energy usage. The maintenance of such practices should essentially go back to a company's code of conduct discussed in Chapter 5.

As international event organisations go about their business, there are a number of SUST measures that would benefit from an immediate review. Essentially, this means considering how a venue operates, considering how engagement is conducted with the event, and considering a product's entire life cycle, whether that be a component of the event or the event itself, from the design phase right through to its disposal. The three areas that would benefit most from a SUST approach are:

- Transportation
- Waste management
- Energy use.

10.9.1 The transportation dilemma

Transportation has been discussed in some depth in Chapter 6. For as long as international events have occurred, the international event industry has traded throughout the world with two priorities in the transportation decision-making process. These are:

1. What is the fastest means of transportation? And,
2. What is the most financially beneficial means of transportation?

There are other considerations for the safety, class and comfort of the product or individual, but these can be considered supplementary to the decision. In previous centuries, this approach was considered fully acceptable based on the available knowledge of the subsequent effects. Today, the impact from international event transportation activities have on the planet is a major SUST issue. It is only when a SUST review is applied that a genuinely sustainable process can be achieved. Therefore, the considerations should become:

1. What is the fastest means of transportation considering the impact on the planet?
2. What is the most financially beneficial means of transportation considering the impact on the planet?

Almost every event business considers some form of sustainable development action in their activities. However, the extent to which these actions have a real impact in reducing their overall contribution to the problem renders most of these efforts largely insignificant. Not only are the international event businesses' efforts insufficient, the global standards businesses follow to meet sustainable targets are weak, easily manipulated, and tokenistic.

10.9.2 Waste management

International events generate massive amounts of waste, with a great deal being brought in and left behind by participants. This has been recognised as one of the most significant impacts of events (Collins *et al.*, 2007). According to the organisation A Greener Festival (2008), waste generated at festivals is one of the most prominent environmental impacts that festivals have. Not only is there a great deal of waste generated at many events, it is often the most visible environmental impact to the festival-goer. Spectator events have had a commonly accepted practice of leaving waste at the point of use. This ranges from drinks and food packages on the ground, to tents and other furniture left at the site. Considering audiences are counted in tens of thousands, the amount of food waste and foodstuffs requiring packaging represents a large amount of disposable products that are left to enter the waste channels.

A SUST review of waste management would include the monitoring of the whole journey – a system that can evidence where all products leaving the event end up. The responsibility for a product is often assumed to have been transferred once it is removed from the premises. International event organisers should avoid waste removal brokers and obtain reassurances from their waste management company that nothing goes to landfill and that recycling assurances are achieved.

10.9.3 Energy use

We have discussed GHG emissions in some detail thus far. It is the production and use of energy that contribute more than any other human activity to the build-up of GHGs in the atmosphere, and future energy development will determine how quickly those levels continue to rise and by how much (El-Ashry, 2014). The UK festival industry alone uses in excess of 12 million litres of diesel annually with 99% of all the energy used contributing to GHG emissions (A Greener Festival, 2012). By applying a SUST approach, considerable reductions can be achieved.

There is no alternative to energy use for international events other than the sourcing of clean energy. Clean energy is simply energy that is produced by any means that does not pollute the atmosphere. While the making of the equipment to source this energy is not included in this definition, these methods include:

- Solar energy from the sun
- Hydro energy from water (rivers or tides)
- Wind energy.

Getting participants to events will remain one of the event organiser's biggest energy dilemmas. This takes us back to the carbon neutral issue discussed above where large-scale international events can benefit from festival-goers, suppliers and artists voluntarily offsetting their fossil fuel travel miles into clean energy. Figure 10.4 indicates the process involved in offsetting and how this is achieved from calculating the miles travelled, to building a community of renewable energy projects that account for the carbon used.

There are a number of companies that assist international events in tackling travel emissions. There are a number of businesses and charities dedicated to assist event organisers and the event attendee in the fight against climate change. Each will have a particular focus such as conferences, festivals and invest up to 100% of all balancing donations in sustainable energy initiatives to replace non-renewable forms of energy such as oil with sustainable, clean energy solutions such as wind and solar energy (ecolibrium, 2019). The responsibility should still arguably remain with the event organisers. However, the more widespread these contributions become, the greener the event.

The sourcing of clean energy for international events continues to gain momentum as new ventures embrace renewable energy sources during the fit-out, and older venues such as convention centres retrospectively target their renewable energy options to improve their sustainability credentials.

10.9.4 Sustainable planning

Arguably, one of the biggest contributing factors to unnecessary carbon waste or SUST lies in the planning and positioning of international events. Formula 1

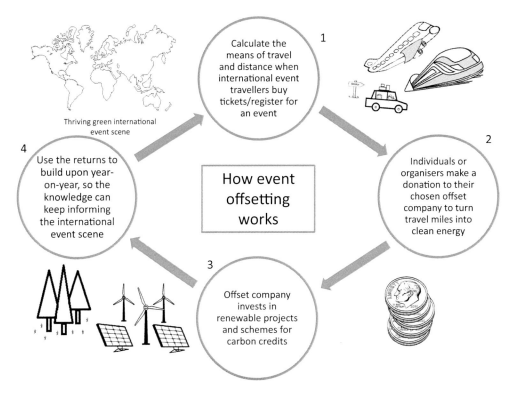

Figure 10.4 Turning fossil fuel travel miles into clean energy

Source: Based on information from ecolibrium, n.d.

motor sport and the Men's World Cup of association football, two of the world's major sporting events on the international events calendar, are indirectly and directly responsible for environmental despoliation (Miller, 2016). Formula 1, however, argues that it contributes technological innovation with advancements that have directly contributed to reductions in GHG emissions and benefitted the wider automotive industry. In 2019 the sport announced a sustainability plan to have a net-zero carbon footprint by 2030 (Formula 1, 2019).

Many international sporting events that are run by organisations with an emphasis on sustainability make what appear to be fundamentally senseless decisions on how the competitions are planned. FIFA (2018) have highlighted their commitment to sustainability by declaring their efforts to take concrete steps towards sustainability by creating best practice for other major sporting events, and hopefully inspire others to pursue and implement sustainability initiatives. UEFA (2017) assert aims to initiate and sustain activities to protect and restore the environment. However, the football clubs that play at the pinnacle of the European leagues and competitions along with their fans are forced to make an enormous impact on the environment due to UEFA decisions.

The planning process for certain international soccer events has meant the appearance of friendly matches and concluding finals in far off destinations from the home supporters. This is discussed in more detail in Chapter 4. Due to the way in which the venues for European football finals are decided, in 2019 football supporters from the UK travelled thousands of miles by road, rail, and air to watch or just be in the city where the teams they support played. Those with tickets who travelled to Spain and Azerbaijan where the two main Association Football European Cup finals were played emitted an estimated 35,000 tonnes of carbon dioxide (Barnes, 2019) in the space of 36 hours.

Four English clubs competed in these finals. Jürgen Klopp, one of the team managers at the time said: 'How can you have finals in Kiev [where Liverpool played Real Madrid in the 2018 Champions League final] and Baku? [Where two teams from London, Chelsea and Arsenal, played in the Europa League final]. I don't know what these travel guys have for breakfast' (McKie *et al.*, 2019).

Figure 10.5 provides details on the bidding nations for the four major European soccer finals. These included, the Champions League, the Europa League, the Women's' Champions League, and the Super Cup.

UEFA have contributed extensively towards sustainable practices during their events and have measured the impact relating to air pollution and the effect on human health, as well as the impact on biodiversity. This multi-indicator approach was said to provide a more complete understanding of the environmental footprint of an event. Similarly, FIFA have highlighted their commitment to sustainability. In 2009, FIFA included sustainability as a topic in future bidding agreements starting with the bidding process for the 2018 and 2022 editions of the FIFA World Cup. All bidders were required to provide comprehensive information on their activities aimed at social development and environmental protection (FIFA, 2019).

From any management perspective, UEFA's efforts to apply environmental or sustainable practices and its decision-making process in awarding finals are at

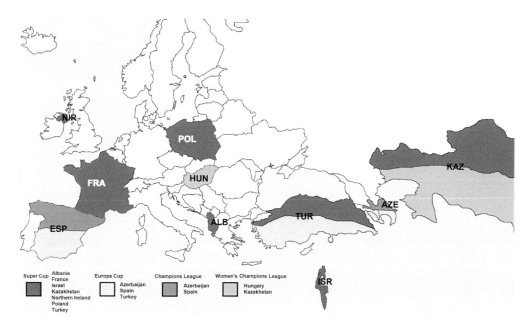

Figure 10.5 Bidding nations to host one of the four major European football finals

Source: Based on information from UEFA, 2019

odds with each other. Any genuine sustainability policy would apply conscious and responsible management processes which would include considering where the greatest carbon emissions are spent and making every effort to reduce them. Awarding Spain host nation status can be understood based on the likelihood of the finalist being relatively local to the potential finalists. However, to choose Kazakhstan as a host nation from a sustainability perspective should at least serve as an opportunity to rectify the absurdities of the venue selection process (Dalaney, 2018). UEFA have publicly admitted the company's biggest contribution to GHG emissions is air travel, but instead of being open about the problem, released data in 2017 that was over ten years old (UEFA, 2017).

10.10 Revising accepted concepts

There are numerous activities that are considered regular or normal in life and international events contribute a great deal to these traditions. In order to reduce the impact international events have on the environment, there are a variety of solutions that could be effortlessly advocated. These range from cancelling the event completely to making small but incremental modifications. However, it is appreciated that the knock-on effect of cancelling an event completely would impact on the international event supply chain affecting jobs, income, and whole communities. This suggests that cancelling the event completely, whether that is a tour or an annual event, would be a last-resort decision made after considerable thought and consultation.

It remains possible, however, to consider a number of possibilities that in the short term would lead to reductions, changes to practice, or even the complete removal of certain normal practices that have a negative effect on the environment. The majority of event organisers are seeking new approaches to event delivery and many of the concepts presented below are beginning to be discussed more widely as genuinely feasible options that are slowly filtering into international event planning. Each suggestion could at some level apply to most if not all international events.

10.10.1 Reconsider where and when mega events are staged

We have discussed the impact mega events have on the environment. Their regularity is to respect the ancient origins of the Olympic Games, which were held every four years at Olympia. As the Olympics is one of the biggest contributors to the problem, there is nothing to stop the IOC from introducing the occasional fallow year or even changing the regularity to five or more years to reduce the impact the event creates. FIFA could adopt a similar approach to the Football World Cup.

10.10.2 Change the travel requirements for business travellers

Due to pressures of work, delegates attending international conferences are usually restricted to sourcing the fastest and most financially beneficial means of travel. As discussed above, this could be reviewed to consider the greenest and then the most financially beneficial means of travel. Many event professionals who attend international events as delegates may make considerable efforts to contribute personally to the GHG problem. Individual actions include: cycling to work, recycling, buying second-hand clothes, not eating meat, making a packed lunch, using reusable containers and so on. Each activity makes a positive incremental impact on the environment, culminating in a noticeable annual contribution. However, as soon as they step on an aeroplane for even the shortest of international trips, the difference in GHG emissions compared to other forms of transport removes the savings from all these efforts in an instant.

For example, a door-to-door journey from London in the UK to Frankfurt am Main in Germany by train is in reality just a few hours longer than the flight. However, the carbon footprint is dramatically different. If the green option is not considered, travelling by aeroplane will always be the preferred choice because it is, on first impressions, quicker and cheaper. Figure 10.6 highlights the difference in various GHG emissions created by three different means of travel between London and Frankfurt.

Similar to this issue, many international event venues emphasise the travelling distance in time from various cities by air on their website to emphasise how accessible the venue is to business travellers. This information would benefit the eco traveller by including the train journey times for comparison.

10.10.3 Exclude the accompanying spouse to meetings

From sports men and women competing in international events to world leaders attending summits, there has been a massive increase in recent years of partners and other family members accompanying the working spouse or family member on business trips. For some of the longer events, the tradition can be considered reasonable, but for two-day summits or three-day conferences, subsidised travel is in some cases both a waste of taxpayers' money and an unnecessary waste of energy and resources.

The global summits that take place around the world arguably create some of the biggest excesses in GHG emissions and waste. The 2010 summit is a case in point. The spouses of world leaders did not attend the G8 summit in Huntsville, Ontario, that year, as it was deemed too difficult for them to 'get around from such an isolated place'. Instead, the world leaders partners travelled, but stayed 230km away in Toronto (Williams, 2019).

10.10.4 Bring to an end the unnecessary hosting of events far away from participants and their followers/fans

As discussed above in section 10.9.4, the host cities for international sporting events could be much more creatively selected to reduce GHG emissions. There are a lot of unknowns during the knockout stages of these events with just a few weeks for cities, venues, and travel companies to prepare for the next stage of the event. A similar approach could be made for the final if a shortlist were

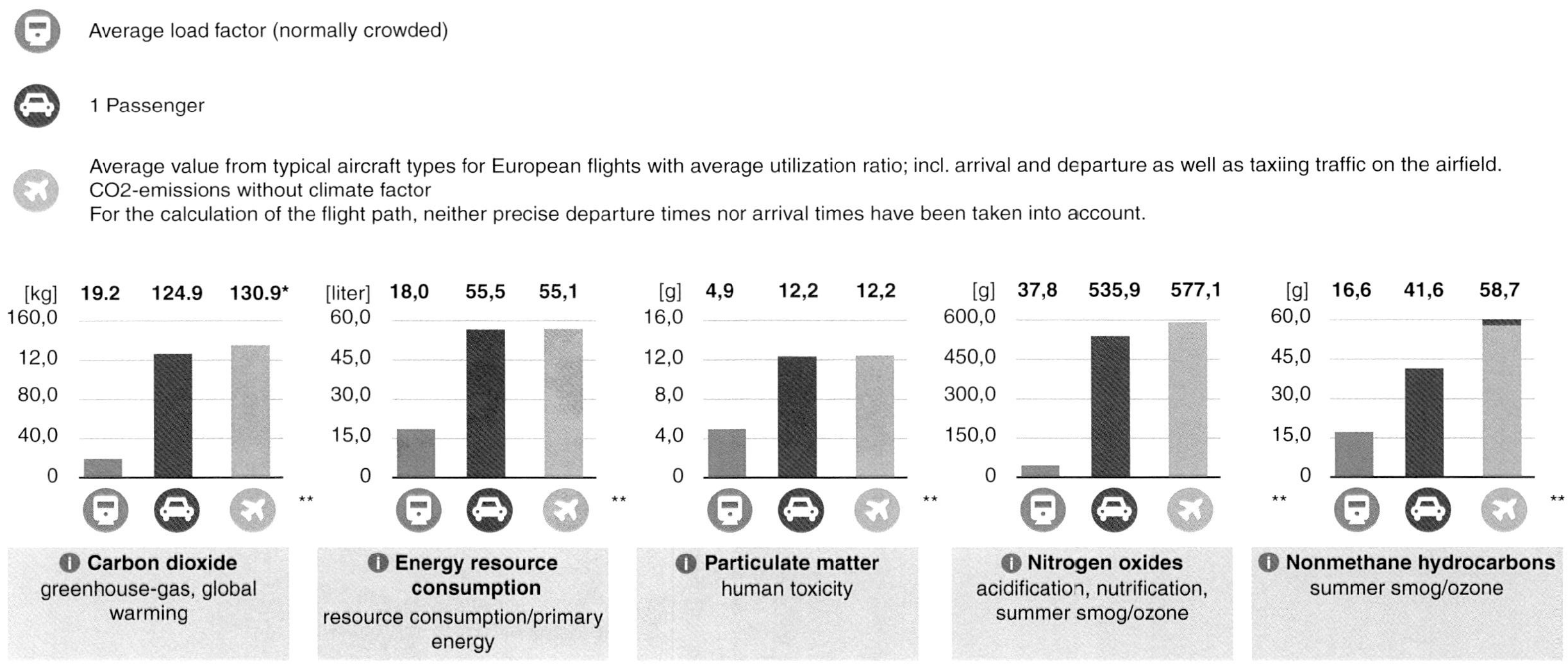

* This does not cover the whole global warming impact of the flight. To consider it totally, select “CO2-emissions with climate factor” in the settings. The RFI Factor takes into account the additional climate effects of other GHG emissions, especially for emissions in high altitudes (nitrogen oxides, ozone, water, soot, sulphur).

** incl. feeder by railway services resp. car

Figure 10.6 Comparison of emissions from a trip from London to Frankfurt by car, train, and aeroplane

Source: ecopassenger.hafas.de, n.d.

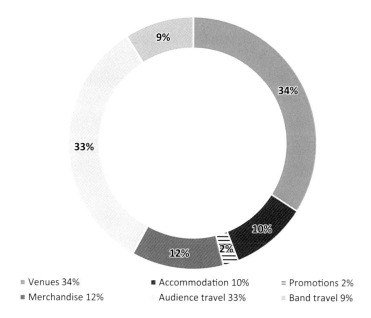

Figure 10.7 How the carbon footprint of a tour is used

Source: Based on Giese and Butz, 2019

made with the most appropriate venue being chosen once the semi-finals had been decided.

In a similar vein and as an attempt to highlight the carbon footprint of a touring band, Coldplay decided to take a break from touring until concerts become more 'environmentally beneficial'. The band's decision did smack of double standards for a British band when they chose to do their non-audience live gigs in the Middle East city of Amman, Jordan. The stunt did make an impression on GHG emissions, however, as greentouring.net revealed that around 33% of GHG contributions from a tour are created by audience travel. Figure 10.7 provides the details of GHG emissions from a typical tour.

10.10.5 Combine the traveller-luggage mass for pricing

There is an old principle of the polluter pays. The polluter-pays principle is part of a set of broader principles to guide sustainable development worldwide that were originally set out at the Rio summit of 1992. The principle is the commonly accepted practice that those who produce pollution should bear the costs of managing it to prevent damage to human health or the environment. The principle does not immediately appear to reduce carbon emissions, but there is good reason to think it will. Essentially, it is the same principle of a bill for a meal when the cost is shared regardless of what was consumed. If everyone is made to pay for what they have consumed, they are more likely to be less indulgent.

Every delegate or spectator who travels internationally will monitor the weight of their own baggage to avoid any excess charges imposed by the carrier. The same goes for all freight that is shipped nationally or internationally with some major penalties for incorrect packaging and weight declarations. There appears to be no reason why airlines could not set the price of a ticket to factor in the weight of the traveller as well as their baggage. By doing so, a more environmentally fair pricing method is created as it is the weight that contributes to increases in carbon emissions. There is also a very good chance passengers will endeavour to reduce their own weight to either increase their baggage allowance or reduce their overall cost. That would mean reducing their food intake to some degree which would have a further positive effect on the environment.

10.10.6 Incentivise green attendance to events

International event organisers spend a great deal of effort marketing and promoting their event in the run-up to the start. It would be a simple addition to detail to include a wide selection of green incentives to delegates, fans or audiences. Incentives could include discounts on entry if there is a fee, special green badges when certain criteria are achieved, or recognition at formal gatherings. The event could then use the data to promote the greening of the event itself.

10.10.7 Reduce the meat content in menus

Animal agriculture and meat consumption are significant contributors to global warming (Vansickle, 2010). By reducing or removing meat from the menu at international events and replacing it with a plant-based menu, not only might health and diet be improved, the environmental impact will be reduced. Considering many international events cater for in excess of 100,000 participants, this would make a significant contribution to the event's sustainability data.

The population of the world is increasing and is expected to hit 10 billion around 2055 (World Population Review, 2019). If the international event organisers in North America and Europe maintained a meat-free/limited menu for any sized event, the impact would be on the wider production of meat. This is important as projections for maintaining current practices for such a large population suggest it will be impossible to create the amount of meat as it would require too much land and water, and lead to unacceptable GHG and other pollutant emissions (Tilman et al., 2011).

Figure 10.8 indicates the results of this dietary modification with the different diets shown in rank order of increasingly positive effects on health. The consumption of more beef increases individual risk of diet-associated mortality by about 1.5%, chiefly due to higher heme consumption (Springmann et al., 2019). Once plant-based food is the basis of the menu, the organisers can go on to consider vegan and other meat-free variations.

10.10.8 Regulate individual carbon emissions by generating personal carbon budgets

If each individual or business had an annual GHG emission limit to use on international events, the way this was spent would be drastically reviewed. This

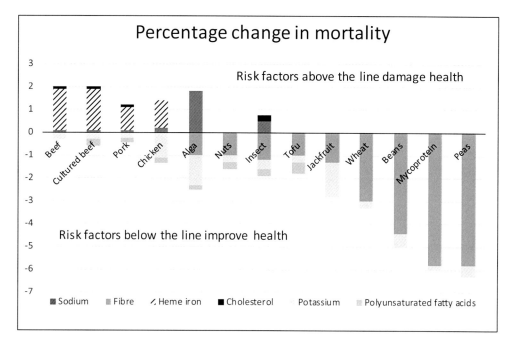

Figure 10.8 The health effects of consuming an additional portion of different alternative proteins

Source: Springmann *et al.*, 2019

would not only impact on the international event industry, but would drastically reduce commuter traffic and spending. This concept may not be acceptable from a fiscal perspective, but by including other suggestions in this section, the GHG emissions would be further reduced limiting the impact on the event. Similar questions are already being asked of individuals in their day-to-day lives. The future of the planet should outweigh the needs of maintaining a consumerist lifestyle.

If 10% of APEs travelling a similar distance were to observe the results in Figure 10.6 above and changed their mode of transport to a conference from an aeroplane to a train, this would reduce carbon dioxide emissions by 200,520 tonnes. To put this into perspective, the average CO_2 emission of a person living in Belgium is 8 tonnes per year (Energuide, n.d.).

10.10.9 Eliminate fossil fuel subsidies

Considering the impact from fossil fuel use in the delivery of international events, it is surprising to discover that Western governments continue to provide fossil fuel subsidies. G7 countries provide about US$100 billion in fiscal support and public finance for fossil fuels each year (Chen, 2018), while the G20 countries provide around US$444 billion (Bloch, 2017). Paradoxically, this is four times the amount of subsidies for renewable energy. In 2016, countries agreed to phase out fossil fuel subsidies by a deadline of 2025. Unfortunately, there has been limited action to address fossil fuel subsidies. In addition, there are limited mechanisms put in place for defining and documenting the full extent of these governments' fossil fuel subsidies and for holding countries accountable for achieving their pledges (Chen *et al.*, 2018). If the use of fossil fuels remains subsidised, organisations will continue to avoid adopting more sustainable practices.

10.11 The adoption of sustainable practices

Arguably, the two most significant contributors to the sustainability pillars discussed above in the event industry include:

1. ASTM/APEX Environmentally Sustainable Meeting Standards
2. ISO 20121 event sustainability management system

The ASTM/APEX is made up of the Convention Industry Council's Accepted Practices Exchange (APEX) and the American Society for Testing and Materials (ASTM). These and the ISO 20121 standards make up a collection of industry standards that specify precisely what it means to plan a green event (Watson, 2014). The ISO 20121 is a voluntary international standard for sustainable event management and specifies the requirements for an Event Sustainability Management System to improve the sustainability of events (Toniolo *et al.*, 2017). Event companies keen to demonstrate a real concern for the environment would set themselves apart from their rivals by setting targets for recycling, saving energy and tackling climate change. However, while the standard provides an opportunity for event businesses to show off their green credentials, the standard is limited to whatever the business chooses to disclose or achieve. Therefore, being awarded an ISO 20121 does not translate to a business being fully sustainable.

In light of recent warnings on climate change, sustainable practices should be incorporated into all activities of an event company and considered in every decision that includes using energy or the need for water, the production of waste, transportation, buildings, and infrastructure.

There are a number of activities an international event company can adopt to improve sustainability and the environment practices, from the office space to the festival or conference site. Some opportunities are far more advanced than others. However, even some of the simplest of returns can be significant in the long term. These include:

- Sending waste to either be recycled or sent to an incinerator and burnt to generate electricity. The recycling contributions from large companies can create enough waste to power homes, or be equivalent to taking numerous cars off the road for a year or to planting hundreds of trees
- Introducing catering facilities that have recyclable or biodegradable dishes and cutlery for takeaways alongside reusable dishes, stainless steel knives, forks and spoons
- Providing opportunities to refill flasks and drinks with an individual's own containers
- Collecting waste cooking oil and convert it into renewable energy

- Recycling waste food through contractors who use anaerobic digestion units to break down waste into biogas and biofertiliser
- Where possible, using and encouraging the use of electric vehicles by providing electric charging points, or by partnering with companies who already do
- Upgrading lighting to energy efficient LED lights
- Install lighting controls that detect absence and presence in all areas.

Where possible, all international event companies should adopt innovative solutions as a showcase for marketing purposes and for clients to observe when visiting the company. International events are usually delivered through multiple companies and agencies and many practices are passed on by learning from each other. Therefore, all procurement activities should highlight the importance of sustainable practices. This should include the wording in tenders for suppliers to state how they are reducing their own carbon footprint, using environmentally friendly or minimal packaging and provide details of their environmental, social and economic impacts and highlight how they are managed.

10.12 Language of compliance

For many activities, international event organisers are guided by codes of practice. These include the Green Guide (SGSA, 2018), The Purple Guide (Purple Guide, 2012), STAR (Secure Tickets from Authorised Retailers (2017), Temporary Demountable Structures (ISE, 2017), and Event Stewarding and Crowd Safety (BSI, 2009) to name just a few. Many international events seek guidance on sustainability and environmental practices from the International Organization for Standardization or ISO standards. These standards offer detailed guidance for event organisers to follow and receive certification that proves that the guidance is being applied to the organisation. However, while ISO standards are making a huge contribution to the difficulties of meeting sustainable targets, the language used in defining an achievement effectively limits the impact the business is actually making.

In the events-related International Standards such as ISO20121 and ISO14001 (ISO, 2015), the following verbal forms are used:

- 'shall' indicates a requirement;
- 'should' indicates a recommendation;
- 'may' indicates a permission;
- 'can' indicates a possibility or a capability.

In order to achieve any of the recommendations set out in the Kyoto Protocol, COP 21 or the 2016 Paris Climate Agreement, the language is far too weak to address the real issues of sustainability. In effect, such an approach makes it easy for any business to meet parts of an international standard. This way, the standards can be met and certificates provided for less than influential contributions to the problems. However, to achieve the necessary goals, the language needs to be much more robust for any effort to have a real effect. Words like 'will', 'must', 'essential', and 'necessary' should replace the weaker, 'shall', 'should', 'may', and 'can' terms.

10.13 Summary

The relationship between international events and sustainability is extremely complicated, but at the same time undoubtedly managed in such a way that is appropriate to the financial demands of the larger international events. We have learned that there are international events that put sustainability at the heart of the event and provide a better understanding for its audience while others play the sustainability card but contribute little to reducing their environmental impact. There is no doubt a great deal of effort has been and continues to be made to reduce the impact international events have on the environment and this has improved both our understanding of and involvement in reducing the damaging effects. However, the power of profit from international events continues to supersede the purpose of sustainability.

International events cannot by definition avoid some of the major contributors to damaging the environment. However, the only way organisers will be able to demonstrate that a sustainability policy is adopted for the event is when the sustainable efforts are not outweighed by other factors being deliberately overlooked.

Case study 10.1 A world and workforce on the move

Millennials, the latest generation of workers have far greater expectations of working internationally. It's a globally consistent trend with 93% of African, 81% of Latin American and 74% of Middle Eastern citizens saying that they would like to work outside their home country at some point in their career. Between 2000 and 2010, the number of mobile employees increased by 25%. In 2010, Price Waterhouse Cooper predicted this was likely to accelerate to 50% by 2020. In the past, the talent has tended to flow from East to West, but as we move forward, a more globally interconnected market will see global talent moving in all directions and working in new ways. The need to migrate is often created by the lack of opportunities available.

Many of the world's fastest growing populations are in the poorest countries, where population growth brings additional challenges in the effort to eradicate poverty, achieve greater equality, combat hunger and malnutrition, and strengthen the coverage and quality of health and education systems. Europe and North America, Northern Africa and Western Asia, and Australia/New Zealand are becoming net receivers of international migrants, while other regions net senders. Some of the largest migratory movements are driven by the demand for migrant workers (Bangladesh, Nepal and the Philippines) or by violence, insecurity and armed conflict (Syria, Venezuela and Myanmar). Belarus, Estonia, Germany, Hungary, Italy, Japan, the Russian Federation, Serbia and Ukraine will experience a net inflow of migrants, helping to offset population losses caused by an excess of deaths over births (population.un.org, 2019).

Migration flows may continue to account for a large proportion of developed countries' population growth. By 2030, 85% of population growth in the G7 economies could be from net migration which could be beneficial to these economies but could also lead to increased social and political tensions as indicated by the UK vote to leave the EU in June 2016, where migration was one of the key issues in the debate (PwC, 2017).

Added to these migration flows is the impact on the environment from the number of flights required as non-resident domiciles travel back and forth between their home country and place of work.

Questions

1. What can the international event industry do to reduce the impact of migrant flows on the environment?
2. How do you think less developed nations will be affected by migration flows?
3. Should millennials review their plans to migrate if the environmental impact is harmful?

10.14 Useful websites

Eco Passenger
http://ecopassenger.hafas.de/bin/query.exe/en?L=vs_uic&

Making events carbon neutral
www.rapiergroup.com/can-you-make-your-event-carbon-neutral/

Institute for Energy and Environmental Research
www.ifeu.de/en/

CO_2 offsetting sites
www.atmosfair.de/en/
https://climatecare.org/
http://carboncounter.org/
www.offsetters.ca/
https://carbonfund.org/projects/

Read the science
https://readthescience.com/

World Population Prospects
https://population.un.org/wpp/

External forces

Political instability
http://uk.reuters.com/article/uk-sri-lanka-politics/sri-lanka-crisis-deepens-with-no-confidence-motion-passed-against-pm-idUKKCN1NJ0F9

Engaging the global event industry in the United Nations Sustainable Development Goals
www.positiveimpactevents.com/

Positive Impact Events survey
https://events.myworld2030.org/

Carbon calculator
www.shameplane.com

Green touring network
http://greentouring.net/

References

A Greener Festival (2012). Communicating green energy at events a greener festival. Energy Fact Sheet #4, *Powerful Thinking*. Retrieved from www.powerful-thinking. org.uk/site/wp-content/uploads/4-Power_Factsheet-Communicating-Green-Energy. pdf Accessed 17th January 2020.

A Greener Festival (2008). Waste management. Retrieved from www.agreenerfestival. com/waste-management/ Accessed 20th December 2019.

Abbasov, F. (2019). *EU shipping's Climate Record: Maritime CO_2 Emissions and Real-World Ship Efficiency Performance*. Brussels: European Federation for Transport and Environment.

Andereck, K. L., & Vogt, C. A. (2000). The relationship between residents' attitudes toward tourism and tourism development options. *Journal of Travel Research, 39*(1), 27–36.

Barnes, J. (2019). Liverpool vs Tottenham Champions League final should be abandoned, claims MEP, *The Express*. Retrieved from:www.express.co.uk/news/uk/ 1134496/Liverpool-Tottenham-Hotspur-Champions-League-Final-abandoned-travel-cost-climate-change Accessed 23rd April 2019.

Bloch, M. (2017). Fossil fuels – billions in subsidies, trillions in health costs, *Solarquotes*. Retrieved from www.solarquotes.com.au/blog/fossil-fuel-subsidies-health-mb0144/ Accessed 20th December 2019.

Bonilla-Priego, J., Font, X., & Pacheco-Olivares, R. (2014). Corporate sustainability reporting index and baseline data for the cruise industry. *Tourism Management, 44*, 149 – 160.

British Standards Institution (BSI) (2009). *BS 8406:2009 – Event Stewarding and Crowd Safety. Code of practice*. London: British Standards Institution.

Caratti, P., & Ferraguto, L. (2011). The role of environmental issues in mega-events planning and management processes: Which factors count? In G. Hayes & J. Karamichas (Eds.), *Olympic Games, Mega-Events and Civil Societies: Globalisation, Environment, Resistance*, 109–125. London: Palgrave Macmillan.

Carbon Trust (2018). Carbon footprinting guide. Retrieved from www.carbontrust. com/resources/guides/carbon-footprinting-and-reporting/carbon-footprinting/ #download-guide Accessed 11th December 2019.

Carmichael, G. R., Soon-Chang, Y., Jones, C., Hochfeld, C., & Oben, T. (2009). *Independent Environmental Assessment: Beijing 2008 Olympic Games*. Nairobi: United Nations Environment Programme.

Carrington, D. (2019). Revealed: microplastic pollution is raining down on city dwellers, *The Guardian*. Retrieved from www.theguardian.com/environment/2019/dec/27/revealed-microplastic-pollution-is-raining-down-on-city-dwellers?CMP=share_btn_link Accessed 28th December 2019.

Case, R. (2013). *Events and the Environment*. Oxon: Routledge.

Chalkley, B., & Essex, S. (1999). Urban development through hosting international events: A history of the Olympic Games. *Planning Perspectives, 14*(4), 369–394. doi:10.1080/026654399364184

Chen, H. (2018). G7 countries waste $100 billion a year on coal, oil, and gas. Retrieved from www.nrdc.org/experts/han-chen/g7-countries-waste-100-billion-year-coal-oil-and-gas Accessed 20th December 2019.

Chen, H., Doukas, A., Gençsü, I., Gerasimchuk, I., Touchette, Y., Whitley, S., et al. (2018). G7 fossil fuel subsidy scorecard. *Natural Resources Defense Council*. Retrieved from www.nrdc.org/resources/g7-fossil-fuel-subsidy-scorecard Accessed 30th December 2019.

Clark, D. (2011). A complete guide to carbon offsetting, *The Guardian*. Retrieved from www.theguardian.com/environment/2011/sep/16/carbon-offset-projects-carbon-emissions Accessed 21st November 2018.

Collins, A., Flynn, A., Munday, M., & Roberts, A. (2007). Assessing the environmental consequences of major sporting events: The 2003/04 FA Cup final. *Urban Studies, 44*(3), 457–476. doi:10.1080/00420980601131878

Cooper, M. (2016). A man-made meteor shower launched by satellite could open the 2020 Olympic Games in Tokyo. Retrieved from https://qz.com/689794/a-man-made-meteor-shower-launched-by-satellite-could-open-the-2020-olympic-games-in-tokyo/ Accessed 22nd October 2016.

Dalaney, M. (2018). Champions League and Europa finals prompt questions of whether Uefa's bidding criteria is fit for purpose. *The Independent*. Retrieved from www.independent.co.uk/sport/football/european/champions-league-final-europa-baku-2019-tottenham-liverpool-arsenal-chelsea-uefa-host-fit-for-a8914336.html Accessed 20th December 2019.

De Brito, M. P. (2018). Festivals are joining the green movement: Sustainability at leisure and events. *Uncover, 2018*(2), 10–11.

Dearden, N. (2015). The UN sustainable development goals miss the point, *New Internationalist*. Retrieved from https://newint.org/blog/2015/09/25/un-sdgs-miss-point Accessed 12th December 2019.

Dhanda, K., & Hartman, L. (2011). The ethics of carbon neutrality: A Critical examination of voluntary carbon offset providers. *Journal of Business Ethics, 100*(1), 119–149. doi:10.1007/s10551-011-0766-4

Dolles, H., & Söderman, S. (2010). Addressing ecology and sustainability in mega-sporting events: The 2006 football World Cup in Germany. *Journal of Management and Organization, 16*(4), 587–600. doi:10.5172/jmo.2010.16.4.587

Earth Overshoot Day (2018). Earth Overshoot Day 2018 is August 1. Retrieved from www.overshootday.org/newsroom/press-release-july-2018-english/ Accessed 14th May 2019.

Eco Passenger (n.d.). Compare the energy consumption, the CO_2 emissions and other environmental impacts for planes, cars and trains in passenger transport, Retrieved from http://ecopassenger.hafas.de/bin/query.exe/en?L=vs_uic Accessed 6th January 2020.

ecolibrium (2019). Energy Revolution. Retrieved from https://ecolibrium.earth/energy-revolution/ Accessed 16th January 2020.

Economist, The (2015). The 169 commandments: The proposed sustainable development goals would be worse than useless. Retrieved from www.economist.com/leaders/2015/03/26/the-169-commandments Accessed 12th December 2019.

Edie (2016). Rio 2016 Olympics: How sustainable is the greatest show on Earth? Retrieved from www.edie.net/library/Rio-2016-Olympics-sustainability-carbon-emissions-air-and-water-quality/6719 Accessed 12th December 2019.

El-Ashry, M. (2014). Energy, climate change and global sustainability. *Environmental Policy and Law, 44*(1/2), 33–37.

Energuide (n.d.). What exactly is a tonne of CO_2? Retrieved from www.energuide.be/en/questions-answers/what-exactly-is-a-tonne-of-co2/2141/ Accessed 28th September 2019.

Erickson, A. (2018). Few countries are meeting the Paris climate goals. Here are the ones that are. *Washington Post*. Retrieved from www.washingtonpost.com/world/2018/10/11/few-countries-are-meeting-paris-climate-goals-here-are-ones-that-are/ Accessed 11th November 2019.

FIFA (2018). Sustainability Strategy of the 2018 FIFA World Cup. Retrieved from www.fifa.com/sustainability/strategy.html Accessed 8th November 2019.

FIFA (2019). 2018 FIFA World Cup Russia: Sustainability Report. Retrieved from https://img.fifa.com/image/upload/ya7pgcyslxpzlqmjkykg.pdf Accessed 20 December 2019.

Formula 1 (2019). Formula 1 announces plan to be Net Zero Carbon by 2030. Retrieved from www.formula1.com/en/latest/article.formula-1-announces-plan-to-be-net-zero-carbon-by-2030.5IaX2AZHyy7jqxl6wra6CZ.html Accessed 10th January 2020.

Friedrich, J., Ge, M., & Pickens, A. (2017). This interactive chart explains world's top 10 emitters, and how they've changed. Retrieved from www.wri.org/blog/2017/04/interactive-chart-explains-worlds-top-10-emitters-and-how-theyve-changed Accessed 28th September 2019.

Gibson, H. J., Kaplanidou, K., & Kang, S. J. (2012). Small-scale event sport tourism: A case study in sustainable tourism. *Sport Management Review, 15*(2), 160–170. doi:10.1016/j.smr.2011.08.013

Giese, J. C. P., & Butz, J. (2019). Green touring guide: A guide for musicians, agents, tour managers, promoters, venues, and booking agencies. Retrieved from http://greentouring.net/downloads/GreenTouringGuide_EN.pdf Accessed 20th December 2019.

Global Footprint Network (2019). National Footprint and Biocapacity Accounts, 2019 Edition. Retrieved from www.footprintnetwork.org/resources/data/

Groves, T. (2008). Reduce, reuse, recycle. *BMJ, 336*.

Haider, S. I. (2011). *Environmental Management System ISO 14001:2004 Handbook of Transition*. Boca Raton: CRC.

Hall, C. M. (2012). Sustainable mega-events: beyond the myth of balanced approaches to mega-event sustainability. *Event Management, 16*(2), 119–131. doi:10.3727/152599512x13343565268294

Harvey, F. (2008). Warning on quality of CO_2 offsets, *The Financial Times,* p. 22.

Hausfather, Z., Drake, H. F., & Schmidt, G. A. (2019). Evaluating the performance of past climate model projections. *American Geophysical Union*. doi:10.1029/2019GL085378

Intergovernmental Panel on Climate Change (IPCC) (2007). Summary for policymakers. Contribution of working group I to the fourth assessment report of the Intergovernmental Panel on Climate Change. In S. Solomon, D. Qin, M. Manning, Z. Chen, M. Marquis, K.B. Averyt, M. Tignor and H.L. Miller (Eds.), *Climate Change 2007: The Physical Science Basis*. Cambridge: Cambridge University Press.

Institution of Structural Engineers (2017). *Fabric Structures* (4th ed.). London: Institution of Structural Engineers.

International Organization for Standardization (ISO) (2015). ISO 14001:2015(en). *Environmental Management Systems*. Retrieved from www.iso.org/obp/ui/#iso:std:iso:14001:ed-3:v1:en Accessed 20th December 2019.

Lancaster, J. (2019). Quality key to industry's sustainable culture. *Association Meetings International, April 2019.*

Laville, S. (2019). European shipping emissions undermining international climate targets. *The Guardian.* Retrieved from www.theguardian.com/environment/2019/dec/09/european-shipping-emissions-in-way-of-nations-meeting-paris-climate-targets Accessed 11th December 2019.

McKie, R., Savage, M., & Cornwall, P. (2019). As English fans get set to cross Europe, anger rises at football's carbon bootprint. *The Guardian.* Retrieved from www.theguardian.com/environment/2019/may/11/anger-carbon-bootprint-english-football-finals-champions-league-europa-league Accessed 11th May 2019.

Metcalf, G. (2019). Carbon taxes: What can we learn from international experience? Retrieved from https://econofact.org/carbon-taxes-what-can-we-learn-from-international-experience Accessed 14th May 2019.

Miller, T. (2016). Greenwashed sports and environmental activism: Formula 1 and FIFA. *Environmental Communication, 10*(6), 719–733.

Mugnier, E., Mairet, A., & Boucher, J. (2010). *Product Carbon Footprinting – a Study on Methodologies and Initiatives. Final report.* Brussels: Ernst & Young and Quantis for Directorate-General for Environment.

O'Brien, D., & Gardiner, S. (2006). Creating sustainable mega event impacts: Networking and relationship development through pre-event training. *Sport Management Review, 9*(1), 25–47. doi:10.1016/s1441-3523(06)70018-3

O'Shea, T., Golden, J. S., & Olander, L. (2013). Sustainability and earth resources: Life cycle assessment modeling. *Business Strategy and the Environment, 22*(7), 429–441. doi:10.1002/bse.1745

Pernecky, T., & Lück, M. (2013). *Events, Society and Sustainability: Critical and Contemporary Approaches.* Oxon: Routledge.

Pettinger, T. (2019). Top CO_2 polluters and highest per capita. economicshelp.org. Retrieved from www.economicshelp.org/blog/10296/economics/top-co2-polluters-highest-per-capita/ Accessed 12th December 2019.

Powell, O. (2019). Sustainability top priority for event industry. *Exhibition News.* Retrieved from https://exhibitionnews.uk/sustainability-top-priority-for-events-industry/ Accessed 22nd May 2020.

Pratley, N. (2019). Saudi Aramco will soon be worth $2tn but it looks plainly overvalued. *The Guardian.* Retrieved from www.theguardian.com/business/nils-pratley-on-finance/2019/dec/11/saudi-aramco-soon-worth-2tn-dollars-but-looks-plainly-overvalued Accessed 12th December 2019.

Prayag, G., Hosany, S., Nunkoo, R., & Alders, T. (2013). London residents' support for the 2012 Olympic Games: The mediating effect of overall attitude. *Tourism Management, 36,* 629–640. doi:10.1016/j.tourman.2012.08.003

Price Waterhouse Cooper (PwC) (2017). A world and workforce on the move. Retrieved from www.pwc.co.uk/issues/megatrends/demographic-and-social-change.html Accessed 15th June 2017.

Purple Guide, The (2012). The Purple Guide to health, safety and welfare at music and other events. Retrieved from www.thepurpleguide.co.uk/ Accessed 23rd March 2017.

Rao, S., & Riahi, K. (2019). The role of non-co2 greenhouse gases in climate change mitigation: Long-term scenarios for the 21st century. *The Energy Journal*, 27, 177–200.

Rapier Group (2019). Can you make your event carbon neutral? Retrieved from:www.rapiergroup.com/can-you-make-your-event-carbon-neutral/ Accessed 30th December 2019.

Riley, G. (2019). Negative production externalities (chain of analysis). Retrieved from www.tutor2u.net/economics/reference/chain-of-reasoning-negative-production-externalities Accessed 14th May 2019.

Ryan, W. G., Fenton, A., Wasim, A., & Scarf, P. (2020). Recognizing events 4.0: the digital maturity of events. *International Journal of Event and Festival Management, 11*(1), 47–68.

Schnitzer, E. (2011). Reduce, reuse, recycle. *Multi-Housing News, 46*(2), 34–35.

Settimi, C. (2016). The 2016 Rio Summer Olympics: By the numbers. *Forbes*. Retrieved from www.forbes.com/sites/christinasettimi/2016/08/05/the-2016-summer-olympics-in-rio-by-the-numbers/ Accessed 12th December 2019.

SGSA (2018). *Guide to Safety at Sports Grounds* (6th ed.). Norwich: Sports Grounds Safety Authority.

Sporting Intelligence (2017). Global attendances: Best attended domestic sports leagues in the world. Retrieved from www.sportingintelligence.com/finance-biz/business-intelligence/global-attendances/ Accessed 28th September 2019.

Springmann, M., Sexton, A., Lynch, J., Hepburn, C., & S., J. (2019). *Meat the Future Series: Alternative Proteins*. White paper prepared by the Oxford Martin School, Oxford University, for the World Economic Forum. Geneva: World Economic Forum.

Thunberg, G. (2019). You come to us young people for hope. How dare you? *Vital Speeches of the Day, 85*(11), 294.

Tilman, D., Balzer, C., Hill, J., & Befort, B. L. (2011). Global food demand and the sustainable intensification of agriculture. *Proceedings of the National Academy of Sciences of the United States of America, 108*(50), 20260. doi:10.1073/pnas.1116437108

Tokyo 2020 (2019). Tokyo 2020 'G-satellite' completed. Tokyo 2020. Retrieved from https://tokyo2020.org/en/news/notice/20191203-02.html Accessed 20th December 2019.

Toniolo, S., Mazzi, A., Fedele, A., Aguiari, F., & Scipioni, A. (2017). Life Cycle Assessment to support the quantification of the environmental impacts of an event. *Environmental Impact Assessment Review, 63*, 12–22. doi:10.1016/j.eiar.2016.07.007

UEFA (2017). Environment. Retrieved from www.uefa.com/insideuefa/social-responsibility/environment/ Accessed 8th November 2019.

UEFA (2019). Evaluation Report: UEFA Club Competition Finals 2019. Retrieved from www.uefa.com/MultimediaFiles/Download/OfficialDocument/uefaorg/Regulations/02/50/17/48/2501748_DOWNLOAD.pdf Accessed 8th Novemvber 2019.

UFI (2019). UFI releases figures showing global economic impact of exhibitions. www.ufi.org/wp-content/uploads/2019/04/23_04_19-UFI-releases-figures-showing-global-economic-impact-of-exhibitions.pdf Accessed 28th September 2019.

UN Department of Economic and Social Affairs (2019). World population prospects 2019: Highlights. Retrieved from https://population.un.org/wpp/Publications/Files/WPP2019_10KeyFindings.pdf Accessed 20th December 2019.

Vansickle, J. (2010). Producing more with less. *National Hog Farmer, 55*(3), 22.

Vanwynsberghe, R. (2015). The Olympic Games Impact (OGI) study for the 2010 Winter Olympic Games: Strategies for evaluating sport mega-events' contribution to sustainability. *International Journal of Sport Policy and Politics, 7*(1), 1–18. doi:10.1080/02601370.2014.988189

Watson, J. (2014). Environmentally sustainable events and green meetings with the APEX/ASTM Standards. Retrieved from https://greeneventninjas.com/the-dojo/apex-astm-green-meetings-standard/ Accessed 28th September 2019.

Wikipedia (n.d.). List of countries by carbon dioxide emissions per capita. Retrieved from https://en.wikipedia.org/wiki/List_of_countries_by_carbon_dioxide_emissions_per_capita Accessed 12th December 2019.

Williams, Z. (2019). The G7 was the final straw – world leaders' wives should refuse to travel with their spouses. *The Guardian*. Retrieved from www.theguardian.com/lifeandstyle/2019/aug/28/the-g7-was-the-final-straw-world-leaders-wives-should-refuse-to-travel-with-their-spouses Accessed 30th April 2019.

World Population Review (2019). World population review. Retrieved from http://worldpopulationreview.com/ Accessed 28th September 2019.

Chapter 11

Digital communication

Contents

11.1 Chapter overview

This chapter will consider the digital communication currently used as well as some future potential in the delivery of international events. International event organisations have embraced digital communication and other technological advancements and are rapidly developing on an unprecedented scale. Many of the developments are carried out behind the scenes while others are the visible or augmented elements of the delivery process. This is completely restructuring how international events are experienced. Becoming more digital has become necessary for all international event organisations to evolve with the times. This has meant the transformation of an industry on every level through the way we deal with data to how we engage with every different aspect of an international event.

11.2 Learning objectives

By the end of this chapter, the student will be expected to:

- Understand the various levels of digital communication in international events
- Understand the contribution of digital communication at international events
- Recognise the significance of Industry 4.0 in contemporary international event delivery
- Appreciate the various, terms, apps and tools used for improving digital communication at international events.

11.3 Introduction

As we advance into what many in business and academia call the fourth industrial revolution (Industry 4.0 or I4.0), the capacity to control and exchange data electronically has extended our ability to create, edit, maintain, transmit, and retrieve information. To this end, modern event organisers are able to exponentially expand the event participant–event–event organiser relationship through digital communication technology and insight through data (Ryan et al., 2020). With this in mind, there is a great deal of evidence to suggest that the field of international events is developing at a phenomenal pace and technological advances have extended into each and every aspect of planning, participation, and delivery. These developments have improved the communication possibilities, putting information, experiences, and collaboration quite literally at everyone's figure tips with mobile apps and cloud communications. Aside from improving collaborative experiences, the planning and delivery stages can all be assisted and accelerated with the use of these technological advancements.

11.4 Coexisting levels of communication

International event organisations and individuals will work and experience digital communication at a number of different levels of maturity (Ryan *et al.*, 2020). These range from a basic level that incorporates the widespread digital technologies such as websites, email, mobile devices and social media, right through to fully integrated systems that are frequently upgraded and data-driven, providing optimised communication that is digitally managed. The model in Figure 11.1 captures the state of digital maturity in events that currently exist and work.

While the model illustrates how Event 4.0 (E4.0) suggests a trend of digital maturity towards data exchange in international events, the ability to fully engage much less digitally coexists at a level that can be considered Event 1.0. This area comprises the majority of consumers and organisers in international events. However, a path towards a more integrated level of engagement remains the objective for most organisations.

11.4.1 Electronic communication

Specific technologies (such as electronic mail) can be compared to their manual counterparts (such as memos) for their relative effectiveness, but the vast range

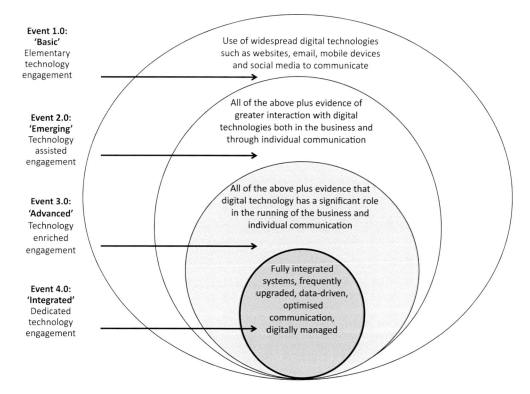

Figure 11.1 Different levels of digital maturity in events

Source: Ryan *et al.*, 2020, adapted from Neuhofer *et al.*, 2013 and Colli, 2018

of systems and products makes such comparisons overwhelming (Dickson *et al.*, 2000). Probably the most evident way digital communication is used in all aspects of life today is the widespread use of electronic communication. The concept itself would appear to be relatively modern. However, the foundations were laid in the 1830s with the development of Morse code.

Electronic communication has developed more in the 21st century than ever before, expanding its scope and reach to include new participants from around the world and provide new ways of communicating (Ramsey, 2013). Today, many electronic communication tools are taken for granted. They are so well integrated into society they form part of most of the world's daily life. These include Wi-Fi, email, apps and websites, but organising these technical constituents and continuing demands for an international event is not as simple as it first appears. In the same way that an event organiser will employ a specialised service provider for sound and lighting or transporting equipment, the responsibility for technology and electronic communication should be outsourced and tailored to the specific requirements of the event.

11.4.2 Wi-Fi

Even though the term and demand for Wi-Fi is now ubiquitous, the knowledge behind its reliability has largely remained a secret only known to the technically minded. When available, the strength of the connection and speed would be a mystery and the larger the audience attending the event, the worse the quality would become. But the overall quality of Wi-Fi at an event is due to the link rate.

The link rate is the maximum speed that data can move across a wireless link. Therefore, events that are dependent on Wi-Fi for operations and attract larger gatherings require a higher link rate. As the technology improved so did the name of the next generation of Wi-Fi. However, the name being used was unclear until 2019 when Wi-Fi 6 was introduced. At the same time, the previous names were retrospectively revised to reflect the generation in the same way computer software is updated. Previously, an international event organiser would struggle to understand if 802.11a (Wi-Fi 2) was more powerful or reliable than 802.11ac (Wi-Fi 5). Table 11.1 lists the new and the old names of the various

Table 11.1 Wi-Fi generation, year of adoption, and the link rate

Wi-Fi generation	Year adopted	Maximum link rate (megabit per second –Mbps)
WiFi 6 (or 802.11ax)	2019	600–9608
WiFi 5 (previously 802.11ac)	2014	433–6933
WiFi 4 (previously 802.11n)	2009	72–600
WiFi 3 (previously 802.11g)	2003	3–54
WiFi 2 (previously 802.11a)	1999	1.5 to 54
WiFi 1 (previously 802.11b)	1999	1 to 11

Source: Based on data from Kastrenakes, 2018

generations, the year of adoption, and the link rate capabilities or data-transfer rate in megabits per second (Mbps).

To put the development of the link rate over the years into perspective, an example is required. If you had a 1 Mbps connection at your event, a 1MB file would have taken eight seconds to download. On a 1 Mbps connection, an MP3 file, which might measure about 6MB, would have taken about 48 seconds to download (Layton, 2017). If 10,000 delegates attempted to do this at the same time, the system would have failed. By improving the link rate at an international event, the congestion created when delegates or fans attempt to use the available Wi-Fi to send and receive data at the same time is reduced.

At international events, multiple devices with varying bandwidth requirements are used on multiple levels. Devices are competing with one another to send and receive data and therefore a robust system is required. Audiences use mobile devices to record, upload, and share videos to social media. Organisers require bandwidth to access email, and the internet, in order to connect with the office. On-site card machines and ticketing functionalities may be required. The event may be providing a bespoke log-in screen to maintain branded communication, or the actual event places even greater demand on the signal as graphics, videos, and live action is streamed as a continuous transmission of audio, data or video files.

Today, most venues have their own dedicated Wi-Fi connection, while outdoor events will require a temporary set-up. (This is discussed in more detail below in section 11.8). Whichever method is in use, some preparation will be essential to ensure the demands of the event have a bulletproof system that maintains a consistent connection at high speed. simpli-fi.co.uk (2018) provide the event organiser with a list of questions to help make a calculated and more informed decision as to whether the venue has the right Wi-Fi service to support the planned event. These include:

- How many wireless access points are installed into the event space?
- Does the Wi-Fi cover the whole event space, including any breakout areas?
- Is there a separate log-in process for the event space?
- Will there be on-site support? What is the process when technical issues arise?
- Is the internet bandwidth on the event wireless network dedicated to this network or shared with the rest of the venue?

With the revised Wi-Fi generation designations, a numeral can now be displayed with the Wi-Fi icon on the receiving device to indicate the technology available. This should improve user experience, while the renaming also contributes to simplifying our understanding of the technology. As the capacity of the network improves, the optimal available throughput becomes visible and provides the user with an indication of how well the available network will handle the massive demands international events can present (Mitchell, 2019).

With the latest generation, Wi-Fi 6, customers and organisers can access the network simultaneously. Wi-Fi 6 removes the competition as each device is simultaneously scheduled to transmit data in parallel (Aruba, 2018). This technology was introduced in the Wi-Fi 5 generation of software and adopts a Multi-user Multiple Input/Multiple Output (MU MIMO) model. Figure 11.2 shows how the technology allows for better flows of data by removing the narrow bottleneck.

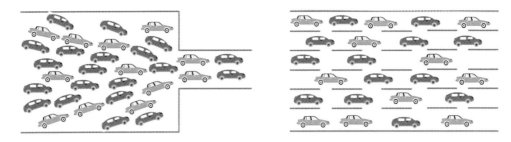

Figure 11.2 Multi-user Multiple Input/Multiple Output (MU MIMO) model
Source: Based on Aruba, 2018

Beyond electronic communication, digital transformation processes have become embedded within many different technologies. These come together under an umbrella term known as Industry 4.0 (I4.0). The term was introduced to indicate how all industries have been transformed in recent years due to a digitally connected world and it is important to understand the impact these developments are having on international events.

11.5 Industry 4.0

Industry 4.0 (I4.0) is the term for the fourth industrial revolution and although it is actually directed towards modern manufacturing (Qin *et al.*, 2016), it has an enormous impact on international events. It has been described as the digitisation and automation of the manufacturing environment (Oesterreich and Teuteberg, 2016) and has numerous elements that play an important role in the phases of international events from planning through to the delivery and legacy.

The term was first introduced by the German government in 2011 and has signalled a new era in manufacturing and the acknowledgement of the fourth industrial revolution. It is said to signify resource optimisation using advanced technologies (Gretzel *et al.*, 2015). The term refers to a wide range of concepts based on leveraging Big Data processing from technologies such as artificial intelligence, mobile internet, robotics, Internet of Things, and cloud computing to provide smart workplace solutions for ongoing efficiency and improvements (Marketresearch.com, 2017). Figure 11.3 displays the various components of I4.0.

I4.0 refers to a wide range of concepts that make up the fourth dimension of industry (mechanisation, mass production, computer and automation, networks and cyber physical systems). I4.0 plays a significant role in strategy to take the opportunities of digitalisation of all stages of production and service systems (Ustundag, 2018). Since its first expression in 2011, I4.0 has galvanised all industries into understanding how to maximise the benefits of automation and data exchange. Today, the 4.0 suffix has become the principle buzzword in the lexicon of cutting-edge organisations (Ryan *et al.*, 2020).

I4.0 has contributed to the development of many aspects of international events, including the demand to reduce costs and deal with the increasingly complex health and safety, technological, sustainability, and regulatory landscape (Ryan and Kelly, 2017). Most of the advancements used are not visible

Figure 11.3 The components of Industry 4.0

Source: Based on Saturno *et al.*, 2018

to the customer and occur much further back up the supply chain. Essentially, everything is potentially digital: business models, environments, production systems, machines, operators, products, and services. It can all interconnect inside the digital scene with the corresponding virtual representation (Alcácer and Cruz-Machado, 2019). Other aspects of I4.0 are utilised in the visual aspect of the show itself. No contemporary product launch would achieve the visual experience without components of I4.0 and some live/hologram events that have been observed in recent years would simply not occur.

Central to the development of digital communication within international events is how people and things communicate, in particular, making communication more efficient between individuals and between the components involved in the delivery of an international event. Digital communication today allows the event organiser to see where a particular piece of equipment is when it is being delivered. Barcodes convert into useful information providing information about an item's origin, service history, last event, and location. Designers can model products in 3D, access and security is improved, and with widespread cyberattacks, sensitive information can be protected.

A good example of how I4.0 meets classic practices is how goods are labelled and sent on tour. Touring in the 21st century allows suppliers to scan a barcode on every piece of equipment at each stage of the journey from the warehouse to the stage and back to the warehouse. With the information being updated at each stage, the customer and business remain constantly up-to-date with the whereabouts of every piece of kit, and when it returns to the warehouse, it can be quality checked and updated on the system. The team then know if the equipment requires servicing or if it can go straight back out on tour in the knowledge that it is unlikely to break down.

Today, each piece of kit usually has a Printed Adhesive Label (PAL^tm) attached that informs the crew where it is going. Modern labels provide space for text and a barcode. The text can be easily read to position the equipment in trucks and on stage at the venue. Figure 11.4 shows how a PAL^tm mix of barcoding and text provides both visual and digital information on a PA company's touring equipment.

Based on I4.0, the upsurge in digital applications gave rise to the terms 'Tourism 4.0' (Boes et al., 2016; Korže, 2019) and Event 4.0 (E4.0) (Ryan et al., 2020). As these components of I4.0 become more prevalent in the event industry, greater audience and business engagement is achieved through digital technologies. International events are in many ways the perfect medium

Figure 11.4 A PAL™ label on a flight case about to leave the warehouse for an international tour

to absorb the benefits of the digital technologies and abilities because there are so many different communication points along the way in an international event, whether that is business to business (B2B), customer to customer (C2C), customer to business (C2B), or business to customer (B2C). With the constant demand to improve experiences and automate the process, I4.0 can assist in providing valuable information, detailed statistics, and a cyber presence in an instant. Lasi *et al.* (2014) detail the sharp development of I4.0 as being on the one hand a huge application pull, inducing a remarkable need for changes due to changing operative framework conditions, while on the other hand constituting an exceptional technology push in industrial practice.

11.6 The digital transformation of international events

There are several reasons why international events have been transformed by digital communication. Like many other industries, international events have benefited from the triple revolution of increased smartphone ownership, social media, and faster internet speeds. Such developments continue to create a more networked and connected experience (Poushter, 2016; Rainie and Wellman, 2012) for people attending events and the organisations which deliver them. In the world of international events, this digital transformation is perhaps epitomised by the return of legends from the afterlife. Audiences all over the world have experienced live virtual performances from Elvis, Whitney Houston, Roy Orbison, and Michael Jackson. Elvis even completed a world tour with the Royal Philharmonic Orchestra, something he never achieved during his life (Clarke, 2017). However, the possibilities technology presents suggests this is just the beginning for the future of live event experiences.

Industry as a whole is becoming more and more driven by internet-connected digital systems and data, which in turn means that real and virtual worlds become 'smart' and grow together (Federal Ministry for Education and Research, n.d.). Smartness emphasises how inter-operable systems can integrate functions that have the ability to manage Big Data and generate value (Boes *et al.*, 2016; Gretzel, 2018).

From a purely technological perspective, these developments can be attributed to integrated circuit device size reduction, the number of transistors on a device and the cost per component. This relates to Moore's Law which is the observation that the number of transistors (space for memory) in a dense integrated circuit doubles about every two years. (Gale Virtual Reference Library, 2012). But it these technological advances are then put to work in pursuit of the ultimate goal to squeeze as much performance in terms of operations per second (or per Watt) out of devices, circuits, and architectures (Ferdinand, 2017). With the additional demand for excellence from all sides, international event organisers are almost obliged to adopt digital communications for their events. This is because the event industry has become an ideal environment to benefit from the implementation of a widespread digitised approach, with numerous organisations improving the overall event experience with the integration of extensive ICT practices and systems (Ryan *et al.*, 2020).

Some international event businesses can benefit from digital communication on a number of levels while others may only require a digital communication approach for promotion and marketing purposes. For example, a concessions trader would be wise to focus on social media investment to maintain the profile of the business online. This investment might be supported by other computer software that assists in the general running of the business. However, a venue would be wise to integrate all operations with digital communication. Ticketing and printing, customer communications, cashless payments, Radio Frequency Identification (RFID) technology, marketing, and data collection, can all be digitalised to assist in the delivery of an event. Each aspect of trading activity can be reviewed against the net gain of a tech investment. An international event organiser will need to decide whether the investment in a digital communications solution will return more than the current effort of the responsible team or individual. To answer this, the company should consider the 3 'i's of digital communication.

11.7 The 3 'i's of digital communication

Digital communication requires considerable investment. Therefore, once the decision has been made to focus on using digital communication as a leading means of engagement, there are three benefits or returns the international event business should expect to achieve. Digital communication should:

1. Improve
2. Integrate
3. Inform.

Each of these characteristics must be provided from the investment in digital communication, otherwise any investment may only serve to increase unnecessary costs. Table 11.2 provides further details on the benefits. In certain situations, an analogue method will be just as suitable. Grabbing a pen and paper will achieve the necessary requirements for a task. However, as soon as the information needs to be transferred, time, effort and cost may signal the value of a technological alternative.

11.7.1 Improve

Improvements from the use of digital technology should develop any existing activities of an international event to make them even better. This might include the upgrading of systems to allow for better control during the planning stages and delivery. It would be expected to speed up any existing processes and make any additional activities or amendments simpler to incorporate.

Any of the processes of an international event could be refined with the adoption of digital technology, allowing for a broader spectrum of uses. For example, the adoption of a digital ticketing system could improve access to a venue by streamlining admissions. Over time, because of the retention of data, the investment should enhance the value of the system by boosting sales through better communication and marketing opportunities with customers.

Table 11.2 The 3 'i's of digital communication

3 'i's: Benefits of digital communication		
Improve	*Integrate*	*Inform*
Planning	Departments	Stakeholders
Quality	Workforces	Audiences
Communication	Communications	Assessments
Speed of processes	Operations	Communications
Time and effort	Responsibilities	Data
Value	Activities	Future events
Access	Procedures	
Progress	Transportation	
Additions or amendments		

11.7.2 Integrate

One of the most useful benefits of digital communication is how software can bring together the various logistical sections of a business or incorporate the different parts to communicate in different directions to create an integrated network. This can be most useful across a number of processes. For example, when equipment is on the road, due for servicing, or stored in a warehouse, information in a barcode can be viewed on a computer for a situational analysis. Barcoding technology allows the tracking of goods for a whole host of reasons and the data contained can even speed up out-of-reach activities such as crossing borders.

Data can also be integrated to improve communications between the planning department, purchasing for finance, or from updating team managers by creating operational efficiency. Access to integrated databases that collate data from various departments into a single space reduces lack of knowledge and facilitates communication. A problem within any organisation that does not benefit from digital integration is the presence of departmental or operational silos. This is discussed in more detail in Chapter 5.

11.7.3 Inform

Francis Bacon is alleged to have said, 'The more one knows, the more one will be able to control events' (Dictionary.com, n.d.). Digital communication provides international event organisers with rapid communication capabilities that go direct to the main stakeholders and customer base. It can provide important information in an instant. It can assist the promotion of sales and reduce the likelihood of danger.

Digital communication can be used to engage, animate, or even inspire audiences. In the run-up to international events, informing the audience by providing updates and increasing communication adds to the overall experience of the event. Digital communication can provide powerful and personalised connected experiences, or reassure audiences through the sharing of information. The ability to inform an audience through digital communication reduces the possibility of knock-on effects from last minute developments or changes.

The data gathered from previous events can also assist in the planning of future events. The more digitally connected the event, the more data there is to be used to develop an awareness of those who do and even do not attend. By combining data gathered prior to an event with data gathered on site, information about event attendees can be used to tailor future events.

11.8 The contribution of digital communication at events

Digital communication can bring many more options to the event in the long run, but there are so many components to an international event that need to come together in a timely fashion for it to work. For participants and organisers, each stage in the process is most likely to raise stress levels. There is also a lot to gain and lose. With reputation at the centre of this fast-paced and highly competitive industry, no self-respecting international event company is going to knowingly underachieve or deliver a sub-standard experience.

Therefore, a considerable amount of investment will be made in constructing the event experience, making each component (from both a production and experience perspective) as stress-free and as widely available as possible, with as much digital communication as possible. Adopting digital communications early can provide further benefits that contribute to improving the overall experience. However, there are two leading difficulties with bringing digital communication to the international event experience. These are:

- Knowing which are the best options for your event
- Balancing the investment with making a profit.

While these two points stand out, a third option could also be included as it is important to consider the balance between the use of technology and a sense of freedom from it. It can be tempting, with the continuous drive to keep up with advancing digital communication, for all international event businesses to invest in a great number of technologies. With this in mind, it is prudent to understand the impact on the end-user, and the value of the investment against the return.

11.8.1 Bandwidth and networks

For many small international event organisations, a business broadband connection should be more than enough to handle the needs of day-to-day digital communications. However, once the company begins to grow, other more substantial options need to be considered such as cloud computing or virtual spaces. Cloud computing provides a network of online servers that host data. This data can then be accessed from anywhere with an internet connection. For international event organisations, office staff can access the same data from several offices in different countries.

As well as using networks for administration and planning purposes, the event venue or destination will require a considerable amount of access to digital networks. In fact, one of the key factors in choosing a destination for hosting international events is the quality of infrastructure, with digital connectivity playing a key role (Gov.uk, 2019). All types of international event create peaks and troughs during the timescale of the event. Low usage can be described as email and basic surfing. Medium usage is the use of web applications, audio streaming and Skype. High usage can be the transfer of large data files and webcasting (Encore, 2018).

The beginning of any live event is likely to create a surge in smartphone communication. When the band plays its biggest hit, or if a conference has a long workshop in the afternoon, the demand on bandwidth will be high or low accordingly. It is important to consider and to take into account these different levels of use. Therefore, a reliable and well-managed internet connection is a must. The bigger the crowd or venue the wider the bandwidth required. Add to this the fact that many international events are held outdoors and no internet infrastructure exists for the attending audience or the workforce to connect to, networks and bandwidth become high on the list of priorities for the international event organiser.

Bandwidth provision is like many other international event services and is outsourced to specialist companies. Any specialist supplier would be able to provide one of three types of supply. These are:

- ADSL (Asymmetric Digital Subscriber Line)
- 3G / 4G and soon 5G Connectivity
- Satellite.

Most outdoor events will require a temporary broadband contract for the duration of the event. The outsourced company with either be, or work closely with, the national telecom and broadband providers. For one-off international events, contracts can be drawn up on a monthly basis and range from standard platforms to local loop unbundled services to provide the highest speeds available. However, for those more adventurous international event organisers, an inspection of the location would be advised to ensure an internet service can be provided.

Just like a home supply, temporary broadband requirements focus on upload speed. With the audience sharing their images and videos, the media sending articles, and staff using mobile devices, uploading or the sending of information to the internet, the critical part of the network is the facility to upload. For smaller international events, a single network will usually cover the amount of traffic. Once the event is webcasting or streaming video to a live stream, much bigger upload bandwidth capacity will be required.

11.8.2 5G

Telecommunication will continue to be one of the fundamental technologies that the delivery of international events will be based and build upon.

Fifth-generation (5G) mobile wireless networks are being rolled out across the world due to the continuing growth in data traffic for mobile networks. However, the roll-out has been met with a number of delays from opponents across the world who support low-radiation living spaces and freedom of choice as opposed to blanket availability of fifth generation cellular network technology (del Sol Beaulieu, 2019; Wendorf, 2019). Many of the fears raised by the protestors such as the scorching of nearby trees and cell phone radiation are yet to be proven.

If 5G technology is proven to be safe, the capabilities of high speed connectivity and networks will enhance current technological activities. This will be fuelled by applications such as ultra-high-definition (UHD) video and augmented reality (AR) (Shankaranarayanan and Ghosh, 2017). UHD is essentially straightforward to understand, but AR's use in international events requires a little more explanation.

Augmented reality consists in 'overlaying virtual imagery onto a physical world scene' (Li and Been-Lirn, 2013). This means that any live event can have images streamed live to a device or screen with additionally overlaid animation or action to create a more immersive and interactive experience. UHD and AR are both in use today, but the widespread availability of 5G will increase the power and speed capabilities.

If we compare the possibilities of 5G and international business events to developments in live sport coverage, the stay-at-home supporter obtains just as high a level of attachment to the event than those who attend the event in person. The atmosphere is virtually captured through the lens. TV coverage provides many benefits as well, including super-slow-motion replays, an abundance of stats on performance, numerous viewpoints, peer-led commentary and interviews, as well as backstage access that is reserved for the very few. Considering the ascendancy of spectator sport through TV subscription, international business events with 5G technology have the potential to defeat the insistent argument for and supersede face-to-face meetings.

Without going into the technology in detail, 5G is the latest generation of wireless technology for digital cellular networks that began being widely deployment in 2019. 5G is expected to be around ten times faster than 4G. This means, for example, that a high-definition film will be downloaded in approximately one second, making most click-through rates instantaneous. The main benefit for international events is the ability to enable virtual reality games and experiences. Japan is expecting to have 5G as a key part of its Summer Olympics including drone-based security (Millet, 2018). From an environmental perspective, the higher bandwidth will allow international events to create greater interest in 'virtual' ticket options (Eventbase, 2018).

11.8.3 Data management

Data management is an administrative process that includes acquiring, validating, storing, protecting, and processing required data to ensure the accessibility, reliability, and timeliness of the data for its users (House of Commons Public Accounts Committee, 2008). At the start of any international event planning process, it is important to consider what and how data will be managed. Getting professional advice should be the first stage in the process and obtaining software for the data management from a professional solutions provider may be the second. Getting professional advice will help create a perspective on where the focus should be – for example, how to make sense of the data collected to assist in understanding attendee behaviour. Professional advice should also highlight the difficulties involved and help an event organiser understand the broader feasibility of digital communication for an event.

All international events are bound to come across snags and problems. The type of event and the planned destination/s should highlight the more likely issues. Problems might stem from border crossings, visas, indoor/outdoor facilities, venue availability, timescale, equipment hire, accommodation, travel times, rest days, ticketing, pricing, marketing, and so on. Relying on individuals to manage each of the major tasks is common, but the organisation will need to document the data involved and plan the sequence of events as a team. The information required for an international event needs to be controlled and shared in a widely accessible manner for the event to be planned and delivered appropriately.

One of the benefits of experience in international event delivery is that many of the activities are replicated for each event delivery process. Using dedicated software will assist with the preparation process. To support this process, a number of event and project management software platforms have been created. Dedicated software will help integrate many of the processes adopted and provide much finer detail of the overall event.

As events grow, more data is collected and, with the right technology partnership, communication can be improved. For example, international events with a technology partner can track social media content and audience sentiment to provide insights and benefits for the event owners. The ability to know who is at the event can allow the event organisers to directly communicate with their customers through their digital devices. This can be anything from thanking them for attending, informing them of upcoming events, or providing them with 'special offers' before they leave.

Some organisations will continue to maintain their events with project management software by producing detailed flow charts, Excel spreadsheets and supporting Word documents. This decidedly basic technology is still multi-layered and more than powerful enough for many international event organisers to deliver successful events effectively. However, data entry is usually manual and can therefore be quite time-consuming. Moreover, the broader benefits from Big Data collection, which are discussed later in the chapter, are not achievable with the manual inputting of data.

There are several websites that provide free event management templates to download while many websites exist to offer free advice to help you choose the right software to purchase for the type of organisation. Once a software package has been purchased, depending on the type of package agreed, software providers may offer training and online support. Once the software is understood by those directly involved, it becomes possible to contribute to the planning process from anywhere around the world. Whichever management tool is chosen, whether digital or manual, the need to regularly back up data remains.

There are many potential drawbacks with event software. These include: knowing what to do with it once you have it, the cost to implement and maintain, the amount of data gathered, and the reliance on a good internet connection or Wi-Fi. If the information is saved to a single computer that is not networked, nobody else can have access to the data. For a sole trader, this may not be an issue, but international events usually require more than one person to manage the various demands. From an international perspective, this can include a team working from different countries. Such a scenario will place greater demand on the need to access information without any barriers or delays while still maintaining security. These issues have led to the use of virtual spaces or 'clouds' where documents can be shared and edited by any number of contributors. However, even while virtual spaces offer access for more people to contribute, uploading and downloading remain reliant on secure networks.

11.8.4 Social media

The term 'social media' refers to new forms of media that involve interactive participation (Manning, 2016). Although its use is relatively widespread today, it is easy to forget just how quickly social media usage has grown. In 2008 just 29% of online adults used social networking sites. By 2013, that figure had more than doubled to 72% (Duggan, 2013). Because of social media's value in communication, it is a central part of an international event company's marketing mix. This makes the setting up of the now ubiquitous social media accounts one of the primary tasks an event company will undertake. Social media is an extremely powerful tool that can increase an event's visibility and improve the organisation's efficiency and productivity while assisting with marketing the company's activities. Social media accounts are usually created long before many other significant necessities of a business and are easily set up without the need for external assistance.

Social media provides the international event organisers with the ability to communicate instantly and directly with their customers. Keeping delegates and fans up-to-date is one method of improving the relationship. Communities, cultures and even individual ways of life are constantly being bombarded with globalised messages from international events that create or reinforce values in society (Jepson and Clarke, 2016). Therefore, it is every international event organiser's responsibility to be prepared to respond to the demands that will inevitably arise and to be able to utilise the latest advances in technology that will assist in the safe delivery of the event.

11.8.5 Apps and digital information

There is much technology used in preparing for international events, from the now ever-present email and texting, to fully branded apps that unlock abundant opportunities to engage with the event and its audience. There is an app for just about everything to assist with international events, but overuse can be considered less valuable than a more streamlined approach. The decision to choose a particular app provider will depend on several questions being answered. These will include:

- Are there a number of pricing and content options?
- Is the technology cloud-based or downloaded to a company's own computer hardware?
- How many users will there be?
- What type of deployment is required?
- Does it suit all devices? (Android, MacOS etc.)
- Can multiple languages be provided?
- Does the app cover the languages you need?
- Can the app be downloaded from anywhere?
- Is the app restricted in any nations?
- Does the event require access to additional features such as customer surveys or session registration?
- Is catering software required?
- Is event check-in software required?
- Is meeting software required?
- Is registration software required?
- Is ticketing software required?
- Is live streaming software required?
- Is venue management software required?

11.8.6 Cloud customer relationship management (cloud CRM)

Many companies engaged in international events today make use of cloud customer relationship management (cloud CRM) technology where the CRM software, CRM tools and the organisation's customer data reside in the cloud and are delivered to end-users via the internet. The cloud CRM is usually provided through an automation development software company who provide a PC-based environment designed for efficient connectivity (Eitel, 2019). This can then be integrated to assist an international event organisation's operations during the planning of large-scale events. Bespoke programmes can be developed, bringing together multiple layers of data to expand the organisation's communication abilities.

Therefore, event organisers have to deal with internet service providers, web-based search services and social media services in the early stages of planning. Data collection and analysis will carry on beyond the life of the event itself and continue to provide vital information for both the current event and any that will occur in the future. For an event organiser who is used to conventional methods of business communication, it can be terribly confusing and often involves considerable negotiation to craft the contours of these product categories (Conrad, 2017). What the event company chooses to integrate would be based on the event itself as a multitude of support mechanisms can be built in, from confirming registration to ongoing access control management.

Cloud CRM provides access to the application via web-based tools or web browser log-ins where the CRM system administrator has previously defined the various access levels across the organisation. To simplify the process, app icons are created to provide a visual anchor for the service provided. Figure 11.5 depicts a typical array of CRM-style computer icons for event apps. Employees can log in to the CRM system, simultaneously, from any internet-enabled computer or

Figure 11.5 A variety of CRM style computer icons for apps that represent the features of an automation program for an international event

Source: Author, based on data from Boomset, 2018

device. Often, cloud CRM provides users with mobile apps to make it easier to use the CRM on smartphones and tablets (Beal, 2017).

11.8.7 Online tools and apps for improved communication

As well as the paid-for apps that support international event delivery, there is also a multitude of freely available support applications that can assist in the planning process. For example, some of the features on both Bing Maps and Google Earth provide excellent planning tools. The actual site for an outdoor event in most destinations can be prepared, while Google Earth allows you to conduct reasonably accurate measurements of many outdoor spaces. These should only be used as estimates, but a good indication of suitability and access issues can be generated. The information available should only be used as a guide prior to a site visit, however.

For a much more detailed level of digital communication, a growing number of support organisations and mobile event applications are available to provide a top-to-bottom digital communication service for any international event. Online marketplace vendors or search engines for apps such as Capterra, GetApp, and G2 serve as an intermediary between buyers and sellers within the software industry. A search on their sites for event management software can suggest over 400 providers that will assist in the digital management of the event. Table 11.3 is a selection of the category leaders in event apps for 2019, with the company's description of their use. The important thing to remember is that there are numerous data analysts, but it is the data itself that adds value to the event.

Mobile event app software allows international event organisers to create their own customised mobile app that can be downloaded from other online marketplace vendors such as the Apple App Store and Google Play. Depending on the level of support or communication required, these downloadable apps

Table 11.3 Popular event apps and their basic description

Eventbrite	Eventbrite is a global ticketing and event technology platform that provides creators of events with tools and resources to seamlessly plan, promote, and produce live experiences.
Bizzabo	Complete web and mobile-based event registration and management solution spanning site building, ticketing, analytics, customer relationship management (CRM) and on-site check-in.
ThunderTix	A seamless cloud based ticketing solution with reserved seating and subscriptions. Embed on your website. Patron and donor tracking. Barcode tickets and scanning.
Purplepass	Purplepass is a full-scale ticketing platform for online presale, marketing, social media, day-of-event sales and admission management.
Brushfire	Brushfire is a customisable online ticketing and event registration platform for churches, non-profits, and secular clients, with conditional forms, assigned seating, email marketing, and more.
Accelevents	Built by event hosts to help you sell more tickets and fundraise more effectively. Our affordable prices come with instant pay-outs and 24/7 support with a real person.
Eventzilla	Eventzilla provides the same top shelf features as industry leading solutions while offering affordable event registration software.
Ticket Tailor	Sell tickets with Ticket Tailor – a white label event ticketing platform with low fees to create a box office for charity fundraisers, concerts, comedy clubs and more.
Eventsquid	Self-serve control over website, apps, registration, payment, check-in, badging, reporting and more. Built with a modern aesthetic, an all-in-one solution for managing a wide array of tasks.
Picatic	Picatic provides a web-based platform to create and publish branded event listings, promote and sell tickets online and view up-to-date sales reports.
Attendify	Attendify helps you elevate the attendee experience and create registration pages quickly and easily.
Cvent	Online event planning and management, web survey and email marketing software across industries, globally. Software supports the entire event life cycle, from marketing to event check-in and beyond.
EventMobi	EventMobi helps event planners create engaging mobile apps with guest registration, check-in, networking and more for trade shows, conferences and events.
EventBank	An all-in-one engagement platform combining event management, membership management, email marketing, customer relationship management (CRM), finance and mobile apps.
Eventtia	Eventtia is an intuitive events management platform which enables small to medium size businesses to plan different networking, academic, corporate or commercial events.

Source: Based on data from GetApp®, n.d.

can provide attendees with detailed event information, from maps of the event space to individual contributor details. Mobile event app creation software is often used as a supplement to other event management platforms or event planning software (G2, n.d.).

11.9 Business intelligence (BI)

At this stage, it becomes easy to get lost in terminology, but once digital communication has been adopted by an international event organisation, there are strategies required to fully exploit the information being gathered. The more technologies used by event organisations for data analysis, the bigger the increase in business intelligence (BI).

Improved decision making, increased profit, market efficiency, and reduced costs are some of the potential benefits of improving existing analytical applications, such as BI, within an organisation (Dedić and Stanier, 2016). BI is considered an umbrella term which should be understood to include all the elements that make up the business environment. However, it is important to point out that some aspects of BI also have a number of issues for end-users, including the software's functional capability, data quality, integration with other systems, flexibility, user access and risk management support (Işik et al., 2013). Table 11.4 lists the most common types of BI technologies with their Wiki definition.

Specialist companies can provide the software and technical support to enable international event organisations to fully apply many of these BI technologies. They can then be applied by the event organisation to support a wide range of operational and strategic business decisions such as evaluation (see Chapter 3), staffing (see Chapter 5), and ticketing (see Chapter 7).

11.9.1 Big Data

Big Data is described as data being made up of a very large size, typically to the extent that its manipulation and management present significant logistical challenges. It is also the branch of computing involving such data (OED, 2020). It has been further defined as the collection and monitoring of extremely large data sets that may be analysed computationally to reveal patterns, trends, and associations, especially relating to human behaviour and interactions (IGI Global, n.d.). When used appropriately, the data has the power to assist with the broader management and communication of international events. Organisations which collect Big Data are over 70% more likely than other organisations to also have BI projects (Tableau, 2019) and can use the data to improve communication. With the advent of Big Data and analytics, new sources of valuable data are available to guide decision-making processes in a more informed manner. Businesses were once looking at historical data, but advances in database technology and system processes have led to near real-time data collection and analytics (Madarasz, 2018).

Digital communication is informed by Big Data and, with the use of other technology such as an application programming interface (API), can be the

Table 11.4 Terms and the Wiki definition of several business information (BI) tools

Term	Wiki definition
Digital reporting	Business reporting or enterprise reporting refers to both the public reporting of operating and financial data by a business enterprise, and the regular provision of information to decision makers within an organisation to support them in their work.
Online analytical processing	Online analytical processing, or OLAP is an approach to answer multi-dimensional analytical (MDA) queries swiftly in computing.
Analytics	Analytics is the discovery, interpretation, and communication of meaningful patterns in data; and the process of applying those patterns towards effective decision making.
Data mining	Data mining is the process of discovering patterns in large data sets involving methods at the intersection of machine learning, statistics, and database systems
Process mining	Process mining is a family of techniques in the field of process management that support the analysis of business processes based on event logs. During process mining, specialised data mining algorithms are applied to event log data in order to identify trends, patterns and details contained in event logs recorded by an information system.
Complex event processing	Event processing is a method of tracking and analysing (processing) streams of information (data) about things that happen (events), and deriving a conclusion from them. Complex event processing, or CEP, is event processing that combines data from multiple sources to infer events or patterns that suggest more complicated circumstances.
Business performance management	Business performance management is a set of performance management and analytic processes that enables the management of an organisation's performance to achieve one or more pre-selected goals. Synonyms for business performance management include corporate performance management (CPM) and enterprise performance management.
Benchmarking	Benchmarking is the practice of comparing business processes and performance metrics to industry bests and best practices from other companies. Dimensions typically measured are quality, time, and cost. Benchmarking is used to measure performance using a specific indicator (cost per unit of measure, productivity per unit of measure, cycle time of x per unit of measure or defects per unit of measure) resulting in a metric of performance that is then compared to others.
Text mining	Text mining, also referred to as text data mining, roughly equivalent to text analytics, is the process of deriving high-quality information from text. High-quality information is typically derived through the devising of patterns and trends through means such as statistical pattern learning. Text mining usually involves the process of structuring the input text, deriving patterns within the structured data, and finally evaluation and interpretation of the output.

continued

Table 11.4 Cont.

Term	Wiki definition
Predictive analytics	Predictive analytics encompasses a variety of statistical techniques from data mining, predictive modelling, and machine learning that analyse current and historical facts to make predictions about future or otherwise unknown events. In business, predictive models exploit patterns found in historical and transactional data to identify risks and opportunities. Models capture relationships among many factors to allow assessment of risk or potential associated with a particular set of conditions, guiding decision-making for candidate transactions.
Prescriptive analytics	Prescriptive analytics is the third and final phase of business analytics, which also includes descriptive and predictive analytics. Referred to as the final frontier of analytic capabilities, prescriptive analytics entails the application of mathematical and computational sciences and suggests decision options to take advantage of the results of descriptive and predictive analytics.

solution to increasingly complex workflows. If the data is managed incorrectly, it can also make things worse (Rachel, 2017). This is why specialist companies provide assistance in gathering and delivering the digital communication. An API is essentially a way to let one piece of technology 'speak' to another. Sharing data and meaning, they can be used together with relative ease. This means it is possible to pick and choose from a number of virtual solutions and have them work together seamlessly (Walker, 2016). With the collection of Big Data available to all organisations, Cambie and Ooi (2009) suggest that the world of communication is changing. It is no longer about the dominance of big players; it is just as much about the local perspective.

Many international event organisations are yet to realise the power of digital communication technology and the potential value it can bring to international events. Failure to adopt aspects of digital communication technology does not necessarily suggest a poor experience or the end for those businesses less digitally mature, because as we have discussed earlier not every international event business relies on this kind of data support to survive (Ryan *et al.*, 2020).

Developments in sport are a good example of how Big Data has improved a team's performance. Sir David Brailsford, when performance director of British Cycling, referred to it as the doctrine of marginal gains according to which the small incremental improvements in any process add up to a significant improvement when they are all added together (BBC, 2015). By collecting data on each aspect, the data collected by Brailsford and his team revealed small areas of improvement in the cyclist's performance, the bike's performance, and even the performance of their clothes, shoes and helmets. These efforts culminated in the dominance of his teams in cycling.

All sporting teams can benefit from Big Data as the technology allows images to create visualisations from data. How many assists did a player make? How much possession, distance travelled, or the amount of space controlled by any one player during a game? All of these activities can be mapped to produce revealing data to improve performance. This is done through the use of analytics.

11.9.2 Analytics

As digital communication allows for the gathering of lots of data, analytics has been identified as one of the four major technology trends in the past few years (IBM, 2011). The bigger the event, the more likely Big Data analytics will be central to a company's operations. Effective analysis of Big Data has become the new magic key to unlocking seriously effective business decisions. The importance and link between business intelligence and analytics are expressed in the acronym BI&A. The ability to effectively analyse critical business data is no easy task and whole university degrees have appeared in response to the demand for this knowledge. This comes as no surprise when such knowledge supports a company's ability to better understand its business and market and make more timely business decisions.

11.10 Summary

The recognition of I4.0 and its component technologies has allowed international events to produce whole new concepts and experiences in the delivery and management processes. As was suggested in Chapter 1, this book has shown how international event companies continue to develop new and innovative ways to connect. International events are absorbing aspects of I4.0 at every stage of the process, pushing the boundaries of event experiences far beyond the physical world. Digital communication is improving the level of performance of business, while Big Data and analytics are transforming performance from manufacturing to the field of play.

International events are increasingly engaging and investing in the use of digital communication. With the level of understanding required to achieve E4.0, it becomes necessary to adopt a cautious approach. The investments in additional technology need to demonstrate significant evidence of the 3 'i's. A much greater focus has been placed on the need for secure networks and appropriate bandwidth to satisfy demand. However, the widespread availability of digital communication, apps, and tools will continue to permeate throughout international events, driving knowledge, improving communication, and reinventing our methods of engagement.

Case study 11.1 Esports and the 2017 World of Legends Final, Beijing

One of the biggest growth areas in international event education and delivery is Esports. Esports is a form of borderless sport competition using video games. One of the leading Esports games is League of Legends (LoL), a multiplayer online battle arena video game developed and published by Riot Games for Microsoft Windows and MacOS (Nguyen, 2009). In 2017 the LoL final was held in Beijing. This final happened to be a rematch from the 2016 final between the teams Samsung Galaxy and SKT T1. Samsung Galaxy were the eventual victors after SKT T1 had won the previous year.

Inspired by the pomp and ceremony of mega events such as the Olympics, the Riot Games created an opening ceremony that included live performances. As it was a gaming event, the entertainers included real and artificial performers. With the focus on Chinese culture, the ceremony was capped off with the performance of the game's theme 'Legends Never Die,' and the introduction of an augmented reality dragon in the middle of the song.

The dragon appeared to land on the roof of the Beijing National Stadium, which is more commonly known as the Bird's Nest. The visual effect was made all the more realistic as shadows reflected off the roof. As the dragon peered over the edge of the roof, it began to roar and then soared down into and around the arena, before landing on the main stage. A 16-metre inflatable replica of the tournament trophy rose up from the stage as the dragon circled the venue. As part of the choreographed dragon entrance, the performers on the stage appeared to duck out of fear and ran for cover as the dominant dragon continued to roar at the audience. After making what appeared to be a final show of defiance to the audience, the dragon flew back onto the stadium roof before disappearing into the sky, cueing the singer to finish the last part of the game title song as the two competing teams were introduced to the stage.

For further information on how this event was created, see the following websites, and for other AR applications at events:

- https://nexus.leagueoflegends.com/en-gb/2017/12/dev-summoning-the-worlds-dragon/
- www.enginecreative.co.uk/integrated-agency-services/augmented-reality/augmented-reality-events/
- https://appreal-vr.com/blog/augmented-reality-for-events/

Questions

1. How important is digital communication in the delivery of an opening ceremony for an international event?
2. What are some of the complications with mixing augmented reality with live action?
3. What do you think the organisers are trying to achieve by bringing augmented reality to live events?

11.11 Useful websites

A Guide to Enterprise Reporting. By Gregory Hill
http://ghill.customer.netspace.net.au/reporting/definition.html

Samsung Galaxy S20 event: How to watch and everything announced
www.pocket-lint.com/phones/news/samsung/140143-watch-samsung-galaxy-
   unpacked-press-conference

8 Event Management and Planning Software That Will Make You a Rockstar.
   By Whova
https://whova.com/blog/free-event-planning-software-make-you-rockstar/

20 Bedford Way
https://20bedfordway.com/news/

Data Analytics Resource library
www.exasol.com/en/community/resources/

Bandwidth calculator
www.encore-anzpac.com/events/calculating-bandwidth-for-meeting-and-event-
   planners-made-easy

Wi-Fi solutions for events
www.madebywifi.com/

References

Alcácer, V., & Cruz-Machado, V. (2019). Scanning the Industry 4.0: A Literature Review on Technologies for Manufacturing Systems. *Engineering Science and Technology, an International Journal, 22*(3), 899–919. doi:10.1016/j.jestch.2019.01.006

Aruba (2018). What is 802.11AX (WI-FI 6)? And why you need it. *Hewlett Packard Enterprise Development*. Retrieved from www.arubanetworks.com/assets/so/SO_80211ax.pdf Accessed 23rd January 2020.

BBC (2015). Viewpoint: Should we all be looking for marginal gains?. Retrieved from www.bbc.co.uk/news/magazine-34247629 Accessed 26th January 2020.

Beal, V. (2017). Cloud CRM – Customer Relationship Management cloud. Retrieved from www.webopedia.com/TERM/C/crm_cloud.html Accessed 2nd March 2018.

Boes, K., Buhalis, D., & Inversini, A. (2016). Smart tourism destinations: Ecosystems for tourism destination competitiveness. *International Journal of Tourism Cities, 2*(2), 108–124. doi:10.1108/ijtc-12-2015-0032

Boomset (2018). Features. Retrieved from https://boomset.com/ Accessed 2nd March 2018.

Cambie, S., & Ooi, Y.-M. (2009). International communications strategy: developments in cross-cultural communication, PR, and social media. In Y.-M. Ooi (Ed.). London: Kogan Page.

Clarke, A. (2017). Elvis, Michael Jackson, Roy Orbison: Technological ghosts return to the spotlight. Retrieved from www.eadt.co.uk/what-s-on/elvis-michael-jackson-roy-orbison-technological-ghosts-return-to-the-spotlight-1-5262953 Accessed 19th January 2018.

Colli, M., Madsen, O., Berger, U., Møller, C., Wæhrens, B. V., & Bockholt, M. (2018). Contextualizing the outcome of a maturity assessment for Industry 4.0. *Ifac-papersonline, 51*(11), 1347–1352.

Conrad, M. (2017). *The Business of Sports: Off the Field, in the Office, on the News* (3rd ed.). Oxon: Routledge.

Dedić, N., & Stanier, C. (2016). 'Measuring the Success of Changes to Existing Business IntelligenceSolutions to Improve Business Intelligence Reporting'. Paper presented at the 10th International Conference on Researchand Practical Issues of Enterprise Information Systems (CONFENIS), Vienna, Austria.

del Sol Beaulieu, J. (2019). Brussels becomes first major city to halt 5G due to health effects. *Take Back Your Power*. Retrieved from www.takebackyourpower.net/brussels-first-major-city-to-halt-5g-due-to-health-effects/?fbclid=IwAR0wXcnpM1l2t-2o0Myx-kY9NsRAM2qZWmyrKxCcxhJQYacHPcop_YnGsPM

Dickson, G. W., DeSanctis, G., & Poole, M. S. (2000). Teams and technology interactions over time. *Research on Managing Groups and Teams, 3*, 1–27.

Dictionary.com (n.d.). Knowledge is power. Retrieved from www.dictionary.com/browse/knowledge is power Accessed 20th January 2020.

Duggan, M. (2013). It's a woman's (social media) world. Retrieved from www.pewresearch.org/fact-tank/2013/09/12/its-a-womans-social-media-world/ Accessed 5th March 2018.

Eitel, L. (2019). Using software for designing and sizing motion-control systems. *Design World Online*. Retrieved from www.designworldonline.com/using-software-for-designing-and-sizing-motion-control-systems/ Accessed 21st May 2020.

Encore (2018). Calculating bandwidth for meetings and event planners made easy. Retrieved from www.encore-anzpac.com/events/calculating-bandwidth-for-meeting-and-event-planners-made-easy Accessed 26th January 2020.

Eventbase (2018). 5G is coming: How will it change your events?. Retrieved from www.eventbase.com/blog/5g-is-coming-how-will-it-change-your-events Accessed 18th January 2020.

Federal Ministry for Education and Research (Germany) (BMBF) (n.d.). Digital economy and society. www.bmbf.de/de/zukunftsprojekt-industrie-4-0-848.html Accessed 2nd July 2018.

Ferdinand, P. (2017). The end of Moore's Law: Opportunities for Natural Computing? *New Generation Computing, 35*(3), 253–269. doi:10.1007/s00354-017-0020-4

G2 (n.d.). Best mobile event apps: What is Mobile Event Apps? Retrieved from www.g2.com/categories/mobile-event-apps Accessed 20th January 2020.

Gale Virtual Reference Library (2012). Moore's Law. In L. J. Fundukian (Ed.) *Gale Encyclopedia of E-Commerce, Vol. 2.* (2nd ed.), 517–518). Detroit: Gale.

GetApp® (n.d.) Discover the best apps to grow your business. Retrieved from www.getapp.com/#popular-categories Accessed 23rd May 2020.

Gov.uk. (2019). Broadband competition for event venues. Retrieved from www.gov.uk/gover nment/publications/broadband-competition-for-event-venues Accessed 21st January 2020.

Gretzel, U. (2018). From smart destinations to smart tourism regions. *Investigaciones Regionales 42*, 171–184.

Gretzel, U., Werthner, H., Koo, C., & Lamsfus, C. (2015). Conceptual foundations for understanding smart tourism ecosystems. *Computers in Human Behavior, 50*, 558–563. doi:10.1016/j.chb.2015.03.043

House of Commons Committee of Public Accounts (2008). *The Budget for the London 2012 Olympic and Paralympic Games*. London: House of Commons, The Stationery Office.

IBM (2011). The 2011 IBM tech trends report: The clouds are rolling in…is your business ready? Retrieved from www.ibm.com/developerworks/techntrendsreport Accessed 1st April 2015.

IGI Global (n.d.). What is Big Data? Retrieved from www.igi-global.com/dictionary/data-knowledge-and-intelligence/39008 Accessed 2nd March 2019.

Işik, Ö., Jones, M. C., & Sidorova, A. (2013). Business intelligence success: The roles of BI capabilities and decision environments. *Information and Management, 50*(1), 13–23.

Jepson, A., & Clarke, A. (2016). *An introduction to planning and managing communities, festivals and events*. London: Routledge.

Kastrenakes, J. (2018). Wi-Fi now has version numbers, and Wi-Fi 6 comes out next year. Retrieved from www.theverge.com/2018/10/3/17926212/wifi-6-version-numbers-announced Accessed 23rd October 2019.

Korže, S. Z. (2019). From Industry 4.0 to Tourism 4.0. *Innovative Issues and Approaches in Social Sciences, 12*(3). doi:10.12959/issn.1855-0541.IIASS-2019-no3-art3

Lasi, H., Fettke, P., Kemper, H.-G., Feld, T., & Hoffmann, M. (2014). Industry 4.0. *The International Journal of Wirtschaftsinformatik, 6*(4), 239–242. doi:10.1007/s12599-014-0334-4

Layton, S. (2017). How to decide what internet speed you need. Retrieved from www.nerdwallet.com/blog/utilities/how-to-decide-what-internet-speed-you-need/ Accessed 23rd January 2020.

Li, N., & Been-Lirn, H. (2013). Cognitive issues in mobile augmented reality: An embodied perspective. In W. Huang, L. Alem & M. A. Livingston (Eds.), *Human Factors in Augmented Reality Environments*, 109–135. New York: Springer.

Madarasz, M. (2018). Why outsourcing social media data is a good thing. Retrieved from https://dataconomy.com/2018/11/outsourcing-social-media-data/ Accessed 20th December 2018.

Manning, J. (2016). Social media. In J. C. Nash (Ed.), *Gender: Love*, 271–287. Farmington Hills, MI: Macmillan Reference USA.

Marketresearch.com (2017). The convergence of 5G, artificial intelligence, data analytics, and Internet of Things https://blog.marketresearch.com/the-convergence-of-5g-artificial-intelligence-data-analytics-and-internet-of-things

Millet, D. (2018). 5G: The hype vs the reality. What will 5G mean for business owners? Retrieved from www.itproportal.com/features/5g-the-hype-vs-the-reality-what-will-5g-mean-for-business-owners/ Accessed 21st May 2020.

Mitchell, B. (2019). 802.11 standards explained: 802.11ac, 802.11b/g/n, 802.11a. Retrieved from www.lifewire.com/wireless-standards-802-11a-802-11b-g-n-and-802-11ac-816553 Accessed 4th January 2020.

Neuhofer, B., Buhalis, D., & Ladkin, A. (2013). A typology of technology-enhanced tourism experiences. *International Journal of Tourism Research, 16*(4), 340–350.

Nguyen, T. (2009). Clash of the DOTAs. Retrieved from https://web.archive.org/web/20111128151953/www.1up.com/features/clash-dotas-league-legends-heroes Accessed 26th January 2020.

OED (2020). Big Data. Retrieved from: www-oed-com.ezproxy.wlv.ac.uk/view/Entry/18833?redirectedFrom=big+data#eid301162177 Accessed 26th January 2020.

Oesterreich, T., & Teuteberg, F. (2016). Understanding the implications of digitisation and automation in the context of Industry 4.0: A triangulation approach and elements of a research agenda for the construction industry. *Computers in Industry, 83*, 121.

Poushter, J. (2016). Smartphone ownership and internet usage continues to climb in emerging economies. Pew Research Center. Retrieved from www.pewresearch.org/global/2016/02/22/smartphone-ownership-and-internet-usage-continues-to-climb-in-emerging-economies/ Accessed 3rd September 2017.

Qin, J., Liu, Y., & Grosvenor, R. (2016). A categorical framework of manufacturing for Industry 4.0 and beyond. *Procedia CIRP, 52*, 173–178. doi:10.1016/j.procir.2016.08.005

Rachel, G. (2017). How to automate your event technology using APIs and integrations. Retrieved from www.eventbrite.co.uk/blog/apis-and-integrations-for-event-technology-ds0c/ Accessed 2nd February 2018.

External forces

Rainie, H., & Wellman, B. (2012). *Networked: the new social operating system*. Cambridge, MA: MIT Press.

Ramsey, J., Wilshere, A. (2013). Impact of electronic communication. Retrieved from http://jackramseyaaronwilshere.blogspot.co.uk/ Accessed 1st March 2018.

Ryan, W. G., Fenton, A., Wasim, A., & Scarf, P. (2020). Recognizing Events 4.0: The digital maturity of events. *International Journal of Event and Festival Management*, 11(1), 47–68.

Ryan, W. G., & Kelly, S. (2017). The effects of Supply Chain Management (SCM) activities and their impact on festival management and the customer experience. In A. Jepson, Clarke, A. (Eds.), *Power, Construction, and Meaning, in Communities Festivals and Events*, 109–128. Oxon: Routledge.

Saturno, M., Pertel, V., & Deschamps, F. (2018). Proposal for new automation architecture solutions for Industry 4.0. *LogForum, 14*(2). doi:10.17270/j.log.266

Shankaranarayanan, N. K., & Ghosh, A. (2017). 5G. *IEEE Internet Computing, 21*(5), 8–10. doi:10.1109/mic.2017.3481346

Simpli-fi (2018). The importance of having the right WiFi network to keep your conference better connected. www.simpli-fi.co.uk/the-importance-of-having-the-right-wifi-network-to-keep-your-conference-better-connected/ Accessed 23rd January 2019.

Tableau (2019). Top 10 Big Data trends. Retrieved from www.tableau.com/asset/top-10-big-data-trends#kOWO8lE0j2zxhr6i.99 Accessed 30th November 2019.

Ustundag, A. (2018). *Industry 4.0: Managing The Digital Transformation*. Cham: Springer International Publishing.

Walker, M. (2016). 10 event technology trends you need to know in 2016 (and beyond). Retrieved from www.eventbrite.co.uk/blog/10-event-technology-trends-you-need-to-know-in-2016-ds00/ Accessed 2nd February 2018.

Wendorf, M. (2019). Swiss citizens to protest 5G cell phone network rollout. *Interesting Engineering*. Retrieved from https://interestingengineering.com/swiss-citizens-to-protest-5g-cell-phone-network-rollout Accessed 3rd November 2019.

Index

Index

Index

Index

Index

Index

Index